Henry George's Legacy in Economic Thought

Frontispiece   Henry George *c*. 1897. Courtesy of Fryer Library, University of Queensland

Henry George's Legacy in Economic Thought

Edited by

John Laurent

Honorary Senior Lecturer, Department of Economics and Resources Management, University of Southern Queensland, Australia

Edward Elgar
Cheltenham, UK • Northampton, MA, USA

Published by
Edward Elgar Publishing Limited
Glensanda House
Montpellier Parade
Cheltenham
Glos GL50 1UA
UK

Edward Elgar Publishing, Inc.
136 West Street
Suite 202
Northampton
Massachusetts 01060
USA

A catalogue record for this book
is available from the British Library

Library of Congress Cataloguing in Publication Data
Henry George's legacy in economic thought / edited by John Laurent.
    272 p.cm.
    Includes bibliographical references and index.
    ISBN 1-84376-885-2
    1. George, Henry, 1839-1897. 2. Economists–United States. 3. Land value taxation. 4. Land reform. 5. Land value taxation–Australia. I. Laurent, John, 1947-

HB119.G4H46 2005
330'.092–dc22   2005049721

ISBN 1 84376 885 2

Printed and bound in Great Britain by MPG Books Ltd, Bodmin, Cornwall

Contents

List of Contributors

Philip D. Day, 3/24 Croydon Street, Toowong, Brisbane, 4006, Australia.

Terry Dwyer, Asia Pacific School of Economics and Government, Australian National University, Canberra, 0200, Australia.

Kirk D. Johnson, Department of Economics, Goldey-Beacom College, Wilmington DE 19808, U.S.A.

Marianne F. Johnson, Department of Economics, University of Wisconsin, Oshkosh WI 54901, U.S.A.

Kirrily Jordan, Political Economy, School of Economics and Political Science, University of Sydney, Sydney, 2006, Australia.

Rob Knowles, School of Classics, History and Religion, University of New England, Armidale, 2351, Australia.

John Laurent, Department of Economics and Resources Management, University of Southern Queensland, Toowoomba, 4350, Australia.

Erin McLaughlin-Jenkins, Department of History, University of Victoria, P.O. Box 3045, Victoria BC, Canada V8W 3P4.

Laurence S. Moss, Economics Division, Babson College, Babson Park, MA 02457, U.S.A.

John Pullen, School of Economics, University of New England, Armidale, 2351, Australia.

Warren J. Samuels, Department of Economics, Michigan State University, East Lansing MI 48824, U.S.A.

Frank Stilwell, Political Economy, School of Economics and Political Science, University of Sydney, Sydney, 2006, Australia.

PART I

Historical Background

1. Introduction

John Laurent

In his contribution to this volume, Phil Day notes the unmistakable stamp of Henry George on the former Lord Mayor of Brisbane, Jim Soorley's observation that the Queensland State Government had 'failed to capture for future generations any of the value it had created' by its spending a billion dollars on upgrading the motorway between Brisbane and the Queensland-New South Wales Gold Coast resort. Yet, in Australia today, Day observes, such Georgist influences are nowhere acknowledged or made explicit, which is perhaps not surprising since George is now unknown to many people, even economics graduates, who can complete their courses without ever having heard his name. As Phil Day notes elsewhere (Day, 2000), despite George's *Progress and Poverty* (George, 1976 [1879]) having been republished in millions of copies since its original appearance in an 'author's edition', and translated into fifteen languages, only a relatively small band of dedicated adherents to his ideas is today familiar with his writings.[1] William Barber's (1979) *A History of Economic Thought* relegates George to a four-line footnote, and Robert Heilbroner's (1991) *The Worldly Philosophers* dismisses George as a 'semicrackpot', whose ideas belong to the 'underworld of economics' (p. 191).

It is true that even at the height of his influence, George (1839–1897) tended to polarize people's attitude towards him and his theories. 'More damneder nonsense than poor Rousseau's blether' was how 'Darwin's Bulldog', Thomas Henry Huxley, described *Progress and Poverty* in 1889, as Erin McLaughlin-Jenkins recounts in her chapter, and instilling 'poison into [working class] minds', was Alfred Marshall's opinion of the book (cited Groenewegen, 1998, p. 586). George Bernard Shaw, on the other hand, acknowledged a profound debt to *Progress and Poverty*: it was a book that led him 'into the Fabian Society and other Socialist bodies' (Shaw, 1928, p. 468), and Beatrice Webb (1930) recalled a similar intellectual path. According to Sidney Webb (1908, pp. 29–30), the arguments of 'John Stuart Mill and Henry George' had 'converted an immense body of public opinion to the Socialist view of the justice of, and urgent necessity for, Nationalization of the land; or, at least, the absorption by the State or Municipality of ground rent, mining royalties, and similar unearned profits

3

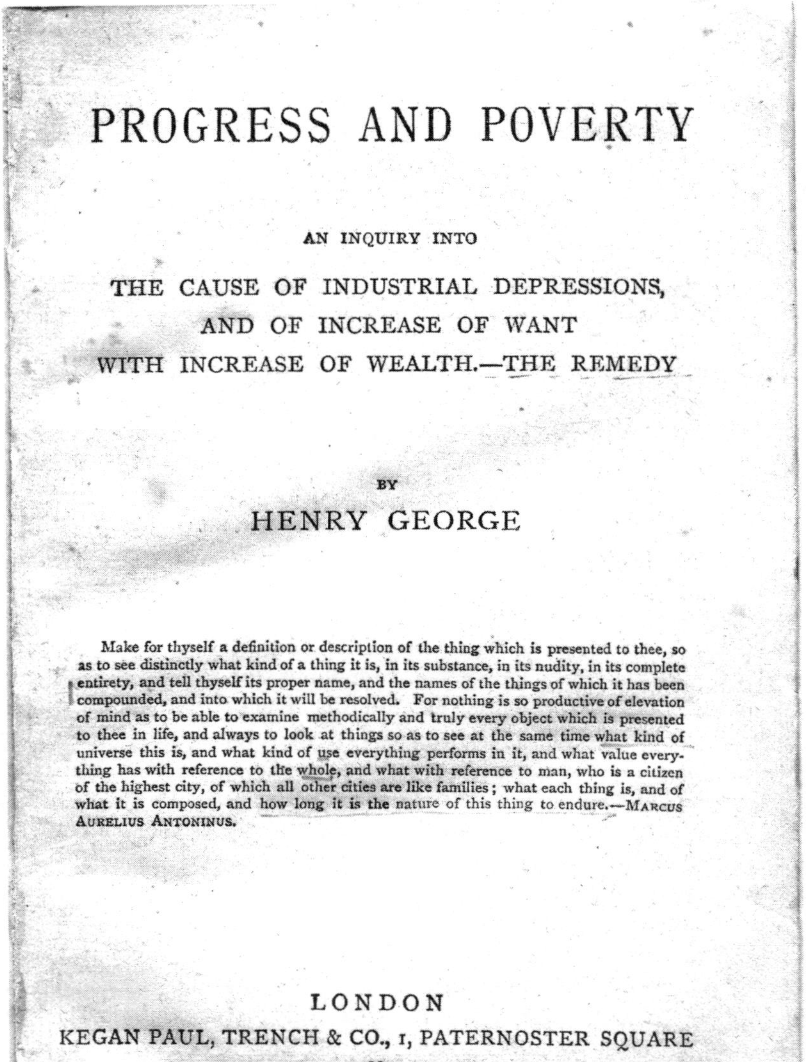

PROGRESS AND POVERTY

AN INQUIRY INTO

THE CAUSE OF INDUSTRIAL DEPRESSIONS,
AND OF INCREASE OF WANT
WITH INCREASE OF WEALTH.—THE REMEDY

BY

HENRY GEORGE

Make for thyself a definition or description of the thing which is presented to thee, so as to see distinctly what kind of a thing it is, in its substance, in its nudity, in its complete entirety, and tell thyself its proper name, and the names of the things of which it has been compounded, and into which it will be resolved. For nothing is so productive of elevation of mind as to be able to examine methodically and truly every object which is presented to thee in life, and always to look at things so as to see at the same time what kind of universe this is, and what kind of use everything performs in it, and what value every-thing has with reference to the whole, and what with reference to man, who is a citizen of the highest city, of which all other cities are like families ; what each thing is, and of what it is composed, and how long it is the nature of this thing to endure.—MARCUS AURELIUS ANTONINUS.

LONDON
KEGAN PAUL, TRENCH & CO., 1, PATERNOSTER SQUARE
1884

Figure 1.1   Title page of an early edition of *Progress and Poverty*.
Photograph: Rob Laurent

from the soil'. For a young Tom Mann (1913, p. 3), *Progress and Poverty* was 'the real stimulus that helped me to a prolonged and continuous study of social economics'. The economist Philip Wicksteed wrote to George that *Progress and Poverty* had opened 'a new heaven and a new earth' for him (cited King, 1988, p. 94); and Leo Tolstoy (see Rob Knowles's chapter) said that George 'was the first to lay a strong foundation for the economic organization of the coming age' (cited in George, 1999 [1871], back cover).

In Australia and New Zealand, in contrast to his current neglect, George was immensely influential. He had visited Melbourne as a young sailor in 1855, and his wife, Annie Fox, whom George met in California in 1861, was Australian born. So when the couple arrived in Sydney in 1890 for a lecture tour by George at the invitation of the Sydney Single Tax Association, it was a significant occasion for both of them. For George, according to his daughter Anna, Australia – notwithstanding an economic downturn at the time – was the land of enlightenment, the great Pacific Continent where 'the secret ballot had originated, where railroad and telegraph systems were publicly owned, and where savings banks and parcel post were part of the postal service' (de Mille, 1972, p. 176). En route to the Southern Continent, the Georges called in briefly to Auckland, New Zealand, where they met the then Premier (former Governor), Sir George Grey, who had read and been greatly impressed by *Progress and Poverty*. The two men struck up a friendship, which arguably smoothed the reception of George's ideas in the country—at any event, when another American, Henry Demarest Lloyd, visited New Zealand a decade later he 'found Henry George everywhere spoken of with the greatest admiration' (Lloyd, 1902, p. 120).

In Sydney, where the Georges arrived in March 1890, Henry was welcomed by large and sympathetic audiences, which continued throughout the Australian colonies during his extensive tour. Amongst his Sydney listeners were a number of notable, or soon to be so, people, including the future Premier of New South Wales, William Holman, and future Prime Ministers of Australia, William Morris ('Billy') Hughes and (later Sir) Joseph Cook. Cook was local secretary of the Clerks' Union at the time, and the following year Hughes became president of the Balmain Single Tax League (Brown, n.d. [*c*. 1956]; Palmer, 1966; Horne, 1983; Grattan, 2000). In Brisbane, George met the Queensland Premier, Samuel Griffith, whose earlier (1884) Pastoral Leases Amendment Bill, aimed at breaking up 'squatters' runs' and encouraging closer settlement, had been influenced by George's ideas (Joyce, 1984). Later that year (1890) Griffith posted George a copy of his radical Natural Law Bill (reproduced by Phil Day in the Appendix to his chapter). Griffith had explained, during the debates surrounding the introduction of his Pastoral Leases Bill, that his object had been 'to give the present tenants a better tenure' but also to make them understand that they 'must make room for others so that the country may be more thickly peopled and its resources more fully developed' (Griffith, QPD, XLI, 1884, p. 390).[2]

Griffith's 'Georgist' policies were widely approved of, including by his political opponents. His 1889 article 'The Distribution of Wealth' in *The Centennial Magazine* referred to 'the gifts or products of nature', like his Natural Law Bill, and observed that, in times past at any rate, 'the products of a man's own labor belonged to himself' (Griffith, 1889, p. 836), both of which views are reminiscent of George, as where, in *Progress and Poverty*: 'The equal right of all men to the use of the land is as clear as their equal right to breathe the air', and 'As a man belongs to himself, so his labour when put in concrete form belongs to him' (thus should not be taxed—George, 1976 [1879], pp. 237, 240)—ideas which George may have gleaned from John Locke (cf. Terry Dwyer's chapter). Hence Griffith's conclusion, in 'The Distribution of Wealth', that '[w]hen more men than one co-operate in, or contribute to, the production of wealth, they are by the law of natural justice partners in the production, and are entitled to share in the product in proportion to their contributions to the partnership' (Griffith, 1889, p. 840). Or, as Griffith worded it in his Natural Law Bill: 'Land is, by natural law, the common property of the community', and 'If more persons than one are concerned in the production [of wealth], the net products belong to them, and are divisible amongst them, in proportion to the value of their respective contributions to the production' (see Appendix to Day, below).

The similarity to, and further development of, George's views here were not lost on the editor of the Brisbane socialist journal *The Boomerang*, who was happy to print an earlier version of Griffith's paper, commenting with satisfaction that '[p]olitical economy is taught now by teachers who regard men as something better than beasts and the world as rather more than a chess-board at which monopolists play with human pawns. It is taught now by Marx...and by Stuart Mill...and by Henry George' (*The Boomerang*, 22 December 1888).

The impression made by George on Griffith left its mark on the Queensland parliament. In 1917 the Queensland Labor Treasurer, E.G.('Red Ted') Theodore – who, according to fellow Labor politician Bill Morrow 'had been strongly influenced by Henry George' (Johnson, 1986, p. 20) – likewise applauded Griffith's position, claiming it as a precedent for his efforts to introduce a supertax on land values to help defray expenses incurred by the First World War. In the debate following Theodore's second reading of a Land Tax Amendment Bill in the Queensland Legislate Assembly in October, the Government member for Bowen, Charles Collins, remarked: 'Was it not a Liberal, sitting on these Treasury benches – Sir Samuel Griffith – who embodied a tax on unimproved values of land in your [the Liberal Opposition's] Local Authority Acts, which every thinker recognises throughout the civilised world as being one of the finest things ever done in any country?' (QPD, CXXVII, 1917, p. 2221). Collins also appealed to the authority of the economist J.A. Hobson. A specific work was not named, but possibly it was Hobson's (1910) *The Industrial System: An Enquiry into Earned and Unearned Income*, which does indeed (p. 224) make a case that 'income that is "unearned" by the individual landowner is "earned" by society' and that, 'in taking rents by a process of taxation, society, through its instrument the State, is taking an income which belongs to it in the same sense wages belong to the labourer, interest to the capitalist, and profit to the employer, viz. because its efforts have made the income'.

Theodore's proposal was that properties with an unimproved ('taxable')value of over £2,500 (which on average was about half their full commercial value) would pay an extra 2d. in the £ levy over and above that already incurred under his Government's Land Tax Act of 1915, whereby all Queensland lands alienated from the Crown and held in fee simple were liable to a tax ranging from 1d. in the £ at £500 to 6d. in the £ at £75,000 and over (with a statutory exemption of £300 allowed).[3] Theodore's argument was that the amendment, besides yielding an annual revenue of about £120,000, would have the added benefits of reducing land values (cf. Frank Stilwell's and Kirrily Jordan's contemporary arguments, Chapter 10) and facilitating repurchase of additional pastoral holdings suitable for cultivation and closer settlement. As Theodore had earlier argued in support of the 1915 Bill – in language which would have pleased George – a land tax 'can be operated to effect certain reforms in the affairs of the State in order to protect the interests of the people', since it 'enables the Government to impose a tax on the truest economic basis, upon the unearned increment in land values' and has the advantage of 'making land more easily available, since it makes it extremely unprofitable for anyone to hold large aggregations of land' (QPD, CXXII, 1915, pp. 2297–8). The tax, Theodore explained, was aimed at the land speculator, who 'denied the community at large the use of valuable land'. It would lower the price of land and 'compel it into use' — an argument fully in accord with George's conception (George, 1976 [1879], p. 308–9; Fitzgerald, 1994, p. 71). In short the Bill, Theodore claimed, would have 'the effect – the incontestable effect – of destroying, or tending to destruction, of private monopolies in land'.

There can be no question that this bipartisan philosophy, borrowing from George, had a major bearing on the future economic development of Queensland. Closer settlement in such areas as the Darling Downs in south-east Queensland was directly influenced by the Georgist ideas of Griffith, Theodore and others enshrined in legislation referred to and such related legislation as a Queensland Agricultural Lands Purchase Act of 1894, and a series of Closer Settlement Acts of 1906–17 (Camm, 1967; Waterson, 1968; French and Waterson, 1982). Under the 1894 Act, where there was considered to be 'demand for land in the neighbourhood for agricultural settlement', and subject to the suitability of the land and 'the permanency of the water supply', the Secretary for Public Lands was authorized to 'make a contract for the acquisition of the land by surrender at the price fixed by the [Land] Board as the fair value thereof or at any lesser price'. (The term of the lease for selectors was set at 20 years, and the rent payable at £7. 12s 10d. annually—Qld Statutes, Vol. III, Sessional Acts, 1894–6, pp. 4988–92.)

Over the 23-year period 1894–1917 the Queensland Government 're-purchased'* 785,310 acres for closer settlement from pastoral estates under these provisions, much of it on the Darling Downs. This land was subdivided into blocks of between around 80 to 640 acres, largely depending on its suitability for dairying – which was promoted by the Government, and popular with settlers because it produced a regular income – in which case it was closer to 80 (Glass, 2004). Among the large pastoral leases thus made available for 'selection' over the period were Glengallan, 1895–1902 (37,120 acres); Mt. Russel, 1901 (45,144 acres); Rosewood, 1903 (20,000 acres); Talgai East, 1912 (22,500 acres); and Cecil Plains, 1916 (120,947 acres) (French and Waterson, 1982; Beal 1993; Ashton, 1999; Raymont, 2004). Associated with these releases of land was a Dairy Produce Act of 1904 authorizing inspection of farms and dairy factories and establishing compulsory grading of butter (enabling guarantees of quality and attainment of a market reputation). Infrastructure and assistance provided by the Queensland Government included a travelling dairy plant giving advice on cream separation and butter and cheese manufacture, bounties on the latter, assistance with refrigeration technology and construction of rail links and sidings. The outcome of these initiatives was highly satisfactory: between 1892 and 1914 the number of dairy cows producing milk on the Darling Downs rose from 10,126 to 85, 588, and butter production increased ten-fold between 1893 and 1918, from 388,000 kg to 3.93 million kg. There were eleven butter factories operating on the Darling Downs in 1916, most of them co-operatives. By the 1920s and 1930s, Queensland, with over 50 factories, was the largest State producer of cheese in Australia (*ibid.*; see also Glass, 1999; Luck, 2004; Stallman, n.d. [*c.* 1980]).[5]

The economist Colin Clark (1958, quoted in Skitch, 2000, p. 25) wrote of Henry George's influence that 'There are no countries in the world in which his ideas have had so much influence as Australia and New Zealand', and it is clear he meant in terms of promoting agricultural settlement. Clark was an economic advisor to the Queensland Labor Government at his time of writing, and was clearly sympathetic to such an interpretation of George, being himself also influenced by the distributivist theories of Hilaire Belloc and G.K. Chesterton. Clark advocated decentralization and closer settlement, and envisioned Australia as a land of yeoman farmers (Fitzgerald, 2003; see also Pearce, 1997).

---

* As Phil Day explains, the term, together with 'resumption', refers to the legal position that upon colonization of Australia the 'Crown' assumed ownership of all land. Following sale or lease it could be resumed, or repurchased, by the government. The same actually applies in England, where all land ultimately belongs to the Crown, so that 'nationalization' of the land—as advocated by A.R. Wallace, for example (see below)—would not strictly involve a transfer of ownership. In Australia today, only about 13 per cent of the total area of the country has been converted to freehold title (MacCallum, n.d. [*c.* 1944] ; Lowe et al., 1997).

Clark had an ally in the Australian geographer Griffith Taylor, who wrote in 1925: 'Australia must make the most of the garland of verdure which surrounds her arid interior. Water conservation and dry farming will broaden this garland. Intense cultivation will produce a yeoman class and promote decentralization' (Taylor, 1925, p. 264).

Notwithstanding what eventually proved to be the impracticality of these theories for Australia (see below), they received an enthusiastic response at the time. Especially was this so when combined with irrigation schemes. George was evidently interested in the possibilities of irrigation, as where he wrote in *Progress and Poverty*: '[W]e are apt to underrate the density of population which the intensive cultivations characteristic of the earliest civilisations are capable of maintaining – especially where irrigation is resorted to' (George, 1976 [1879], p. 79). Nevada, he noted, had land in cultivation 'which will hardly yield a crop three years out of four without irrigation' (*ibid.*, p. 105). And concerning financing of the same, George's reply to a question from the audience during his Australian tour is pertinent. Regarding Government expenditure of revenue raised by land value taxation, George said: 'Many ways would be found of spending it advantageously to the community. They could expend it partly for educational purposes, for increasing the useful public works in the colony [etc.]' (*Wagga Wagga Advertiser*, 25 March 1890, cited in Pullen, 2003, p. 20).

While irrigation schemes were not specifically part of George's single-tax concept, they could be interpreted as compatible with it. In any event, this was one way in which George was interpreted in Australia. In Joseph Cook's (*supra*) understanding, for example, 'the land would in effect be nationalized and thrown open for closer settlement' (Grattan, 2000, p. 92). Another early 20th Century Australian Prime Minister, Alfred Deakin (P.M. 1903–1910), had a similar understanding. According to Deakin's biographer, Walter Murdoch (1999) [1923], Deakin 'avowed himself a disciple, in a general way, of Henry George' (p. 87) — and irrigation was his speciality: In 1884, as Commissioner of Public Works and Minister of Water Supply in the Victorian Parliament, Deakin visited the United States and viewed irrigation works in California, Colorado and Nevada and published a report, 'Irrigation in Western America', which was to serve as a blueprint for the initiation of similar schemes on the Murray River. In New South Wales, Labor Premier William Holman introduced a sliding-scale land tax in 1915 utilizing such prior legislation as a Closer Settlement Act of 1901 and a Crown Lands (Amendment) Act of 1908 to inaugurate the Murrumbidgee Irrigation Scheme (M.I.A.). Under this 1908 Act a constituted board could advise on whether portions of pastoral land (on 'scrub-leases') within fifteen miles of a railway had the capacity 'for agriculture or other profitable use', and on 'the number of farms into which it could be suitably subdivided, and the possibility of irrigation' (Briely and Irish, 1909). By 1912 work on the Burrinjuck Dam and a system of canals to farms was sufficiently advanced for settlers to begin taking up perpetual leaseholds for fruit growing and mixed farming on properties varying from 24 acres to 740 acres, in a total area thrown open for irrigation of 371,000 acres (Smith, 1914).

E.G. Theodore, in Queensland, similarly interpreted George in the context of irrigation schemes. As Ross Johnston (1982, p. 165) quotes Theodore's (1922) reaffirmation of 'a belief in the yeoman ideal of the nineteenth century':

> No one has a greater claim to be regarded as a worker than the man who tills the soil, and no one is more entitled to participate in shaping the policy of governing the affairs of the State than the members of that great and influential class. The farmer is the mainstay of our civilization and the most indispensable member in the community...
> The industry must be greatly extended for only in that way can an additional population be absorbed; and it is only by increasing the population that we can reduce our per capita financial burdens (*Brisbane Courier*, 22 February, 1922).

With a view to increasing the population density of the inland, Theodore enthusiastically took up the advice that an irrigation scheme in the Dawson Valley in south-east Queensland could sustain a population of 50,000 on 300,000 acres of land, based on 5,000 irrigated farms of from 10 to 24 acres, suitable for vegetable growing, and 2,000 attached 'dry' farms (provided with bores or dams) of 80 to 500 acres suitable for dairying and mixed farming. After an Irrigation Act of 1922 was introduced by Theodore (now Queensland Premier), the 'Woolthorpe' squatter's lease of 34,000 acres was resumed by the Government and work was begun on a weir and channelling, and construction of a new town (after the manner of Leeton and Griffith in the M.I.A.), 'Theodore' – the 'first model garden city of Australia' – was begun on the Dawson River flats.

'All that is required to enable Queensland to take advantage of her unique position is increased population', Theodore (1920) repeated on another occasion in good Georgist terms (see below in this Introduction, and Chapter 4). The Federal Bruce–Page (conservative) Government of the day thought similarly: its Development and Migration Commission set up in 1926 recommended outlays totalling £6,000,000 for various land-settlement, rail-construction and irrigation schemes, of which the Dawson Valley project received favourable attention as 'one of the most far reaching of all the schemes propounded for the absorption of immigrants on a large scale' (*Telegraph* [Brisbane], 26 March 1927). And George's ideas clearly informed Theodore's plans for *financing* the project. As Theodore put it in another defence of an increased land-value tax (finally passed in 1922 when the upper house in the Queensland Parliament, the Legislative Council, was abolished): 'The Land Tax is a boon to the Farmers. It prevents wealthy persons from becoming Land Monopolists, and it makes it unprofitable for anyone to hold land in idleness for speculative purposes' (Theodore, n.d. [*c.* 1925], p. 1). Figures provided by Theodore (*ibid.*, pp. 3–4) show that the revenue obtained through the tax on unimproved land values in 1924–5 in

Queensland was £427,362, of which farmers owning less than 500 acres paid only £9,900 altogether. And it is clear that at least some of this revenue was meant to help pay for settlers taking up Dawson Valley allotments: they were granted perpetual leases and paid no land tax (Partridge, 1926).

With the onset of Depression in 1929, Theodore's perhaps slightly grandiose scheme stalled, and with the voting in of a conservative government (under A.E. Moore) hostile to the scheme that same year, the project was almost abandoned. The first Commissioner of Irrigation and Water Supply, Archibald Partridge, personally appointed by Theodore, was dismissed in 1933, and a commission of enquiry into the scheme found that '[t]he present economic conditions in Australia [did] not foster unaided agricultural or pastoral development, except in the production of wheat or wool' (Anon., 1933). A more damning assessment of the scheme appeared in the conservative Sydney *Sunday Observer* (28 May 1933): 'An expensive bubble has been burst by the Land Administration Board (acting for the Queensland Government) in its report on the Dawson Valley Irrigation Settlement Scheme. After expenditure of £1,053,057, an average of £8,492 for each of the 124 settlers so far established, the scheme has been pronounced to be fifty years ahead of its time. In other words, it has failed'. The *Sunday Observer* recommended postponement of the scheme for 'at least 25 years'. Interestingly, the projected Nathan Dam on the Dawson River, never completed, is just now being re-assessed by the Queensland Government, a draft evaluation of the proposal being that it was 'economically viable and ecologically sustainable' and 'clearly superior' to a number of other irrigation proposals presently being considered for the region (Anon., 2004, pp. 42–3).

The question of ecological sustainability clearly impinges on George's conception of land use which, as we have seen, encompassed operating 'to force improvement'.[7] In the 1920s, 'improvement' included tree clearing, 'considerable progress' in which the Queensland Irrigation and Water Supply Commission was pleased to report in 1927 and which is depicted in a photograph in the Commission's promotional booklet, *The Dawson Valley Irrigation Scheme* (Partridge, 1926) published the previous year. It was in fact a *condition of lease* that settlers carry out such 'improvements' on their blocks (*ibid.*). The Queensland Government would be unlikely to set such requirements today. Tree clearing is a highly contentious issue in Queensland currently, the Beattie Labor Government, under pressure from the Green lobby, having passed a Natural Resources and Other Legislation Amendment Bill in 2003 (and further clarifying legislation since) providing for forfeiture of lease to landholders guilty of breaching tree clearing restrictions. A moratorium was imposed on the granting of any further permits for clearing in May 2003 (see Giskes, 2004), and at present a ballot for permits is in operation, successful applicants having between 18 months and two years to complete their clearing. 'Working' of the land, it seems, has reached unsustainable levels.

Yet three contributors to this book, Frank Stilwell, Kirrily Jordan and Phil Day, argue for a revisiting of George's ideas in terms of their usefulness in *preserving* the environment. Stilwell and Jordan, citing Binning and Young (1993), acknowledge that in Australia today any increase in land taxes could encourage landowners to increase the productive capacity of their land in order to cover the additional costs – as indeed George advocated – and that this could have an adverse effect on the natural environment. On the other hand, Stilwell and Jordan argue, land tax could be seen as an 'environmental tax', in that it taxes the use of a natural community resource, like a carbon tax, or a resource rental tax. Introducing changes to land taxes aimed at encouraging socially, economically and environmentally responsible activities and discouraging destructive activities, Frank Stilwell and Kirrily Jordan conclude, may sensibly involve a planned mix of such taxes. Phil Day finds that similar arguments were mooted by a committee set up by the Major Conservative Government in the U.K. in 1995: the committee recommending 'a gradual move away from taxes on labour, income, profits and capital towards taxes on pollution and the use of resources' (quoted Day, below).

In his book *Land: The elusive quest for social justice, taxation reform & a sustainable planetary environment*, Phil Day (1995) suggests that there are today arguments for a Georgist philosophy which were not available in 1879 and which reinforce the Georgist position. Among these are arguments arising from the advent of town planning, which controls the uses to which land can be put and thus has a major bearing upon the value of a given parcel of land. Specifically, Day argues, the possibility of windfall profits being appropriated by private landholders is more readily apparent than in George's day, but at the same time, there now exists a greater awareness of the value of public land and the importance of its protection as a community resource. This can involve action to eliminate development pressures which are motivated primarily by the prospect of windfall profits. Interestingly, Day (1995, pp. 97–8) cites the beginnings of large-scale planning in the U.K. under the war-time Prime Ministership of Winston Churchill in this context, which involved the production of the Ministry of Town and Country Planning's White Paper, *Control of Land Use* (see also McCallum, c.1944) – which made the radical, Georgist, proposition that beneficiaries of increased land value resulting from zoning should pay 80 per cent of the 'betterment' – and also its *Greater London Plan 1944* (Abercrombie, 1945), which recommended 'new powers for planning…including powers for the control of land values'(p. 5) and the acquisition of land for the establishment of 'Green Belts' in outer suburban areas (plates between pages 110 and 111). Day notes that Churchill's position on these subjects was consistent with that which he had taken earlier in his career when, as President of the Board of Trade in the Asquith Liberal Government, he denounced land monopoly as 'the mother of all other forms of monopoly' and a 'toll upon all other forms of wealth and upon every form of industry' (Day, 1995; Churchill, 1970 [1909], pp. 117, 121; Roberts, 1941).

The similarity of Churchill's rhetoric to that of George was noticed by Elwood Lawrence who, in his *Henry George in the British Isles* (Lawrence, 1957), points out that Churchill's (1909) *The People's Rights* (a collection of speeches) and the arguments in favour of the taxation of land values in the Liberals' 1910 Budget – obstructed by the Lords, and for which the Asquith Government went to the country (and won) – closely paralleled the arguments of *Progress and Poverty*. Particularly was this so of Churchill's speeches in Dundee and Edinburgh, and it is tempting to see some intended link here with the impression made by George during his several visits to Scotland between 1882 and 1890. As H.J. Hanham (1968) recounts, George had drawn attention to what he described as the plight of the Skye crofters in early 1882, when he was in Ireland in support of the Irish Land League, and in 1884 he spoke in a number of Scottish cities and towns, including Portree, Dundee, Edinburgh and Glasgow, his address in the last – in which he proclaimed 'the grand truth that every human being born in Scotland has an inalienable and equal right to the soil of Scotland' (Hanham, 1968, p. 41) – resulting in the immediate formation of the Scottish Land Restoration League, with branches soon to follow in Dundee, Aberdeen, Inverness, Edinburgh and Greenock. In an earlier report to the New York-based *Irish World*, George had described the process of enclosure of extensive areas of the Highlands in the 18th Century (see chapter by Warren Samuels and Marianne and Kirk Johnson, below, on George's dispute with the large landowner, the Duke of Argyll), when land once owned in common became the private property of lairds who depopulated the land by rack-renting and eviction to make room for deer parks (Lawrence, 1957). Friedrich Engels (1977)[1891], too, asserted that from about the time of the Jacobite revolt in 1746 in Scotland there was a breakdown in the traditional way of life of many people 'in their use of lands in common, in the fidelity of the clansman to his Chief and of the members of the clan to each other' (p. 132). In Ireland also, according to Engels, up to the 17th Century, when English jurists were sent to the country to transform the clan lands into domains of the English King, the land 'had been the common property of the clan or gens, except where the chiefs had already converted it into their private domain' (*ibid.*, p. 130).

Can these claims of common ownership in antiquity be sustained, and how relevant are they to George's arguments? Certainly George believed that in the British Isles, at any rate, 'the vast majority of…people have no right whatever to their native land save to walk the streets or trudge the roads'(George, 1976 [1879], p. 271), and that this situation can be traced back to the Norman Conquest (*ibid.*, p. 243). 'Historically', George insisted, 'as ethically, private property in land is robbery. It nowhere springs from contract; it can nowhere be traced to perceptions of justice or expediency; it has everywhere had its birth in war and conquest' (*ibid.*, p. 263). George elaborated: 'In California our land titles go back to the Supreme Government of Mexico, who took from the Spanish King, who took from the Pope [i.e., Pope Alexander VI, who divided the Americas between Spain and Portugal in 1493]...or, if you please, they rest upon conquest. In the Eastern States they go back to treaties with Indians, and grants from English Kings...while in England they go back to the Norman conquerors' (*ibid.*, p. 243). This picture, according to George, is vastly different from earlier times:

> Wherever we can trace the early history of society, whether in Asia, in Europe, in Africa, in America, or in Polynesia, land has been considered...as common property, in which the rights of all who had admitted rights were equal. That is to say, that all members of the community...had equal rights to the use and enjoyment of the land of the community. This recognition of the common right to land did not prevent the full recognition of the particular and exclusive right in things which are the result of labour, nor was it abandoned when the development of agriculture had imposed the necessity in recognising exclusive possession of land in order to secure the exclusive enjoyment of the results of labour expended in cultivating it. The division of land between the industrial units, whether families, joint families, or individuals, only went so far as was necessary for that purpose, pasture and forest lands being retained as common, and equality as to agricultural land being secured, either by periodical re-division, as among the Teutonic races, or by prohibition of alienation, as in the law of Moses (George, 1976 [1879], p. 263).[8]

George cites further historical examples of this 'primary adjustment', and goes on to claim that it still existed in the village communities of various countries including India, the mountain cantons of Switzerland, and among the Kabyles of North Africa and the native populations of Java and New Zealand.[9] For his sources for this information George draws principally on the work of the Belgian professor of political economy, Emile de Laveleye (1822–92), whose *Primitive Property* (Laveleye, 1878) is cited extensively in *Progress and Poverty*. But as Roy Douglas (2003) has shown, Laveleye, notwithstanding his appreciation of George's citations, begged to differ from George on one point. His criticism rested on an essential difference of opinion between the two on the question of land *nationalization*. While George could insist – as he does in his distancing himself from Herbert Spencer's position in *A Perplexed Philosopher* – 'I am not a land nationalisationist, as the English and German and Australian land nationalisationists well know' (George, 1893, p. 91); he nevertheless sometimes left himself open to misunderstanding on this subject. As Douglas explains, Laveleye clearly saw a major difference between his solution to the loss of access to land by the poor, and George's solution. For Laveleye, 'there is but one true cure for the social evil; it is individual property generalized and assured to all', or as Douglas phrases it, 'peasant-proprietorship' (Douglas, 2003, pp. 55–6).

George, on the other hand – notwithstanding his support for the crofters of Skye and Ireland – preferred to emphasize land as a public thing, which included its being subject to taxation and redistribution. As Elwood Lawrence (1957) has noted, before George's first visit to the British Isles, his pamphlet, *The Irish Land Question* (George, 1965[1881], p. 64), demanded 'the nationalization of the land by the simple means I have proposed – nay, as the discussion goes on, makes inevitable – an irresistible combination...of labor and capital against land-lordism'. And in dispatches to the *Irish World* of February and July 1882 George again extolled land nationalization, and applauded the proposals of the scientist Alfred Russel Wallace's recently founded Land Nationalization Society.

As Douglas argues, part of the problem of interpretation of George stems from George's association with the Irish Land-Leaguer, Michael Davitt. George and Davitt shared the platform on a number of occasions, including in Manchester in May 1882 and in London in November 1884; and George made little attempt to disassociate himself from Davitt's call for land nationalization, as opposed to fellow Land-Leaguer Charles Parnell's campaign for peasant proprietorship. Davitt's appeal for 'the land for the people' was seen by George as striking the right note, whatever the precise details of his (Davitt's) cause. Over the next decade or so British socialists were similarly little concerned with what they saw as nuances of meaning. The program of the Independent Labour Party (I.L.P.), according to its Secretary, Tom Mann, in 1895, included the securing that '[l]and values, urban and rural' were to be 'treated as public property' (Mann, 1895, quoted Lawrence, 1957, p. 19). In an election speech as I.L.P. candidate in North Aberdeen in 1896 Mann declared that 'the surface land must be common property. Land was not made by man or woman. It is the gift of Nature...'; but he was prepared to admit that the day was 'some distance off when land nationalisation is likely to be successfully carried through the British House of commons'. In the meantime, Mann called for County Councils and District Councils 'to obtain from the present owners such land as the residents in the respective districts may be willing to cultivate collectively, paying rent (for rent will always have to be paid) to the recognised communal authority, and therefore securing to the community all the advantages of the unearned increment which hitherto has gone to the mere landlord'(Mann, 1896, p. 15). In all, according to Elwood Lawrence (1957, p. 119), socialists 'supported the taxation of land values as a matter of course, for they interpreted a tax on the unearned increment in land as a form of nationalization'.

So when writers in the London *Spectator* (12 January 1884) and Sowerby Bridge *Chronicle* (11 January 1884) took issue with 'the Socialist lecturer, Mr George' (both), who '[l]ike Michael Davitt...is a strong advocate of the nation-alisation of the land' (*Chronicle*), their confusion is perhaps understandable .The *Spectator's* journalist further maintained that 'Mr George would, to begin with, have the Legislature confiscate all land within the United Kingdom, including not only agricultural land but all mines and forests' and especially 'all ground upon which cities or houses have been built'. But '[h]e would not take the houses', the *Spectator* continues, for anything 'which a man creates is sacred property'.

Land, by contrast, 'he does not create', and therefore 'the community alone, as beneficiaries deriving from God, can without crime own land'. Ownership 'is in fact, in Mr George's mind, burglary', according to the *Spectator's* account, and George would accordingly 'tax all up to the full amount payable by a yearly tenant', thereby meriting his description as the 'embodiment in flesh of all the Socialistic feeling in the air'.

Whether George would have objected to this account of his position is not at all clear (and for the distinction between 'ownership' and 'possession' in George's conception, see Pullen, below). In *Protection or Free Trade* (George, 1886), he says in a footnote that: 'The term "socialism" is used so loosely that it is hard to attach to it a definite meaning. I myself am classed as a socialist by those who denounce socialism...[f]or my own part I neither claim nor repudiate the name' (p. 324); and in the main text of this book George avers that '[s]ociety ought not to leave the telegraph and the railway to the management and control of individuals' (p. 325), a regime that, as was noted above, he was pleased to find operated in Australia. George in fact, during his lecture tour of Australia, complemented the country for being ahead of America in that respect (Pullen, 2003); and indeed, to a question put to him in Goulburn, New South Wales, George answered that he had 'no objections to make the State the sole landlord' (*ibid.*). But this doesn't necessarily make him a socialist. Perhaps part of the enduring attraction of George's writings, (*Progress and Poverty* has never been out of print, as far as I am aware) for many people is their capacity to accommodate a range of views.

Thus George is perceived by many to still have worthwhile things to say about environmental issues, notwithstanding his argument for 'working' the land, as discussed above. He was well aware of the importance of preserving the natural environment, as I discuss at the end of Chapter 4. This element in George's thought also appears in his treatment of the 'commons' issue. As already indicated, George was deeply interested in this subject, especially in terms of its importance for traditional communities, as with the practice of 'pasture and forest lands being retained as common', a subject also of interest to Laveleye (Douglas, 2003, pp. 53–4). 'Historically, as ethically', George insists, 'private property in land is robbery' — it has 'everywhere had its birth in war and conquest'; it 'nowhere springs from contract', and it is not the natural state of things (George, 1976 [1879], p. 263). George pursued this theme at length in *Progress and Poverty*. Beneath the feudal system of the Middle Ages in Europe, he argues, an older system, 'based on the common rights of the cultivators', took root and has 'left its traces all over Europe':

This primitive organisation which allots equal shares of cultivated ground and the common use of uncultivated ground, and which existed in Ancient Italy as in Saxon England, has maintained itself beneath absolutism and serfdom in Russia, beneath Moslem oppression in Servia, and in India has been swept, but not entirely destroyed, by wave after wave of conquest, and century after century of oppression (George, 1976 [1879], pp. 266–7).

Legally, George argued, traces of these ancient arrangements could still be found, 'like the still existing remains of the ancient commons of England':

The doctrine of eminent domain (existing as well in Mohammedan law), which makes the sovereign theoretically the only absolute owner of land, springs from nothing but the recognition of the sovereign as the representative of the collective rights of the people; primogeniture and entail, which still exist in England, and which existed in some of the American States a hundred years ago, are but distorted forms of what was once an outgrowth of the apprehension of land as common property. This very distinction made in legal terminology between real and personal property is but a survival of a primitive distinction between what was originally looked upon as common property and what from its nature was always considered the peculiar property of the individual (*ibid.*, p. 270).

The environmental lawyer Thomas Sterner (2003) would seem to be in agreement with George here—only he would take the term 'real' back a step further to include the notion of the sovereign as the embodiment of the people in its reference to *regal*, or that which is owned by the King (or the 'Crown'). Sterner (*ibid.*, p. 61) also notes, in agreement with George's point about Mohammedan law, that in Spain from the 8th to the 15th Centuries 'Moorish rule...imparted the practice of communal management'. And both Sterner and George carry their analyses back further still, to the Hispano-Roman and Germanic law of the 6th and 7th Centuries, under which, for example, on the question of commons – in this case, concerning water courses – it is stated that:

No one shall for his own private benefit, and against the interests of the community, obstruct any stream of importance; that is to say, one in which salmon and other sea-fish enter, or into which nets may be cast, or vessels may come for the purpose of commerce (*Visigothian Water Code*, Law 29 of Book 8, Title 4, quoted in Sterner [2003], p. 61).[10]

Sterner goes on to point out that such statutes ultimately heavily influenced laws in the Spanish colonies, including in North America, and indeed, as we have seen, George was aware of the influence of Spanish law in California. Incorporated into this law was the Roman doctrine of *res communes*, expressed by George in these terms: '[M]an has...the right – declared by the fact of his existence – to the use of so much of the free gifts of nature as may be necessary to supply all the wants of that existence, and as he may use without interfering with the equal rights of any one else....This right is natural; it cannot be alienated. It is the free gift of his Creator' (George, 1999 [1871], p. 59). Or, as George approvingly cited Pope Leo XIII's Encyclical, *Rerum Novarum*:

The land...of every country is the common property of the people of that country, because its real owner, the Creator who made it, has transferred it as a voluntary gift to them....Now, as every individual in that country is a creature and a child of God, and as all his creatures are equal in his sight, any settlement of the land of a country that would exclude the humblest man in that country from his share of the common inheritance, would be not only an injustice and a wrong to that man, but, moreover, would be an impious resistance to the benevolent intentions of his Creator (Leo XIII, quoted George, 1891, p. 47).

A few pages further on in his 'Open Letter' to the Pope, George repeats his arguments concerning the ancient *res communes* status of land: 'Examination will show that wherever we can trace them, the first perceptions of mankind have always recognized the equality of right to land', and that 'whenever individual possession became necessary to secure the right of ownership in things produced by labour', some

> method of receiving equality sufficient in the existing state of social development was adopted. Thus, among some peoples, land used for cultivation was periodically divided, land used for pasturage and wood being held in common. Among others, every family was permitted to hold what land it needed for dwelling and for cultivation, but the moment that such use and cultivation stopped, any one else could step in and take it on like tenure. Of the same nature were the land laws of the Mosaic Code (George, 1891, pp. 59–60).

So how was this equitable situation to be restored in the 19th Century? George answers this question unambiguously further on in *The Condition of Labour*:

> There is one way, and only one way, in which in our civilisation working people may be secured a share in the land of their country, and that is the way that we propose — the taking of the profits of land-ownership for the community (*ibid.*, p. 115).

That is to say, the Single Tax. As George explains in *Progress and Poverty*: 'If the land belongs to the people, why continue to permit land-owners to take the rent?...Consider what rent is. It does not arise spontaneously from land; it is due to nothing that the land-owners have done. It represents a value created by the whole community'. Rent, George explains – the creation of the whole community – 'necessarily belongs to the whole community'. Thus was George able to ingeniously provide a 19th Century solution to what he saw as the injustice of the loss of the age-old access to the land enjoyed by the community at large. The 'unearned increment' – land-value increases resulting from exogenous factors such as population increase, rather than from any activity on the part of the landowners themselves – could be recouped by the community through taxation on unimproved values, thus providing recompense for the loss of those benefits once held in common.

The matter of population increase brings us to the vexed question of George's discussion of Malthus, and whether his (some would say, misguided) criticisms of Malthus vitiate his broader argument. I address this subject at the end of Chapter 4, but perhaps some further remarks here are warranted. When, in *The Condition of Labour*, George (1891, p. 136) condemns theories 'like that to which the English clergyman, Malthus, has given his name' and which 'assert that Nature (they do not venture to say God) brings into the world more men than there is provision for', presumably he hoped to find a sympathetic ear in Pope Leo XIII. George and the Pope no doubt disagreed on many things, but they were at one here, as they were on Malthus with an unlikely colleague, Marx (1909, p. 465). Tom Mann, too, sided with George: he believed that *Progress and Poverty* 'seemed to give an effective answer to Malthus' (Mann, 1967 [1923], p. 16); and Alfred Russel Wallace, in a letter to Charles Darwin (see Chapter 4), thought that 'Mr. George, while admitting [that] the main principles [of Malthus's population theory]' were 'self-evident' and 'actually operat[ed] in the case of animals and plants', had nevertheless shown that the theory does not apply 'in the case of man, still less that it has any bearing on the vast social and political questions which have been supported by a reference to it' (Wallace to Darwin, 9 July 1881).[11]

Malthus himself had been uncompromising. In his *Essay on the Principle of Population* he had argued that since 'food is necessary to the existence of man' and 'the passion between the sexes is necessary and will remain nearly in its present state', it can be assumed that:

> [T]he power of population is indefinitely greater than the power of the earth to provide subsistence for man. Population, when unchecked, increases in a geometrical ratio. Subsistence increases only in an arithmetic ratio....By this law of our nature which makes food necessary to the life of man, the effects of these two unequal powers must be kept equal....This implies a strong and constantly operating check on population from the difficulty of subsistence (Malthus, 1926 [1798], pp. 13–14).

Malthus went on to cite figures which he said demonstrated that where subsistence *was* available – as with the thinly populated and fertile United States at the time – population *had* in fact increased geometrically, doubling in 25 years, and in some parts of the country in as few as 15 years (*ibid.*, pp. 20, 106). Applying these findings to his own land, Malthus continued:

> If I allow that by the best possible policy, by breaking up more land and by great encouragement to agriculture, the produce of this Island [Great Britain] may be doubled in the first twenty-five years, I think it will be allowing as much as any person can demand.
>
> In the next twenty-five years, it is impossible to suppose that the produce could be quadrupled. It would be contrary to all our knowledge of the qualities of the land. The very utmost that we can conceive is that the increase in the second twenty-five years might equal the present produce. Let us take this for our rule....The most enthusiastic

speculator cannot suppose a greater increase than this. In a few centuries it would make every acre of land in the Island like a garden (*ibid.*, pp. 21–2).

As we have seen, George was all in favour of making deer parks etc. available for cultivation: here Malthus expressed doubts as to whether this would make any difference in the long term to the needs of a geometrically increasing population. But was the human population increasing geometrically anywhere at George's time of writing? Marx (1909, p. 465), for one (writing at about the same time as George) did not think so (and the rapid growth of the United States could surely be attributed in part to immigration). Perhaps it was true that populations of animals and plants had the *potential* to grow geometrically, or exponentially, but George doubted that this applied to humanity. Regarding the 'reproductive force' of various species, he wrote in *Progress and Poverty*:

> [A] single pair of salmon might, if preserved from their natural enemies for a few years, fill the ocean...a pair of rabbits would under the same circumstances soon overrun a continent...many plants scatter their seeds by the hundred fold, and some insects deposit thousands of eggs; and...everywhere through these kingdoms each species constantly tends to press and when not limited by the numbers of its enemies evidently does press against the limits of subsistence....(George, 1976 [1879], p. 94).

But, George asks, is this 'analogy' valid?

> Does not the fact that all things that furnish man's subsistence have the power to multiply many fold—some of them many million or even billion-fold—while he is only doubling in numbers, show that, let human beings increase to the full extent of their reproductive power, the increase of population can never exceed subsistence? (*ibid.*, pp. 94–5).

Again, as I argue at the end of the Chapter 4, George was half right: Malthus's argument concerning the 'arithmetic' increase of subsistence (i.e., additive —presumably referring to the area of land cultivated), as compared with the geometric growth of population, has proved to be not entirely applicable since Malthus's time—fertilizers, genetic modification of food crops, etc. have enormously increased food production since 1798, increases which are geometric to an extent anyway (since it is biological reproduction of plants and animals that we are talking about).

The mention of Malthus also points to another subject of major interest to George, that of evolutionary theory. George's proviso that a pair of salmon might 'fill the ocean' with its offspring, and a pair of rabbits soon overrun a continent, '*if preserved from their natural enemies*' suggests the essence of Darwinism. Darwin himself wrote in *The Origin of Species*:

> A struggle for existence inevitably follows from the high rate at which all organic beings tend to increase. Every being, which during its natural lifetime produces several

eggs or seeds, must suffer destruction during some period of its life, and...on the principle of geometrical increase, its numbers would quickly become so inordinately great that no country could support the product. Hence, as more individuals are produced than can possibly survive, there must in every case be a struggle for existence, either one individual with another of the same species, or with individuals of distinct species, or with the physical conditions of life. *It is the doctrine of Malthus applied with manifold force to the whole animal and vegetable kingdom*; for in this case there can be no artificial increase of food, and no prudential restraint from marriage. Although some species may be now increasing, more or less rapidly, in numbers, all cannot do so, for the world would not hold them (Darwin, 1901 [1859], pp. 58–9).

The phrase 'struggle for existence', which Darwin uses here and also as the title of the chapter from which this paragraph is taken, is in fact Malthus's (Malthus, 1926 [1798], p. 48) — which indeed Darwin effectively acknowledges in the lines I have italicized. And the phrase is a critical one for Darwin: it is the *success* in this struggle of some individuals (and perhaps social groups, and even species),[12] as against other less well-equipped individuals (and groups and species), that provide the raw material for evolutionary change. As I mention in chapter 4 (note 13), George quotes these italicized lines from Darwin, as well as an 1872 address by Jean Louis Agassiz before the Massachusetts State Board of Agriculture, in which Agassiz refers to Darwinism as 'Malthus all over' (George, 1976 [1879], p. 74), and George is prepared to admit that 'the Malthusian theory has received new support in the rapid change of ideas as to the origin of man and the genesis of species' (*ibid.*, p. 73). So he was well aware of the central tenets of Darwin's theory, and the cogency of its basis in Malthus's argument. One can only assume then, that for George, population increase, while undoubtedly pressing on scarce resources, was at the same time an essential ingredient in the process of wealth creation. *Malthusianism*, as such, George dismisses as an ideological weapon 'eminently soothing and reassuring to the classes who, wielding the power of wealth, largely dominate thought' (George, 1976 [1879], p. 72; see also King, 1988, p. 87).

What in the final analysis, then, can be said of George's legacy? This Introduction has concentrated on George's influence in the Antipodes (Australia and New Zealand), these countries being that part of the world most familiar to me, but also, arguably – as Colin Clark was quoted above as saying – because they were those countries most conspicuous for their taking up of George's ideas for a variety of reasons, including their late settlement by Europeans and the large role assumed by government in their economic affairs (cf. Butlin, 1959). However this may be, New Zealand very quickly accepted the principle of a land value tax, initially by George's friend George Grey, and following him by John Ballance, Premier 1890–2. The tax was in operation when Henry Demarest Lloyd visited the country a decade later, achieving its objectives of 'making the [large] landowners pay their share of the cost of government and of the public works which made them rich, and...break[ing] up the monopolies'

(Lloyd, 1902, p. 105). George kept a close eye on these developments. In 1894 he wrote in the *North American Review* that he was pleased to see that 'New Zealand is today the one country which enjoys anything like prosperity in the midst of a universal depression', a circumstance he attributed to 'the partial application of the single-tax principle' (*Review of Reviews*, Australasian Edition, April 1894, p. 276).

Five months earlier George had written to the Labour member for Buller, P.J. O'Regan, a Georgist, that he was 'glad to learn...that the single taxers of New Zealand are not going to rest content with the small instalment which Mr. Ballance was able to secure'.[13] In 1896, under the Premiership of Richard Seddon, who had taken over from Ballance, a Land Valuation Department was established—believed to be the world's first. As at 1902, a land tax of 1d. on every £1 of an estate's unimproved ('ground') value applied on properties valued at over £500, increasing in steps to 2d. in the £ (Reeves, 1902, p. 260). As in Queensland at the time, the explicit aim of the Government with this tax was to break up large estates and to make them available to small holders: from 1891 onwards, the Government 'pursued a policy of State re-purchase of private lands for settlement—buying up the large, over-valued under-worked holdings and splitting them up for the small man to use' (Stewart et al., 1938, p. 37). As in Queensland too, this policy was closely aligned with encouragement of the dairy industry, operating on a co-operative basis. Concentrated in the South Auckland and Taranaki regions of the North Island, areas ideally suited to small farming, dairying developed rapidly from the 1890s, with the Government, especially following a Dairy Industry Act, 1908, applying itself to improved transport and export facilities, and to the education of farmers in the latest methods. By 1902 there were 222 butter and cheese factories operating in the country as a whole, and by 1927 the total value of butter and cheese exports reached £16,498,000, representing 34.6 per cent of total commodity exports (Irvine and Alpers, 1902; Stewart et al., 1938; Stamp, 1960).

While Georgist philosophies can be confidently said to have strongly influenced radical governments in Australia and New Zealand well into the 20th Century, this was, as I have argued, mainly in the sense of varying *interpretations* of George's theories. For example, in the 1930s the New Zealand Labour Party's platform officially included land nationalization which, while never actually implemented, no doubt influenced the thinking of Georgists within the Party, including (Sir) Walter Nash, Minister of Finance in the Michael Savage Labour Government of 1935–8, who was involved in a change to land-value rating in New Plymouth, Taranaki, in 1937 (Bob Keall, personal communication). The prospect of full-blown land nationalization also prompted Rolland O'Regan, surgeon and Georgist son of P.J. O'Regan, to emphasize the virtues of universal Crown-leasehold tenure rather than freehold in New Zealand, citing a paper advocating such a concept by Justice Else-Mitchell, Chairman of a

Royal Commission on Rating, Valuation and Local Government Finance in New South Wales. (Else-Mitchell's arguments are discussed by Phil Day, below.) A change to universal leasehold in New Zealand and Australia, O'Regan argued, was a 'practical political objective', and would 'harmonise with the Georgist objective of an economically free society and would have none of the dreaded features of Marxist-type nationalisation' (O'Regan, 1968, p. 4).

O'Regan pointed out a difficulty with land-value taxation as it existed in New Zealand and Australia at his time of writing, which was that it operated at both national and local levels, so that the latter reduced the base on which the former fell. In Australia, O'Regan explained, the situation had been even more difficult prior to 1952, when the tax had been imposed at federal, state and local levels. The federal tax, which had operated since 1910, when it had been introduced by Australia's first majority Federal Labour Government (the Fisher Government, which according to former Federal Minister for Labour Clyde Cameron [1984] 'was actually elected over the sole issue of the taxation of unimproved land values'), was abolished in 1952,[14] and land tax had been gradually reduced at state level since that date up to O'Regan's time of writing (1968). This had left the burden of the taxation remaining with the municipalities, which in O'Regan's view was a good thing. Colin Clark, too, writing in 1958, noted that in Australia 'the municipalities derive practically the whole of their revenue from taxes imposed, exactly as Henry George advocated, solely on the unimproved value of the land, exempting buildings and cultivations' (Clark, 1958, cited in Skitch, 2000, p. 25).

This is no longer true—local government authorities in Australia currently receive on average about 50 per cent of their revenue through rating on unimproved land values;[15] but the principle has been actively re-examined by State authorities of late, in particular by the Victorian and New South Wales State Governments. Frank Stilwell and Kirrily Jordan, in Chapter 10, make an eloquent case for strengthening land taxes (they do not necessarily restrict themselves to unimproved values, but are mainly concerned with these) as a means of not only protecting the natural environment, but also, and specifically within an Australian context, of containing runaway inflation of property values. In an Appendix to their chapter they provide figures showing the land-tax rate on unimproved values in all the Australian States and Territories as at 2003–4. These show that, in New South Wales, no tax was payable at that date on land with an unimproved value of up to $260,999 (Australian dollars): on $261,000 and over, the rate was $100 plus 1.7 cents for every $1 of value exceeding $261,000. This is considerably less than the tax of 1d. in the £ (in constant money terms) on unimproved value of land provided for under a Local Government Act of 1905 in that State, with *no* statutory exemption allowed (Murray, 1966, p. 55). Likewise in Victoria—the nil tax on 0–$149,999, and the $150 plus 0.1 cents for every $1 of value between $150,000 and $199,999 (rising to $54,880 plus

5 cents for every $1 of value exceeding $2,700,000) is less than the ½ d. in the
£ on values over £250 imposed in 1910 (*ibid.*).

It is not surprising, therefore, that New South Wales has this year (2004)
announced an overall increase in land-tax rates (0.4 cents in each $1 of value
up to $399,999, $1,600 plus 0.6 cents in each $1 from $400,000 to $499,999,
and $2,200 plus 1.4 cents in each $1 in excess of $500,000); and the Victorian
Government is resisting complaints from property owners that they are suffering, in terms of land tax payable, from the effects of rapid rises in land prices in
that State, especially for coastal properties (*Business Review Weekly* [Sydney],
15–21, July 2004; *Australian Financial Review*, 11 March 2004). And this
renewed interest in land tax is not restricted to Australia. Another article in the
Australian Financial Review (15 March 2004) discusses the current housing
price boom in the U.K. where, notwithstanding land tax having 'acquired a
bad name because of the loopy disciples of Henry George', the idea is being
touted as a serious device for dealing with the potential problem of runaway
inflation. The writer goes on to say: 'As the British are beginning to realise, a
comprehensive land tax could discourage property price bubbles. And it could
do it more efficiently than some of the alternative measures suggested such as
restrictions on the negative gearing of residential property investment'.

This is hardly high theory, but it is a testament to George's ongoing influence
at various levels of economic discussion, whether or not consciously recognized
(and that George was capable of making signifigant theoretical contributions
is affirmed in Laurence Moss's chapter). George could hardly have imagined
that his campaign for land reform in the British Isles in the 1880s might be
translated into a method of dealing with serious macroeconomic problems in
the 21st Century. Yet this has eventuated. In the intervening 120 years, he has
inspired economists, politicians and innumerable others, including Leo Tolstoy,
the scientists Alfred Russel Wallace and Ludwig Büchner (Silagi, 1993), and
the South Australian Independent parliamentarian, Edward Craigie (M.H.A.
1930–41), who argued, *c*.1932, that 'Our present system of taxation and unjust
laws are strangling production and the only remedy is to make the land the only
source of taxation' (Schubert, n.d., p. 16; see also McGillick, 1980), and who,
in turn, inspired the Hon. Clyde Cameron, A.O., Australian Federal Minister
for Labour in the E.G. Whitlam Labor Government, 1972–5. Clyde Cameron
became Secretary of the Gawler, South Australia, branch of the Henry George
League at sixteen years of age in 1929, and '[r]ight from those early days [has]
remained a constant supporter of governments collecting the unimproved rental
value of land in place of the present unfair direct and indirect taxes that weigh
so heavily upon our lower and middle income groups' (Clyde Cameron to the
editor, 20 July 2004). George would surely have been pleased with this eloquent
endorsement of his central idea.

NOTES

1. According to Richard Hoggart (1971), 60,000 copies of *Progress and Poverty* were sold within four years of its first appearance, and an article in the *Christian Science Monitor* of 1 September 1929 commemorating the 50th anniversary of the book's first publishing claims that 'more than 3,000,000 copies' of the book had been issued (clipping of the article contained in noted socialist, Alf Mattison's copy of *Progress and Poverty*, Mattison Collection, Brotherton Library, University of Leeds). Clyde Cameron (see above) has said (1989) that the book 'became the world's best seller in the field of political science and economic reform'.

2. The Bill limited pastoral leases to 20,000 acres, agricultural selections to 960 acres, and suburban housing lots to 5 acres (Joyce, 1984). QPD refers to Queensland Parliamentary Debates (Legislative Assembly).

3. See Murray (1966), p. 57.

4. The average acreage of holdings on one page of the Rosalie Shire (established 1880) Valuation Register for 1893, for instance, was 190 (Glass, 2004).

5. As early as 1906 the Pittsworth Dairy Co. was shipping butter to London; and by 1934 small factories like the Moola Co-operative Dairy Association, near Maclagan, Queensland, were shipping over 6 tons of cheese a month to various U.K. ports. By 1954 the Downs Co-operative Dairy Association, with factories in Toowoomba, Miles, Clifton, Dalby, Crow's Nest, Goombungee and Jandowae, was producing around 258 tons of butter a month. (Pittsworth Dairy Co. Ltd. *Minutes*, 14 February 1906; Moola Co-operative Association Ltd. Shipping register, 17 April 1934; *Unity Co-operator*, July 1954). On refrigeration technology, see Springett (1921).

6. E.G. Theodore to A.F. Partridge, 24 December 1929 (Queensland State Archives).

7. In *Progress and Poverty* George had contended: '[T]o shift the burden of taxation from production and exchange to the value or rent of land would not merely be to give new stimulus to the production of wealth; it would be to open new opportunities. For under this system no one would care to hold land unless to use it...taxation, instead of operating, as now, as a fine upon improvement, would operate to force improvement' (George, 1976 [1879], pp. 308–9). William Lane, author of the socialist novel *The Workingman's Paradise*, paraphrased George's argument thus: 'George's...scheme...works this way. You tax the landowner until it doesn't pay him to have unused land. He must either throw it up or get it used somehow and [the effect of] the demand for labour thus created is to lift wages and put the actual workers in what George evidently considers a satisfactory position' (Lane, 1948 [1892], p. 116).

8. cf. Leviticus 25.23: 'The land shall not be sold for ever: for the land is mine; for ye are strangers and sojourners with me'.

9. The Australian economist R.F. Irvine (1933, p. 29), in an account of the organization of 'primitive' societies, including the Maoris of New Zealand, argues that 'the group was paramount', that there was 'complete community of goods as well as of labour' and that '[l]and was common'.

10. D.E. Fisher (2004, p. 203) has recently drawn attention to the treatment of water and other commons in Roman Law as a backdrop to the present discussions on water 'rights' in Australia (a major issue, especially in connection with what many see as the unsustainable drawing of water from the Murray-Darling system by several States—see Wahlquist, 2004, but also see Dwyer, 2004). As Fisher notes, according to the Institutes of Justinian, 'the air, running water, the sea and subsequently the seashore' were 'by natural law common to all'. This unregulated common property regime, Fisher observes, reflected a situation where abundance and purity of water were not major concerns. In his notes to the Institutes, J.B. Moyle (1949) argues that 'the history of Roman Law alone...convinces us that among primitive peoples absolute private ownership is a thing at first unknown, and that when it has been developed, alienation is the exception, not the rule' (p. 198). Alison Burford (1993) has pointed out that ancient Greek has no word for 'landowning' or 'landowner', and even aristocratic property holders, such as the *geomoroi* of Samos and the *gomoroi* of Syracuse were literally 'land*sharers*', not owners. The Church Father St. John Chrysostom (*c.* 347–407 A.D.), in an exposition of the story of Ananias and Sapphira (Acts 5.1–10), outlines, according to Emil Brunner (1961, p. 161) 'an absolutely communistic theory, which even extols communal consumption as the

most natural method'. In describing the early Christian community, Chrysostom (1989, p. 47) himself wrote: 'This was an angelic commonwealth, not to call anything of their's their own....No talk of "mine" and "thine"....Neither did they consider their brethren's property foreign to themselves...nor again deemed they aught their own, all was the brethren's'.
11. See note 1, Chapter 4.
12. See Wynne-Edwards (1986); Sterelny (2001); Eldredge (2004).
13. Copy of letter kindly supplied by Bob Keall, Takapuna, New Zealand.
14. The tax, as it originally operated, was on the basis of 1d. in the £ of unimproved value for unoccupied land up to £5,000 in value, increasing to 7d. in the £ at £80,000 plus in value. Occupied land up to £5,000 in value (increased to £8,750 by 1952) was exempt. Only £62,352 in Commonwealth land tax was collected in Queensland in 1949–50, compared with £430,687 in State land tax (Murray, 1966; *Commonwealth Law Reports*, Vol. 14, 1911–1912, pp. 348–54; *Queensland Year Book*, 1951, p. 360; Clyde Cameron, personal communication, 26 November 2004).
15. This varies considerably. The Crow's Nest Shire, Queensland, in which I reside, has currently budgeted for a total income of $17 million in 2004–5, of which rates on land values are expected to contribute $4.2 million. In the nearby Pittsworth Shire, on the other hand, rates on land are 'the major component of the Council's income', rural landholders paying 1.844 cents per dollar of land valuation, and urban residents paying between 1.945 cents and 2.413 cents (*Highfields Herald*, 29 June 2004; *Pittsworth Sentinel*, 28 July 2004).

REFERENCES

Abercrombie, P. (1945), *Greater London Plan 1944*, London: His Majesty's Stationery Office.
Anon. (1933), *Theodore Irrigation Settlement: Review of Terms and Conditions of Holdings* (typescript, Queensland State Archives, Loc. No. LAN/118).
Anon. (2004), Queensland Govt, Dept of Natural Resources, Mines and Energy, *Central Queensland Regional Water Supply Study, Information Paper No. 3* (draft).
Ashton, R. (1999), *Dairy and Cheese Making Factories of the Pittsworth District*, Pittsworth, Qld: Pittsworth Shire Council.
Barber, W.J. (1979), *A History of Economic Thought*, Harmondsworth, Middlesex: Penguin.
Beal, D.J. (1993), *The Making of Rosalie*, Toowoomba, Qld: University of Southern Queensland Press.
Binning, C. and M. Young (1999), *Conservation Hindered: The Impact of Local Government Rates and the State Land Taxes on the Conservation of Native Vegetation*. National R & D Program on Rehabilitation, Management and Conservation of Remnant Vegetation, Research Paper 3/99, Canberra: Environment Australia.
Brierly, E.W. and T.W. Irish (1909), *The Crown Lands Acts of New South Wales*, Sydney: The Law Book Company of Australasia, Ltd.
Brown, F.C. (n.d. c. [1956]), *They Called Him Billy: A Biography of the Rt. Hon. W.M. Hughes, P.C., M.P.*, Sydney: Peter Huston.
Brunner, E. (1961), *The Divine Imperative: A Study in Christian Ethics*, London: Lutterworth Press.
Burford, A. (1993), *Land and Labor in the Greek World*, Baltimore and London: Johns Hopkins University Press.
Butlin, N.G. (1959), 'Colonial Socialism in Australia, 1860-1900', in Hugh G.T. Aitkin (ed.), *The State and Economic Growth*, New York: Social Sciences Research Council, pp. 26–78.
Cameron, Hon. Clyde R. (1984), 'How Labor Lost Its Way', *Progress*, June 1984, pp. 1–4.

Cameron, Hon. Clyde R. (1989), *Revenue That is Not a Tax: Speech Given at the Official Opening of the New Western Australian Headquarters of the Georgist Education Association (Inc.) at 10 Broome Street, South Perth, on 31 March 1989* (typescript).

Camm, J.C.R. (1967), 'The Queensland Agricultural Land Purchase Act 1894 and Rural Settlement: A Case Study of Jimbour', *Australian Geographer*, **10**, 263–74.

Chrysostom, St. (1989), 'Homilies on the Acts of the Apostles and the Espistle to the Romans', in P. Schaff (ed.), *A Select Library of the Nicene and Post-Nicene Fathers of the Christian Church*, Vol. XI, pp. 1–348, Grand Rapids, Michigan: Wm. B. Eerdmans Publishing Company.

Churchill, Rt. Hon. W.S. (1970) [1909], *Liberalism and the Social Problem*, London: Hodder and Stoughton.

Churchill, Rt. Hon. W.S. (1970) [1909], *The People's Rights*, London: Jonathan Cape.

Darwin, C. (1901) [1859], *The Origin of Species*, London: Ward, Lock, & Co., Limited.

Day, P.D. (1995), *Land: The elusive quest for social justice, taxation reform & a sustainable planetary environment*, Brisbane: Australian Academic Press.

Day, P.D. (2000), *Hijacked Inheritance*, unpublished Ph.D. thesis, University of Queensland.

De Mille, Anna George (1972), *Henry George: Citizen of the World*, New York: Greenwood Press.

Douglas, R. (2003), 'Laveleye: A Critic Ripe for Conversion', in Robert V. Andelson and Laurence S. Moss (eds), *Critics of Henry George* (2 vols), Oxford: Blackwell Publishing, Vol. 1, pp. 47–59.

Dwyer, T. (2004), 'State Abuse of Monopoly Power in Water', *Australian Financial Review*, 25 October.

Eldredge, N. (2004), *Why We Do It: Rethinking Sex and the Selfish Gene*, New York: W.W. Norton.

Engels, F. (1977) [1891], *The Origin of the Family, Private Property and the State—In the Light of the Researches of Lewis H. Morgan*, Moscow: Progress Publishers.

Fisher, D.E. (2004), 'Rights of Property in Water: Confusion or Clarity', *Environmental and Planning Law Journal*, **21**, 200–26.

Fitzgerald, R. (1994), *'Red Ted': The Life of E.G. Theodore*, St Lucia, Qld: University of Queensland Press.

Fitzgerald, R. (2003), *The Popes Battalions: Santamaria, Catholicism and the Labor Split*, St Lucia, Qld.: University of Queensland Press.

French, M. and D.M. Waterson (1982), *The Darling Downs: A Pictorial History 1850-1950*, Toowoomba, Qld: Darling Downs Institute Press.

George, H, (1999) [1871], *Our Land and Land Policy* (ed. K. Wenzer), East Lansing: Michigan State University Press.

George, H. (1976) [1879], *Progress and Poverty*, London: Dent.

George, H. (1965) [1881], 'The Irish Land Question', in *idem*, *The Land Question (And Other Essays)*, New York: Robert Schalkenbach Foundation.

George, H. (1886), *Protection or Free Trade: An Examination of the Tariff Question with Especial Regard to the Interests of Labor*, New York: Henry George & Co.

George, H. (1891), *The Condition of Labour: An Open Letter to Pope Leo XIII*, London: Swan Sonnenschein & Co.

George, H. (1893), *A Perplexed Philosopher, Being, An Examination of Mr. Herbert Spencer's Various Utterances on the Land Question, with some Incidental Reference to his Synthetic Philosophy*, London: Kegan Paul, Trench, Trübner & Co.

Giskes, R. (2004), *An End to Broadscale Clearing by 2006 under the Vegetation Management and Other Legislation Amendment Bill 2004 (Qld)*, Queensland Parliamentary Library Research Brief No. 2004/06.

Glass, G.J. (1999), *Couriers, Mailmen and Bush Telegraph: The Story of the Cream Carters of Goombungee*, Goombungee, Qld: Rosalie Shire Historical Society Inc.

Glass, G.J. (2004), *Landholders in Rosalie Shire 1880 to 1940s* (C.D.), Goombungee, Qld: Rosalie Shire Historical Society Inc.

Grattan, M. (ed.) (2000), *Australian Prime Ministers*, Sydney: New Holland Publishers.

Griffith, S.W. (1884), Speech at Pastoral Leases Act of 1869 Amendment Bill — Second Reading, 19th February. Queensland Parliamentary Debates, Vol. XLI, Brisbane: Government Printer.

Griffith, S.W. (1889), 'The Distribution of Wealth', *Centennial Magazine* (Sydney), July, pp. 833–42.

Groenewegen, P. (1998), *A Soaring Eagle: Alfred Marshall, 1842–1924*, Aldershot, Hants.: Edward Elgar.

Hanham, H.J. (1968), 'The Problem of Highland Discontent, 1880–1885', *Transactions of the Royal Historical Society*, **19** (fifth series), 21–65.

Heilbroner, R.L. (1991), *The Worldly Philosophers: The Lives, Times and Ideas of the Great Economic Thinkers*, Harmondworth, Middlesex: Penguin.

Hobson, J.A. (1910), *The Industrial System: An Enquiry into Earned and Unearned Income*, London: Longmans, Green & Co.

Hoggart, R. (1971), *The Uses of Literacy*, Harmondsworth, Middlesex: Penguin.

Horne, D. (1983), *Billy Hughes: Prime Minister of Australia 1915–1923*, Melbourne: Black Inc.

Irvine, R.F. (1933), *The Midas Delusion*, Adelaide: Hassell Press.

Irvine, R.F. and O.T.J. Alpers (1902), *The Progress of New Zealand in the Century*, Toronto and Philadelphia: Linscott Publishing Company.

Johnson, A. (1986), *Fly a Rebel Flag: Bill Morrow 1888–1980*, Ringwood, Victoria, Australia: Penguin.

Johnston, W. Ross (1982), *The Call of the Land*, Milton, Qld: The Jacaranda Press.

Joyce, R.B. (1984), *Samuel Walker Griffith*, St Lucia, Qld: University of Queensland Press.

King, J.E. (1988), 'Henry George (1839–1897)', in *idem*, *Economic Exiles*, London: Macmillan, pp. 82–108.

Lane, W. (1948) [1892], *The Workingman's Paradise*, Sydney: Cosme Publishing Co.

Laveleye, Émile de (1878), *Primitive Property*, London: Macmillan.

Lawrence, E.P. (1957), *Henry George in the British Isles*, East Lansing: Michigan State University Press.

Lloyd, H.D. (1902), *Newest England: Notes of a Democratic Traveller in New Zealand, with some Australian Comparisons*, New York: Doubleday, Page & Co.

Lowe, I. et al. (1997), *State of the Environment Australia 1996*, Collingwood, Australia: CSIRO Publishing.

Luck, A. (2004), 'Sunnyside Cheese Factory and Hugh Sharpe's General Store'. Talk given at Centenary of Muniganeen State School commemoration, Muniganeen, Queensland, 4 December 2004.

Malthus, T.R. (1926) [1798], *First Essay on Population* (with notes by James Bonar), London: Macmillan and Royal Economic Society.

Mann, T. (1896), *The Socialists' Program (A Speech delivered at North Aberdeen, on Saturday, April 25th, 1896)*, Manchester: Labour Press Society.

Mann, T. (1913), *From Single Tax to Syndicalism*, London: Guy Bowman.

Mann, T. (1967) [1923], *Memoirs*, London: MacGibbon & Kee.

Marx, K. (1909), *Capital: A Critique of Political Economy*, Vol 3, Chicago: Charles H. Kerr & Co.

McCallum, I.R. (ed.) (n.d. *c*. [1944]), *Physical Planning*, London: The Architectural Press.

McGillick, T. (1980), *Comrade No More: The Autobiography of a Former Communist Party Leader*, West Perth, Western Australia: The Author.

Moyle, J.B. (ed.) (1949), *Imperatoris Justiniani Institutionum*, Oxford: Clarendon Press.

Murdoch, W. (1999) [1923], *Alfred Deakin*, Melbourne: Bookman.

Murray, J.F.N. (1966), *Principles and Practice of Valuation*, Sydney: Commonwealth Institute of Valuers.

O'Regan, R. (1968), *State Leaseholds – The Basis for Land Reform*, Wrexham, U.K.: New Zealand Unimproved-Value Rating Association.

Palmer, V. (1966), *The Legend of the Nineties*, Melbourne: Melbourne University Press.

Partridge, A.F. (1926), *The Dawson Valley Irrigation Scheme and What It Offers to Settlers*, Brisbane: Irrigation and Water Supply Commission (Qld).

Pearce, J. (1997), *Wisdom and Innocence: A Life of G.K. Chesterton*, London: Hodder & Stoughton.

Pullen, J. (2003), *Henry George's Lecture Tour of Australia in 1890*, Paper presented at History of Economic Thought Society of Australia Conference, Australian Catholic University, Melbourne, 16 July 2003 (Typescript).

Raymont, P. (2004) 'With No Shoes on Their Feet: Off to a Queensland One-Teacher Country School in the 1960s', *Educational Historian*, **17**(3), 7–18.

Reeves, Hon.W. Pember (1902), *State Experiments in Australia and New Zealand* (2 vols), London: George Allen & Unwin Ltd.

Roberts, B. ('Ephesian') (1941), *Winston Churchill*, London: Hutchinson & Co.

Schubert, A.I. (n.d.), *An Appreciation of the Political Life of E.J. Craigie*, Adelaide: The Printing Press.

Shaw, G.B. (1928), *The Intelligent Woman's Guide to Socialism and Capitalism*, London: Constable and Company Ltd.

Silagi, M. (1993), 'Henry George and Europe', *American Journal of Economics and Sociology*, **52**, 119-127.

Skitch, R.F. (2000), *Encouraging Conservation through Valuation* (2 vols), Brisbane: Qld Dept of Natural Resources.

Smith, S.H. (1914), *Second Book of Geography*, Sydney and Brisbane: William Brooks & Co. Ltd.

Springett, B.H. (1921), *Cold Storage and Ice Making*, London: Pitman.

Stallman, J. (n.d. *c* [1980]), *A Brief History of the Cheese Making Industry in the Pittsworth District 1896–1980*, Pittsworth, Qld: Pittsworth and District Historical Society.

Stamp, L.D. (1960), *The Econcomic Geography of the Leading Countries*, London: Longmans.

Sterelny, K. (2001), *Dawkins vs. Gould: Survival of the Fittest*, Duxford, Cambridge, U.K.: Icon Books.

Sterner, T. (2003), *Policy Instruments for Environmental and Natural Resource Management*, Washington, D.C. and Stockholm: Resources for the Future, World Bank and Swedish International Development Corporation Agency.

Stewart, W.D. et al. (1938), *Contemporary New Zealand*, Auckland, N.Z.: New Zealand Institute of International Affairs.

Taylor, G. (1925), *Australia in its Physiographic and Economic Aspects*, Oxford: Oxford University Press.

Theodore, E.G. (1920), *Policy Speech, 10 September 1920*, Brisbane: Anthony James Cumming, Government Printer.

Theodore, E.G. (n.d. *c*. [1925]), *Who Pays The Land Tax?* Brisbane: Anthony James Cumming, Government Printer.

Wahlquist, A. (2004), 'Irrigators Turn The Currents', *Weekend Australian*, 21–22 August.
Waterson, D.B. (1968), *Squatter, Selector, and Storekeeper: A History of the Darling Downs 1859–93*, Sydney: Sydney University Press.
Webb, B. (1930), *My Apprenticeship*, London: Longmans, Green & Co.
Webb, S. (1908), *The Basis & Policy of Socialism* (Fabian Socialist Series, No.4), London: A.C. Field.
Wynne-Edwards, V.C. (1986), *Evolution through Group Selection*, Oxford: Blackwell.

ACKNOWLEDGEMENTS

Again I am grateful to my contributing authors for their forbearance and to the friendly staff at Edward Elgar's, especially Alexandra Minton, for their help and patience in the preparation of this book. Peter Pegg formatted the manuscript and provided editorial advice, and Robin Neill read the manuscript and made helpful suggestions. Thanks also to colleagues at the University of Southern Queensland, Geoff Cockfield, Ian Eddington, Ann Firth and Richard Temple-Smith, to former colleagues at Griffith University, Ian Lowe and Max Standage, and to Roy MacLeod for their support and encouragement. I am indebted also to the staff of Cambridge University Library, the Brotherton Library, University of Leeds, the Fryer Library, University of Queensland, the library of the University of Southern Queensland, the Queensland Parliamentary Library and Queensland State Archives, and to Jill Bowie, Clyde Cameron, Margaret Campbell, Roslyn Cox, Nicole Dixon, Emma Dorrough, Geoff Edwards, John Hall, Geoff Hodgson, Greta Jones, Richard Joseph, George Jukes, Bob Keall, John King, Mike Kirk, Rob, Sal and Nathan Laurent, Andrea and Nola Luck, John Marsden, Jim Moore, John Morgan, John Nightingale, Doug Ogilvie, Adam Perkins, Hilary Perrott, John Pullen, Oliver Pickering, Richard Sanders, Mary Seefried, George and Yvonne Simmons, Nell Smith, Jim Thompson, David and Isabella Thorpe, Maira Turraids, Godfrey Waller and Ken Wenzer for all their help in many ways.

John Pullen's chapter, 'Henry George's Land Reform: The Distinction between Private Ownership and Private Possession' originally appeared in the *American Journal of Economics and Sociology*, and I am grateful to the editor of that journal, Laurence Moss, and to its publisher, Blackwell Publishers Inc., for permission to republish it in this book.

2. Henry George and Darwin's Dragon: Thomas Henry Huxley's Response to *Progress and Poverty*

Erin McLaughlin-Jenkins

'More damneder nonsense than poor Rousseau's blether'. Thomas Henry Huxley was not always this clear, and rarely so brief, in his condemnations of rival philosophies, but this simple invective conveyed to James Knowles, editor of the periodical *The Nineteenth Century*, said it all.[1] Huxley was, of course, speaking of Henry George's *Progress and Poverty*, an enormously popular book among the working classes and an entirely irksome bit of 'fudge' from Huxley's point of view (Huxley, 1968d, p. 376). Dismissed as another errant Rousseauian, Huxley accused George of treading 'perilously near the boundary which divides blunders from crimes' in his promotion of 'social discord'. *Progress and Poverty* he dismissed as '*a priori* political speculation' and an 'interesting museum of political delusions' that showed more poverty than progress (*ibid.*, pp. 337–8, 362; Huxley, 1968a, p. 170). Concerned that the masses were in need of a little 'common sense', Huxley wrote four articles for Knowles attacking Rousseau, Quesnay, the Physiocrats, socialism, individualism, and any other irresponsible philosophy he could toss in to make his point.[2] George figured prominently in two of these articles – 'Natural Rights and Political Rights' (Huxley, 1968d) and 'Capital: The Mother of Labour' (Huxley, 1968a) – being treated to generous servings of scorn, mockery, and patronizing analogies.

For George's part, he was more interested in undermining Herbert Spencer's sociology in *A Perplexed Philosopher* (1892), offering little commentary on Huxley's ideas other than to note that the dispute between Huxley and Spencer printed in the London *Times* (November 1889) indicated that Huxley was bullheaded and seemed not to have a very solid grasp of Spencer's philosophy (George, 1892, pp. 94–5). Any other offending comments made by George remained indirect as general comments on versions of Darwinian sociology (see below). So why the smoke and fire from Huxley? Was it simply a philosophical dispute? Huxley might have chosen from any number of pro-labour theorists, but he chose George: why? On the simple level, Huxley's condemnation of George can be seen as a matter of rival philosophies, but a closer look reveals that it was about much more than this: it was a multi-layered defence of personal goals, ideals, and scientific authority. This chapter begins with an analysis of Huxley's philosophical and economic arguments, followed by an exploration of the personal and professional motivation behind the attack on George. Ultimately, the 1890s essays are less instructive with respect to their political and economic insights than for what they tell us about the impact of Huxley's emotional and physical health on his prose, his loss of control over the scientific community and popular opinion, and his outrage with George's irreverence towards science in general and Darwinism in particular.

The four 1890 essays became part of Huxley's intention to publish, at his wife's suggestion, a 'Primer of Politics' to dissuade workers from falling prey to socialism's 'political fictions'.[3] The first article, published in the January issue of *Nineteenth Century* was 'The Natural Inequality of Men'. It refutes the doctrine of natural rights along with its central assumption that all men are born free and equal. Based on the obvious differences in people's innate abilities, Huxley asserted that inequality is both a natural and political reality in which 'Witless will serve his brother' (Huxley, 1968c, p. 309). The last instalment appeared in May under the title 'Government: Anarchy or Regimentation', and it pitted socialism against its opposite, individualism (Huxley, 1968b). Both extremes were, according to Huxley, equally dangerous but in different ways. The second and third articles focused, more or less, on the ideas in *Progress and Poverty*, though both begin with lengthy discussions of Rousseau, Quesnay, and the Physiocrats.

The first of these, 'Natural Rights and Political Rights', repeats the philosophical approach found in 'The Natural Inequality of Men', while 'Capital: The Mother of Labour' diverges to some extent by attempting to grapple with economic theory. This last article is rarely mentioned in historical analysis, which is unfortunate because it forcefully, though selectively, confronts some of the more practical elements of Henry George's program. Also, it offers a rare moment of human frailty in Huxley's polemics revealing his awkwardness with the topic and his almost hysterical irritation with Henry George. For these reasons, 'Capital' is in some ways a more instructive text, though 'Natural Rights and Political Rights' outlines the intellectual pedigree behind Huxley's foray into economic theory.

In 'Natural Rights and Political Rights', Huxley reproduced his summary of Rousseau's basic principles from 'The Natural Inequality of Men' with the necessary alterations to accommodate George's version:

'The Natural Inequality of Men'	'Natural Rights and Political Rights'
1. All men are born free, politically equal, and good, and in the 'state of nature' remain so; consequently it is their natural right to be free, equal, and (presumably, their duty to be) good.	1. All men have equal rights.
2. All men being equal by natural right, none can have any right to encroach on another's equal right. Hence no man can appropriate any part of the common means of subsistence – that is to say, the land or anything which the land produces – without the unanimous consent of all other men. Under any other circumstances, property is usurpation, or, in plain terms, robbery.	2. There is no foundation for any rightful title to ownership except this: That a man has a right to himself; to the use of his own powers; to the enjoyment of the fruit of his own exertions; therefore, to whatsoever he makes or produces.
3. Political rights, therefore, are based upon contract; the so-called right of conquest is no right, and property which has been acquired by force may rightly be taken away by force (pp. 304–5).	3. The right to that which is produced is 'vested' in the producer by natural law. It is also a 'fundamental law of Nature that her enjoyment by man shall be consequent upon his exertion'.
	4. Land is a gratuitous offering of Nature, not a thing produced by labour; all men therefore have equal rights to it. These rights are inalienable, as existing men cannot contract away the rights of their successors. Every infant who comes into the world has as good a right to landed estates as their present possessors, by whom he is, in fact, robbed of his share (pp. 360–61).

Comparing the lists reveals some important differences. As Roy Douglas points out, the first list contains ideas similar to George's in some respects, but there are crucial points of disagreement over property rights, the use of force, and the basis of equality. George's solution to monopolization of land was not forceful seizure, but a single tax on ground rent. Moreover, as Douglas notes, the foundation of George's economic philosophy and the meaning behind his assertion of a man's natural rights to himself, the products of his labour, and open access to Nature's bounty was equality in the eyes of God, entitling all to civil equality and the blessings of God's gifts to humanity. It was ethical justice and Christian brotherhood that underpinned his enquiry into the causes of poverty and the remedial potential of a single tax on land (Douglas, 1979, p. 141). This was in no way part of Rousseau's philosophy, and Huxley had to take a very narrow view of what constitutes equality to confuse the two.[4]

In 'Natural Rights and Political Rights', Huxley acknowledged that George's and Rousseau's philosophies were 'in principle, though by no means in all its details, identical', but the details were overshadowed by the dangerous similarity in the principles and type of reasoning. In Huxley's view, George's 'political philosophy...exhibits, in perfection, the same *a priori* method, starting from highly questionable axioms which are assumed to represent absolute truth'. Moreover, George was 'asking us to upset the existing arrangements of society on the faith of deductions from those axioms' (Huxley, 1968d, p. 338). All of this rested on the doctrine of natural rights, which was, in Huxley's mind, the assumption stoking the flames of socialist propaganda and labour unrest. The details be damned! He had to confront the foundation and destroy it once and for all: *Progress and Poverty* had to be shown for the 'mischievous' collection of 'political delusions' it was (*ibid.*, p. 355). Not that he was without anything positive to say about George: aside from the 'superfluous rhetorical confectionery' that weakened its prose, it was 'clearly and vigorously written' (*ibid.*, p. 338). Twenty-one pages later – pages mainly consisting of philosophical bluster – Huxley had to remind his readers what the topic was!

Huxley argued that there are two kinds of rights: natural and civil. Natural rights are linked to natural law – the 'pitiless "struggle for existence"' – while civil laws, based on a social contract, dictate the moral and ethical imperatives that George mistakenly derived from *a priori* axioms. Using an analogy of a tiger to demonstrate natural rights, Huxley claimed that the 'rights of tigers' must include 'the exercise and enjoyment of the faculties with which nature has endowed them'. If this includes eating a man, then man is part of the tiger's natural foodstuff and is consumed under the tiger's right to preserve its existence. Similarly, a man has the right to shoot the tiger if he is equipped to do so in order to preserve his existence. These rights are 'diametrically opposed', and so the stronger will exercise his rights while the other will perish (*ibid.*, pp. 343–8). This is the only natural right that Huxley recognizes.

Extending his analogy to social relations, Huxley drew upon the Robinson Crusoe analogy employed with different conclusions by Henry George in *Social Problems* (1902 [1884]). On the island, Crusoe and another man, Will Atkins, must sort out their right of property. Stalking the same goat, they are 'in the same position of two tigers, slinking after the same Hindoo, so far as the law of nature is concerned'. In the absence of civil law, they will have 'to fight for the goat'. This 'extreme and logical individualism means isolation and war', and if the men follow 'the commonest common sense' they will choose to cooperate and 'renounce natural law' for a social contract, placing themselves 'under a moral and civil law'. George's error was in 'confounding natural with moral rights' (*ibid.*, pp. 354–5). Perhaps men have a moral right to their freedom, but what this means is determined by civil arrangements. If the existing order is inhibiting the freedom of individuals, then by all means we should set about reforming it in rational and peaceful ways (*ibid.*, pp. 361–2). Huxley's lifelong commitment to educational reforms, the promotion of science, and reward for merit without regard for class barriers are examples of his commitment to achieving more equitable social relations.

Huxley saw this as a real dividing line between his ideology and George's; but more accurately, it reveals the narrow dualistic framework Huxley was applying to George's comprehensive survey of modern economic contradictions and problems (Douglas, 1979, p. 141). George's rationale for natural rights followed a line of reasoning beginning with the idea that God created nature for the use of all His creatures. All are born with an equal reliance on the earth's resources, just as all need oxygen to breathe. Everyone must remain free to exercise the right of access to these resources and to retain the products of their labour. Just as society would not tolerate a monopoly in oxygen, it was 'preposterous' to George that any one inhabitant of this 'rolling sphere' would be allowed to monopolize the soil (George, 1902, p. 194; see also pp. 185–95). George offered by way of analogy the example of Robinson Crusoe and Friday sharing an island (*ibid.*, p. 141). If Crusoe claims the entire island for his own property, then Friday is left without resources and is, therefore, a mere slave, subject to the whimsy of Crusoe. George's argument for freedom and equality is an anti-slavery message, not an advocacy of economic and political levelling. There are always ranks in society, but a tax on land would re-invest wealth in the community, stimulate and stabilize the economy, and soften the gap between the rich and the poor. Moreover, George asserted that natural sociability was a feature of humanity; man is more than a mere animal or plant (*ibid.*, pp. 203–07). The 'Master Workman' created natural laws of progress, brotherhood, and cooperation, and these overrode Huxley's law of the jungle. Man's natural right was to enjoy the 'gifts of the Creator' (*ibid.*, pp. 206, 208). Huxley might have been on safer ground if he had challenged George's egalitarian natural theology rather than his tentative links with Rousseau and Quesnay.

Huxley's argument in 'Natural Rights and Political Rights' remains at the philosophical level. He does not mention the single tax advocated by George and, in fact, misrepresents George's land policy. Huxley claims that George supported the 'eviction of all several landowners and the confiscation of that which is, and, for many centuries has been, regarded as their undoubted property' (Huxley, 1968d, p. 359). This is a gross misreading and is only one of many errors. Roy Douglas has concluded that 'in his eagerness as a controversialist, he misunderstood the implications of George's teaching' (Douglas, 1979, p. 147). Huxley failed to see that many of George's views were compatible with his own – e.g., liberal capitalism, educational reform, civil contract, legal equality, peaceful reforms – and he did not make the necessary distinction between land and capital (*ibid.*, pp. 144–5). Furthermore, Huxley's historically based defence of property was so lacking in 'substantive information' that it left Douglas 'mystified' (*ibid.*, p. 148). Not only was it unsubstantiated, it was, as Douglas claims for much of Huxley's commentary, more concerned with winning an argument than it was with a clear enumeration of the 'ideas which lay at the root of his social thought' (*ibid.*, p. 151). Douglas attributed this to Huxley's 'bitter' competitive nature, and though this may be true to a limited degree, Douglas did not have, in 1979, the benefit of the full and rich biography of Huxley written by Adrian Desmond. Desmond's study of Huxley makes clear the complex forces behind the great dragon's liberal reformist beliefs and his personal struggles in the last years of his life. Set against a backdrop of revolutionary agitation from socialists and the 1880s generation of labour activists, and afraid that the lessons of Darwinism were being forgotten, Huxley had much more at stake than mere controversy (Desmond, 1997).

In March 1890, 'Capital: the Mother of Labour' appeared in *The Nineteenth Century*. Modelled presumably on George's statement that 'production is the mother of wages', Huxley weaned himself off philosophical one-upmanship to the best of his ability, displaying awareness that the terms of the debate were shifting (George, 1953, p. 56). This new generation demanded more than high-minded recitations of Hume, Kant, Hobbes, Locke, and Rousseau—the language of modern economics was reframing the discussion. For Georgists, the forces of production provided the arena in which equal rights are determined. Speculation on a 'state of nature' was set aside for the realities of the current state of capitalist economics and the uneven distribution of wealth. Whether or not Huxley understood George's economics is questionable, but it is evident Huxley perceived that, while he might still dazzle his readers with a puff of Hume and flourishes of smoky Hobbesian rhetoric, the 'too ready-fisted' workers required some attention to the relationship of labour to capital and other similarly mundane issues (Huxley, 1968d, p. 380).

Despite this attempt to adapt to the times, 'Capital: The Mother of Labour, An Economical Problem Discussed from a Physiological Point of View' is plagued with stylistic and theoretical gaffes. In the simplest terms, Huxley missed the point of *Progress and Poverty*. Nowhere in this economic critique did he mention the single tax on land. This is the climactic point that George's analysis of economics, production, poverty, and progress is striving to reach. It was the remedy to the disease. Huxley did not address that section of the book, basing his review on a mere two chapters of Book I, which deal mainly with the meaning of economic terms. Moreover, substituting extra servings of inappropriate analogies for his customary historical lessons, and replacing philosophical illustration with irrelevant physiological examples, Huxley flails about in 'Capital' like a beached rhetorical fish. Adding further confusion, his flippant and all too hasty dismissals of George's ideas create abrupt shifts in his thinking. Huxley had pushed hard the limits of disrespect for George in 'Natural Rights and Political Rights', but 'Capital' took ridicule to a new pitch. Beneath this ill-considered assault are signs of a lack of confidence, if not lack of familiarity, with the practical application of economic theory.

The first half of 'Capital' lines up a series of analogies that includes thermo-dynamics, the relationship between mother and infant, a wandering savage, and a shepherd.[5] Beginning at the beginning, Huxley explains that 'the first act of a new-born child is to draw a deep breath'. This observation is followed by a mechanical explanation of respiration, with the added notation that all classes of people undergo this same lifelong exertion of energy (Huxley, 1968a, pp. 147-48). The point of this illustration is two-fold. Huxley was associating exertion with work and labour, linking human physiology to thermodynamics and productive labour. Having made this connection, he demonstrates that each of these relies on pre-existing material or 'vital capital supplied by others': material supplied by the mother, transference and conversion of energy, and economic capital, respectively. This frames his first thrust at George in the easily recognizable terms of mother and child while simultaneously bringing the economic issues under scientific authority. The wandering savage example and the shepherd anecdote follow the same pattern, adding a touch of historical development to further solidify his premise (*ibid.*, pp 152–55):

Recipient:	Infant	Savage	Shepherd	Labourer
Supplier:	Mother	Nature	Flock	Capital
Productive Output:	None	None	None	Unspecified
Labour Expended:	Locomotive	Negligible	Negligible	Negligible

In each of these illustrations, Huxley's point is that despite 'what labour he bestows' upon the pre-existing materials, the infant, the savage, the shepherd, and the labourer must 'borrow the capital he needs' (*ibid.*, p. 152). The infant returns nothing to the mother while consuming a great deal of her 'food-stuffs' (*ibid.*, pp. 150–51). The savage devotes what little labour he expends to the 'destruction' of natural resources (*ibid.*, 153). The shepherd's labour is a 'mere accessory of production of very little consequence'; more likely the sheep are the actual producers (*ibid.*, pp. 153, 154). Extended to labour, 'vital capital is essential' and the 'importance of human labour may be so small as to be almost a vanishing quantity' (*ibid.*, 158). This negates the importance of labour in relation to production, thereby undercutting George's claim that 'production is the mother of wages', and labour is the antecedent of production (George, 1953, p. 56). Naturally, or perhaps typically, Huxley couched his analogies in a highly manipulative and obscurantist context, such as setting the shepherd in ideal conditions without predators, economic competitors, or any of the real life problems that beset farmers. Still, it is mystifying that Huxley eliminated the laborious nature of farm work, and that in his acknowledgement that the shepherd lived on 'milk, cheese, and flesh which [the sheep] yield', he gives the impression that these products appear as if by magic, ready for consumption (Huxley, 1968a, pp. 153–5).

If this were not enough, Huxley finally reaches a nearly hysterical crescendo when he questions the productive autonomy of the sheep by directing attention first to their reliance on grass, and more precisely, the dependence of the grass on the sun. Locating the ultimate supplier of vital resources, the sun is designated as 'the primordial capitalist' (*ibid.*, p. 155).

For Huxley's rhetorical climax to this fanciful storytelling, readers are treated to a shocking parade of circuitous logic and false premises. Using an island analogy, as did George in *Social Problems*, he borrowed loosely from three of the Canary Islands to construct communities with different conditions and productive specialties. Refining his premise, he adds that these islands are 'cut off from the rest of the world' (*ibid.*, p. 163). Gran Canaria is a lush grain-producing island. Tenerife, home to a cattle-breeding community, also enjoys a lush pastoral environment. Lanzerote, on the other hand, is a barren island of manufacturers. Huxley gives Gran Canaria and Tenerife all of the materials necessary for independent existence, but leaves the residents of Lanzerote with only their manufacturing abilities and no capacity to feed themselves. The inhabitants of the self-sustaining islands not only supply the necessary materials for manufacturing, such as timber or wool, they also have the option of doing without manufactured goods entirely. Under these circumstances, the Lanzerotians are forced to accept the trade conditions imposed by their independent neighbours or 'starve'. Production on Lanzerote cannot exist without pre-existing 'vital capital' and 'food-stuffs' from Gran Canaria and Tenerife (*ibid.*, pp. 164–5). Of course, if the earlier analogies are applied, then both of the imaginary autonomous islands are not truly independent because they are dependent recipients of the vital stock of the primordial capitalist; but why confuse this circular and 'superfluous rhetorical confectionery' with its own contradictions?[6] This is clearly not Huxley at his best. His argument is fallacious and sophistical. The assignment of ideal autonomy to two islands and total dependence for one reflects, more than anything else, Huxley's growing concern over the labour agitation and the tension between employers and employees. As economic analysis, it fails; as an expression of anxiety, it succeeds.

Twenty-three pages into his critique, Huxley finally arrives at the point that he can no longer avoid: Henry George's economic ideas. After pages of problematic analogies and enough fire and smoke to choke the entire population of Lanzerote, Huxley confronts the 'museum of political delusions' (Huxley, 1968a, p. 169) contained in *Progress and Poverty*; or does he? More accurately, he isolates what he considers a definitive statement, mocks it briefly, and then dismisses it as unworthy of further consideration. This is only a partial engagement of the text, but at least it is on topic.

Huxley begins his analysis of George's central propositions that wages are not drawn from capital, but from the products of labour, and that production precedes enjoyment. Sweeping these notions aside, Huxley states:

The doctrine respecting the relation of capital and wages, which is thus opposed in 'Progress and Poverty', is that illustrated in the foregoing pages; the truth of which, I conceive, must be plain to any one who has apprehended the very simple arguments by which I have endeavoured to demonstrate it. One conclusion or the other must be hopelessly wrong…(*ibid.*, pp. 169–70).

Enough said. The analogies have made his point. Moving along to the next major issue – the definition of wealth – Huxley recalls George's statement that 'Nothing which nature supplies to man without his labour is wealth' (*ibid.*, p. 170), to which Huxley offers the objection:

I take it that native metals, coal and brick clay, are 'mineral products'; and I quite believe that they are properly termed 'wealth'. But when a seam of coal crops out at the surface, and lumps of coal are to be had for the picking up; or when native copper lies about in nuggets or when brick clay forms a superficial stratum, it appears to me that these things are supplied to, nay almost thrust upon man without his labour. According to the definition, therefore, they are not 'wealth'. According to the enumeration, however, they are 'wealth': a tolerably fair specimen of a contradiction in terms.

Further to this, Huxley indignantly asks if we are to believe that by breaking off a piece of coal and carrying it away, wealth is somehow conferred upon the coal that would otherwise not have been if the coal had been left untouched. This notion, according to Huxley, is 'a fallacy which needs no further refutation….So much for the doctrine of "Progress and Poverty" touching the nature of wealth' (*ibid.*, pp. 170–71).

The section of *Progress and Poverty* from which Huxley selected these apparent fallacies concerns the distinction between 'actual and not merely relative value'. According to George, natural resources that have been 'adapted by human labor to human use or gratification…[that is] secured, moved, combined, separated, or in other ways modified by human exertion' constitute actual value or wealth. Natural products that remain unmodified by labour have a potential value that has not yet been transformed into wealth. The coal or oil that needs mining but cannot be reached, or is without labour to dig or pump it, is wealth only in a relative sense. George also differentiates between capital and wealth, asserting that while 'all capital is wealth, all wealth is not capital' (George, 1953, pp. 41–2). Capital is 'that part of wealth devoted to production', or looking at it in a different way, 'capital is wealth in the course of exchange'. George is, therefore, distinguishing between articles of wealth designated for consumption and wealth 'devoted to production' (*ibid.*, p. 48). Huxley avoided these details, preferring generalities to in-depth analysis, and as a result, he missed his mark much as he missed the point.

One of the key distinctions George made was that between land and capital. Huxley cites this passage from *Progress and Poverty* as representative:

A fertile field, a rich vein of ore, a falling stream which supplies power, may give the possessor advantages equivalent to the possession of capital; but to class such things as capital would be to put an end to the distinction between land and capital (Huxley, 1968a, pp. 175–6).

In response, Huxley exclaims, 'Just so. But the fatal truth is that these things are capital; and that there really is no fundamental distinction between land and capital'. Again, Huxley shows a failure to distinguish among productive factors, collapsing wealth, land, and labour under the heading of capital:

Is it denied that a fertile field, a rich vein of ore, or a falling stream, may form part of a man's stock, and that, if they do, they are capable of yielding revenue? Will not somebody pay a share of the produce in kind, or in money, for the privilege of cultivating the first royalties for that of working the second; and a like equivalent for that of erecting a mill on the third? In what sense, then, are these things less 'capital' than the buildings and tools...? (*ibid.*, p. 176).

This is a revealing list of questions deserving a Georgist response. Assuming we accept, as Huxley does, the right to claim land as private property, the richness of the natural resources on that property constitute a kind of wealth or potential value. If the fertile field, ore, and stream are left uncultivated, without application of labour, they remain in a potential state. They become part of 'a man's stock' when and if labour is added to them. An apple tree may contain potential wealth either for consumption or exchange (potential capital), but unless someone picks and moves the apples, they are bird food and compost. Huxley, despite his protestations to the contrary, shows some awareness of this. Deconstructing his language, the necessary divisions are embedded in his commentary. The land is capable of 'yielding revenue', but it is not revenue itself. Someone must 'pay a share' – capital paid as rent – for 'cultivating' the ore deposits or 'erecting' a mill by the stream—labour. Just as tools and buildings are natural resources transformed by labour into exchangeable goods, or goods devoted to the increase of wealth, so the field, ore, and stream must be transformed by labour into wealth for consumption or exchange. The three factors of production are separate, and rent is the wild card upsetting the balance of forces. Though Huxley intended to disagree with George, he unintentionally supports George's definitions of land, labour, and capital while highlighting the role of rent in creating wealth for the landowner and barring both capital and labour from reaping the full reward of their effort (George, 1953, p. 38).

Not all of Huxley's criticisms were this weak. He took issue with George's concluding statement at the end of a long dissertation on the meaning of 'capital', i.e. that his 'digression' is 'not of any importance' because he 'is not writing a text-book'. Huxley pounced on this and rightly so. In a section devoted to terminological clarity, the suggestion that a full explanation of a central concept is a digression confuses the reader. Most likely, George meant that he had wandered off on a seven-page tangent about some of the finer points of disagreement among political economists. But as none of the information provided seems tangential, the statement weakens the concluding section. Huxley made great rhetorical capital of this, charging George with holding the opinion that 'it is less important to be clear and accurate when you are trying to bring about a political revolution than when merely academic interest attaches to the subject treated'. Furthermore George, as quoted by Huxley, claims that he 'is only attempting to discover the laws which control a great social problem'. Huxley saw this as 'intellectual muddlement', because though he knows of 'laws that control other "laws"', he is not aware of '"laws" which control a "problem"' (Huxley, 1968a, p. 172). Huxley has obvious fun in this section, and why not! He is on safe grounds: the elements of debate. Still the keen intellectual predator in his final years, he could smell a writing error from great distances. Unfortunately, his expository gifts and his understanding of the topic were not up to their usual standards; the dragon was getting old.

But was it that he was simply getting old? Aside from his age and his evident unfamiliarity with economic theory – or at least well below the level of George's expertise – were there other reasons for the sophistry and histrionics? What was happening to Huxley both personally and professionally? Can the context and motivation behind Huxley's determination to publicly undermine Henry George help to explain what he represented to Huxley? Certainly there were any number of popular pro-labour economists, political theorists, social reformers, and working-class activists that Huxley could have challenged. Why was George so dangerous?

Huxley always had an 'itch to be fighting'.[7] Writing to Knowles about *Progress and Poverty*, Huxley looked forward to the opportunity to 'cut and come again at this wonderful dish'.[8] His pugilistic spirit was reignited; but it came late in Huxley's life, during a time of personal struggles with family illnesses and death, ailing friends, and his own physical and psychological maladies that robbed him of his energy, forcing him to reduce his professional activities and, arguably, weakening his rhetorical powers (Desmond, 1997, especially chapters 8 and 9). In his final years, he was fighting to preserve his lifelong objectives of scientific authority, liberal meritocracy, and acceptance of Darwinism. Juggling mutinies from all quarters, Huxley fought to control dissension from within the Ethnological and Anthropological Societies while simultaneously adjudicating the potentially explosive conflict over women entering the scientific societies, medical professions, and universities: an issue for which Huxley had mixed feelings (Richards, 1989; Desmond, 1994, p. 272, and 1997, pp. 246–7). At the same time, personal and ideological conflicts undermined the solidarity of the Darwinians. Alfred Russel Wallace had wandered off from the inner circle, associating with Henry George, socialists, and spiritualists. The co-discoverer of evolution by natural selection was turning out to be something of a rebel.

Writing to Darwin in 1881, Wallace praised *Progress and Poverty* as 'the most startling novel and original book of the last twenty years' (Marchant, 1916, Vol. 1, p. 260). Moreover, Wallace wrote a letter to *The Times*, publicly declaring his support for George's 'fundamental position' that poverty increases as wealth increases.[9] Further fissures were in the offing as the tumultuous 1880s progressed: tension between Huxley and Herbert Spencer that had been building for years finally exploded in 1889, ending their friendship of more than three decades (Fichman, 1997; Desmond, 1997, pp. 191–2).

On another front, agnosticism – a term originated by Huxley in 1869 as a useful 'rhetorical strategy' for distancing scientific questions from religious matters – was being misinterpreted by positivists and secularists 'inspired by Spencer's vision of an Unknowable deity'. Spencer's 'theistically oriented agnosticism' had little in common with Huxley's intended meaning (Lightman, 2002, pp. 284–5). Huxley's meaning was simple: science cannot explain metaphysical beliefs in or out of existence due to insufficient data. Irritated by the increasingly popular theistic revisions of his commonsense 'ism', Huxley wrote three essays for Knowles in early 1889 attempting to 'regain control of his coinage'. It was one more battle to fight among many, and the essays, according to one of Huxley's longtime associates, T. A. Hirst, 'lacked depth' (*ibid.*, p. 271).

These pressures bore down on Huxley while socialists and labour advocates were shouting from the stumps and rioting in the streets. Between 1886 and 1891, major crises in class relations had Huxley worried that 'the industrial classes' were showing 'a certain want of sanity'.[10] Trafalgar Square saw labour riots in February 1886 and February 1887, the first of which found Huxley on an omnibus attacked by rioters (Desmond, 1997, pp. 166, 178). In 1888, the Matchgirls' Strike, led by Annie Besant, ignited public support for factory reform and unionism. The following year, encouraged by the matchgirls' success, the London Dockers went out on strike for better pay and hours. Supported by pro-labour organizations as far away as Australia, the dockers' main demands were finally met after five weeks. All of this agitation and violence was part of an alarming trend affecting Huxley: his long-time working-class audience was drifting to the Left, sending him letters of reprobation for his antiquated views. One of these letters came from J. D. Christie, a pastry cook incensed by 'Natural Rights and Political Rights'. Knowles printed it in *The Nineteenth Century* in March 1890 as 'A Working Man's Reply to Professor Huxley' (Christie, 1890, pp. 476–83). The letter begins with a warning: 'working-class votes now outnumber all the others combined', and the 'masses' would 'use their influence on terms of equality when they arrive at the ballot box' (*ibid.*, p. 476). Even if Huxley could not 'for the life of him see any good' in Henry George's program and the doctrine of natural rights, both gave workers 'great hopes for the future, and hope is one of the most effective safety valves' in times of potential revolution. Christie did not want revolution, just a cure for the 'misery' that stems from some 'maladjustment in the social organism'. Offering Huxley a brief history lesson on the mid-century challenge to aristocratic authority, he reminded him that the 'Tory privileged of to-day were very well satisfied with the then existing order of things; but they suffered for their blindness', as would Huxley's class if they did not act quickly and appropriately. But how could 'the Professor' understand the workers' suffering when he 'is placed too high up in the social scale...to examine the foundations of a structure' (*ibid.*, p. 477)?

These warnings are only the beginning of Christie's reply and not nearly the most incendiary points of contention; these he saved for a critique of Huxley's demeanour and style in 'Natural Rights and Political Rights'. Christie's outrage lights up his prose. He begins his critique with a short passage from 'Natural Rights and Political Rights' into which he cannot resist inserting a question:

> Political philosophy is identical with Rousseauism, the same *a priori* method, starting from highly questionable axioms which are assumed to represent truth, and asking us [Who is meant by us?] to upset the existing arrangements of society on the faith of those axioms (*ibid.*).

Christie's embedded question makes the point that Huxley does not speak for workers but for the class interests of 'well-fed dukes and professors', too remote from the realities of real labour to do anything more than 'philosophize over abstract principles' (*ibid.*, p. 478). As to the accuracy of Huxley's claim, Christie asserts, 'These are very good phrases, yet to me they just seem to describe the position the Professor himself takes up' (*ibid.*, p. 477). Highlighting several short passages from Huxley's article, Christie accuses him of 'vague' prose, 'verbose gyrations', 'hiding his meaning', 'lamentable twaddle', and being 'out of his groove in taking up politics' (*ibid.*, pp. 478, 480, 482–3). Rejecting one of Huxley's favourite rhetorical strategies, Christie declares, 'There is no use telling us about Quesnay, Dupont de Nemours, or going back 130 years; it is of now and the future we have to think' (*ibid.*, p. 479). This dismisses approximately one-third of the arguments in Huxley's 1890 essays. Disposing of another third, Christie described Huxley's use of analogy as 'defective', and countered with a humorous parody of Huxley's tiger analogy in which a tigress carries off a villager as a training tool for her cubs. In Christie's version, a 'capitalist seizes a fellow-creature and carries him off to his sweater's den' where he is subsequently forced to labour under starvation conditions while the capitalist and his 'offspring thrive and grow fat'. Huxley is chided for his attempt to put 'the whole matter in a nutshell oh! so nicely to suit [his] purpose', and Christie cautions the Professor that these tricks will 'not pass unchallenged at this time of the day' (*ibid.*, pp. 479-80).

By Christie's account, Henry George's theory 'seems to the minds of millions well calculated to solve the social problem'. If Huxley objects to 'the doctrine of natural rights being used as a fulcrum on which to rest the lever which is to

change the basis of society', then he must 'show us a better one, for changed it
must be' (*ibid.*, pp. 477–8). Nor was Christie alone in his assertion that Huxley
was meddling in areas beyond his expertise. In 1887, 'Mechanic' wrote a letter
to *The English Mechanic* questioning Huxley's right to meddle in trade-related
matters and workplace control over technical training:

> Professor Huxley is a very able man; as a biologist, none but his enemies admit that
> he has a rival. His monograph on the anatomy of the frog is perfection. But as an
> authority on trade matters or commercial questions, his opinion is not worth more
> than that of the Llama of Thibet or the Archbishop of York.[11]

Similar complaints were sent directly to Huxley, each complaining that he
had lost touch with the workers (McLaughlin-Jenkins, 2001, p. 68). Huxley,
who had always been the champion of merit regardless of class background,
was now placing obstacles in the way of the 'ever onward and upward' development of 'political principles'(Christie, 1890, p. 483). Huxley had become
one of 'them', while George was giving voice to the sorrows and aspirations
of the people.

Henry George was problematic for Huxley on several fronts. Aside from
George's association with Wallace, he was quickly replacing Huxley as a hero
of the working classes, fuelling their radical demands, and thrusting them into a
confrontation with the liberal industrial elite, with whom Huxley was chummy
to say the least (Desmond, 1997, pp. 4–5, 106–7). Huxley was a progressive
thinker, but he remained convinced that a liberal capitalist meritocracy guided
by scientific authority was the best hope humanity had in the 1890s, and no
Rousseauian *a priori* speculator was going to change that, unless violent revolution and dictatorship were preferred to progress and stability. More importantly,
George not only reminded Huxley, and wrongly so, of Rousseauian socialists
– whatever that means – he had the temerity to challenge the authority of science in general and Darwinists in particular. Though George was no socialist
and was, on the contrary, a pro-capitalist, anti-monopolist, single-tax advocate
guided by Jeffersonian republicanism and egalitarian natural theology, his gross-
est insult was to dismiss social Darwinism as limited in its explanatory power.
Natural selection, Malthusian population theory, materialism, and meritocracy
were insufficient pillars on which to build a progressive, thriving society because they had not and could not explain why poverty was increasing despite
enormous gains in production and wealth. These ideas might explain the animal
and vegetable kingdoms, but humanity was special; we have Mind, and as such,
are guided by the 'Master Workman' (George, 1902, p. 207). Not only were
George's views the antithesis of everything Huxley had worked for, they could
be seen as anti-science. Moreover, his popularity was undeniable and growing
all the time. It is to this threat rather than in his economic recommendations
that Huxley's fury is to be traced.

George devoted an entire section of his book to Malthus's population theory and its implications for social science and economics. Pointing out, first, that Malthusianism is linked to the 'utterly baseless' wages doctrine – i.e., wages are determined by the ratio between capital and labour, with an increase in the latter tending to reduce wages – George claims that both concepts 'mutually blend with, strengthen, and defend each other' and have become 'scientific dogma' even among the most 'acute thinkers' (George, 1953, pp. 91–2). Additional support was provided by 'analogies in the animal and vegetable kingdoms', with the great triumph of this multi-faceted dogma being that it is 'soothing and reassuring' to the wealthy and powerful classes still living in fear of another French Revolution. The Malthusian dogma provided the elite with a rationale for inaction and a free conscience by establishing that there could be no solution to the poverty question; attempts to ameliorate conditions would only make them worse. Like the law of gravitation, the disproportionate growth of population to subsistence was heralded by its adherents as a universal law (*ibid.*, p. 99). Henry George saw this purported principle more as a reflection of the 'greed of the rich and the selfishness of the powerful' (*ibid.*, p. 100). If this failed to get Huxley's attention, the next argument surely would have done the job.

George recognized that 'new support' for Malthusianism and the wages doctrine was coming from 'the rapid change of ideas as to the origin of man and the genesis of species'. In *The Origin of Species*, Darwin explicitly aligned his concept of struggle in nature with the 'doctrine of Malthus', and George cited, in addition to Darwin, Louis Agassiz, the biologist and critic of Darwinism, who described natural selection as 'Malthus all over' (*ibid.*). The 'authority of natural science' helped to construct popular rationales for poverty, but just how secure was this pillar? According to George, there was a fundamental contradiction between Darwinism and Malthusianism. In essence, development theories gave progressive accounts of nature and human history, whereas population theories presented a fixed socioeconomic order or system that limited progress to the growth of industry and arts under elite stewardship. If natural selection is the force that has 'in the course of unnumbered ages developed the higher from the lower type, differentiated the man and the monkey, and made the Nineteenth Century succeed the age of stone', how could the Malthusian Darwinians now claim that systemic change had reached its zenith? Besides, this naturalized economic explanation for 'social phenomena' was just one theory in a long succession of antiquated theories, such as 'the fixity of the earth' or 'the facts of geology' derived from 'the literal inspiration of the Mosaic record' (*ibid.*, pp. 101–2). Scientists were not infallible. What, if any, were the limitations of analogies between man and beast, and how were errors in this increasingly dogmatic assertion contributing to false projections of human progress?

Plainly and unambiguously stated, in a style the like of which we might have expected from the younger Huxley, George declares that naturalized Malthusianism 'springs from a false analogy':

> That vegetable and animal life tend to press against the limits of space does not prove the same tendency in human life. Granted that man is only a more highly developed animal; that the ring-tailed monkey is a distant relative, and the hump-backed whale a far-off connection who in early life took to the sea—granted that back of these he is kin to the vegetable, and is still subject to the same laws as plants, fishes, birds, and beasts. Yet there is still this difference between man and all other animals—he is the only animal whose desires increase as they are fed; the only animal that is never satisfied (*ibid.*, p. 134).

In this statement, George rejects what he saw as Malthus's scientific pretensions along with some fundamental precepts of Darwinism. He does not reject evolution, only its failure to grasp the nature of human progress, where man and beast 'part company':

> The beast never goes further; the man has but set his feet on the first step of an infinite progression—a progression upon which the beast never enters; a progression away from and above the beast (*ibid.*, p. 135).

In this passionate and poetic section of *Progress and Poverty*, George asks if the 'gulf' is not 'too wide for the analogy to span'? (p. 136). Man is not a beast: the theoretical limitations of Malthusianism and Darwinism are clear.

George returns to this question of man's status in the final section of *Progress and Poverty* with the intention of determining the 'laws of human progress'. His starting point for analysis is the 'prevailing belief' that man has undergone a process of evolution, but he questions the explanatory limitations of this belief. Whether evolutionism explains man's genesis and the way in which he has 'crossed the wide chasm which now separates him from the brutes' is not a useful question because 'inference cannot proceed from the unknown to the known'. We must study man 'just as he is found' now and through known history. What is evident is that humanity possesses some qualities in common with animals and some which are unique. Humans think, make tools, transform natural resources into commodities, and increase their capacity for language, knowledge, and invention. As 'men improve' and become 'more civilized', learning to 'co-operate in society', so 'great cities rise' and improvements increase (*ibid.*, pp. 476–7). Dogs simply cannot make this leap despite their rudimentary emotions and intelligence. Humans are social, intelligent, and ambitious in ways that make us exceptional; whether or not our ancestry can be traced to apes is uncertain, and so practically immaterial.

On the other hand, it is entirely plausible to view 'civilization' from an evolutionary standpoint. Herbert Spencer's development theory of 'progress from an indefinite, incoherent homogeneity to a definite, coherent heterogeneity' was unquestionably valid in this respect; however, 'to say this is not to explain or identify the causes which forward or retard it'(i.e., 'progress'):

How far the sweeping generalizations of Spencer, which seek to account for all phenomena under terms of matter and force, may, properly understood, include all these causes, I am unable to say; but, as scientifically expounded, the development philosophy has either not yet definitely met this question, or has given birth, or rather coherency, to an opinion which does not accord with the facts (*ibid.*, p. 478).

Spencer's Lamarckian observation was, in George's view, reasonable, but it was breeding vulgar generalizations about innate capacities among men and races as the cause for unequal distribution of wealth: wealthy men, races, and nations are more highly developed, more civilized, because they are innately superior in 'will and ability'. Unfortunately, this 'scientific formula' was in complete accord with the 'existing prejudices both of rich and poor'. Scientifically bolstered, political economists had embraced the 'development theory' so thoroughly that its 'wonderful spread since the time Darwin first startled the world with his "Origin of Species" has not been so much a conquest as an assimilation' (*ibid.*, pp. 478–9). Questioning the efficacy of this new orthodoxy, George likens it to natural theology:

On this theory, the differences between man and the animals, and differences in the relative progress of men, are now explained as confidently, and all but as generally, as a little while ago they were explained upon the theory of special creation and divine interposition (*ibid.*, p. 479).

Shades of Paley.[12] This could not have but infuriated Huxley. Accused of what amounts to *a priori* inferences from the unknown details of man's genesis, Darwinists had produced a partial developmental model that was mired in generalities, false analogies, and shallow reasoning. Superficial in their penetration of the cause and laws of human progress and regress, they were ultimately supporting an ideology of socioeconomic fixity, much like the natural theologians whose authority the Darwinians had undermined in the first half of the century. Instead of carrying a banner of progress into the future, Darwinians had fallen victim to 'fatalism', in which man's progress depended on war, famine, and misery (*ibid.*, pp. 480–81). The irony seems not to have been missed by Huxley.

Not only was Henry George challenging the Darwinian Dragon and Spencerian sociobiology at a time when working-class opinion was being mobilized against liberal capitalist apologists, people were listening to him, as Huxley was well aware.[13] George spoke the words that labouring men and women needed to hear:

In every civilized country, pauperism, crime, insanity, and suicides are increasing. In every civilized country the diseases are increasing which come from overstrained nerves, from insufficient and monotonous occupations, from premature labour of children, from the tasks and crimes which poverty imposes upon women (George, 1953, p. 541).

Elitist justifications for unequal distribution of wealth based on innate capacities, with only minor amelioration possible for the lower ranks through 'education and...prudence' (George, 1953, p. 100), sounded hollow and selfish next to George's dedication for *Progress and Poverty*:

> TO THOSE WHO, SEEING THE VICE AND MISERY THAT SPRING FROM THE UNEQUAL DISTRIBUTION OF WEALTH AND PRIVILEGE, FEEL THE POSSIBILITY OF A HIGHER SOCIAL STATE AND WOULD STRIVE FOR ITS ATTAINMENT

George's identification of the problem, its cause, and its remedy, was appealing: poverty was caused by the current monopolization of wealth and land. A single tax on the land would divert substantial resources back to the State and then into the community, where poverty would be eradicated. It meant real systemic change and did not require working Britons to understand complex philosophies or take out membership in foreign-based revolutionary political organizations; it was about the land. It was elegantly simple and imminently compatible with British working-class traditions in freethought, radicalism, and affinity with the soil. How could Huxley compete? His promises of progress in the 1860s had, during the 1880s and 1890s, dissolved into Malthusian rationales for the existing order. Huxley was yesterday's hero. Whether or not George slew the mighty dragon, or the dragon impaled himself on the sword of anti-poverty anger, is hard to judge.

Given the personal and professional challenges Huxley was juggling in 1890, it is not surprising that his rhetorical powers were diminished. The battles were raging, but he was weary of the war. He had, perhaps, only one or two blasts of smoke and fire in him, and socialism was a worthy target. The problem was that his limited economic knowledge and his conflation of modern socialism, Rousseau, and George's program weakened the relevance and impact of his 1890 essays. He missed his target and relied on worn-out rhetorical devices tinged with frustration and a hint of hysteria. As social, economic, or political commentary, they have little value, which working-class readers and left-wing intellectuals were only too happy to point out. However, the submerged message – the defence of liberal capitalist meritocracy, scientific authority, and social Darwinism – makes this collection of Huxleyan inflammatory prose crucial to an understanding of his personal beliefs and professional schemes in Huxley's later years when, for various reasons, he was forced to defend socioeconomic fixity in a rapidly changing world.

NOTES

1. T.H. to James Knowles, 14 December 1889, in Leonard Huxley, *Life and Letters of Thomas H. Huxley* (New York: D. Appleton and Company, 1901), Vol. II, pp. 260–61.
2. T.H. to Joseph Hooker, December 1889, *ibid.*, p. 261.
3. T.H. to Joseph Hooker, December 1889, *ibid.*; T.H. to James Knowles, 14 December 1889, *ibid.*, pp. 260-61.
4. The same can be said about Huxley's comparison of Quesnay, the Physiocrats, and George's land policy. They are vaguely related in some of their language, but dissimilar in content and implementation.
5. Interestingly, George drew upon thermodynamics in *Progress and Poverty* but to a much better effect (George, 1953, p. 133).
6. This is one of Huxley's criticisms of *Progress and Poverty* in 'Natural Rights and Political Rights', p. 338.
7. James Knowles to Huxley, cited in Desmond, *Huxley*, Vol. II, p. 197. See also pp. 186, 189, 204.
8. T.H. to James Knowles, 14 December 1889, in L. Huxley, *Life and Letters*, pp. 260–61.
9. *The Times* (London), 29 January 1884, p. 3, reprinted in Charles H. Smith, *The Alfred Russel Wallace Page*, www.wku.edu/~smithch/wallace/S369.htm.
10. *Trades' Unionist*, June 1891, reprinted in Binderman and Joyce, Clark University, *The Huxley File*, http://aleph0.clarku.edu/huxley/UnColl/PMG/PMGetal/BusStrike.html.
11. *The English Mechanic*, **45** (1887), 575–7. This technical and scientific periodical was edited by J. Passmore Edwards. It ran from 1865 to 1926, with an approximate circulation of 80,000 to 100,000. For more, see E. McLaughlin-Jenkins, *Common Knowledge: The Victorian Working Class and the Low Road to Knowledge, 1870-1900* (2001), Ph.D. dissertation, York University, Toronto, Canada.
12. William Paley, English natural theologian (1743–1805).
13. T.H. to James Knowles, 14 December 1889, in L. Huxley, *Life and Letters*, Vol. II, p. 261.

REFERENCES

Christie, J. D. (1890), 'A Working Man's Reply to Professor Huxley', *The Nineteenth Century*, March, pp. 476–83, from The Huxley Files, created by Charles Blinderman and David Joyce: http://babbage.clarku.edu/huxley/comm/19th/Christie.html.

Desmond, A. (1994), *Huxley: The Devil's Disciple*, London: Michael Joseph.

Desmond, A. (1997), *Huxley: Evolution's High Priest*, London: Michael Joseph.

Douglas, R. (1979), 'Huxley's Critique from Social Darwinism', in R.V. Andelson (ed.), *Critics of Henry George: A Centenary Appraisal of Their Strictures on Progress and Poverty*, New Jersey and London: Associated University Presses, pp. 137–52.

Fichman, M. (1997), 'Biology and Politics: Defining the Boundaries', in B. Lightman (ed.), *Victorian Science in Context*, Chicago: University of Chicago Press, pp. 94–118.

George, H. (1953) [1879], *Progress and Poverty: An Inquiry into the Cause of Industrial Depressions and of Increase of Want with Increase of Wealth*, New York: Robert Schalkenbach Foundation.

George, H. (1902) [1884], *Social Problems*, London: Kegan Paul, Trench, Trübner & Company.

George, H. (1965) [1892], *A Perplexed Philosopher*, New York: Schalkenbach Foundation.

Huxley, L. (1901), *Life and Letters of Thomas Henry Huxley* (2 vols.), New York: D. Appleton and Company.

Huxley, T.H. (1968a) [1902], 'Capital: The Mother of Labour', in *idem*, *Collected Essays*, Vol. IX, New York: Greenwood Press.

Huxley, T.H. (1968b) [1917], 'Government: Anarchy or Regimentation', in *idem*, *Collected Essays*, Vol. I, New York: Greenwood Press.

Huxley, T.H. (1968c) [1917], ' The Natural Inequality of Men', in *idem*, *Collected Essays*, Vol. I, New York: Greenwood Press.

Huxley, T.H. (1968d) [1917], 'Natural Rights and Political Rights', in *idem*, *Collected Essays*, Vol. I, New York: Greenwood Press.

Lightman, B. (2002), 'Huxley and scientific agnosticism: the strange history of a failed rhetorical strategy', *British Journal for the History of Science*, **35**, 271–89.

McLaughlin-Jenkins, E. (2001), *Common Knowledge: The Victorian Working Class and the Low Road to Knowledge, 1870–1900* , Ph.D. dissetation, Toronto: York University.

Marchant, J. (1916), *Alfred Russel Wallace: Letters and Reminiscences* (2 vols), London: Cassell.

Richards, E. (1989), 'Huxley and woman's place in science: The "woman question" and the control of Victorian anthropology', in James R. Moore (ed.), *History, Humanity and Evolution*, Cambridge: Cambridge University Press, pp. 253–84.

3. Tolstoy's Henry George: 'a step on the first rung of the ladder...'

Rob Knowles

> After him [Henry George] it is impossible to prevaricate; one must directly take a stand on his or on the other side. My demands go much further than his; but his are a step on the first rung of the ladder that I'm climbing (Leo Tolstoy, 1885).

A great deal has been written about connections between the American political economist Henry George (d. 1897) and the Russian literary writer and social critic, Leo Tolstoy (d. 1910), in their own time especially. More recently, some writings have also sought to highlight their intellectual relationship – from the perspectives of both George and Tolstoy – including an argument that Tolstoy adopted a 'Georgist spiritual political economy' (e.g. Wenzer, 1997c; Wenzer, 1997a, chapter 1; Wenzer, 1997b, chapter 2; Redfearn, 1992, especially chapter 12; Simmons, 1960, e.g. pp. 77, 201–2, 363–5; Maude, 1961). What is typically not taken very thoroughly into account are the profound differences between George and Tolstoy with respect to the political and socio-economic contexts into which each of them was interpreting the potential effectiveness of George's 'Single Tax' scheme.[1] These contexts are historical sites of great significance if one is going to attempt to draw conclusions about the intellectual connections between the two thinkers.

When it is understood that Henry George's context was that of a capitalist, liberal-democratic society, however flawed, and that of Tolstoy was a monarchical absolute autocracy which retained much of the legacy of serfdom, it can be suggested that each man was confronting and seeking to solve different problems. Further, while George did not propose any fundamental change in the institutional structures of society, Tolstoy was openly a communitarian anarchist in his visions for a future society (e.g. Tolstoy, 1948 [1900], pp. 112–27). It follows that they each had profoundly different ultimate goals. This does not imply that they could not and did not share some ethical beliefs or many views of existing society, whether within an autocratic regime or a liberal democracy, but it does suggest that it is not possible to reach unqualified conclusions about connections between them as far as political economy is concerned.

It appears that the first time Tolstoy expressed his support for Henry George's 'Single Tax' system was the passage from which an extract is quoted above, from 1885. Tolstoy had by then read George's *Social Problems* and also his earlier work *Progress and Poverty* (Simmons, 1960, p. 77). At that early moment in the short history of their intellectual relationship, Tolstoy had taken a firm stand with respect to the value of George's work, as he interpreted it, but he also clearly implied that his eventual path would be different from that of George. In the short twelve years between that time and the death of George in 1897, the two men corresponded rarely and they never met in person. Tolstoy did, however, read most of George's published work and he was thoroughly aware of its content (Wenzer, 1999, p. xv).

It is not clear how much of Tolstoy's work, especially his social criticism, was read by George. As many of Tolstoy's critical essays could not be published in Russia at the time of writing due to extremely tight censorship constraints (Simmons, 1960, p. 78), and much was written after George's death, it is unlikely that George read much of Tolstoy's social criticism. Kenneth Wenzer has demonstrated that George was aware of some of Tolstoy's work, extracts from which George published in his American journal *The Standard* in 1888–9, but Wenzer also points out that George was aware of Tolstoy's rejection of state control of taxation of land. As Tolstoy had stated: 'If you could get angels from heaven to administer the taxes from the land you might do justice and prevent mischief. I am against all taxation' (cited in Wenzer, 1997b, p. 23). This fundamental difference between the thinking of George and Tolstoy cannot be lightly dismissed. Ultimately, how could Tolstoy fundamentally embrace a scheme which had state taxation at its core?

The essential nexus between the two men's thinking and their social concerns was their shared Christian ethics and their shared concern for the alleviation of poverty and social inequity which each believed stemmed primarily from existing patterns of ownership of land. Without holding similar views about the essence of Christianity and the basic irrelevancy or even distortion of social thinking by church teachings, it is unlikely that their views about a means of alleviating or removing the problems of land ownership would have been shared. It was the fact that they could, virtually without speaking, understand each other's ethics and thus a crucial dimension of their interpretative frameworks, that made possible Tolstoy's embracing of George's 'Single Tax' project. For Tolstoy, the ethics were at least as important as George's ideas about solving the land problem (e.g. Rose, 1968, p. 155). In Henry George, Tolstoy had found comfortable, satisfying, solid ethical ground. As only one example of many, he approvingly cited George in his 1905 essay 'A Great Iniquity': 'Until there be correct thought there cannot be right action, and when there is correct thought right action will follow...'

(Tolstoy, 1961 [1905], p. 301). That this 'correct thought' was accompanied by what Tolstoy considered to be a clever and immediately practical project which could cut through the constraints to solving the land problem in Russia – which was his major, but not exclusive, concern – was enough to make Tolstoy effusive in the way he expressed support for George's scheme.

GEORGE'S 'SINGLE TAX' SCHEME

George's America of the late nineteenth century had only just seen the outcome of the Civil War and the end of slavery. It was still very much a period of exploration of new land and the rapid spread of population and infrastructure across the newly-opening states. At the forefront of much of this expansion was the construction of railroads, accompanying or closely following the annexation, occupation or purchase of productive land. Cities were growing rapidly and so were urban populations. America, like most of western Europe, was rapidly industrializing. Politically, the United States of America had a Declaration of Independence and a new Constitution on which its political institutions and democratic politics were based. There was, with the exception of intrinsic racial discrimination, universal male suffrage. The government and the President were popularly elected. There were complex systems of taxation and duties, applied across all segments of society and, in that period of largely unfettered capitalism at work, there were inevitably winners and losers, socially and financially (Hobsbawm, 1975, pp. 137–46).

Henry George's primary concern was to find a means to alleviate the suffering and inequities being experienced by those who were 'losers' as a result of the financial and political power wielded by those who were 'winners'. He sought a way to cut through the entrenched inequalities and to emancipate the average individual from the constraints of freely applied economic power and that of government—which he saw as being not only ineffective in realizing the productive capacity of the new nation, but also in many respects corrupt (George, 1904 [1880], pp. 8–10, 414–5). One of the major consequences of this political and socio-economic context in action was increasing poverty amongst increasing wealth. He was most acutely aware of this relationship in 1868–9 in New York, seeing the contrast on the streets, and again on his return to California, when he saw the effects of soaring land prices through the land boom which was then in full swing (George Jr., 1904, pp. 191–5). George's Christian ethics focused his mind sharply on the problem of poverty and eventually his proposed solution became his 'Single Tax' plan.

Here is the way George summarized the characteristics and consequences of his scheme in *Progress and Poverty*, a position from which he essentially never wavered throughout the remainder of his life:

What I therefore, propose, as the simple yet sovereign remedy, which will raise wages, increase the earnings of capital, extirpate pauperism, abolish poverty, give remunerative employment to whoever wishes it, afford free scope to human powers, lessen crime, elevate morals, and taste, and intelligence, purify government and carry civilization to yet nobler heights, is—*to appropriate rent by taxation.*

In this way the State may become the universal landlord without calling herself so, and without assuming a single new function....No owner of land need be dispossessed, and no restriction need be placed upon the amount of land any one could hold. For, rent being taken by the State in taxes, land...would be really common property, and every member of the community would participate in the advantages of its ownership (George, 1904 [1880], pp. 403–4).

His remedy would involve the elimination of all other taxes: '*To abolish all taxation save that upon land values*'. In allaying fears that land would be taken from individual ownership and nationalized, he stated that: 'I do not propose either to purchase or to confiscate private property in land...Let the individuals who now hold it still retain, if they want to, possession of what they are pleased to call *their* land. Let them continue to call it *their* land...We may safely leave them the shell, if we take the kernel. *It is not necessary to confiscate land; it is only necessary to confiscate rent*' (*ibid.*, p. 403, see also George, 1981 [1883], pp. 208–12).

So the plan, for Henry George, was to tax all land according to its unimproved value ('irrespective of improvements'), with all tax income being collected by the state for redistribution in the common interest of all. Tax revenue would be divided between local governments, state governments and the 'general government' (Wenzer, 1997a, pp. 65–6). For George, above all, this Single Tax on land value would release productive capacity that was currently bound up by the extent of the existing taxation imposed on the average working individual. The Single Tax would replace all other taxation, including tariffs and customs duties which were inhibiting free trade. He envisaged that such a simplified tax scheme would lead to a great reduction in the bureaucracy needed to collect and administer taxes, and also contribute greatly to a reduction in corruption in government, which could currently be bought by the wealthy and influential few. For the individual, the reduction of taxation would release a greater capacity for spending as well as provide self-run or small-scale business opportunities and, for the mass of producers, it would lead to less taxation and thus greater means available to them for investment. Those who made their wealth out of speculating in or holding land and not making productive use of it would be unable to afford to continue in their ways. George noted, however, that in America 'there are few, if any, individuals who belong exclusively to this class' (*ibid.*, p. 59). He observed that most of the large land owners in America were also capitalists. The land which was tied up in unproductive hands would be released for others to be able to acquire it for productive use, and the land price increases which were constantly and artificially occurring through speculation would be eliminated. Overall, there would be a more just distribution of wealth across society (George, 1904 [1880], pp. 446–51).

Behind this scheme was George's profound belief that the land, like air and water, 'is the indispensable element necessary to the life of every human being' (Wenzer, 1997a, p. 60). And as land was made by God, it belongs to all: 'As no man made the land, so no man can claim a right of ownership in the land'. He did, however, believe equally deeply in the right to property which is the result of human labour: 'Whatever any individual, by the exercise of his powers, takes from the reservoirs of nature, molds into shapes fitted to satisfy human needs, that is his; to that a just and sacred right of property attaches'. Violation of that right to property would be a violation of the 'sacred command, "Thou shalt not steal"' (*ibid.*, p. 61).

The concentration of population in the towns and cities, with consequent high levels of poverty, would be alleviated by the new opportunities this tax reform would enable for individuals taking up land. For George:

> This life of great cities is not the natural life of man. He must, under such conditions, deteriorate, physically, mentally, morally. Yet the evil does not end here....This unnatural life of the great cities means an equally unnatural life in the country.... The tendency everywhere that this process of urban concentration is going on, is to make the life of the country poor and hard, and to rob it of the social stimulus and social gratifications that are so necessary to human beings (George, 1981 [1883], pp. 235–6).

George believed that implementation of his Single Tax scheme would ultimately lead to a more even distribution of the population: 'With the resumption of common rights to the soil, the overcrowded population of the cities would spread, the scattered population of the country would grow denser' (*ibid.*, p. 238).

Implementation of his scheme was envisaged by George to be a 'gentle and gradual process'. He was sufficiently a realist to acknowledge that although the aim should be a 'single tax unlimited' – that is, involving a complete implementation of the scheme, without exceptions – in practice it might be necessary to settle for a 'single tax limited'. This possibility, however, should not diminish the aim, which must be to 'take the whole of economic rent "as near as might be"' (Wenzer, 1997a, pp. 64, 83).[2] He also asserted that the plan was not only applicable to America: 'it is a world-wide matter'. He stated his noble goal as follows:

> What we are battling for is the freedom of mankind; what we are struggling for is for the abolition of that industrial slavery which as much enslaves men as did chattel slavery. It will not take the sword to win it. There is a power far stronger than the sword and that is the power of public opinion....What enslaves men everywhere is ignorance and prejudice (*ibid.*, p. 64).

George did acknowledge that, in circumstances where few landholders had power, they would be able to demand whatever they wanted from their enslaved workers and, in that event, all taxes, including the Single Tax, would be 'irrelevant'. He noted, however, in 1890, that 'today, in the countries with which we are concerned, there is not that concentration or combination of land ownership which gives that absolute power to which I have referred...' (*ibid.*, p. 71). In contrast, Tolstoy, in 1902, referred to Russia 'where the land retained by the large landed proprietors would suffice for all the factory working men in Russia and in the whole of Europe...' (Tolstoy, 1905 [1902], p. 139).

There arises a very important question here. The structure of Russian society under Tsarist autocracy, which had been reinforced by Tsar Nicholas II, was very much a concentration and combination of authoritarian power of the nobility and large land ownership and consequently power over the mass of the peasantry, despite the apparition of the emancipation of the serfs in 1861 (Fitzpatrick, 2001, p. 15; Hosking, 1998, pp. 320–2). Was Henry George including or excluding Russia amongst his 'countries with which we are concerned'? He was not at all clear on this important question. He did, however, point out that the 'essence and fundamental power of landlordism as we are confronted with it, is its appropriation of economic rent'. In opposition to 'landlordism' he argued that 'to take rent by taxation on the value of land would destroy all the power there is in landlordship as we know it for its pressure would force competition between landowners, and destroy the expectations which has the effect of combination' (Wenzer, 1997a, p. 72). In a state such as Tsarist Russia, any scheme which could possibly break down the power of the landlords would potentially appeal to any of the radical social reformers. A special attraction of such a scheme to a vehement advocate of non-violence such as Tolstoy was the accompanying possibility of such reforms taking place in the absence of violent revolution.

Given that socialism was being strongly advocated towards the end of the nineteenth century, across most of the world, both George and Tolstoy were required to confront it. From their different political and socio-economic perspectives, they each rejected the doctrines and aspirations of the then hegemonic Marxist socialism. The primary basis of Tolstoy's rejection of socialism was that its doctrines ignored the issue of land for the peasantry; yet for him that was the most pressing issue for all Russia. Tolstoy saw that socialism would constrain workers to the cities, to factory work, while he advocated 'the return of the working men to an agricultural life' (Tolstoy, 1905 [1902], pp. 136–42). Tolstoy had a deep-seated belief that fruitful and fulfilled life related to the land:

> The possibility of living on the land, of gaining one's sustenance from it by means of one's own labour, has always been and always will be one of the chief conditions of a happy and independent human life. This all men have always known, and so all men have always striven and never stop striving and always will strive, like a fish for the water, at least for the semblance of such a life (*ibid.*, pp. 137–8).

George objected to the socialists' concentration on capital rather than land as 'the great robber of labor', and their insistence on socializing the means of production (Wenzer, 1997a, p. 160). Socialist criticism understood that capital would remain in private hands under George's system, such that there would remain the intrinsic confrontation between capital and labour, leaving in place the struggle between employers and employees. George was accused of seeing capital and labour as 'friends, not enemies' and ignoring the fact that their interests are antagonistic – even if latent – and can burst out (*ibid.*, p. 160). For all his rhetoric about the 'abolition of industrial slavery' by means of his Single Tax system of taxing land value, George was in many respects a voice among a muted few, surrounded by loudly proclaimed socialist dissent. The socialists simply did not believe that his scheme went far enough, nor did it attack the central issue (for them) of capital. He was seen by many to be a captive of bourgeois society (Lawrence, 1957, p. 63).

George rejected such criticism because he believed that 'the requisites of production are simply land and labour. These are the two primary factors in all production. Capital is but a derivative factor, formed from their combination' (Wenzer, 1997a, p. 167). George was, however, a thorough capitalist, rejecting the need to 'nationalize' capital. He expressed his belief this way:

> The equitable principles already exist in natural laws, which, if left unobstructed, will with a certainty that no human adjustment could rival, give to each who takes part in the work of production that which is justly his due, and leave to the community and applied to purposes of general benefit, and to the assurance of all against the accidents of life, that 'unearned increment' which can be justly claimed by the individual, but is due to the growth and improvement of the community as a whole (*ibid.*, pp. 166–7).

There was no place here for socialized means of production or the 'nationalization of capital'. His was a strong *laissez-faire* claim on behalf of all individuals in society, which was reflected in his insistence on free trade and his aim to minimize government bureaucracy and interference in society by replacing the widespread intrusion of a wide range of taxes with his proposed Single Tax.

Occasionally George thought he could glimpse the possibility of a socialist or cooperative future society:

> The ideal of socialism is grand and noble; and it is, I am convinced, possible of realization; but such a state of society cannot be manufactured—it must grow. Society is an organism, not a machine. It can live only by the individual life of its parts. And in the free and natural development of all the parts will be secured the harmony of the whole. All that is necessary to social regeneration is included in the motto of those Russian patriots sometimes called Nihilists—'Land and Liberty' (George, 1904 [1880], p. 319).

When George wrote these words, in 1879, there were many socialisms.[3]

Marxist state socialism had not yet attained dominance in Europe or elsewhere, and communitarian anarchist ideas were frequently syncretized with statist socialist thought (Knowles, 2004, pp. 9–11). It is not clear just which 'ideal of socialism' George had in mind. There is also an underlying theme of individualism in this passage which would not necessarily have appealed to communitarian thinkers. Tolstoy could have been attracted to George's statement that society could 'approach the ideal of Jeffersonian democracy, the promised land of Herbert Spencer, the abolition of government' but, for George, there was always a simplified state ('government') at its core, even if only as 'the administration of a great co-operative society…merely the agency by which the common property was administered for the common benefit' (George, 1904 [1880], pp. 453–4).[4] Edward Rose (1968, p. 64) has astutely characterized George's scheme as an 'attempt to harmonize the individualism of capitalist economics with the communalistic goals of Christian charity'. As George had said: 'It is no mere fiscal reform that I propose; it is a conforming of the most important social adjustments to natural laws' (George, 1981 [1883], p. 213). However, as noted earlier, the collected Single Tax would be distributed throughout a hierarchy of local, state, and 'general government', although within this context he did consistently advocate 'the decentralized democracy of Jefferson' through maximizing 'local self-government' (Rose, 1968, p. 19; George, 1981 [1883], p. 174).

This was neither a communitarian anarchist nor a state socialist enterprise. Henry George and his system were always embedded in a capitalist, free trading, *laissez-faire*, economic context within a popularly elected liberal-democratic state with a hierarchical set of government institutions. By the late 1880s in Britain, his scheme – still confused by the public as belonging to socialist or land nationalization movements – had begun to attach itself, as did Henry George himself, to British Liberal politics (Lawrence, 1957, pp. 63, 73). From 1880 to the end of that decade, apart from promoting his project in America, George had concentrated his efforts on Britain with special focus on the land issue in Ireland and Scotland (e.g. George, 1999 [1885], p. 146). In developing a political program which advocated his Single Tax idea, he 'proposed nothing less than a union of Irish, Scottish, and English workers to drive landlordism out of the British Isles' (Lawrence, 1957, p. 9). His program of lecture tours and speeches during 1884 and 1885 is instructive. Of visits to 44 cities in Britain during that period, 30 were in Scotland, 12 in England and 2 in Ireland (Irish focus had changed from the land question to Home Rule by this time). Of the 75 speeches he made, 50 were in Scotland, 23 in England, and 2 in Ireland. As Elwood Lawrence (*ibid.*, p. 36) has observed: 'The most enduring accomplishment of George's campaign in 1884 and 1885 was the founding of the Scottish and English Land Restoration Leagues.' At this time, George was approaching the zenith of his popularity in Britain.[5] He was in no respect advocating violence or revolution; it was his hope that workers would use their voting power to bring about his scheme gradually. He was completely respectful of the parliamentary system of Britain. So how did George's system translate into a project which was so attractive to the communitarian anarchist Leo Tolstoy in terms of the social problems Tolstoy confronted and sought to solve in autocratic Tsarist Russia?

TOLSTOY: SOCIAL JUSTICE, HENRY GEORGE, AND THE LAND QUESTION

Christian ethics, as asserted earlier, was the essential underpinning of the relationship between George and Tolstoy. In the absence of this common ground, it is unlikely that Tolstoy would have become so enamoured of George and his scheme. By the mid-1880s, when he first encountered George's writings, Tolstoy had been through his personal crisis, his *Confession* of 1879, and had resolved to his satisfaction an interpretation of the Gospels which led him to reject organized religion (Knowles, 2004, pp. 277–9). He embraced what was, for him, the basic law of human society; the 'law of reciprocity':

> Two thousand years ago a law of God became known to men, the law of reciprocity, that *one should act unto others as one wishes others to act to oneself*, or, as it is expressed by the Chinese teacher Confucius, 'Do not do unto others that which you do not wish others to do unto you' (Tolstoy, 1905c [1901], p. 51).

In rejecting institutionalized Christian religious teachings, Tolstoy concluded that the 'harm of [this] innocuous, false Christianity consists chiefly in this, that it prescribes nothing and forbids nothing' (Tolstoy, 1905b [1900], p. 219). He, however, was determined to prescribe the most fundamental role possible for his distilled Christian beliefs, embodied in the single law of reciprocity: 'The deductions from this law are infinitely beneficent and varied, defining all possible relations of men among themselves, and everywhere putting concord and mutual service in the place of discord and struggle' (Tolstoy, 1905 [1901], p. 249). In this way Tolstoy identified the ground upon which he constructed his vision for a future society, the ground upon which the feet of his metaphorical ladder stood firm.

Taking his own independent path, Henry George had arrived at a similar position in his Christian beliefs. For George, 'The laws of this universe are the laws of God, the social laws as well as the physical laws, and He, the Creator of all, has given us room for all, work for all, plenty for all'. Included in this 'room' and 'plenty' for all was land (George, 1999 [1887], p. 168). In distinct parallel with the fundamental beliefs of Tolstoy, George embraced the same 'law of reciprocity'. In asserting that the Kingdom of God on earth must imply a kingdom of justice, he stated:

> No one can think of it without seeing that a very kingdom of God might be brought

on this earth if men would but seek to do justice—if men would but acknowledge *the essential principle of Christianity, that of doing to others as we would have others do to us*, and of recognising that we are all here equally the children of one Father, equally entitled to share His bounty, equally entitled to live our lives and develop our faculties, and to apply our labour to the raw material that He has provided (George, 1999 [1889], p. 198).

With respect to connections between the church and the 'upper classes', George attacked that 'unholy alliance', arguing that Christian teachings were intrinsic to justifications for and perpetuation of poverty. For George, however, this was not a failure of Christianity: 'The failure has been in the sort of Christianity that has been preached' (Lawrence, 1957, pp. 47–8; George, 1999 [1889], p. 199). Just as Tolstoy had argued that 'all possible relations of men among themselves' could be deduced from a single law, George argued that 'if the loving God does reign, if His laws are the laws not merely of the physical but of the moral universe, there must be a way of carrying His will into effect, there must be a way of doing equal justice to all His creatures. And so there is' (*ibid.*). His answer was his own Single Tax scheme. It was a huge claim, but one in which he profoundly believed.

Beyond the common ground of Christian ethics, as they each interpreted it, was the history of Tolstoy's concern about the condition of the peasantry in Russia. As a wealthy Russian nobleman, who for much of his life had lived and acted typically – with his own inherited estate at Yasnaya Polyana to which were attached numerous peasant workers and their families – Tolstoy was intimately aware of the traditional relationship between the peasantry and the land. Through his own personal enlightenment he had questioned that relationship and sought various means of helping to alleviate it, on his own lands as well as more generally (Knowles, 2004, p. 269).[6]

As early as the mid-1850s, long before Henry George had experienced his own questioning of the relationship between poverty and wealth and the relevance of land ownership to that relationship (which had most visibly begun in 1868–9), Tolstoy had been thinking about and discussing the basic land question. In 1856, during his first travels in western Europe, Tolstoy had been reading fictional works, the Gospels, and political and historical works, amongst which was the work of the French communitarian anarchist, Pierre-Joseph Proudhon (Simmons, 1949, p. 180). Of Proudhon's work Tolstoy probably at least read his well-known 1840 book *What is Property?*, the answer to which was, for Proudhon, 'Property is Theft!' This, Proudhon argued, was a consequence of the illegitimate usurpation of a right to property, and the raising of a rent or interest on that property, at the expense of the occupier or possessor (Knowles, 2004, p. 99). Interestingly, in discussing the ethics which informed his ideas, in 1851 Proudhon also argued:

Instead of a million laws, a single law will suffice...*Do not to others what you would not they should do to you: do to others as you would they should do to you. That is* the law of the prophets. But it is evident that this is not a law; it is the elementary formula of justice, the rule of all transactions (Proudhon, 1989 [1851], p. 134, emphasis in original).

Here was another, but earlier, espousal of the fundamental significance of the 'law of reciprocity' with respect to social justice which both Tolstoy and George were later to assert.

In 1861 Tolstoy met Proudhon in Brussels, where Proudhon was living in exile and, incidentally but perhaps significantly for Tolstoy's later ideas, writing a book which he had titled *La Guerre et la Paix* [*War and Peace*]: *Recherches sur le principe et la constitution du droit des gens* (Simmons, 1949, p. 213). A passage from Tolstoy's diary in 1865 indicated Tolstoy's debt to Proudhon for his argument against property, and identified the role he saw for Russia in advancing change on a larger scale:

The mission of Russia in world history consists of bringing into the world the idea of a socialized organization of land ownership. '*La propriété—c'est le vol*' ['Property is theft'] will remain a greater truth than the truth of the English constitution, as long as mankind exists. It is an absolute truth, but there are relative truths resulting from it—applications. The first...is the Russian people's conception of property. The Russian people refuse to recognize property in land... (Novak [ed.], *c*. 1958, p. 122).

Note Tolstoy's association of the notion of theft or stealing with ownership of land—just as Proudhon had done and as George was later to do. Note also the central role Tolstoy perceived for Russia, at least at that time, in dealing with the land question. This diary note was written by Tolstoy a few years before Henry George had experienced his own revelations about the relationship between wealth and poverty, and the connection of that problem to ownership of land, and twenty years before Tolstoy became aware of George's ideas.

During a visit to Moscow in 1881, Tolstoy explored for himself the conditions of the poor in that city. He found himself face to face with the contradiction between wealth and poverty: 'I had spent my life in the country, and...the sight of town poverty surprised me. I knew country poverty, but town poverty was new and incomprehensible to me' (Tolstoy, 1991 [1884–6], p. 1). Tolstoy's contact with a peasant named Syutaev opened up to him the futility of charity to help the poor. It was this peasant's suggestion to Tolstoy that real charity involved working with the peasantry, and thus learning from each other, which was profoundly instrumental in Tolstoy's decision to begin to do just that. For Tolstoy, such an approach was nearer to the tenets of Christianity than anything else he had done. In 1884–5, back home on his estate Yasnaya Polyana, Tolstoy turned his hands to making shoes and practical farming, and began dressing in peasant clothes (Novak [ed.], *c*. 1958, p. 25; Simmons, 1949, pp. 399–400, 423–5). At this time, Tolstoy still had not encountered Henry George's ideas or his writings.

In an essay in 1902, Tolstoy acknowledged the existence of various other works on the land question; he cited the 'project of the Englishman, William Ogilvie, who lived in the eighteenth century'; followed shortly afterwards by another Englishman, 'Thomas Spence...[who] solved the land question by recognizing the land to be the property of parishes which could dispose of it as they pleased. In this way the private possession of separate individuals was completely abolished'. Tolstoy asserted that the land question 'was similarly solved by...Thomas Paine' who proposed that land would become the property of the nation upon the death of an owner. After Paine, Tolstoy noted Patrick Edward Dove who perceived the value of land arising from 'two sources—to the property of the land itself and to the work put into it'. He also noted the Japanese Land Reclaiming Society which had a scheme relating payment of a tax to the amount of land apportioned to an individual. At this point Tolstoy, with knowledge of these precursors, extolled the virtues of Henry George's scheme in this way: 'I personally consider Henry George's project the justest, most beneficent, and, above all, most easily applied of all the projects of which I know anything' (Tolstoy, 1905 [1902], pp. 160–1).[7]

It is apparent that, whether with hindsight after George's death in 1897, or in the progressive formation of his own awareness of the problems of the peasantry and his profound dissent against 'landlordism', Tolstoy did not exclusively rely on the work of Henry George. He had developed and experienced his own aversion to the social structure of the nobility and its consequences for the peasantry, not needing George to have brought it to his attention. He had accepted the idea of property as theft before Henry George had expounded that notion, just as he had earlier observed and understood the coexistence of poverty with wealth. He did not need to engage with George's Single Tax scheme to enable him to bring together his own ideas and remedies for the ills of society as he perceived them. For Tolstoy, George's scheme was an instrument, a 'project', a weapon or a tool, a means to an end. Obviously, as evidenced by Tolstoy's own enthusiastic promotion of the Single Tax idea, it was an important weapon in his arsenal if it could be implemented, but it was not more than that.

There are many instances which can be cited of Tolstoy praising the Henry George scheme (see Wenzer, 1997b, chapter 2 for a wide selection of samples), but there are also many instances of his being critical of that scheme or being very cautious in the way he expressed support for it. The apparent changes in Tolstoy's enthusiasm for, or at times even apparent rejection of, the Single Tax project have presented a dilemma to some of those who have written about the relationship between Henry George's scheme and Tolstoy's support for it (e.g. Wenzer, 1997b, pp. 22–4; Redfearn, 1992, pp. 93–5). Yet if the communitarian anarchist beliefs of Tolstoy are kept in sharp focus, such dilemmas do not arise. It is only through trying to force the extent of the connections between the two reformers that unclear issues occur. The different goals and different contexts of each man simply gave rise to different perspectives of and different aims for the Single Tax scheme.

Elwood Lawrence (1957, p. 75) has called George 'an American apostle of frontier individualism and free trade' whom history has acknowledged as 'a catalyst for British socialism....Socialist pioneers agreed that George was a powerful influence upon them'. Edward Rose (1968, p. 159) has pointed out: 'Henry George's philosophy is essentially an American world-view, true to the tradition of the American Dream. He saw no reason why the entire world could not become – if men were willing – the promised land of milk and honey, like the fruitful and ever bountiful plains of North America'. Tolstoy did not have an equivalent perception of Russia and his vision for a future Russian society was not at all compatible with George's vision for America and Britain.

Tolstoy was disparaging in his views of America and Britain. Poverty and wealth continued to coexist there, just as they did in Russia, despite the existence of democratic political institutions. People were not free in those states. They obeyed laws which were made by their political representatives and imagined they were free, but he argued that he was more free in Russia because he had played no part in the making of laws and thus he was free not to obey them. He expressed his opinion of parliamentary government in this way: 'To ask me what I think about parliamentary government is just like asking – I won't say the Pope – but some monk his opinion as to how prostitution ought to be regulated' (Simmons, 1960, p. 364). In an essay written in 1902, five years after the death of Henry George, Tolstoy argued that, just as serfdom and slavery had been abolished by governments in the past, in Russia and elsewhere, so could governments order the abolition of the ownership of land; yet such action was unlikely ever to be taken. He was certain that it would not be possible in Russia:

> In Russia the power is nominally in the hands of the Tsar; in reality it is in the hands of a few hundreds of fortuitous men, relatives and near friends of the Tsar, who compel him to do what pleases them. Now all these men own immense tracts of land, and so they will never allow the Tsar, even if he should wish to do so, to free the land from the power of the landed proprietors....[Thus] it is impossible to expect the emancipation of the land from the government in general, and in Russia from the Tsar (Tolstoy, 1905 [1902], pp. 145–6).

This was not a new revelation for Tolstoy, suddenly arising in his twilight years. It was a reflection of his own early life as a noble landowner and also of his anarchist thought which had been with him for decades. As early as 1865 he had written in his diary: 'All governments...are in equal measure good and evil. The best ideal is anarchy' (Simmons, 1949, p. 183). Was he not also describing here, in Russia, that tight concentration of ownership of immense tracts of land and thus power in the hands of a few which George had earlier admitted would be fatal to his Single Tax scheme?

Neither George nor Tolstoy denied their intrinsic national roots. Just as George remained consistent in his fundamental world-view, running for Mayor of New York in 1886 and 1897 and thus exhibiting his commitment to the 'rule of law' and to the hierarchical government institutions of the United States (Rose, 1968, pp. 119–122, 139–141), so Tolstoy remained true to his vision of, and belief in, a possible future for Russia without overarching government authority and without the existence of institutionalized state violence to protect either land or capital (e.g. Tolstoy, 1948 [1900], pp. 106–7, 112–3, 124, 127). He knew of course that he could not alone act to remove the imperial Russian state apparatus, and he was wholly unsupportive of revolutionary socialism's imperative to do so, but he did believe that, through living his life as an example of, and preaching, his religion of brotherly love and non-violence, he could help to erode it.

Tolstoy's suggestion to the Tsar that he should consider implementing the Single Tax scheme has often been cited as an example of the extent of Tolstoy's commitment to George's project: if this Christian anarchist could go so far as to deny his own stated anarchist beliefs, he must truly be a 'disciple' of Henry George. Yet Ernest Simmons has pointed to the context within which Tolstoy made his decision, and it is instructive: 'He did this not because he had any love for autocracy, for he condemned all governments. But he was willing to compromise with his own ultimate ideals, for he feared the violence of revolution...' (Simmons, 1960, p. 364). There had indeed been a violent revolution in Russia in 1905, and the consequent actions of the Tsar in establishing the Duma as a democratic institution with only an illusion of its holding devolved power fooled none of the radical reformers in Russia and few of the people (Fitzpatrick, 2001, pp. 32–5). There was every possibility of another, more comprehensive, revolution. In a letter to his then close friend, Grand Duke Nikolay Mikhaylovich in 1902, through whose hands he had earlier that same year sent his letter to the Tsar, Tolstoy again argued in favour of implementation of George's scheme through Tsarist authority (Tolstoy, 1978 [1902], pp. 615–7). This letter, and the letter to the Tsar, were tactical; Tolstoy was not in any way resiling from his deeply entrenched Christian anarchist beliefs. In his 1902 letter to the Tsar, Tolstoy argued that 'I think that its [ownership of the land] abolition will place the Russian people on a high level of independence, well-being, and contentment. I also think that this measure will undoubtedly get rid of all the socialist and revolutionary agitation which is now flaring up among the workers and threatens the greatest danger both to the people and to the government' (cited in Wenzer, 1997b, pp. 113–4). As late as 1909, well after the 1905 revolution, Tolstoy had not retreated from his position:

> Our Government, I am convinced, is acting very foolishly in not putting Henry George's theory into practice, for the principle that the land ought never to be the private property of individuals has always had its advocates, and is an article of faith today among the peasants of Russia. Had measures been taken with this end in view,

it would have done more than all their deeds of cruelty and violence to pacify the people and so to make the further spread of revolution impossible (Tolstoy, 1931 [1909], pp. 283–4).

He was seeking to achieve a step forward, a release of pressure from below, in the context of the spectre of state socialist and violent revolution.

A similar contextual caveat should be applied to Tolstoy's oft-cited interaction with the imperial Minister for Interior Affairs, Pyotr Stolypin, in 1907, when Tolstoy again advocated implementation of George's Single Tax scheme (Alexandra Tolstoy, 1975 [1953], p. 456). His constructive engagement with the Russian government was to seek urgent relief for the working people and the peasantry from oppression while at the same time attempting to steer the whole of Russian society away from the imminent prospect of violent socialist revolution. It was not evidence of an erosion of Tolstoy's Christian anarchist beliefs, nor was it evidence of uncritical support for George's Single Tax scheme. Already, in 1905, Tolstoy had written an essay titled 'The End of the Age: An Essay on the approaching Revolution' in which he not only explicitly expounded his anarchist beliefs, including 'the abolition of States with their coercive power' (Tolstoy, 1948 [1905], p. 253), but he also advocated non-violence and non-involvement in government or revolutionary activities, and he set out his vision of the life which the peasantry of Russia should adopt:

> The peasants, the majority of the Russian people, should continue to live as they have always lived, in their agricultural, communal life, enduring all violence, both governmental and non-governmental, without struggle, but not obeying demands to participate in any kind of governmental coercion; they should not willingly pay taxes, they should not willingly serve in the police, the administration, the customs, in the army, in the navy, nor in any coercive organisation whatever....It is only the non-participation of the people in any violence whatever which can abolish all coercion from which they suffer, and prevent all possibility of endless armaments and wars, and also abolish private property in land (*ibid.*, p. 257).

Tolstoy was not looking to George's Single Tax project here as a solution to the social problems or even to solving the land problems of the peasantry — 'they should not willingly pay taxes'.

There was never a possibility that George's Single Tax scheme could be introduced unchanged into the profoundly different political and socio-economic structures of imperial Russia at the end of the nineteenth century. Just as Marxist socialism was naturalized to Russian conditions and syncretized with Russian populism by some early Russian socialists and then by the Bolshevik leaders, both in terms of doctrine and in terms of practical politics (Hosking, 1998, pp. 361–3), so also the philosophy and project of Henry George needed to be naturalized. Tolstoy was always very much aware of this and said so in various different ways on many occasions (e.g. Tolstoy, 1905 [1902]; Tolstoy, 1961 [1905]).

TOLSTOY'S 'HENRY GEORGE'

Despite the obvious and significant differences between George and Tolstoy when it came to respect for parliamentary political systems, or even government by a state in any form, George's Single Tax project did have resonance for Tolstoy as a first step on the rung of the ladder he was climbing. His enthusiasm for the Single Tax project was a reflection of his deep feelings for the plight of the peasantry as well as its being embedded in Christian ethics as he understood and practised them. He saw it as a morally driven and non-violent but partial and expedient means of quick release of the peasantry – and for the 'working people' more generally – from the shackles of 'landlordism' and thus some relief from their structured poverty. For at the top of Tolstoy's ladder was a clear vision of communitarian anarchist society for all humanity.

Tolstoy believed that the 'enlightenment of conscience as to the utilization of land, and the practical application of that new consciousness...' was 'one of the chief problems of our time'. He saw Henry George as having been 'the leader and organizer' of a movement in that direction which Tolstoy asserted had been growing (as 'a process') in 'Christendom' at the end of the 18th Century and into the beginning of the 19th. For Tolstoy, 'in this lies his immense, his pre-eminent, importance'. George had not only contributed to this awakening but also helped to 'place it on a practical footing'. Here he presented George as a prime mover in the development of working-class consciousness of its plight with respect to land ownership and the ill-effects of 'landlordism' on its welfare. Tolstoy knew that others had expressed these same ideas earlier but the valued contribution of Henry George was as a 'leader and organizer', driven by evangelistic fervour in promoting his ideas, and the fact that his scheme was, for Tolstoy, 'practical' (Tolstoy, 1961 [1897], p. 192).

As a critic of the role of religious teachings and the science of political economy, Tolstoy asserted: 'The service rendered by Henry George is that he has not only mastered the sophistries by which religion and science try to justify private ownership of land, and simplified the question to the uttermost...but he was also the first to show how the question can be solved in a practical way' (*ibid.*, p. 194). With respect to the role of religion, in 1884, for example, George had stated: 'The people had not merely been taught by their masters and pastors that this was a natural state of things....The name of God has been called in to show that it was His will that some should be rich and some should be poor...' (cited in Lawrence, 1957, p. 47). Tolstoy also believed that George 'first gave a clear and direct reply to those excuses used by the enemies of every reform, to the effect that the demands of progress are unpractical [sic] and inapplicable dreams'. Tolstoy argued that the practicality and clarity of George's project were such that it could be implemented immediately, given the political will to do so. He believed: 'The need for altering the present system has been explained, and the possibility of the change has been shown (there may be alterations and amendments of the Single-Tax system, but its fundamental idea is practicable)....It is only necessary that this thought should become public opinion...' (Tolstoy, 1961 [1897], p. 194).

Note here the caveat which Tolstoy applied to the single tax project. He was certainly convinced of the 'fundamental idea', and also of the essential practicality of it, but he had reservations – sufficient to deliberately note their existence – about the details if it was implemented. Note also how Tolstoy was convinced of the necessity for 'this thought' (not necessarily the entire single tax project?) to 'become public opinion'. It was necessary to spread 'this thought' widely; to enhance the collective consciousness of the peasantry and the working people with respect to the way in which a tax on the value of land, as the only tax, would free the land from idle landowners, give the peasants and workers more equitable access to it, and thus enable it to be put to fruitful use. And Tolstoy certainly played a substantial role in the Russian and in the international attempt to achieve this objective. In 1905 he lamented the lack of interest in George's work:

> Very striking...is the fate of the activity of the remarkable man who appeared towards the end of the last century – Henry George – who devoted his immense mental powers to elucidating the injustice and cruelty of the institution of landed property and to indicating means of rectifying that injustice under the forms of government now existing in all countries. He did this by his books, articles, and speeches, with such extraordinary force and lucidity that no unprejudiced person reading his works could fail to agree with his arguments... (Tolstoy, 1961 [1905], pp. 284–5).

However, Tolstoy's support for George's project – or, more precisely, the 'fundamental idea' behind it – did not extend to his uncritical embracing of George's political economy, nor even to an uncritical, nor even complete, acceptance of George's 'Single Tax' project. A diary note by Tolstoy in 1906 is indicative of his contingent support for George's project: 'It isn't the system which is valuable (although not only do I not know a better one, but I can't imagine one), but *what is valuable is the fact that the system establishes an attitude to land which is universal* and the same for everybody' (cited in Redfearn, 1992, p. 98, emphasis added).

Tolstoy's Christianity and his communitarian anarchist beliefs enabled him to generalize his emancipatory aspirations for Russian working people and the peasantry to all those in the world who were oppressed by land ownership (e.g. Tolstoy, 1905 [1901], especially pp. 241–2). Despite Tolstoy's stated global imperative, Russia was the primary focus of his work and of his visions for the future. In 1905, for example, he wrote:

> The Russian people, owing to their agricultural environment, their love of this form of life, and their Christian trend of character, and also because, almost alone among European nations, they continue to be an agricultural people and wish to remain so

– are as it were providentially placed by historic conditions in the forefront of the truly progressive movement of mankind in regard to what is called the labour question (Tolstoy, 1961 [1905], p. 293).

Russia was Tolstoy's homeland and it was his primary, or at least his most immediate, concern.

The key to understanding just why Tolstoy was so enamoured of George's 'fundamental idea' was the way he set out this summary of George's project and its positive outcomes if implemented:

1. That no one would be unable to get land for use.
2. That there would be no idle people owning land and making others work for them in return for permission to use that land.
3. That the land would be in the possession of those who use it, and not of those who do not use it.
4. That as the land would be available for people who wished to work on it, they would cease to enslave themselves as hands in factories and workshops, or as servants in towns, and would settle in the country districts.
5. That there would be no more inspectors and collectors of taxes in mills, factories, refineries, and workshops, but there would only be collectors of the tax on the land, which cannot be stolen, and from which a tax can be most easily collected
6. (and most important) That the non-workers would be saved from the sin of exploiting other people's labour (in doing which they are often not the guilty parties, for they have from childhood been educated in idleness and do not know how to work), and from the still greater sin of all kinds of shuffling and lying to justify themselves in committing that sin; and the workers would be saved from the temptation and sin of envying, condemning, and being exasperated with the non-workers, so that one cause of separation among men would be destroyed (Tolstoy, 1961 [1897], pp. 190–1).

This was Tolstoy's description of the benefits of George's scheme for a Russian peasant.

The way Tolstoy expressed item 6 is telling; it sounded almost Biblical and he pointedly asserted that it was the most important of all the outcomes he envisaged. So much sin would be averted by abolishing the ownership of land through implementing George's scheme. Tolstoy had stated a related ethical sentiment earlier, in 1886, in a diary note he made after re-reading George's *A Perplexed Philosopher*: 'Became very vividly aware again of the sin of owning land' (cited in Redfearn, 1992, p. 91), and the ethic was repeated later, in his 1902 essay 'To the Working People', for example: 'I do not propose a strike, but a clear consciousness of the criminality, the sinfulness of the participation in the ownership of land…' (Tolstoy, 1905 [1902], p. 150). Ernest Simmons (1960, p. 365) has pointed out that in the period leading up to the 1905 revolution, the 'land hunger of the peasants was driving them on to kill landowners'. Tolstoy's response was an essay, 'The Great Sin', which again advocated the implementation of George's Single Tax 'solution'. This need for freedom from sin—most profoundly the sin of unrestrained ownership of land and the inequitable consequences which flowed from that—was a consistent theme for

Tolstoy and for George. However, as David Redfearn observes (1992, p. 93), with reference to Tolstoy's summary above of George's project, 'Some of this is not quite according to Henry George...'. Redfearn refers to the inconsistencies between Tolstoy's exposition of George's project and the scheme as consistently explained by Henry George as 'inaccuracies of detail' but that is a distortion of what had actually happened. Tolstoy had naturalized George's project into the political and socio-economic conditions of Russia of his time and reconciled George's 'fundamental idea' with his own vision for Russian society.

Here, in a neat summary, was Tolstoy's 'Henry George'. It was a solution to the exploitation of Russia's peasantry by idle landowners, it was a means of the workers and peasants gaining access to land which they could work for themselves, it was a means of working people being able to leave the 'slavery' of factory work in towns and cities and being able to move to rural areas, and – 'above all else' – it was a means of both 'non-workers' and workers avoiding, or escaping from, the necessity to sin against God's will. Not only had Tolstoy seen in the Single Tax idea the possibility of an expedient and practical first step towards emancipation of workers and peasants from under the heel of the non-working nobility and, concurrently, towards his ideal communitarian anarchist society, but he had seen, most profoundly, a project which he had reconciled comfortably with his Christian ethics and which made a contribution to the removal of the necessity for sin. Tolstoy's enthusiastic support for the Single Tax idea was most definitely neither an uncritical nor complete acceptance of Henry George's Single Tax project nor of his political economy.[8]

Tolstoy and George, given their evangelistic projects, must each be acknowledged as having had the right to have acted, spoken, and written polemically and strategically from time to time. Tolstoy had his own vision for society, his own goals, his own political economy – and, when carefully read into the socio-economic and political context of their time, these did not fit closely with the vision for society, goals, and political economy of Henry George. Where Tolstoy's and George's minds and hearts did meet most securely was that place which Edward Rose (1968, 'Preface') has insightfully identified with respect to Henry George:

> George's success...was traceable to the way in which he expressed his theory as much as to the concept itself. For this reason, it is an unforgivable error to equate the whole of George's philosophy with the idea of the Single Tax. George was a gifted writer and a powerful speaker who was endeavouring to express a vision of man – not simply a fiscal policy.

NOTES

1. Use of the label 'Single Tax' is not being simplistic but reflects both Tolstoy's and George's shorthand expression for George's scheme. Tolstoy variously referred to George's proposals as a 'project', a 'system', a 'scheme', or even just an 'idea'. Although Henry George acknowledged that his scheme could be labelled 'land rent tax' or some similar phrase, by the mid-1880s he had adopted the shorthand expression 'Single Tax' as it 'more fully expressed' his idea, although it still needed to be understood that this was not an additional tax but a tax to replace all others. He also liked the term's implicit association with 'those great Frenchmen [the Physiocrats], ahead of their time, who, over a century ago, proposed the *impôt unique* as the great means for solving social problems and doing away with poverty…' (Rose, 1968, p. 133; Wenzer, 1997a, p. 50).
2. George understood 'economic rent' to equate to 'natural rent'; that is, distinct from 'monopoly rent' which was possible due to a 'power to extract a rent' (Wenzer, 1997a, p. 63).
3. Ironically, in the same year (1879) that George wrote of this group of 'Russian patriots'—the Land and Liberty group, or *Zemlia i Volia*—a majority of their delegates meeting at a secret congress voted in favour of a program of systematic terror, to include the assassination of leading members of the government. Tsar Alexander II was condemned to death and the group eventually succeeded in assassinating him in 1881 (Hosking, 1998, pp. 346, 357–8).
4. George's reference to Herbert Spencer here is to anarchistic ideas expressed in the first edition of his book *Social Statics*. He later retreated from that position and omitted the offending chapter from the second edition of the book. Anarchists early in the twentieth century published the omitted material as a pamphlet, Herbert Spencer (1913), *The Right to Ignore the State*, London: Freedom Press.
5. For an indication of Tolstoy's social reform popularity in Britain at about the same time, especially Tolstoyan community experiments of the 1890s, see W. Gareth Jones (ed.) (1995), *Tolstoi and Britain*, Oxford: Berg Publishers.
6. A begging question is, given his Christian anarchist beliefs and his opposition to land ownership, did Tolstoy remain the owner of the Yasnaya Polyana estate? He answered the question himself in a letter he wrote in 1906: 'In order to rid myself of landed property which was reckoned to be mine, I decided to act as though I were dead….The fact is that about 20 years ago my heirs each took what was due to him by law, and I kept nothing myself, and since then I have neither owned nor had control of any property except my own clothes'. He informed his correspondent that his wife owned and was in control of Yasnaya Polyana (Tolstoy, 1978 [1906], p. 656).
7. Tolstoy had used John Morrison Davidson's *Precursors of Henry George* for the source of his knowledge of most of these earlier similar ideas about land ownership (see 'Author's Note' in Tolstoy, 1905 [1902], p. 160).
8. For a similar, though thinly argued, conclusion see, for example, Leo Hecht (1976), *Tolstoy the Rebel*, New York: Revisionist Press, p. 176, note 31.

REFERENCES

Fitzpatrick, Sheila (2001), *The Russian Revolution*, 2nd edn, Oxford: Oxford University Press.
George, Henry (1999) [1871], 'Our Land and Land Policy', reprinted in *Our Land and Land Policy: Speeches, Lectures, and Miscellaneous Writings by Henry George*, Kenneth C. Wenzer (ed.), East Lansing: Michigan State University Press.
George, Henry (1904) [1880], *Progress and Poverty: an inquiry into the cause of industrial depressions and of increase of want with increase of wealth: The Remedy*, 4th edn., New York: Doubleday Page & Company.
George, Henry (1981) [1883], *Social Problems*, New York: Robert Schalkenbach Foundation.

George, Henry (1999) [1885], 'The Crime of Poverty', reprinted in Kenneth C. Wenzer (ed.), *op. cit.*

George, Henry (1999) [1887], 'Thou Shalt Not Steal', reprinted in Kenneth C. Wenzer (ed.), *op. cit.*

George, Henry (1999) [1889], 'Thy Kingdom Come', reprinted in Kenneth C. Wenzer (ed.), *op. cit.*

George, Henry Jr. (1904), *The Life of Henry George: First and Second Periods*, New York: Doubleday Page & Company.

Hobsbawm, E.J. (1975), *The Age of Capital 1848–1875*, New York: Charles Scribner's Sons.

Hosking, Geoffrey (1998), *Russia: People and Empire 1552–1917*, London: Fontana Press.

Knowles, Rob (2004), *Political Economy from Below: Economic Thought in Communitarian Anarchism, 1840–1914*, New York: Routledge.

Lawrence, Elwood P. (1957), *Henry George in the British Isles*, East Lansing: Michigan State University Press.

Maude, Aylmer (1961), 'Introduction', in *Recollections and Essays by Leo Tolstoy*, Aylmer Maude (trans.), London: Oxford University Press.

Novak, D. (ed.) (*c.* 1958), 'An Unpublished Essay on Leo Tolstoy by Peter Kropotkin', *Canadian Slavonic Papers III*, Ottawa: Canadian Association of Slavists.

Proudhon, Pierre-Joseph (1989) [1851], *General idea of the revolution in the nineteenth century*, London: Pluto Press.

Redfearn, David (1992), *Tolstoy: Principles for a New World Order*, London: Shepheard-Walwyn.

Rose, Edward J. (1968), *Henry George*, New York: Twayne Publishers.

Simmons, Ernest J. (1949), *Leo Tolstoy*, London: John Lehmann.

Simmons, Ernest J. (1960), *Leo Tolstoy*, Vol. II 'The Years of Maturity 1880–1910', New York: Vintage Books.

Tolstoy, Alexandra (1975) [1953], *Tolstoy: A Life of My Father*, Massachusetts: Nordland Publishing Company.

Tolstoy, Leo (1991) [1884–6], *What then must we do?* Bideford, Devon: Green Books.

Tolstoy, Leo (1961) [1897], 'Letters on Henry George', reprinted in *Recollections and Essays*, Aylmer Maude (trans.), *op. cit.*

Tolstoy, Leo (1948) [1900], 'The Slavery of Our Times', reprinted in *Essays from Tula by Leo Tolstoy*, London: Sheppard Press.

Tolstoy, Leo (1905a) [1900], 'Where Is The Way Out?', reprinted in *Miscellaneous Letters and Essays*, Leo Wiener (ed.), *op. cit.*

Tolstoy, Leo (1905b) [1900], 'Need It Be So?', reprinted in *Miscellaneous Letters and Essays*, Leo Wiener (ed.), *op. cit.*

Tolstoy, Leo (1905c) [1901], 'The Only Means', reprinted in *Miscellaneous Letters and Essays by Count Lev N. Tolstoy*, Leo Wiener (ed.), London: J.M. Dent & Co.

Tolstoy, Leo (1978) [1902], 'To the Grand Duke Nikolay Mikhaylovich', reprinted in R.F. Christian (ed.), op. cit., Letter 485.

Tolstoy, Leo (1905) [1902], 'To the Working People', reprinted in *Latest Works, Life, General Index, Bibliography*, Leo Wiener (ed.), London: J.M. Dent & Co.

Tolstoy, Leo (1948) [1905], 'The End of the Age', reprinted in *Essays from Tula*, *op.cit.*

Tolstoy, Leo (1961) [1905], 'A Great Iniquity', reprinted in *Recollections and Essays by Leo Tolstoy,* Aylmer Maude (trans.), London: Oxford University Press.

Tolstoy, Leo (1978) [1906], 'To A.S. Marov', reprinted in *Tolstoy's Letters, Volume II 1880-1910*, R.F. Christian (ed.), London: Athlone Press, Letter 532.

Tolstoy, Leo (1931) [1909], 'A Letter on the True Solution of the Land Problem', in *New*

Light on Tolstoy: Literary Fragments, Letters and Reminiscences not previously published, René Fülöp-Miller (ed.), London: George G. Harrap, 283–284.

Wenzer, Kenneth C. (1997a), *An Anthology of Henry George's Thought*, New York: University of Rochester Press, Vol. I of the Henry George Centennial Trilogy.

Wenzer, Kenneth C. (1997b), *An Anthology of Tolstoy's Spiritual Economics*, New York: University of Rochester Press, Vol. II of the Henry George Centennial Trilogy.

Wenzer, Kenneth C. (1997c), 'Tolstoy's Georgist spiritual political economy (1897–1910): anarchism and land reform', *The American Journal of Economics and Sociology*, **56**, 639–67.

Wenzer, Kenneth C. (1999), 'Preface', in *Our Land and Land Policy: Speeches, Lectures, and Miscellaneous Writings by Henry George*, Kenneth C. Wenzer (ed.), East Lansing: Michigan State University Press.

4. Henry George: Evolutionary Economist?

John Laurent

'Evolutionary' economics has by now (I am writing this in June 2004) established itself as a major force in current economic thinking, and has achieved the status of a respected alternative or heterodox paradigm alongside such fields as Institutionalist, post-Keynesian and behavioural economics (cf. Earl, 1983; Jones and Stilwell, 1986; Panico and Salvadori, 1993; Pullen, 1997; Hodgson, 1993, 1999, 2004a; Foster and Metcalfe, 2001; Lawson, 2003). Henry George is recognized as an important heterodox economist, but not usually in an evolutionary context. Geoff Hodgson, it is true, in his ground-breaking manifesto for an institutional and evolutionary direction in economics, *Economics and Evolution*, does refer to George's 'enormous...intellectual influence' (Hodgson, 1993, p. 281), and indeed, as illustrative of this influence Hodgson cites a letter from Alfred Russel Wallace (co-discoverer with Charles Darwin of the principle of evolution by natural selection) to Darwin strongly commending George's *Progress and Poverty* and saying that he (Wallace) had 'never been so impressed with a book' — to which Darwin replied that he would 'certainly order' the book[1]. One could hardly find oneself in more illustrious evolutionary company than this! Yet Geoff Hodgson's account of this episode in a footnote is probably appropriate: George's legacy lay largely outside the texts of 'Evolutionary Economics', strictly speaking.

In other academic contexts, such as politics, George's evolutionary interests have received somewhat more notice. In David Stack's (2003) *The First Darwinian Left*, for instance, Stack refers to George having been 'imbued with the general evolutionary ethics of the age' (p. 31), though I would challenge Stack's quick qualification that George 'had little interest in science' and 'was no more a socialist than he was a Darwinist' (*ibid.* — see below, and Erin McLaughlin-Jenkins's chapter about T.H. Huxley's criticisms of George in this volume). In an earlier era, George's evolutionism was in fact well recognized. Robert Blatchford, for example, who argued fervently for his particular vision of socialism from a Darwinian perspective (Blatchford, 1903, 1914), commended

George's *Progress and Poverty* to readers, along with A.R. Wallace's (1883) *Land Nationalisation: Its Necessity and Its Aims* — which also commended George — and Prince Kropotkin's *Fields, Factories and Workshops*, in which the author argues for, amongst other things, the effectiveness of agricultural co-operatives made possible by the evolution of human co-operativeness (Blatchford, 1902; Kropotkin, 1912 [1898]), a subject also of interest to George.[2]

The term 'evolution', of course, can mean many things (as can 'evolutionary economics' — see below). It does not necessarily refer to Darwin's theories. An examination of George's most well-known book, *Progress and Poverty*, therefore, might be helpful in finding just how prominent a theme evolution is in that book, and what George apparently meant by the term.

As readers will know, the last 'Book' in *Progress and Poverty* (and at 50 pages the longest such division in the volume) — Book X — is titled 'The Law of Human Progress'. Its 'evolutionary' tenor, at least in some broad sense, is thus inferred right from the beginning, and this impression is confirmed from a perusal of the Book's first few pages. On the third page, for example, we read that:

> The prevailing belief now [i.e., 1879] is that the progress of civilisation is a development or evolution, in the course of which man's powers are increased and his qualities improved by the operation of causes similar to those which are relied upon as explaining the genesis of species – viz. the survival of the fittest and the hereditary transmission of acquired qualities (George, 1976 [1879], p. 337).

To which George goes on immediately to add in the next paragraph:

> That civilisation is an evolution — that it is, in the language of Herbert Spencer, a progress from an indefinite, incoherent homogeneity to a definite, coherent heterogeneity — there is no doubt (*ibid.*).

And a few pages further on:

> The lower the stage of social development, the more society resembles one of those lowest of animal organisms, which are without organs or limbs, and from which a part may be cut and yet live. The higher the stage of social development, the more society resembles those higher organisms in which functions and powers are specialised, and each member is vitally dependent on the others (*ibid.*, p. 363).

There is much to consider in these lines. Herbert Spencer (1820–1903), author of *First Principles* (first published in 1862), which George is here citing, was, as Geoff Hodgson (1993) points out, probably more important in popularizing the term 'evolution' in the 19th Century than Darwin, however out of fashion he may be today. The Italian socialist Antonio Labriola, writing to colleagues in 1897, for instance, referred to 'the *First Principles* of the now indispensable Spencer', and later to the '*inevitable*' Spencer (Labriola, 1980 [1897], pp. 97, 121, my emphasis). In any event, Spencer used the term as early as 1851 — eight years before Darwin's *The Origin of Species* (and Darwin did not employ the word 'evolution' until the fifth [1869] edition of this work). Spencer introduced the word in his first book, *Social Statics*, and also in an article on 'The Development Hypothesis' in *The Leader* of 20 March 1852 (see Richards, 1987)—a phrase which in turn seems to have been popularized even earlier in Robert Chambers's *Vestiges of the Natural History of Creation* (1844).[3] And it is clear from Spencer's early writing that his conception of human societal evolution was essentially as conveyed by George. Coming from a background in journalism rather than science as such—he was a sub-editor of *The Economist* from 1848 to 1853[4]—Spencer was clearly impressed with Adam Smith's understanding of the division of labour in 'civilized' societies, which he saw as organic wholes, characterized by strong interdependence of 'functions'. In another essay published in 1852 Spencer had written as follows:

> [T]he 'physiological division of labour', as it has been termed, has the same effect of the division of labour amongst men. As the preservation of a number of persons is better secured when, uniting into a society, they severally undertake different kinds of work, than when they are separate and each performs for himself every kind of work: so the preservation of congeries of parts, which combining into one organism, respectively assume nutrition, respiration, circulation, locomotion, as separate functions, is better secured than when these parts are independent, and each fulfills for itself all these functions (Spencer, 1852, quoted Richards, 1987, p. 271).

While Spencer appears to be here making a case for the organization of an individual organism, such as a human being, in terms of specialized cells grouped into organs, each having a role in the 'division of labour' paralleling the organization of modern societies— i.e., that models from *social* phenomena can be brought to bear on *biological* questions[5]—the point is that Spencer saw close similarities between the two spheres. And George evidently subscribed to Spencer's notion in the social realm. Spencer's terms 'social organism' and 'super-organism' appear throughout *First Principles* and *Progress and Poverty*, and it is clear that Spencer remained one of George's chief sources of ideas about evolution, notwithstanding a later falling out between the two over the subject of access to land, which episode should now be discussed briefly.

George also read Spencer's *Social Statics*. We know this because George quotes long stretches of text from three editions of the book – 1851, 1868 and 1892 – in George's book, *A Perplexed Philosopher, Being, an Examination of Mr. Herbert Spencer's Various Utterances on the Land Question, with some Incidental References to his Synthetic Philosophy* (George, 1893), in which he castigates Spencer for his later repudiation of his case for land nationalization made in the two earlier editions of *Social Statics*. Notwithstanding their disagreement (they met in London in 1882, and George was disappointed that he could not interest Spencer in the cause of the Irish Land Leagues—see Duncan, 1908; Spencer, 1904; George, Jr., 1900), and Spencer's condemnation

of 'Communistic theories...of land tenure', George could still approvingly quote
Social Statics as follows, in which Spencer employs his organic, or 'corporate'
model of society:

> But to what does this doctrine, that men are equally entitled to the use of the earth,
> lead? Must we return to the time of unenclosed wilds, and subsist on roots, berries,
> and game? Or are we left to the management of Messrs. Fourier, Owen, Louis Blanc,
> and Co?
>   Neither. Such a doctrine is consistent with the highest state of civilization...and
> need cause no very serious revolution in existing arrangements. The change required
> would simply be a change of landlords. Separate ownership would merge into the
> joint-stock ownership of the public. Instead of being in the possession of individuals,
> the country would be held by the *great corporate body—Society* (George, 1893, p.
> 23, my emphasis).

To George's dismay, however, these paragraphs, from a chapter titled 'The
Right to the Use of the Earth' (Spencer, 1868, pp. 131–44) in the earlier editions
of *Social Statics*, were omitted from the 1892 edition and replaced with a series
of essays originally appearing in the *Contemporary Review* and later published
as a separate book under the title *The Man versus The State*. In *A Perplexed
Philosopher* George expresses his disappointment with Spencer over this, but
nevertheless tries to understand Spencer's about-face. Referring to Spencer's
essay 'The Coming Slavery', and vigorously repudiating the association of his
name with 'communistic theories', George quotes these lines:

> Communistic theories, partially indorsed by one Act of Parliament after another...
> are being advocated more and more vociferously by popular leaders, and urged on
> by organized societies. There is movement for land nationalization which, aiming at
> a system of land-tenure, equitable in the abstract, is, as all the world knows, pressed
> by Mr. George and his friends with avowed disregard for the just claim of existing
> owners (George, 1893, p. 91).

Notwithstanding this seeming damning of his position, George still sees
some hope in these words, with their 'admission that the movement for land
nationalization is "aiming at a system of land-tenure equitable in the abstract"'.
Spencer had not 'reached the point of utterly denying the truth he had seen',
George goes on to say, '[t]he abolition of private property in land he still admits
is equitable in the abstract' (*ibid.*).

But whatever George's precise interpretation of Spencer's 'great corporate
body' idea, there is no question that he was happy to retain it in *A Perplexed
Philosopher*, however strong his criticisms of his mentor. On pages 141–2 of
A Perplexed Philosopher, in an overview of Spencer's 'Synthetic Philosophy',
George repeats Spencer's definition of 'evolution' — that the term refers to 'an
integration of matter, and a concomitant dissipation of motion, during which the
matter passes from an indefinite, incoherent homogeneity to a definite, coherent

heterogeneity' — and he notes that Spencer's philosophy can further be described as a fusion of Laplace's nebular hypothesis (an early attempt to explain the origin of the solar system) with 'what is best known as the Darwinian hypothesis of the development of species'. A few pages further on, it is true, George qualifies his acceptance of Spencer's concept of evolution, which he says 'differs as widely from [the ideas] held by such evolutionists as Alfred Russell [*sic*] Wallace, St. George Mivart, or Joseph Le Conte, as it differs from the idea of special and direct creation', and George wants it to be understood that he wishes to preserve a place for the soul in his understanding of evolution (as with the three authors he mentions). George writes:

> We all see that the oak is evolved from the acorn, the man from the child. And that it is intended for the evolution of something is the only intelligible account that we can make for ourselves of the universe. Thus in some sense we all believe in evolution, and in some sense the vast majority of men always have. And even the evolution of man from the animal kingdom offers no real difficulty so long as this is understood as only the form or external of his genesis (George, 1893, p. 146).

George's progressivism, then, is always present, even as he attempts to soften the role of evolution in human nature. And when he is dealing with the evolution of human *society*, and feels on surer ground, George has no difficulty in subscribing to Spencer's understanding of the workings of evolution at that level. Thus, in a discussion of Spencer's concept of justice, George approvingly summarizes Spencer's notion of the evolution of this quality, albeit curiously combining Spencer's belief in the inheritance of acquired characteristics (now regarded as erroneous — see Dawkins, 1982) with Darwin's more enduring theory of the natural selection of socially beneficial traits:

> Our feeling that we ourselves ought to have freedom to receive the results of our own nature and consequent actions...results from inheritances of modifications produced by habit, or from more numerous survivals of individuals having nervous structures which have varied in fit ways, and from the tendency of groups formed of members having this adaptation to survive and spread. Recognition of the similar freedom of others is evolved from the fear of retaliation, from the punishment of interference prompted by the interests of the chief, from fear of the dead chief's ghost, and from fear of God, when dead-chief-ghost worship grows into God worship, and, finally, by the sympathy evolved by gregariousness (George, 1893, p. 168).

Spencer's principle that we 'ought to have freedom to receive the results of our own nature and consequent actions' is seen by George as a consistent theme in his mentor's writings, going back to the original version of *Social Statics*, notwithstanding Spencer's recantation of his advocacy of land nationalization in later editions of this work. On page 15 of *A Perplexed Philosopher* George notes Spencer's *a priori* declaration, in *Social Statics*, that 'every man may claim the full liberty to exercise his faculties compatible with the possession of like liberty by every other man', and how, as a corollary, this meant that 'exclusive possession of the soil necessitate[d] an infringement of this right' since 'men who cannot "live and move and have their being" without the leave of others, cannot be equally free with those others' (George, 1893, pp. 15–17). For George, Spencer's conception of equal access to justice being part and parcel of 'civilized' society and the evolution of societies to this state was consistent with the condemnation of private property in land. Indeed, George emphasizes this argument with a long citation from Spencer's *Principles of Ethics* which seeks to demonstrate that the 'principle of natural equity...limited only by the like freedom of all' can be seen in operation even in non-human societies (a position that a number of ethologists today would whole-heartedly endorse—see, e.g., de Waal, 1998; Constable, 2000[6]). The quote reads in part as follows:

> Various examples have made clear the conclusion manifest in theory, that among gregarious creatures this freedom of each to act has to be restricted; since if it is unrestricted there must arise such clashings of actions as prevents the gregariousness. And the fact that, relatively unintelligent though they are, inferior gregarious creatures inflict penalties for breeches of the needful restrictions, shows how regard for them has come to be unconsciously established as a condition to persistent social life (Spencer, 1890, quoted George, 1893, p. 171).

These remarkable lines from Spencer, approvingly quoted by George, are further evidence of the assiduity with which George read the evolutionary writers of his day, whatever the idiosyncrasies of his own understanding of evolution. Spencer may be out of fashion today, but he was greatly respected in his own time, and while George may have been annoyed and disappointed with him for his abandonment of his earlier advocacy of common ownership of land, George could still find much in Spencer's voluminous writings with which he could strongly agree. Does this make George an 'evolutionary' economist? Possibly; it at least provides a perspective on George's writing not usually taken into account. Such a perspective, I would suggest, can be helpful in trying to penetrate George's mental world, which was even more strongly imbued with the evolutionary *motif* than is apparent from a perusal of *Progress and Poverty*.

Even this last work contains more evolutionary material than has already been indicated. The long quote from *Social Statics* containing Spencer's reference to 'the great corporate body – society', for example, is included in this work as well as in *A Perplexed Philosopher*, as is the Spencerian notion that '[a]ccumulated wealth seems to play just such a part in relation to the social organism as accumulated nutrition does to the physical organism' (George, 1976 [1879], pp. 108, 287). Cities such as Chicago or St. Louis are described as 'the heart, the brain, of the vast social organism' (*ibid.*, p. 172), and on page 228 of this most widely read of George's books he ventures the suggestion that 'The ideal of socialism is grand and noble; and it is, I am convinced, possible of realisation, but such a state of society cannot be manufactured—it must grow. Society is an organism, not a machine'.

This kind of language permeates George's other writing as well. Notwithstanding his apparent sympathy for socialism, he could write, in *Protection or Free Trade*, 'competition plays just such a part in the social organism as those vital impulses which are beneath consciousness do in the bodily organism' (George, 1886, p. 329). In *Social Problems* we read that 'Between the development of society and the development of species there is a close analogy...as life rises into higher manifestations, simplicity gives way to complexity, the parts develop into organs having separate functions and reciprocal relations'; that 'The rude society resembles the creatures that though cut into pieces will live'; and that 'As in the development of species, the power of conscious, coordinated action of the whole being must assume greater and greater relative importance to the automatic action of parts, so it is with the development of society' (George, 1887, pp. 1, 4, 168).

In *The Condition of Labour* George wrote: 'We who call ourselves single-tax men...see in the social and industrial relations of men not a machine which requires construction, but an organism which needs only to be suffered to grow' (George, 1891, p. 93); and in *The Science of Political Economy* we learn about 'the social organism, or economic body' which 'grows, as the tree grows, as... man himself grows, by virtue of natural laws inherent in human nature and in the constitution of things', and also that:

> by virtue of the same power of discerning causal relations which leads the primitive man to construct tools and weapons, the individual desires of men, seeking satisfaction through exchange with their fellows, would operate...to unite individuals in a mutual coöperation that would weld them together as interdependent members of an organism (George, 1898, p. 36).

In *The Science of Political Economy* George further tells us that 'what the blood is to the physical body, wealth...is to the body economic', and that 'to [the] economic body, [exchange] is what the nerves or perhaps the ganglions are to the individual body' (*ibid.*, pp. 71, 399). George's talk of men uniting in 'mutual co-operation...as interdependent members of an organism' is reminiscent of Spencer's 'sympathy evolved by gregariousness', as quoted above; and what Spencer apparently means by this is explained in a chapter headed 'The Law of Evolution' in *First Principles*, where Spencer describes those 'organic integrations' which transcend a single organism, i.e., those 'by which organisms are made dependent on one another'. In Spencer's words:

> More or less of the gregariousness tendency is general in animals; and when it is marked, there is, in addition to simple aggregation, a certain degree of combination. Creatures that hunt in packs, or that have sentinels, or that are governed by leaders, form bodies partially united by co-operation (Spencer, 1870, p. 315).

Thus we have what Spencer means by gregariousness in *sub*-human species, and it is only a short step in thought to appreciating the evolutionary significance of the other word that he uses — sympathy — in terms of the natural forces which keep a troop of baboons, pack of wolves etc. together. Presumably Spencer also intends this terminology to apply to humans, but he does not so employ it in *First Principles*. However, Spencer does come closer to using the term ' sympathy' in an evolutionary context as applied to humans in *Social Statics*, where he cites Adam Smith's usage of the term in *The Theory of Moral Sentiments*, noting, for example, that ' the aim of that work [is] to show that the proper regulation of our conduct to one another is secured by means of a faculty whose function it is to excite in each being the emotions displayed by surrounding ones' (Spencer, 1868, p. 114). And George clearly has Spencer's (and possibly Smith's, though he doesn't cite *The Theory of Moral Sentiments*) terminology in mind when he refers to situations where, in humans, '[s]atisfactions become possible that in the solitary state were impossible'. George goes on to say:

> There are gratifications for the social and the intellectual nature – for the part of the man that rises above the animal. The power of sympathy, the sense of companionship... open a wider and fuller and more varied life. In rejoicing, there are others to rejoice; in sorrow the mourners do not mourn alone (George, 1976 [1879], pp. 169–70).

George may also have been thinking of Darwin's *The Descent of Man*, published the year following the edition of *First Principles* cited two paragraphs back. Whatever the case, there is no doubt that Darwin's chapter (IV) on 'The Moral Sense' (which approvingly cites Smith's *Moral Sentiments*) is precisely about what Spencer and George are getting at, and has obvious implications for 'evolutionary economics'. Like Spencer, Darwin is convinced of the evolutionary significance of gregariousness and sympathy in social species, including humans. As Darwin (1875, pp. 100–1) argues:

> Animals of many kinds are social [and] render...important services to one another: thus wolves and some other beasts of prey hunt in packs, and aid one another in attacking their victims. Pelicans fish in concert. The Hamadryas baboons turn over stones to find insects, etc., and when they come to a large one, as many as can stand round, turn it over together, and share the booty. Social animals mutually defend each other. Bull bisons in N.America, when there is danger, drive the cows and calves into the middle of the herd, whilst they defend the outside.

With regard to the 'impulse' that 'leads certain animals to associate together' (*ibid.*, p. 104), Darwin draws upon Smith's 'all important emotion of sympathy' (*ibid.*, p. 106) operating between the members of baboon troops, wolf packs etc. in competition with other such groups (or 'communities'). In Darwin's words:

In however complex a manner this feeling may have originated, it is one of high importance to all those animals which aid and defend one another, it will have been increased through natural selection; for those communities which included the greatest number of the most sympathetic members would flourish best, and rear the greatest number of offspring (*ibid.*, p. 107).

Darwin is thus reserving a place for competition and the 'struggle for exis-tence' in these 'social' animals, only now it is at the level of groups rather than individuals. 'Group selection' might currently be out of favour in biological circles (see, e.g., Sterelny, 2001; Pinker, 2002 — but cf. also Hodgson, 1993, pp. 186–194; Rose and Rose, 2001), but clearly Charles Darwin was comfortable with the notion. For Darwin, the principle of natural selection is preserved in competition between groups, even if it is *co-operation* within groups that is the focus. And humans, the social species *par excellence*, have probably inherited, in Darwin's view, these co-operative propensies from primate ancestors: 'Every one will admit that man is a social being', Darwin continues, and although our species has few special instincts, 'this is no reason why he ['man'] should not have retained from an extremely remote period some degree of instinctive love and sympathy for his fellows'. As man is a social animal, Darwin concludes,

it is almost certain that he would inherit a tendency to be faithful to his comrades, and obedient to the leader of his tribe; for these qualities are common to most social animals. He would consequently possess some capacity for self-command. He would from an inherited tendency be willing to defend, in concert with others, his fellow-men; and would be ready to aid them in any way which did not too greatly interfere with his own welfare or his own strong desires (*ibid.*, p. 108).

The Descent of Man is not cited by George, but it is fairly clear that George was fully cognizant of Darwin's view, of which he may have become aware through some of the other authors he mentions (e.g., A.R. Wallace, who had a similar understanding to Darwin's — see below). However this may be, George's observations, in *Progress and Poverty*, that '[m]an is social in his nature'; that '[m]en tend to progress just as they come closer together, and by co-operation with each other increase the mental powers that may be devoted to improve-ment'; that '[t]he incentives to progress are…inherent in the wants of [man's] sympathetic nature'; and that the 'division of labour and all the economies which come with the co-operation of increased numbers' (George, 1976 [1879], pp. 358–9) are clearly close to Darwin's view. In *The Condition of Labour* George writes of 'the social nature of man', and of how he is 'a social being, or, as Aristotle called him, a political animal' (George, 1891, pp. 86–7); in *Social Problems* George (1887, p. 204) says that '[m]an is driven by his instincts and needs to form society'; in *Protection and Free Trade* that '[t]he human being is by nature a social animal' (George, 1886, p. 279); and in his posthumously published *The Science of Political Economy* George (1898, p. 21) argues that 'man is more than an individual. He is a social animal, formed and adapted to live and co-operate with his fellows'.

But George is also anxious to combine these insights, perhaps partly learnt from Darwin, with Spencerian metaphors in a manner reminiscent of current usage of organic analogy in evolutionary economics (see below). Thus a few lines down the page from the last quoted sentences from *The Science of Political Economy* George refers to the

> co-operation of effort that even in its crudest forms gives to man powers that place him far above the beasts and that tends to weld individual men into a social body, a larger entity, which has a life and character of its own and continues its existence while its components change, just as the life and characteristics of our bodily frame continue, though the atoms of which it is composed are constantly passing away from it and as constantly being replaced (George, 1898, p. 21).

While Darwin would be happy with the first part of this quote, he would, I suggest, have difficulties with George's use of Spencer's 'social body' idea, with a 'life of its own'. Darwin in fact had little time for Spencer's grand theorizing based on 'first principle' assumptions rather than experimental or observational evidence, notwithstanding Darwin's reference to 'our great philosopher' (Spencer) in *The Descent of Man*.[7] But Spencer was not the only source of organic analogy or metaphor. It was common currency in George's time, among writers of both 'Left' and 'Right' persuasion (whatever those labels might have referred to at the time). The important 'Historical School' economist Werner Sombart (see Hodgson, 2001; Peukert, 2003), for example, wrote of the Italian Campagna as the 'Campagna organism' (Peukert, 2003, p. 69), and Sombart's contemporary, Gustav Schmoller, described economies as 'social organs' (Backhaus, 2003, p. 10). In more picturesque language the British socialist Edward Carpenter (1894) likened his country's industries' 'evolv[ing] out of their present chaos' to a butterfly emerging from a chrysalis.

Such imagery is not altogether foreign to some of the overblown language of evolutionary economics today, in everything from motivational business litera-ture to academic monographs. Joel Mokyr (1990, p. 104), for example, draws analogies between micro- and macroinventions in technological change, and micro- and macro*mutations* in biotic evolution. 'Species change gradually in a continuous accumulation of micromutations', Mokyr writes, '[m]acroinventions rarely emerge in one single blow...between Papin and Trevithic a number of clear-cut steps can be identified...the emergence of the steam engine created a "species" which was not in existence a century before'. In business literature one could cite Seth Godin's *Survival Is Not Enough*, in which Godin (2002, pp. 24–5) uses terminology similar to Henry George's in a discussion of how an organization may *deal* with technological change: 'Our organizations are not independent machines, standing in the middle of a stable field. Indeed we work for companies that are organisms. Living, breathing, changing organisms that are interacting with millions of other living, breathing, changing organisms'.

Godin's book is actually a more sophisticated treatment of the evolutionary theme than this quote might indicate. In a chapter on memes (Richard Dawkins's [1982] proposed cultural equivalent of genes), for example, in which Godin suggests that '[t]he speed of memetic evolution is now the speed of our evolution', the author goes on to acknowledge that the comparison of memes and genes is entirely hypothetical, and that it is not at all clear what a *unit* meme consists of, or how it should be defined (Godin, 2002, pp. 36–7). This is an improvement on the unrestrained use of biological analogy by some writers. To some extent this has been brought about by a lack of precision in definition which has led to wide disagreement concerning alleged parallels with the life sciences. What, for instance, constitutes a 'species' in evolutionary economics?—is it a new invention, as Mokyr argues, or a new technique or a commodity (Boulding, 2003)? And what are the units of selection (in Darwinian terms)—memes, routines, the 'organization' or institutions? (cf. Nelson and Winter, 1991; Bryant, 1998; Witt, quoted Peukert, 2003).

George, of course, knew nothing about genes or mutations (the words were coined in 1909 and [in a biological sense] in 1901 respectively), but the basic process of 'variation' and selection proposed by Darwin (and which underlies our current understanding) was familiar enough to him and complements his citations of Spencer. So while George was not averse to using analogy and metaphor to describe economic processes, he was also keen to bolster his arguments where possible with illustrations from what he saw as the relevance of Darwin's discoveries for theories of human nature and implications of the same for economics. Thus in *The Science of Political Economy* George says, rather bluntly, that 'political economy is an exposition of certain invariable laws of human nature'. What he means by this is elaborated on throughout the book, but one key idea is that with the appearance of *Homo sapiens* evolution entered a new dimension: as George expresses it, 'after the evolution which finds its crown in the appearance of man himself, a new and seemingly illimitable field of progress [became possible]' (George, 1898, p. 27). The idea is that *culture*, whether in the form of oral tradition, artefacts, written records, etc., has overtaken genetic change in human evolution to a large extent. Darwin had clearly expressed the idea as follows:

> Of the high importance of the intellectual faculties there can be no doubt, for man mainly owes to them his predominant position in the world. We can see that in the rudest state of society, the individuals who were the most sagacious, who invented and used the best weapons or traps, and who were best able to defend themselves, would rear the greatest number of offspring. The tribes, which included the largest number of men thus endowed would increase in number and supplant other tribes.

To which Darwin had added, importantly:

> Now, if some one man in a tribe, more sagacious than the others, invented a new snare or weapon, or other means of attack or defence, the plainest self-interest...*would prompt the other members to imitate him; and thus all would profit* (Darwin, 1875, pp. 128–9, my italics).

Here we have the application of group selection to the cultural sphere. As Geoff Hodgson (1994, pp. 426–7) has suggested, '[g]iven the possibility of group selection in biology [cf. also Wynne-Edwards, 1962, 1986], it can be conjectured that the same phenomenon occurs in the socio-economic sphere....Indeed, it could be argued that group selection is more likely with cultural inheritance in human society than with genetic inheritance....Cultural transmission is more collective...than genetic transmission'. The subject is controversial, but not so clear-cut (in the negative) as some theoreticians (Williams, 1966; Hamilton, 1964; Hirshleifer, 1977; Becker, 1976) would have us believe. Indeed, recent contributions to the debate, notably from Ernst Fehr and Urs Fischbacher (2002, 2003[8]) have specifically linked the notion of group selection with culture in humans in studies of collective behaviour in Ultimatum and similar games, and have concluded that 'cultural selection between groups', *not* necessarily involving a genetic component, is a viable concept, avoiding the difficulties with group selection at the biological level (Fehr and Fischbacher, 2003, p. 789). See also Pagel and Mace (2004).

Another important theorist in this whole area is A.R. Wallace. As I have argued previously (Laurent, 2003), there is good evidence that Darwin learnt something of his understanding of cultural evolution from Wallace, especially from Wallace's 1864 paper, 'The Development of Human Races under the law of Natural Selection' (Darwin's copy of which is heavily underscored, and Darwin did not publish his ideas on *human* evolution until *The Descent of Man*, in 1871). In this paper (which was later republished in the collection, *Natural Selection and Tropical Nature*), under the heading 'Different Effects of Natural Selection on Animals and on Man', Wallace argues that

> man...is social and sympathetic....Some division of labour takes place; the swiftest hunt, the less active fish, or gather fruits; food is, to some extent, exchanged or divided. The action of natural selection is therefore checked....
>
> In proportion as...physical characteristics become of less importance, mental and moral qualities will have increasing influence on the well-being of the race....[In competition with prey] man does not require longer nails or teeth, greater bodily strength or swiftness. He makes sharper spears, or a better bow, or he constructs a cunning pitfall, or combines in a hunting party to circumvent his new prey [etc.] (Wallace, 1895 [1864], pp. 173–4).

The similarities with Darwin's later writing are obvious. But Wallace goes further than this, arguing in another paper, 'The Limits of Natural Selection as

Applied to Man', that with the emergence of modern man (today believed to have been about 100,000 years ago — see Gould [1991]) from pre-human ancestors, 'genetic' selection for all intents and purposes ceased to operate. Wallace quotes T.H. Huxley's (1863) *Evidence as to Man's Place in Nature* concerning the Engis skull (found in a cave in Belgium in the 1830s, and 'surrounded...on all sides' by the bones of rhinoceros, hyena and other species long extinct in Europe), viz., that it was 'a fair average skull, which might have belonged to a philosopher, or might have contained the thoughtless brains of a savage' (Wallace, 1895 [1870], p. 189). In another paper, originally published in 1876, Wallace draws attention to the exquisite works of art found in European caves — 'drawings representing a variety of animals, including horses, reindeer, and even a mammoth, executed with considerable skill on bone, reindeer-horns, and mammoth tusks' (Wallace, 1895 [1876], p. 421). In all, Wallace was convinced, it was difficult to believe that man had 'evolved' in any biologically meaningful sense since the Upper Palaeolithic (to use his friend John Lubbock's [1865] terminology).

All indications are that George entirely concurred with Wallace's view. As we have seen, George at least mentions Wallace in *A Perplexed Philosopher*; and the two corresponded and met during a visit to America by Wallace in 1886 (Shermer, 2002). But whatever George's debt to Wallace in this respect, it is certain that George was of the view, as he expresses it in *The Science of Political Economy*, that '[f]rom as far back as we can see, human nature has not changed' (George, 1898, p. 136). In *Progress and Poverty* (1976 [1879], p. 396) George opines that 'the nature of man seems, generally speaking, always the same'; and likewise, in an 1890 address in San Francisco, George (1999 [1890], p. 220) declared that 'We cannot change human nature; we are not so foolish as to dream that human nature can be changed. What we mean to do is to give the good in human nature its opportunity to develop'. This last sentence seems connected with George's — and, as we have seen, Darwin's — view concerning the 'moral sense', as in George's succinct summary of the Darwinian argument in *Protection or Free Trade*: 'Moral perceptions are implanted in our nature as a means whereby our conduct may be instinctively guided in such a way as to conduce to the general well-being' (George, 1886, p. 37).

The 'moral sense' in humans, then, in George's view, would seem to be a biological trait which has evolved over millennia for its social utility: those communities of pre-human ancestors that were well-endowed with this trait were at a collective advantage in the 'struggle for existence' *vis-à-vis* those that weren't. This is strict Darwinism, as is the argument that competing cultures can result in the death of individuals (and their heredity), thus resulting over time in the natural selection of more 'sagacious' types and the gradual 'improvement' of the race. George summarizes this position as follows:

> The view that dominates the world of thought is this: That the struggle for existence, just in proportion as it becomes intense, impels men to new efforts and inventions.

> That this…capacity for improvement is fixed by hereditary transmission, and extended by the tendency of the best adapted individuals, or most improved individuals, to survive and propagate…and of the best adapted or most improved tribe, nation, or race to survive in the struggle between social aggregates. On this theory the differences between men and the animals, and differences in the relative progress of men, are now explained as confidently…as a little while ago they were explained upon the theory of special creation and divine interposition (George, 1976 [1879],   p. 338).

It is difficult to avoid the impression that George is to some extent parodying Darwin here—certainly the bellicose statements of extreme 'social Darwinists' of the time and later were totally out of kilter with the Darwin of *The Descent of Man*, who could *also* write that '[a]s man advances in civilisation…the simplest reason would tell each individual that he ought to extend his social instincts and sympathies…to the men of all nations and races' (Darwin, 1875, p. 122),[9] and it is not clear whether George's reference to 'improvement…fixed by hereditary transmission' is to as found in Darwin's writing (which, it has to be said, it can be), or to as in Spencer (where it predominates). Whatever the case, it is plain that for George culture is inextricably bound up with 'human nature' and that it has played a decisive role in human cultural and economic evolution. Innumerable instances confirming George's view here can be cited from his books. In the 'Law of Human Progress' section of *Progress and Poverty*, for example, George argues, in an illustration reminiscent of Marx's 'architect and bee' homily,[10]

> [t]he beaver builds a dam, and the bird a nest, and the bee a cell; but while beavers' dams, birds' nests, and bees' cells are always constructed on the same model, the house of the man passes from the rude hut of leaves and branches to the magnificent mansion replete with modern conveniences.…We know of no animal that uses clothes, that cooks its food, that makes itself tools of weapons, that breeds other animals that it wishes to eat, or that has an articulate language [etc.] (George, 1976 [1879], p. 336).

And concerning the *transfer* of this knowledge to later generations in a process paralleling biological inheritance, George wrote later, in *The Science of Political Economy*, 'Being held in the memory, [this knowledge] is transferable by speech; and as the development of speech leads to the adoption of means for recording language, it becomes capable of more permanent storage and of wider and easier transferability – in monuments, manuscripts, books, and so on' (George, 1898, p. 42).[11]

Furthermore, for George, *all* 'men', unless physically or intellectually handicapped, have these capacities, and have always had them as far as can be determined, as is evidenced in the great civilizations of the past: 'The Hindoos and the Chinese were civilised when we were savages. They had great cities, highly organised and powerful governments, literature, philosophies, polished manners, considerable division of labour, large commerce, and elaborate arts when our ancestors were wandering barbarians' (George, 1976 [1879], p. 340). George adverts to the various theories proposed to account for the rise and fall of advanced cultures, citing, among other works, Walter Bagehot's (1873) *Physics and Politics*, with its hypothesis of the 'hardening' of laws and traditions resulting in the suppression of progressive ideas; but however this may be, in George's view the central point is that human 'progress' has everywhere and at all times been made possible by cultural rather than biological advance since the appearance of our species. George concludes: '[T]here is nothing whatever to show any essential race improvement. Human progress is not the improvement of human nature. The advances in which civilisation consists are not secured in [changes in] the constitution of man, but in the constitution of society' (George, 1976 [1879], p. 398).

In adopting this position on the all-importance of culture in human affairs, George also shows that he has moved beyond Spencerian models to some extent. It is true that George remained wedded to Spencer's organic model of society, but he was prepared to at least modify this model in line with his Darwinian insights. Thus, in the 'Law of Human Progress', he quotes Spencer on the 'super-organic environment' where, according to George, a 'body of traditions, beliefs, customs, laws habits and associations…surround every individual' and is 'the great element in determining national character'. It is this environment, George goes on to say, '*rather than hereditary transmission*' which makes 'the Englishman differ from the Frenchman, the German from the Italian, the American from the Chinaman, and the civilised man from the savage man' (George, 1976 [1879], p. 349, my emphasis).

George is here diverging considerably from Spencer's 'survival of the fittest' (Spencer's phrase) biologism, in which Spencer thought that cultural changes were brought about by physical changes in human beings. George's increasing distance from Spencer in this respect is in fact specifically addressed in *Progress and Poverty*, where George cites Spencer's *The Study of Sociology* as averring that '[w]ar, slavery, tyranny, superstition, famine, and pestilence…are the impelling causes which drive man on, by eliminating poorer types and extending the higher; and hereditary transmission is the power by which advances are fixed, and past advances made the footing for new advances' (George, 1976 [1879], p. 339). In George's later *A Perplexed Philosopher*, his extended criticism of Spencer's views, he reproduces this passage, adding:

Some years after this was written…I [was] talking one day with the late E.L. Youmans, the great populariser of Spencerianism in the United States [about the] political corruption of New York…and of [the rich's] readiness to submit to it, or to promote it wherever it served their money-getting purposes to do so…. I said to him, 'What do you propose to do about it?'

Of a sudden his manner and tone were completely changed, as remembering his Spencerianism, he threw himself back, and replied, with something like a sigh, 'Nothing! You and I can do nothing at all. It's all a matter of evolution. We can only wait for evolution. Perhaps in four or five thousand years evolution may have carried men beyond this state of things. But we can do nothing' (George, 1893, pp. 163–4).[12]

But for all his sophistication of understanding of evolutionary theory, George retained a large blind spot towards a major influence on Darwin's thinking: Malthus. The place of Thomas Malthus in Darwin's (and initially Wallace's — see Jones, 2002) theory of natural selection is well attested to, and acknowledged by biologists and economists alike (Gordon, 1995 [1989]; Hodgson, 1993). Darwin himself wrote concerning the importance of Malthus in the development of his theory as follows:

> In October 1838, that is, fifteen months after I had begun my systematic enquiry, I happened to read for amusement Malthus on *Population*, and being well prepared to appreciate the struggle for existence which everywhere goes on from long continued observation of the habits of animals and plants, it at once struck me that under the circumstances favourable variations would tend to be preserved, and unfavourable ones to be destroyed. The result would be the formation of a new species. Here, then, I had at last got a theory by which to work (Darwin, 1995 [1902], p. 40).

Economics and some branches of the life sciences are of course all about scarce resources, and there is bound to be much in common between the disciplines. Whether this vitiates Darwin's theory as being simply a reflection of the thought-forms of the age (e.g., Young, 1995 [1968]; cf. Marx, 1993 [1862]) is a moot point. Perhaps Stephen Jay Gould (1980) is entitled to the last word on the subject with his observation that 'the source of an idea is one thing; its truth or fruitfulness is another....Darwin may have cribbed the idea of natural selection from economics, but he may still be right'. But however this may be, there is no question that Darwin learnt much from Malthus, and indeed that Malthus's ideas are pivotal to Darwin's theory. (For an excellent discussion on this whole subject see Hodgson, 1993, pp. 62–72. See also Hodgson, 2004b.) And George was aware of this importance of Malthus for Darwin.[13]

So it is curious that George seems to have felt it necessary to *rebut* Malthus with all the force of his noted eloquence. Especially is this so when it is considered that George's bugbear, the 'unearned increment', or inflation in land values was largely brought about by population growth — as George himself conceded, and for which he acknowledged a debt to Ricardo.[14] George in fact wrote, citing Ricardo, in *Progress and Poverty* that 'it is unquestionably true that the increasing pressure of population...compels a resort to inferior points of production', and that this was a primary source of increase in rents (George, 1976 [1879], pp. 162–3, 299). In *Social Problems* George (1887, p. 150) wrote of the abolitionist Thaddeus Stephens's 'forty acres and a mule' for freed slaves that such a scheme 'in the course of time, *and as the pressure of population increased*' would fail (my emphasis). And in *Protection or Free Trade* George acknowledges that a tax on unimproved land values involved 'a taking for the use of the community of a value' that arises 'not from individual exertion *but from the growth of the community*' (George, 1886, p. 308, my emphasis).

George, then, is admitting that there is such a thing as population pressure.

What he is not conceding, however, is that this is necessarily a problem. Rather than being the primary cause of the immiseration of the poor—as held by 'Malthusians' like Annie Besant (George, 1976 [1879], p. 81)—George argued that population growth can contribute to the *solution* of the 'social problem' of the growing disparities in wealth between the rich and poor in industrialized countries like England and the United States.

Phil Day, a contributor to this volume, has written that George's 'extensive refutation of Malthus…is outdated' (Day, 2000), and perhaps this is true. Certainly the world is a much more crowded place than it was in 1879, when George was writing. The world's population was then somewhat less than 1.4 billion (to use Smithsonian Institute figures provided by George[15]); it is now over 6 billion. And conditions are rapidly reaching the point where it will no longer be possible to argue that it is not the production of food that is the problem, but its distribution. Perhaps that point has already been reached (Ehrlich and Ehrlich, 1990; Linas, 2004; Hasthorpe, 2004). And along with this growth has been the steady destruction of the environment that has become so depressingly familiar. Actually, George wrote forcefully on this subject, in a surprising paragraph in *Social Problems* that does not sit well with his enthusiasm for population expansion:

> Nor must it be forgotten that, while our population is increasing, and our 'wild lands' are being appropriated, the productive capacity of our soil is being steadily reduced, which, practically, amounts to the same things as reducing its quantity. Speaking generally, the agriculture of the United States is an exhaustive agriculture. We do not return to the earth what we take from it; each crop that is harvested leaves the soil the poorer. We are cutting down forests which we do not replant; we are shipping abroad, in wheat and cotton and tobacco and meat, or flushing into the sea through the sewers of our great cities, the elements of fertility that have been embedded in the soil by the slow processes of nature, acting for long ages (George, 1887, p. 27).

The resolution of this apparent tension in George's writing, I would suggest, lies in his insistence on 'man's' unique capacity to find novel solutions in dealing with his material needs made possible by his intelligence and accumulated knowledge, techniques, etc. As we have seen, Darwin, too, to some extent, felt able to concede this uniqueness. Such a view is at least consistent with George's confidence in man's ability to deal with problems that might be associated with a burgeoning population. Most obviously pertinent in this connection is the ability to grow crops and raise animals, which can *increase* the availability of food, something which no other species has evolved to be able to do. As George finely writes:

> Of all living things, man is the only one who can give play to the reproductive forces more powerful than his own, which supply him with food. Beast, insect, bird, and fish take only what they find. Their increase is at the expense of their food.…But unlike that of any other living thing, the increase of man involves the increase of his

food.…[W]ithin the limits of the United States alone, there are now forty-five millions of men where…in the time of Columbus…there were only a few hundred thousand, and yet there is now within that territory much more food per capita for the forty-five millions than there was then for the few hundred thousand. It is not the increase of food that has caused this increase of men; but the increase of men that has brought about the increase of food (George, 1976 [1879], pp. 95–6).

To a point, of course, George is right. But the law of diminishing returns seems to have asserted itself since his day; indeed it was already becoming apparent in his time with the declining fertility of the soil in over-worked land that he himself described (see also Attenborough, 2002, chapter 10). However, attempts to defend George *against* Malthus today — as with Jim Horner (1997), for instance, who describes Malthus's (1926 [1798]) *Essay on the Principle of Population* as a 'reactionary work', intended to 'promote inequality in defence of a landed aristocracy' (*ibid.*, p. 595) — wear a bit thin as Malthus's spectre, rather than having been discredited (as Horner asserts), looms ever larger. It may be that evolution has been a major part of the problem. As Linas (2004) quotes the British essayist John Gray, 'The destruction of the natural world is not the result of global capitalism, industrialisation, "Western civilisation" or any flaw in human institutions. It is a consequence of the evolutionary success of an exceptionally rapacious primate'. But this doesn't help us much either. Perhaps it's time for a little more Georgist optimism.

NOTES

1.   Wallace to Darwin, 9 July 1881 (Darwin Archive, Cambridge University Library, Cat.No. DAR 106/7 [ser. 2]:154–5); Darwin to Wallace, 12 July 1881 (British Library, Add. MSS 46434, copy held in Darwin Archive). Wallace's letter is reproduced in full on page 1 of Anna George de Mille's (1972) biography of her father.
2.   George discusses productive and distributive co-operation at some length in Book VI — 'The Remedy' in *Progress and Poverty* (George, 1976 [1879], pp. 225–7).
3.   See Chambers (1884) [1844], pp. 179–237. The novelist Charles Kingsley's *Alton Locke* (Kingsley, 1983 [1850]) has a remarkable dream sequence in which the tailor-poet hero in delirium relives the evolutionary process through madrepor (coral), soft crab, remora, ostrich, mylodon, monkey and man. In *Two Years Ago* Kingsley (1889 [1857]) refers to 'the development theory of the *Vestiges*' (p. 150).
4.   The journal was founded in 1843, and saw its role as taking part in 'a severe contest between intelligence, which presses forward, and an unworthy, timid ignorance obstructing our progress' (*The Economist*, 21 February 2004, p. 5).
5.   The idea of specialized groups of cells performing complementary functions may be familiar enough to us today, but it was a new understanding in the young Spencer's day: it was not until 1839 that Mattias Schleiden and Theodor Schwann identified the function of the cell as the building block of living systems.
6.   Frans de Waal (1998) says of 'chimpanzee politics': '[C]himpanzee group life is like a market in power, sex, affection, support, intolerance and hostility. The two basic rules are 'one good turn deserves another' and 'an eye for an eye, a tooth for a tooth'.…[R]eciprocity among chimpanzees is governed by the same sense of moral rightness and justice as it is among humans' (p. 207).

7. Darwin self-deprecatingly said of his own 'gemmules' theory of heredity that it was 'wildly abominably speculative' and 'worthy even of Herbert Spencer' (Desmond and Moore, 1992).
8. I am grateful to John Nightingale for drawing my attention to Fehr and Fischbacher's work.
9. In an anonymous review of David Starr Jordan's *War and the Breed* in the New York Times Book Review of 3 October 1915, Major Leonard Darwin, Charles Darwin's son, is quoted as strongly repudiating the association of his father's name with 'the pseudo-scientific theory of "social Darwinism"', citing *The Descent of Man* to prove his point. In *Democracy and World Relations* (Jordan, 1918), Jordan castigates that 'Social Darwinism [which] applies the law of survival to races and nations, and makes it a national duty to assist evolution by war and conquest' (p. 52).
10. Marx wrote in Volume I of *Capital*: 'A spider conducts operations that resemble those of a weaver, and a bee puts to shame many an architect in the construction of her cells. But what distinguishes the worst of architects from the best of bees in this, that the architect erects his structure in imagination before he erects in reality. At the very end of every labour-process, we get a result that already existed in the imagination of the labourer at its commencement' (quoted Appelbaum, 1988, pp. 72–3).
11. The role of language in human evolution was also explained by the Scottish naturalist Henry Drummond in his (1894) *The Ascent of Man*: '[Before language], [e]volution...had only one way of banking the gains it won—heredity'. With language, 'there arose...a new method of passing on a step in progress. Instead of sowing a gain on the wind of heredity, it was fastened on the wings of words' (p. 191). See also Moore (1986).
12. Geoff Hodgson (2004a, p. 78) has helpfully clarified Spencer's understanding of the role of evolution in human 'progress'. For Spencer, Hodgson writes, 'social evolution operated ultimately in terms of human biological characteristics. Consequently, the speed of the under-lying evolution constrained the pace of socio-economic development. Spencer...thus argued [Hodgson is quoting Spencer's *The Study of Sociology*] that "society cannot be substantially and permanently changed....[S]ocial evolution is limited by the rate of organic modification of human beings"'.
13. In his chapter on 'The Malthusian Theory, its Genesis and Support' in *Progress and Poverty* George quotes Darwin as writing in *The Origin of Species*, 'the struggle for existence is the doctrine of Malthus applied with manifold force to the whole animal and vegetable kingdoms' (George, 1976 [1879], p. 74).
14. I am grateful to John Marsden, former Executive Secretary of the Linnean Society of London, for helpful discussions on Ricardo.
15. George's figures are from the Smithsonian Report for 1873. The Institute estimated a world population of 1,377,000,000 at the time, at an average density of 26.64 people to the square mile (George, 1976 [1879], p. 83).

REFERENCES

Appelbaum, R.P. (1988), *Karl Marx* (Masters of Social Theory, Vol. 7), Beverly Hills, CA: Sage.
Attenborough, D. (2002), *The Life of Mammals*, London: BBC.
Backhaus, J.G. (2003), 'Growth or Development: The Concept of the Historically Writ-ing Economist', in J.G. Backhaus (ed.), *Evolutionary Economic Thought: European Contributions and Concepts*, Cheltenham, U.K. and Northampton, MA, U.S.A.: Edward Elgar, pp. 4–23.
Bagehot, W. (1873), *Physics and Politics, or, Thoughts on the Application of the Principles of 'Natural Selection' and 'Inheritance' to Political Society*, London: Henry S. King & Co.
Becker, G.S. (1976), 'Altruism, Egoism, and Genetic Fitness: Economics and Sociobiol-ogy', *Journal of Economic Literature*, **14**(2), 817–26.

Blatchford, R. (1902), *Britain for the British*, London: Clarion Press.
Blatchford, R. (1903), *God and my Neighbour*, London: Clarion Press.
Blatchford, R. (1914), *Not Guilty: A Defence of the Bottom Dog*, London: Clarion Press.
Boulding, K. (2003)[1950], 'Religious Perspectives in Economics', in P. Oslington (ed.), *Economics and Religion* (2 vols.), Cheltenham, U.K. and Northhampton, MA, U.S.A.: Edward Elgar, Vol. II, pp. 5–23.
Bryant, K. (1998), 'Evolutionary Innovation Systems: Their Origins and Emergence as a New Economic Paradigm', in K. Bryant and A. Wells, *A New Economic Paradigm? Innovation-based Evolutionary Systems*, Canberra, Australia: Department of Industry, Science and Resources, Science and Technology Policy Branch, pp. 53–84.
Carpenter, E. (1894), 'The Way Out of the Present Social State' (address at Bradford Labour Church), *Yorkshire Factory Times*, 23 February.
Chambers, R. (1884) [1844], *Vestiges of the Natural History of Creation*, Edinburgh: W. & R. Chambers.
Constable, T. (2000), *Chimpanzees: Social Climbers of the Forest*, London: BBC.
Darwin, C. (1875), *The Descent of Man and Selection in Relation to Sex*, London: John Murray.
Darwin, C. (1995) [1902], 'Autobiography', in F. Darwin, *The Life of Charles Darwin*, London: Senate, pp. 5–54.
Dawkins, R. (1982), *The Extended Phenotype*, Oxford: Oxford University Press.
Day, P.D. (2000), *Hijacked Inheritance*, Unpublished Ph.D. thesis, University of Queensland.
de Mille, A.G. (1972), *Henry George: Citizen of the World*, Westport, Connecticut: Greenwood Press.
Desmond, A. and J. Moore (1992), *Darwin*, New York: Warner Books.
de Waal, F. (1998), *Chimpanzee Politics*, Baltimore, MD: Johns Hopkins University Press.
Drummond, H. (1894), *The Lowell Lectures on the Ascent of Man*, London: Hodder & Stoughton.
Duncan, D. (1908), *Life and Letters of Herbert Spencer* (2 vols.), New York: D. Appleton and Company.
Earl, P. (1983), 'A Behavioural Theory of Economists' Behaviour', in A. Eichner (ed.), *Why Economics is Not Yet a Science*, London: Macmillan, pp. 90–125.
Ehrlich, P. and A. Ehrlich (1990), *The Population Explosion*, New York: Simon and Schuster.
Fehr, E. and U. Fischbacher (2002), 'Why Social Preferences Matter – The Impact of Non-Selfish Motives on Competition, Cooperation and Incentives', *Economic Journal*, **112**, C1–C33.
Fehr, E. and U. Fischbacher (2003), 'The Nature of Human Altruism', *Nature*, **425**, 785–791.
Foster, J. and J.S. Metcalfe (2001), *Frontiers of Evolutionary Economics: Competition, Self-organization and Innovation Policy*, Cheltenham, U.K. and Northampton, MA, U.S.A.: Edward Elgar.
George, H. (1976) [1879], *Progress and Poverty*, London: Dent.
George, H. (1886), *Protection or Free Trade: An Examination of the Tariff Question with Especial Regard to the Interests of Labor*, New York: Henry George & Co.
George, H. (1887), *Social Problems*, London: Kegan Paul, Trench & Co.
George, H. (1999) [1890], 'Justice the Object—Taxation the Means', in H. George, *Our Land and Land Policy: Speeches, Lectures, and Miscellaneous Writings* (ed. Kenneth C. Wenzer), East Lansing, MI: Michigan State University Press, pp. 203–20.

George, H. (1891), *The Condition of Labour: An Open Letter to Pope Leo XIII*, London: Swan Sonnenschein & Co.

George, H. (1893), *A Perplexed Philosopher, Being, An Examination of Mr. Herbert Spencer's Various Utterances on the Land Question, with some Incidental Reference to his Synthetic Philosophy*, London: Kegan Paul, Trench, Trübner & Co.

George, H. (1898), *The Science of Political Economy*, London: Kegan Paul, Trench, Trübner & Co.

George, H. Jr. (1900), *The Life of Henry George*, London: Reeves.

Godin, S. (2002), *Survival is Not Enough: Zooming, Evolution and the Future of Your Company*, New York: The Free Press.

Gordon, S. (1995) [1989], 'Darwin and Political Economy: The Connection Reconsidered', in G. M. Hodgson (ed.), *Economics and Biology*, Aldershot, Hants, U.K.: Edward Elgar, pp. 234–56.

Gould, S.J. (1980), 'Darwin's Deceptive Memories', *New Scientist*, **21**, 577–9.

Gould, S.J. (1991), *Life's Grandeur: The Spread of Excellence from Plato to Darwin*, London: Vintage.

Hamilton, W.D. (1964), 'The Genetical Evolution of Social Behaviour' (I and II), *Journal of Theoretical Biology*, **7**, 1–16, 17–52.

Hasthorpe, G. (2004), 'Overpopulation the Problem', *Gatton Star* (Queensland), 7 January.

Hirshleifer, J. (1977), 'Economics from a Biological Viewpoint', *Journal of Law and Economics*, **20**, 1–52.

Hodgson, G.M. (1993), *Economics and Evolution: Bringing Life Back into Economics*, Cambridge, U.K.: Polity Press.

Hodgson, G.M. (1994), 'Hayek, Evolution and Spontaneous Order', in P. Mirowski (ed.), *Natural Images in Economic Thought*, Cambridge, U.K.: Cambridge University Press, pp. 408–47.

Hodgson, G.M. (1995), *Economics and Biology*, Aldershot, Hants, U.K.: Edward Elgar.

Hodgson, G.M. (1999), *Evolution and Institutions: On Evolutionary Economics and the Evolution of Economics*, Cheltenham, U.K. and Northampton, MA, U.S.A.: Edward Elgar.

Hodgson, G.M. (2001), *How Economics Forgot History: The Problem of Historical Specificity in Social Science*, London: Routledge.

Hodgson, G.M. (2004a), *The Evolution of Institutional Economics: Agency, Structure and Darwinism in American Institutionalism*, London and New York: Routledge.

Hodgson, G.M. (2004b), 'Hayekian Evolution Reconsidered: A Response to Caldwell', *Cambridge Journal of Economics*, **28**, 291–300.

Horner, J. (1997), 'Henry George on Thomas Robert Malthus: Abundance vs. Scarcity', *American Journal of Economics and Sociology*, **56**, 595–607.

Jones, G. (2002), 'Alfred Russel Wallace, Robert Owen and the Theory of Natural Selection', *British Journal of History of Science*, **35**, 73–96.

Jones, E. and F. Stilwell (1986), 'Political Economy at the University of Sydney', in B. Martin et al., *Intellectual Suppression: Australian Case Histories, Analysis and Responses*, Sydney: Angus & Robertson, pp. 24–38.

Jordan, D.S. (1918), *Democracy and World Relations*, New York: World Book Company.

Kingsley, C. (1983) [1850], *Alton Locke: Tailor and Poet*, Oxford: Oxford University Press.

Kingsley, C. (1889) [1857], *Two Years Ago*, London: Macmillan.

Kropotkin, P. (1912) [1898], *Fields, Factories and Workshops*, London: Thomas Nelson and Sons, Ltd.

Labriola, A. (1980) [1897], *Socialism and Philosophy*, St. Louis, MO, U.S.A.: Telos Press.

Laurent, J. (ed.) (2003), *Evolutionary Economics and Human Nature*, Cheltenham, U.K. and Northampton, MA, U.S.A.: Edward Elgar.

Lawson, T. (2003), *Reorienting Economics*, London: Routledge.

Linas, M. (2004), 'A Plague of Human Proportions', *Australian Financial Review*, 27 February.

Lubbock, J. (1865), *Prehistoric Times*, London: Williams and Norgate.

Malthus, T.R. (1926)[1798], *First Essay on Population* (with notes by James Bonar), London: Macmillan and Royal Economic Society.

Marx, K. (1993) [1862], Letter to F. Engels, 18 June 1862, quoted G.M. Hodgson, *Economics and Evolution*, Cambridge, U.K.: Polity Press, p. 73.

Mokyr, J. (1990), *Twenty-Five Centuries of Technological Change*, Chur, Switzerland: Harwood Academic Publishers.

Moore, J. (1986), 'Evangelicals and Evolution: Henry Drummond, Herbert Spencer and the Naturalisation of the Spiritual World', *Scottish Journal of Theology*, **38**, 383–417.

Nelson, R. and S. Winter (1991), 'An Evolutionary Theory of Economic Change', in L. Putterman (ed.), *The Economic Nature of the Firm*, Cambridge, U.K.: Cambridge University Press, pp. 179–190.

Pagel, M. and R. Mace, (2004), 'The Cultural Wealth of Nations', *Nature*, **428**, 275–8.

Panico, C. and N. Salvadori (1993), *Post Keynesian Theory of Growth and Distribution*, Aldershot, Hants, U.K.and Brookfield, U.S.A.: Edward Elgar.

Peukert, H. (2003), 'W. Sombart's System Approach and Evolutionary Economics: A Comparison', in J.G. Backhaus (ed.), *Evolutionary Economic Thought: European Contributions and Concepts*, Cheltenham, U.K. and Northampton, MA, U.S.A.: Edward Elgar, pp. 64–113.

Pinker, S. (2002), *The Blank Slate: The Modern Denial of Human Nature*, London: Allen Lane.

Pullen, J. (1997), 'The Teaching of Economics: The Art of Paradigm Protection and Suppression', *Journal of Economic and Social Policy*, **2(1)**, 28–40.

Richards, S. (1987), *Darwin and the Emergence of Evolutionary Theories of Mind and Behaviour*, Chicago: University of Chicago Press.

Rose, H. and S. Rose (2001), *Alas Poor Darwin: Arguments Against Evolutionary Psychology*, London: Vintage.

Shermer, M. (2002), *In Darwin's Shadow: The Life and Science of Alfred Russel Wallace*, Oxford: Oxford University Press.

Spencer, H. (1868), *Social Statics; or, The Conditions Essential to Human Happiness Specified, and the First of Them Developed*, London: Williams and Norgate.

Spencer, H. (1870), *First Principles*, London: Williams and Norgate.

Spencer, H. (1904), *An Autobiography* (2 vols.), London: Williams and Norgate.

Stack, D. (2003), *The First Darwinian Left: Socialism and Darwinism 1859–1914*, Cheltenham, U.K.: New Clarion Press.

Sterelny, K. (2001), *Dawkins vs. Gould: Survival of the Fittest*, Duxford, Cambridge, U.K.: Icon Books.

Wallace, A.R. (1883), *Land Nationalisation – Its Necessity and Its Aims*, London: W. Reeves.

Wallace, A.R. (1895), *Natural Selection and Tropical Nature—Essays on Descriptive and Theoretical Biology*, London: Macmillan.

Williams, G.C. (1966), *Adaptation and Natural Selection*, Princeton, NJ, U.S.A.: Princeton University Press.

Wynne-Edwards, V.C. (1962), *Animal Dispersion in Relation to Social Behaviour*, Edinburgh: Oliver and Boyd.
Wynne-Edwards, V.C. (1986), *Evolution through Group Selection*, Oxford: Blackwell.
Young, R.M. (1995) [1968], 'Malthus and the Evolutionists: The Common Context of Biological and Social Theory', in G.M. Hodgson (ed.), *Economics and Biology*, Aldershot, Hants, U.K. and Brookfield, U.S.A.: Edward Elgar, pp. 179–211.

PART II

Theoretical Issues

5. The Duke of Argyll and Henry George: Land Ownership and Governance

Warren J. Samuels, Kirk D. Johnson and Marianne F. Johnson

The objective of this essay is to consider, place in context, and otherwise interpret one aspect of the social and legal-economic theory of rent developed by David Ricardo and Henry George. The aspect is the crucial relationship between land ownership and the system of governance. Ricardo and George opposed in different ways and to different extents the system of land ownership and the system of governance by a landed aristocracy. The abstract issues are whose customs and whose interests will be protected, in part as private property, as the basis of both the distribution of rent and the system of governance. The issues are more than abstract. At stake is the role of a landed aristocracy, in fact if not in name, and later, the role of a propertied – landed and non-landed – aristocracy in fact if not in name. Also at stake is whether the political-economic system is a democracy *and* whether democracy is only some combination of legitimizing the status quo and/or a safety valve for a plutocracy *or* whether democracy is only the form in which Vilfredo Pareto's circulation of the elite takes place.

One means of pursuing that interpretation will be a comparison with Henry George of some of the ideas of George Douglas Campbell, the 8th Duke of Argyll. Argyll and George actively debated the nature and role of land ownership, both as they apply to the production process and as they apply to the organization of society. Their most direct and revealing exchange came in *Property in Land: A Passage-At-Arms between the Duke of Argyll and Henry George* — see George (1982) [1884].

The best-known aspect of George's theory is the Single Tax. The tax involves differential rates on unimproved and improved land. An example of serious critique is Pullen (2004). Perhaps the least-known aspects are George's moral-philosophical approach to justice in which he adhered to a belief in natural law, and his acceptance of free trade and other doctrines of the Classical economists. His radicalism in advocating the capture of socially produced rent was justified by him on conservative grounds; his other ideas were largely consonant with 19th Century economic conservatism (see below). Much of George's economic analysis turns on the concept of the unearned increment. The doctrine is simultaneously conservative and radical. It is radical to someone like Argyll, who emphasizes possession and that the rental income received by possessors testifies to their productivity. It is radical to someone like George, who emphasizes that land is inelastic in supply and yields increasing rent because of the growth of population and the shift of the demand for land to the right, hence unearned by the possessors, whoever they are institutionalized to be.

THE ECONOMIC AND SOCIAL THEORY OF RENT

David Ricardo – among others, including Thomas Robert Malthus and Richard Jones – developed a theory of rent in the early 19th Century. The theory embodied the principle of diminishing returns and concluded that rent was the sum of the supra-marginal returns, its level driven by population growth vis-à-vis the supply of land. As population increased, resort would be made to land on the extensive and intensive margins of decreasing productivity, or at increasingly costly levels of production. Rent was equal to the sum of the differences between market price and unit cost throughout the supra-marginal levels of production. Such rent was called pure or economic rent, and eventually designated Ricardian rent. Pure rent is not what the ordinary person thinks of as rent, which typically includes a return to capital (profit) and always is a matter of the institutions governing the distribution of rent; i.e., not all economic rent goes to the nominal owner of the land (Samuels, 1992a).

The theory of rent stood on its own. However, its application depended on the systemic assumption with which it was combined. Malthus and others assumed a society governed by a land-owning aristocracy; their receipt of rent helped support that aristocracy. Ricardo and others assumed a commercial and industrial society governed, in substantial part, by the middle class; rent had the effect of lowering the profits, which helped support the middle class.

Several issues comprise the context within which the foregoing has meaning. The constitutional issue was the distribution of governing power between the landed aristocracy and other owners of land, on the one side, and the middle-class owners of non-landed property consisting of plant and equipment and of financial instruments such as stocks, bonds, and commercial paper, on the other side. The legislative issue was the Corn Laws, whose intended functions were, first, to maintain the level of domestic grain prices, and therefore rent, by limiting the import of grain, and, second, thereby to maintain the rental incomes of landowners. Pervading both issues was the ownership – especially in England and Scotland – of an extremely high percentage of the land by an extremely low percentage of families. Such concentration led some people to think of rent as a monopoly return.

The theory of rent postulated a given supply of land, that the return to investments in improvements of land was profit (and irrelevant to discussions of pure rent), and that the level of pure rent was driven by the demand for food, itself driven by population growth, against the supply of food grown on land—a function of the supply of land, the rate of decreasing returns, and the level of technology. In short, the theory involved a rightward moving demand-for-land function and a relatively given and inelastic supply-of-land function. One implication of the theory was that the level of rent is independent of the ownership of land. The landowner did nothing to earn his or her rent; rent is unearned, increases in rent are unearned increments. The level of rent is a function of the growth of society, specifically a function of the growth of population. Even the cost-lowering results of improved technology would accrue to the owner of land.

A further implication was that no ontologically given or fundamental connection existed between land ownership, receipt of rent, and governance by landowners. That England and Scotland were then principally governed by rent-receiving landowners was a matter not of the economics of pure rent but of the institutions controlling the distribution of pure rent and the institutions controlling the distribution of the powers of governance.

The Whigs sought not only repeal of the Corn Laws but change in the distribution of governing power. They used the theory of rent to disparage both increases in rent levels and the unnecessary need for the rental income of landowners to finance an unnecessary and undesirable governing class. The owners of land, on the other hand, sought to maintain the status of landed property on three grounds: that landed property was their ownership protected by law, that among the interests so protected was that of receiving rent, and that another was the role of the landowners, in the unwritten constitution, to comprise, as they then were in the early 19th Century, a vast majority in Parliament, or as they became in the late 19th Century, still a majority therein. At issue then, were, in ascending order, the receipt of rent, the ownership of land (full rights, in the minds of owners), and the control of government and thereby of government policy.

A further significance of the theory of rent has had to do with taxation. That part of the theory, which portrays rent as an unearned increment, implies that it was a fit subject of taxation. This conclusion shares some similarities with that of the Physiocrats, as will be discussed later in this chapter. The theory portrays rent as a residual, after the payment of wages and profits, and implies that taxing rent will have no adverse incentive effects. In a world in which government expenditures in peacetime were around 3 per cent or so of gross national product, the idea that taxing rent could likely finance much if not all of those expenditures was a logical possibility. The idea did not readily come to mind for most people, but it did for Henry George.

George accepted the Ricardian theory of rent and used it to develop his proposal of a Single Tax, his diagnosis of social ills, and his social philosophy. The proposal for a tax on rent which would at least substantially finance the cost of government is clear enough. George's diagnosis of social ills centred on the idea of poverty amidst plenty, some or much if not all of the poverty being caused by inequality in the distributions of wealth, especially private property in land, and of income, especially through private receipt of rent. That no one factor is the cause of social problems does not render inequality à la George irrelevant. His social philosophy proceeded from the values of equality amongst hard-working, employed people. The values of George's social philosophy were largely those of the Protestant Ethic, centring on hard, honest work as the basis of income and the ownership of property. This view has long roots in American economic thought, deriving originally from the Puritan mindset of New England and evident in the work of Francis Wayland. In this and other respects, George was both a Classical economist and a conservative. What distinguished George from many other conservatives was that he wanted all individuals, not merely a favoured few, to benefit from the system. His key point was that the existing institution of private ownership of land, inclusive of the private receipt of land, prevented that result.

George's argument – at the very least that private property in land was questionable and especially morally dubious in a world in which a relative handful owned land – called for the taxation of economic rent. In practice, this came to mean taxing unimproved land and the land portion of improved land at higher rates than the improvements, e.g., buildings. Landowners who learned of the Ricardo–George theory of rent and especially of George's proposals to extract from land ownership the right to receive and fully retain rent, saw such as an attack on their property, a confiscation if ever there was one, as tantamount to the loss of their property and as a threat to all other property. Even worse, George, in challenging the origins, the fact, and the social consequences of private ownership of land, as diagnosed by him, sometimes appeared to be calling not merely for the taxing away of one right of land ownership – receipt of rent – but for ending the institution of land ownership as a whole.

George could readily be seen as radical, as a socialist, or a communist. He portrayed land and other natural resources as economic assets whose benefits in terms of rent should be shared by all, in the form of paying for the cost of government. He justified the tax on rent on the grounds that land was originally the property of all people. These views seemed aptly to describe his views as being socialist or communist. This is the position taken by Argyll, who accuses George of being a communist in a vituperative attack in *Property in Land* (1982) [1884].

George was anathema to the owners of landed property, to those who envisioned their children, if not themselves, as owners of landed property, and, as it seemed, to economists (Lissner and Lissner, 1991; Gaffney, 1994). There are speculative reasons why Georgist ideas did not widely take hold. Interestingly, for all the invective hurled by economists at George, a surprising diversity of conservative and liberal economists have believed in taxing land rent. So long as George could be lumped together with Karl Marx, however, economists sensitive to the reputation and safety of economics as a professional discipline refused to accept his ideas—what could be more unsafe than association with someone deemed a threat to the institution of private property? But that is only one hypothesis (Samuels, 2003). The same sort of views are held today by taxpayers: that while they might not currently be in the top tax bracket or subject to the estate tax, they either hope they will or that their children will, and therefore support lowering these tax rates. This seems to be a particularly American point of view.

But George believed precisely the opposite of those who sensed socialism. Taxation of rent did in effect nationalize rent. But it did not constitute confiscation because land rent was not produced by the owners, land ownership actually should not have been theirs to begin with, especially if it included the right to receive rent, moreover, taxing rent would have no disincentive effects, for the reason given above. The taxation of rent would actually promote the values usually affirmed for the market or capitalist system, those of hard work and therefore productivity; this in contrast to rent as an unearned income.

Two conflicting theories of productivity were involved in the debate over the taxation of rent. According to one theory, income was and of right ought to be a function of productivity and receipt of income was understood, in the light of this theory, to connote productivity. That circular reasoning was involved – one identifies income as due to productivity and the test of productivity being that income was received – did not much diminish the rhetorical force of a line of reasoning seemingly so consonant with both the Protestant Ethic and the urging of self-importance. The theory applied, however, not only to labour but to the ownership of property; it assumed that property – all property, including land – was productive in the same sense and that the productivity was due to the owner. The two theories of productivity have one characteristic in common. The term 'productivity' having honorific status, each theory is used to rationalize certain institutional arrangements, the difference being that one equates productivity with the institution of ownership and the other with earned income.

Of course, to George, land was not productive of rent, and the landowners did not earn their rent; income from land did not constitute evidence of productivity. Land ownership was a matter of past conquest coupled with inheritance and purchase and sale. Rent was not a matter of productivity. George believed that the capitalist system did work on the basis of productivity—except in the matter of land and its rent. Land and its rent, instead of being an example, like much other property,[1] was inconsistent with distribution according to capitalism's principles and, moreover, a threat to those principles. Earned income was the key to productivity; unearned income was both its negation and a transfer of income from producers to non-producers.

The fact of the matter is that at the level of pure economic theory both theories of distribution in terms of productivity are incomplete if not wrong — though our point does not disturb the putative difference between the two theories. The theories are at least misleading on the following reasoning. Let marginal income be equal to the marginal revenue product. Marginal revenue product is a function of marginal physical product multiplied by product price. Marginal physical product is a function of technology and of the process which yields technology. Product price is a function of demand and supply under a variety of market types and structures. What is normally thought of as productivity — George had a labour theory of value, which is also not meaningful — is almost entirely misleading. Agricultural technology is now only slightly private-farm developed; product price is a function of many variables, one of which is consumer demand. So a comprehensive account would include the circularity of productivity producer and consumers as producer. Moreover, while one theory identifies productivity with earned income, the other identifies productivity with ownership, and ownership is a matter of institutions. Improvements in technology, for example, can come from many different sources and thus have many different claimants; the actual distribution depends on institutions, including those institutions which both help form and operate through markets. The distribution of rent is a function of custom and law, i.e., of power and institutions (see Ezekiel, 1957; Samuels, 1992a).

George's doctrine of the unearned increment is simultaneously both conservative and radical. It is radical in its attack on the major form of property for untold generations. It is conservative in its affirmation of certain basic values — saccharine but not fully descriptive — of the last several hundred years. The two theories of productivity help us to understand four alternative emphases of conservatism — also saccharine, but neither fully accurate nor meaningful. One emphasis is on maintaining the continuity of received institutions, whatever they are, and thereby of the distribution of income based on them. The second emphasis is on the distribution of income believed to *ipso facto* reward the productivity of ownership. The third emphasis is on productivity defined as earned income. The fourth emphasis is on widespread ownership of land, widespread receipt of pure rent, and widespread control of government.

The foregoing account of the theory of economic rent and its implications is overwhelmingly conventional in works on rent theory and on the history of economic thought. One recent example, authored by a distinguished historian of economic thought, comments on 'the passage from classical to neo-classical economics':

> In the classical view things had value because of their direct and indirect labour costs at the margin. Land qua land (rural and urban) has no labour cost of pro-

duction—it is a free gift of Nature. But it commands a price. The difference is Ricardian rent; a pure surplus arising from its fixity and scarcity relative to demand. Unlike commodities, a rise in the price of land has no tendency to be reversed by a rise in supply (though land-saving innovations might shift down the demand). As a pure surplus, there is an economic and ethical case for collecting these community-created rents for state revenues: the impot unique, anybody? Then along came the neo-classicals. There is no surplus. Intra-marginal land might attract high rents, but you could use it for either corn or potatoes, or for an office or a cinema. Look to the opportunity cost, and the surplus largely disappears. A much more comfortable theory for the property-owning classes (Sandilands, 2004).

Before concluding this section, we should point out that Argyll's complaint about taxing land applied not only to Ricardo and George but to Adam Smith. In his *Wealth of Nations*, Smith proposed that rents on land (ground rents) were a suitable object of taxation, the entire burden of which falls on the landowner, 'who acts always as a monopolist' (Smith, 1976a, Vol. II, p. 843). It was Smith's view that such rents, 'so far as they exceed the ordinary rent of land, are altogether owing to the good government of the sovereign ...' (Vol. II, p. 844). It is good government that 'by giving both the most perfect security ... and by procuring ... the most extensive market' (Vol. II, p. 833), enables the receipt and enjoyment of rent: 'Nothing can be more reasonable than that a fund which owes its existence to the good government of the state should be taxed peculiarly, or should contribute something more than the greater part of other funds, towards the support of that government' (Vol. II, p. 844). Further, contrary to Argyll's positive view, Smith had a negative view of the landlords' efforts to improve the land, saying, 'It seldom happens, however, that a great proprietor is a great improver' (Vol. II, p. 385; see also Smith, 1977, p. 32, and Young, 1997, pp. 174–5).

TWIN NINETEENTH-CENTURY REACTIONS TO THE MIDDLE-CLASS TRANSFORMATION OF ECONOMY AND SOCIETY

After several hundred years during which the foundations of modern commercial and industrial capitalism were laid in Great Britain and the United States, by the time of Adam Smith and then Ricardo, the new economic system was well under way. The system was for all practical purposes new but it was more than an economic system, it was an economic and political system, a new legal-economic nexus. The then-recent centuries comprised a period of both nation building and national-economy building. The economy was transformed, organized religion was transformed, the law was transformed, the system of social belief was transformed, and the nation-state was transformed. One fundamental characteristic of all these transformations was the blossoming of individualism. Another was the development of policy consciousness; probably more the spread of policy consciousness than its initial development. For centuries, even millennia, rulers knew that social arrangements were a matter of social construction, of choice, of policy; indeed, their activities as rulers were largely devoted to reconstruction of social arrangements to their felt advantage.

At any rate, by the time of Ricardo and his friend James Mill, in the early 19th Century, the transformations were well under way in England and Scotland, products of several centuries of conflict, centring on control of the monarchy, control of Parliament, and reformation of law, religion, and belief systems. By the time of the Reform Act in England in 1832 it was reasonably clear that the landowning class, titled and untitled, but a very small slice of the population, was going to have to share the powers of government, have its body of landed property law further expanded to include non-landed property, and face an expanded suffrage. (One historian points out that although the American colonists did not accept 'Britain's hereditary class structure', they did have 'the belief that the ownership of land, or the possession of enough other property to ensure an independent livelihood, was a prerequisite to the full rights and duties of citizenship' [McDonald, 2004, p. 169; see also Williamson, 1960]). All that basically took another century; in fact, it is still going on, as membership in and the power of the House of Lords faces further restrictions. Arguments of claimed right have become increasingly transformed into arguments of claimed utility on pragmatic grounds.

Eventually, in the 20th Century, the responses to these and other developments came to include the regulatory state, so-called, and the welfare state. In the 19th Century, however, the pertinent responses included: (1) German and English romanticism, a return to a fancied golden era, which need not concern us here (Argyll does not fit in with this view); (2) socialism of various types; (3) the trade union movement, which also need not concern us here; and (4) land reform. Our present interest concerns the fourth but it must be seen as an alternative to the second. By the third decade of the 19th Century, a further historic change was taking place. When the inferior nobility, for several centuries, competed with the monarch for power, they were in effect continuing the struggle for power among local rulers, one of whom had defeated his rivals and become king. When the middle class grew in number and in economic power, in their contest with the landed aristocracy and monarchy, they emulated the rhetoric of the earlier struggle. That rhetoric proceeded as if they spoke for all the disadvantaged members of society. In the language of the French Revolution, they sought liberty, equality and fraternity. The rhetoric succeeded in mobilizing the incipient political psychology of the masses. The masses believed that they, too, would participate in a relatively free and open society, and no longer suffer the pains inflicted by the *Ancien Régime*.

In time, however, it became clear to increasing numbers of members of the working class and peasantry that the middle class had intended no such thing. The middle class was now intent on establishing concentrations of economic and political power in its hands, no longer, if possible, in the hands of the landed aristocracy, and certainly not sharing power with the masses. Instead of the rhetoric-marketed free society, the middle class sought to substitute its hegemony for that of the landed aristocracy, or at least join with the latter in a system of governance dominated by property, landed and non-landed. Republican government already compromised the promise of democracy. Economic concentration would further erode the promise of a free society. What had been, or was becoming, the victory of commercial and industrial capitalism over a post-feudal agrarian regime and of middle-class over aristocratic control of government was also coming to be seen as the consolidation of the rule of capital in both economic and political matters. The new rulers were no better than the ones they were displacing.

In the second quarter of the 19th Century, two movements in particular formed in reaction to the foregoing. One focused on landed property. As seen above, the Classical economists, representing one part of the middle-class Whig movement, focused on the repeal of the Corn Laws in order to enhance the profits of non-landed property and to reduce the social and political power of the landed interest. The attack on land did not begin with them but their chapter in the history of economic thought became an important part of that history. Eventually a series of underground chapters, as it were, was written. The two principal figures were the Italian, Achille Loria, and the American, Henry George. (American land views at this point in time differed significantly from those of Europe as the Western Expansion continued unabated, aided by Land and Homestead Acts and a universal American belief in Manifest Destiny.) In sum, both traced the social problems of their respective continents to the history of the institutionalization of land. In Europe, the history either ran through or started with feudalism and ended with the then-present stratified society ultimately driven by private property in land and its grossly unequal distribution. In the United States, though lacking feudalism, land-based stratification was clearly visible. The ability to use Ricardo's theory of rent reinforced lines of reasoning whose genesis resided in other considerations. In both continents the masses were repressed by having to submit to extortion as the price of the use of land owned by others.

The land-oriented movement had numerous adherents, but it did not come to dominate social reform. Among the likely reasons was the increasing opportunity for people of modest means to purchase land; the institution of land banks and mortgage instruments to finance purchase and improvement had much to do with the increasing opportunity. In the United States institutions to help finance home ownership gave many people the opportunity to generate equity for themselves rather than for landlords; and if this did not significantly affect the percentile distribution of wealth by income class, and one or another index of concentration, it did give people a sense of being owners of property. The intent of some institutional innovators was to create a more conservative working class, and, as it turned out, they correctly foresaw that coming to pass. Nonetheless, it is this movement, and certain of its aspects, that are the focus of this chapter.

The other movement, socialism, is so well known, because it was so central to 19ᵗʰ and 20ᵗʰ Century history, that not much need be said about it in order to appreciate its juxtaposition with the land-oriented movement. Whereas the centre of gravity of the Loria and George movements was the conflict between the masses and the owners of land, that of socialism was the conflict between the masses and the owners of capital. Common to both movements is a determination that the privileges of a few become the rights of all. The differences turn on the framework of thought through which each movement expresses, philosophically and technically, its point of view. Each framework rested on a particular foundational determination. The Georgist framework of thought was based on the notion of rent as an unearned income to which land ownership provided access. The Marxist framework of thought was more complex. It rested on the notion that the profits of capital, and rent, derived from the creation of surplus value consequent to the power of capital to compel workers to work each day more hours than was necessary to repay the capitalist for the value of the labour power they advanced; profit too was unearned by those to whom ownership of capital provided access.

Also common to both positions was the belief that mainstream economics, though not necessarily all mainstream economists, provided the legitimizing rationalization of the regnant, exploitative economic system and the institution of property on which it rested. Not surprisingly, many mainstream economists said foul things about the two theories of unearned income, provoking the heretics' claim that the economists were the 'hired guns' of the capitalists. What also happened during the second quarter of the 19ᵗʰ Century was the marriage of accommodation and convenience between the owners of landed property and of non-landed property. They would continue to struggle over the control and use of government to promote their respective interests. But they would unite to confront the third major group in society, the masses, the working class, the class of those without property.

LAND OWNERSHIP

One major characteristic of data on landownership is how little is available. The second major characteristic concerns the difficulties imposed on assembling and publishing data on landownership. The third major characteristic is that data on landownership must be compiled but before it can be compiled – as is usually the case with data construction – significant decisions must be made concerning a multiplicity of definitional and recording issues. The fourth major characteristic is the concentration of landownership in many areas of the world.

Among the crucial decisions are: the definition of owning unit, limits on land registration and reporting, the treatment of varieties of common land, and so on. Also important are the widely different views towards land acquisition, ownership, and availability in Great Britain and the United States in the 19th Century. Because so much discussion pertinent to this chapter relates to Britain, especially to England and Scotland, we provide a rough summary of conclusions for this area. Because the state of Hawaii has such a dramatically high level of concentration, and for other reasons, it has been intensively studied, and a summary of conclusions for it is also provided. For reasons already noted, the data are indicative rather than accurate, notwithstanding the greater or lesser precise comparability of some numbers.[2]

Britain

The content, limits, mode of presentation and summary of the data depend on the manner of its collection:[3]

- Some 6,000 landowners – mostly landed aristocrats but also large institutions, including the Crown – own about 40 million acres, about two-thirds of the 60 million acres of land of the country.
- Of the 59 million people who live on those 60 million acres, some 99.9% live on less than 10% of the land, possibly on as little as 4.4 million acres.
- An additional 14.6 million acres are designated as woodland, mountain, waste, roads and so on.
- The remaining 40 million or so acres are owned by 189,000 individuals or families. The 59 million people, minus the members of those families, live on land at an average density of 12 to 13 persons per acre. The land of the group owning two-thirds of the land has an average density of one person per 90 acres.
- In 1875 – in the midst of the period in which Argyll and George were writing – the English journal *The Spectator* used a four-volume report, 'The Return of Owners of Land, in England, Scotland, Ireland and Wales', to calculate that 710 persons possessed one-quarter of the land in England and Wales.
- Currently almost 26 million acres of land in England and Wales are occupied by almost 160 thousand individuals or families. This 0.28% of the population owns 64% of the land.
- The Duke of Buccleuch and Queensberry owns some 270,700 acres; the Duke of Westminster owns 129,300 acres, including parts of Belgravia and Mayfair in central London; the Queen owns 73,000 acres and Prince Charles, 141,000 acres; the Duke of Northumberland owns 132,200 acres.

The policies and programs that led to such concentration included various episodes of land assignment, such as the division of land by William the Conqueror among himself, the Church and the lesser nobility; Henry VIII's distribution of expropriated land held by Catholic monasteries to some 1,500 favoured families; and the Acts of Enclosure. The policies that accompany such concentration attest to the legislative and judicial influence of the beneficiaries. The benefits of policies appear to include the following: Many wealthy landowners pay no taxes on their land holdings. Many receive grants and subsidies on the basis of their land ownership. The subsidies to the 189,000 individuals or families amount to about £4 billion, or £12,000 or so per year. They pay some £103 million annually in council (property) tax, whereas the 59 million people who live on perhaps 4.4 million acres pay somewhat over £10 billion or an average of £550 such tax per household per year.

The Blair government continued the reform of the House of Lords, excluding hereditary peers, thereby severing some 785 of the wealthiest families, owning perhaps one-third of the land, from these positions of government power.

Hawaii

Recent statistics (Government of Hawaii, 1987) indicate the following:

Federal land	280,000 acres	7.1%
State land	1,122,000 acres	28.5%
County land	14,000 acres	0.4%
Private land	2,515,000 acres	64.0%
	3,931,000 acres	

In 1986, the six largest private owners held title to 938,000 acres, or 23.9% of all land and 37.3% of all private land. The largest single owner, the Bishop estate, held 341,000 acres.

The facts on Great Britain are very interesting and telling, but parallel structure ideally demands similar facts for the United States, which are not available. Hawaii is interesting, but is not representative of the United States.

LAND OWNERSHIP AND GOVERNANCE

That those in control of government will seek to use government to advance what they consider to be their interests is an aspect of a general principle: that government is an instrument of use and therefore an object of control by those who would use it as an instrument for their own gain or advantage (Samuels, 1992b). This is not necessarily nefarious, though it may involve conflict of interest and corruption.

People will tend to promote – vote for – their own interests. When membership in state government legislatures disproportionately favoured rural and agricultural interests, legislation tended strongly to promote those interests; reapportionment tended to change the profiles of membership and of the interests promoted.

One curious feature of the property tax in some states of the United States is that only landed property owners may vote on the level of the property tax used to finance public education, police and fire protection, and other government services. Those without ownership of landed property cannot vote. This feature of the property tax is curious for two reasons. The first reason is a matter of the shifting and incidence of taxation. Owners of landed property both remit the tax and bear its burden; there is no further transaction through which they can shift the tax to others. People who lease landed property—apartments, houses—do not remit any tax; the tax is literally paid by the owners of the leased property. But since there is a further transaction, the monthly 'rental' payment, the owner is able to shift the tax to the lessee. Some states recognize the shifting process and that, therefore, the lease payment includes rent, and takes that into account in other provisions of the tax code. In any event, insofar as the final resting place of the property tax is generally concerned, there is no difference between the owner who cannot shift and the lessee to whom the tax is shifted and who cannot further shift it; both bear the tax. But only one can vote on the tax.

The property tax in such jurisdictions is curious for a second reason. In giving the right to vote on the tax only to the owner of the landed property, it is giving only to the owner the power to determine spending on various government programs. The owner of landed property has power that one would think belongs to all citizens. Most state constitutions provide for the latter, in effect rejecting the former as unjust. The presently interesting aspect of this unusual tax arrangement is that it presents a microcosm of the way things were when the suffrage, the right to vote, was limited to those who owned landed property. It was these people, and basically only these people, who controlled what the government did and for whom it did it. It was a government of, by and for the landed property owners.

An example at the federal level comparable for present purposes involved cotton and other farmers having the power to determine the levels of both crop subsidy payments and supply-control measures (i.e., reduction of planted acreage). Farmers wanted subsidies but bristled at controls over supply, necessary if the level of payments was not to become exorbitant. Two relevant features of various pieces of legislation may be identified. First, only the landlords voted on the two levels; no other citizen could vote. Second, an early (1934–1935) Act left in the hands of the landlords the division of payments between landowners and sharecroppers and the division of the burden of the reduced demand for sharecropper labour that resulted from the reduction in planted acreage (Schweikhardt, 2004, pp. 6–7). Again, landownership conveyed powers of governance. A final example is from Europe. From at least the 14th Century onward, the governing class of towns and cities was recruited from those who owned land. Considered Patrician, they included traders and artisans—so long as they were landowners.

Let us turn to the first school of economic thought, the French Physiocrats, who wrote in the middle of the 18th Century (for Argyll's treatment of the Physiocrats, see Argyll, 1893b, pp. 468ff.). They tended to write of the natural order to which government policy should adhere, of a minimal level of government (specifically legislative) activity, and of a philosophy of non-intervention or *laissez-faire*. Their *bête noire* were the several French versions of Mercantilism and Protectionism. They sought to establish in their place an agricultural system, one populated by rich farmers, in order to enable them to adopt capitalist methods of operation. In this system, they wrote, the government has only three principal duties. One is to uphold and put into effect the natural order, and with it the right of possession, i.e., a system of secure private property. The second is to provide for the education of the people, especially instruction in the natural order. The third is the provision of public works, as a form of foundational investment (Gide and Rist, 1948 [1915]).

It has since been shown that this articulation of the economic role of government in the Physiocratic system is extremely misleading. To say that government policy should adhere to the natural order and establish the agricultural system called for by the natural order is to say that government is a top-down instrument of social reconstruction, hardly the minimalist institution one might think from reading their writings. Actually, the functions of government put forth in their practical as distinct from their esoteric grandiose statements, were: government as an instrument of social change, including the construction of an agricultural kingdom, the reorganization and redirection of the state itself; and government having an agenda of both economic development and economic stability (Samuels, 1962). Naturalist language does not preclude governmental activism; naturalist language facilitates the making of governmental activism seem nonpolitical, i.e., derived from the nature of things—something rebutted by a sense of policy consciousness.

Several aspects of the foregoing situation warrant our attention. First, it is clear that the Physiocrats considered themselves the teachers of all citizens and especially the Crown as to what the natural order required on every issue. They were to be the power behind the throne. Second, while the power of the legislature was to be constrained – in language seemingly laden with non-interventionism (*laissez-faire, laissez-passer*) – no such constraint was to apply to the sovereign, the Crown. That the Crown was to act on the basis of the natural order, as specified by the Physiocrats, may have sounded saccharine but it did not negate the absolute authority of the Crown. They seemingly had no idea that the French Revolution, a few years later, would attack – though by no means precisely eliminate – the principle of monarchical absolutism.

Let us turn to Gide and Rist, whose famous textbook, *A History of Economic Doctrines*, identified the Physiocrats as the first founders of the discipline (and also gives an extended account of Henry George's doctrines and of different lines of criticism [pp. 562–570]). Their way of raising our problem is to ask, 'How can we explain this apparent contradiction and such love of despotism among the apostles of *laissez-faire*?' (p. 35). Gide and Rist develop the problem to that point in the following manner. First, they identify the nature of their natural order:

> ... the 'natural order' was that order which seemed obviously the best, not to any individual whomsoever, but to rational, cultured, liberal-minded men like the Physiocrats. It was not the product of the observation of external facts; it was the revelation of a principle within. And this is one reason why the Physiocrats showed such respect for property and authority. It seemed to them that these formed the very basis of the 'natural order' (p. 9).

Such a system, they claimed, was endowed with the 'double attributes of universality and immutability' (p. 10). Of course, this system as yet existed nowhere, and it had to be brought into existence by properly instructed rulers. By calling their system of privilege the 'natural order' they were utilizing a venerable, if question-begging, mode of rhetorical absolutist legitimization and obfuscation, in part to promote 'faith in a pre-established order' (p. 11). Second, Gide and Rist note that the Physiocrats claimed that within such a system particular private interests will be harmonious with the common interest of all, thus facilitating spontaneous activity by all citizens (p. 11). 'This is,' they write, '*laissez-faire* pure and simple' (p. 11). Third, this is not a philosophy of non-interventionism:

> Laissez-faire does not of necessity mean that nothing will be done. It is not a doctrine of passivity or fatalism. ... It is true that there will not be much work for the Government, but the task of that body will by no means be a light one, especially if it intends carrying out the Physiocratic programme. This included upholding the rights of private property and individual liberty by removing all artificial barriers, and punishing all those who threatened the existence of any of these rights; while, most important of all, there was the duty of giving instruction in the laws of the 'natural order' (pp. 11–12).

What these rights were and what was artificial depended on the substance of the Physiocrats' conception of the natural order. Fourth, the Physiocrats' natural order, Gide and Rist remind their readers, was comprised of three classes: (1) the productive class of farmers, fishermen and miners, especially the first, who create the net product; (2) the proprietary class; and (3) the sterile class of merchants, manufacturers, domestic servants, and members of the professions (p. 19). For the Physiocrats, and therefore for us, the proprietary class includes:

...not only landed proprietors, but also any who have the slightest title to sovereignty of any kind—a survival of feudalism, where the two ideas of sovereignty and property are always linked together (p. 19; see also p. 38).

The property that counted in the Physiocrats *royaume agricole* was that of land, not of capital. This is evident in the Physiocrats' *Tableau économique* in which, as described and critiqued by Gide and Rist:

> the class which enjoys two-fifths of the national revenue does nothing in return for it. We should not have been surprised if such glaring parasitism had given to the work of the Physiocrats a distinctly socialistic tone. But they were impervious to all such ideas. They never appreciated the weakness of the landowners' position, and they always treated them with the greatest reverence. The epithet 'sterile' is applied, not to them, but to manufacturers and artisans! Property is the foundation-stone of the 'natural order.' The proprietors have been entrusted with the task of supplying the staff of life, and are endued with a kind of priestly sacredness. It is from their hands that all of us receive the elements of nutrition. It is a 'divine' institution—the word is there. Such idolatry needs some explanation.
>
> One might have expected – even from their own point of view – that the premier position would have been given to the class which they termed productive, *i.e.* to the cultivators of the soil, who were mostly farmers and *métayers*. The land was not of their making, it is true. They had simply received it from the proprietors. This latter class takes precedence because God has willed that it should be the first dispenser of all wealth (pp. 21–2).

The landowners are held in reverence for their organization and management of production. They *do* do *something*.

But the landowners are also legitimized for their second role. They do something else as well, they rule: The nobility, together with the throne, constituted the upper levels of the social hierarchy – the 'sovereign authority in the guise of a hereditary monarchy' (p. 35) and class of lesser nobility – and it was these levels of the hierarchy that governed—even if to the myopic Physiocrats this meant inculcating and ruling in accordance with their principles and not some other set. The landowners received payments in the Physiocratic system because their rights of property were simultaneously rights of ownership and rights of sovereignty, rights of economic governance and rights of political governance.

> Knowing only feudal society, *with its economic and political activities governed and directed by idle proprietors,*[4] they suffered from an illusion as to the necessity for landed property similar to that which led Aristotle to defend the institution of slavery (p. 22, emphasis added).

Fifth, Gide and Rist identify the subtle nature of the legislative role. When the Physiocrats argued for reducing 'legislative activity to a minimum' one must read into this not the ordinary, literal meaning of words but their meaning in the Physiocratic system. Legislation is to put into place that which is required – according to the Physiocrats – by the natural order, i.e., 'copies of the unwritten laws of Nature'. Legislatures are to 'abolish useless laws,' i.e., useless in terms of the Physiocratic system (p. 33). It is in this system-specific sense, therefore, that one must read Gide and Rist's further summarizing point: 'Neither men nor Government can make laws, for they have not the necessary ability. Every law should be an expression of that Divine wisdom which rules the universe. Hence the true title of lawgiver, not law-maker' (pp. 33–4).

What does this mean in practice? The philosophical realist argues that mankind does not choose between different idealist versions of social reality. Social reality exists independent of mankind. But in a world in which everyone was a philosophical realist, people would still disagree as to what constituted social reality. Thus, in a Physiocratic state, legislators would still disagree as to what constituted the Physiocratic system, e.g., when Physiocratic principles conflicted. (Gide and Rist illustrate this situation in comparing A.R.J. Turgot's positions on issues with the positions of other Physiocrats [pp. 47ff.].) Governance would still involve choice in a context of conflict. Even absent conflict about the details of the Physiocratic program, conflict would occur between it and all other programs and proposals. Which brings us, finally, to the problem of 'apparent contradiction and such love of despotism among the apostles of *laissez-faire*'. Gide and Rist's explanation runs in two parts, as follows. First, a prelude to despotism and the basis for the contradiction:

> What they wanted to see was the minimum of legislation with a maximum of authority. The two things are by no means incompatible. The liberal policy of limitation and control would have found scant favour with them. Their ideal was neither democratic self-government, as … in the Greek republics, nor a parliamentary *régime* such as we find in England. Both were detested.
>
> On the other hand, great respect was shown for the social hierarchy, and they were strong in their condemnation of every doctrine that aimed at attacking either the throne or the nobility. What they desired was to have sovereign authority in the guise of a hereditary monarchy. In short, what they really wanted—and they were not frightened by the name—was despotism (pp. 34–5).

For example:

> There is no mention of representation as a corollary of taxation. This form of guarantee, which marks the beginnings of parliamentary government, could have no real significance for the Physiocrats. Taxation was just a right inherent in the conception of proprietary sovereignty, a territorial revenue [i.e., based on land ownership], which was in no way dependent upon the people's will (p. 35).

Second, the nature of despotism and of freedom:

> Despotism, in the eyes of the Physiocrats, had a peculiar significance of its own. It was the work of freedom, not of bondage. It did not signify the rule of the benevolent

despot, prepared to make men happy, even against their own will. It was just the sovereignty of the 'natural order' — nothing more (p. 35).

... At bottom the system affords a barrier against the autocracy of the sovereign — a barrier that is much more effective than a parliamentary vote (p. 44).

One is free to do what the natural order requires, as articulated in the principles enunciated by the Physiocrats and legislated, as it were, through a society governed in its economic and political activities by a government in which property and sovereignty were indistinguishable. George Douglas Campbell, the 8th Duke of Argyll, was no Physiocrat but he did represent, and defend, the agrarian way of life and as much economic and political governance by land-owners as could be secured in the modern world. Henry George, on the other hand, would have been influenced by the Physiocratic tradition in America, handed down in the writings of Benjamin Franklin, Thomas Jefferson, and the agrarians of the late 18th Century.

Argyll wanted so to define landownership as to render it productive. One way was to portray the landowner as a factor in/of production. Another was to emphasize the role of landowners in government/governance, going beyond the admonition that wealth carries responsibilities. Still another was to denigrate the ideas of unearned income and the associated life-style of a leisure class of conspicuous consumption then being identified by Thorstein Veblen. Surely Argyll would have resisted the economics of leisure in which leisure is treated as a normal good in the sense that people work less if their unearned income rises (Mirrlees, 1974, p. 258)?

THE DUKE OF ARGYLL AND LAND OWNERSHIP AND GOVERNANCE

This section considers a number of Argyll's positions pertinent to the topic of landownership and governance. We take up Argyll's major writings in chrono-logical order.

Essay on ... Contracts for the Hire of Land (1877)

Argyll wrote a great deal on a wide range of issues. He was recognized as a formidable debater, a rhetorician of considerable skill. One of his tactics was to concede a point in order to render more palatable another point or position specific to the issue at hand. For example, in his *Essay on ... Contracts for the Hire of Land* (1877), he wants to have the rights of tenants and of owners 'taken as they are' (p. 2), because he wants to minimize the impact of two bod-ies of fact; one concerning how the landowners became landowners, and the other, the evolution of the relative rights of tenants and owners. Insofar as the latter is inexorably present, by 'taken as they are' he means, and says, 'they are what they are defined to be, not by the antiquarians, but by the judge' (p. 2). The 'antiquarians' are those who would look to history. But Argyll would have discussion focus on the judge—because the judiciary then largely came from the landowning class. No wonder he is willing to insist – concede, as it were – that, as for 'the right of the State to restrict individual freedom.... I know of no abstract limit to the right of the State to do anything' (p. 6). Insofar as this means political choice as between conflicting claimants of rights and also surrenders all invocation of abstract natural law, the result is one meaning of arbitrary, one meaning of coercion, and/or despotism as discussed by Gide and Rist—and acceptable to Argyll because of the safe class position of the judges. (This does not prevent Argyll from distinguishing between the economic and moral ends of legislation as a constraint upon the State [pp. 8ff.]. For the irrelevance of matters relating to the vesting of ownership and of the identity of landowners, see p. 4.)

In *Essay on ... Contracts for the Hire of Land* the issue is how to provide adequate security for capital invested in the cultivation or improvement of their holding by persons [called occupiers, tenants or farmers] hiring land by contract [from owners of land] for agricultural purposes (Argyll, 1877, p. 21). Argyll presents the landowners' case against giving further protection to tenants for their capital invested through improvements to land they only lease. One of his lines of argument ultimately presumes the inherited benevolent treatment by the superior in a relation of deference and thus the situation of harmony in the relation of owner and tenant. It is a favourite line of argument, evidenced by its frequent articulation and invocation. We thus read of:

> That equitable spirit which is essential to the conduct of life in every calling, and which is perhaps more habitually exercised in the relations between owner and occupier of land than in any other business whatever (p. 41).

Argyll emphasizes that 'under the influence of favour and of personal feeling' owners give an allowance 'in the form of abated rent' (p. 42). Of this practice he insists, 'Nor is it just to attach any prejudice to such feeling by calling it feudalism' (p. 42); that it would be 'a dangerous presumption' to think 'that abated rents ... far below the fair letting value are comparatively rare. ... on the contrary, such cases are very common ... the preference given to old tenants is often very large' and 'probably equals more than an average of 10 per cent' (p. 43). We also read of:

> those personal and hereditary feelings on which I have now been dwelling as a special and exceptional security to tenants, the extent and prevalence of which is little known (p. 47).

and again:

> So sound, indeed, and so healthy have the relations hitherto been, both in England
> and Scotland, between the owners and occupiers of the soil, so habitual and rooted
> have been the traditional and customary feelings, which are the best foundation for
> business relations of such endurance as these must always be, that possibly even the
> most unwise law might not at once put an end to cheap and abated rents (p. 52).

Several considerations immediately arise in the modern mind. One consideration in question form is, if the claimed harmony and benevolent treatment
exists, why has the reform legislation been proposed? Another consideration is
precisely the matter of feudal relations: the lessees are treated more like feudal
subjects than independent economic actors with rights in competitive markets.
Still another consideration is reminiscent of claims made by segregationists
in the 1960s that the majority of American blacks were happy with the status
quo, and that the only complainants were a relatively few 'malcontents' and
'outsiders.'

Actually, Argyll wants the best of both worlds, that of a set of contented
and deferential tenants and rent-maximizing behaviour (pp. 42ff., 51, 54ff., 59,
63ff.). He also notes that some tenants 'have never been accustomed to look
upon their business as a commercial one at all' and that owners 'dislike part-
ing with the discretionary power of determining tenancies altogether—even
although practically this power is very rarely or even never exercised' (p. 90).
Both dislikes reflect the situation of superior and inferior in a structure of hierarchical relations.

The Physiocrats' postulate of a landowning class with a claim to income
grounded in their ownership per se and further legitimized by reference to their
economic, as well as political, function, is echoed in the following position
articulated by Argyll:

> It is quite true that ... the farmer or hirer of land can say with justice to the owner,
> 'It is my labour that has given to your soil this largely increased return.' But it is
> equally true that the owner can reply with justice to the farmer, 'It is the quality and
> situation of my land which has yielded to your labour this rich and unusual reward'
> (pp. 30–31).

No clearer affirmation of rent distribution as a function of ownership could
be stated. The Ricardian position, also that of George, is that rent is driven by
population growth. Ownership has nothing to do with the genesis of rent, only
with its distribution. With this position Argyll will have nothing to do; he must,
by the nature of his position, affirm rent as a matter of the yield on his land
–'my land', Thus, apropos of 'the doctrine that improvements executed by an
occupier upon an owner's land are to belong exclusively to the occupier', Argyll
argues, 'This doctrine can only be defended on the ground that the contribution

of ownership is no contribution at all' and that landed property does not have 'the character or the incidents which belong to capital in every other form' (p. 70; the issue is whether the increased productivity due to farmer-hirer invest-ment is a joint result of other, owner investments).

The Land Question (1884)

Argyll felt compelled to defend property in land against the assault levelled on it by Henry George, and George, in his turn, prepared a reply.[5] Both men were at the peak of their rhetorical powers and were amply motivated. Although both men appealed to natural law and both were conservative, their conceptions of what constituted natural law and of what conservatism meant differed widely. Thus, Argyll is able to say, first, of George's *Progress and Poverty* that it 'was directed to prove that almost all the evils of humanity are to be traced to the very existence of landowners, and that by divine right land could only belong to everybody in general and to nobody in particular' (Argyll, in George, 1982 [1884], p. 10); if true, these evils traced to landownership would constitute a hitherto unseen foundation of society. Argyll's second revelation is that George is one of those who 'have an interest, very personal indeed, in believing that they have a right to appropriate a share in their neighbor's vineyard' (p. 10). The irony here is that Argyll elsewhere acknowledges that titles of ownership in land ultimately trace to conquest; but here as elsewhere Argyll wants for discussion to start with landownership as it is in the present; in other words, he prefers to keep the origins of the distribution of land unseen. More than that, he finds George's analysis to be communist in nature (pp. 11–12). Argyll com-posed mighty rhetorical blasts in George's direction but received from George as good as he gave.

The Prophet of San Francisco, by the Duke of Argyll

One charge brought by Argyll is that George neglects the fact that the institution of property pervades, however unseen, relations between people and between people and government:

> It is one thing for any given political society to refuse to divide its vacant territory among individual owners. It is quite another thing for a political society, which for ages has recognized such ownership and encouraged it, to break faith with those who have acquired such ownership and have lived and labored, and bought and sold, and willed upon the faith of it (1884, pp. 17–8).

This is a rationalistic and legitimizing view of the history of an institution early and still laden with conquest and coercion; the late-19th Century development of the institution in the American West was in territory hardly previously unoccupied (as he puts it (p. 18)). That, too, remains unsaid and unseen. Every history has been given multiple interpretations, each yielding its own combination of the seen and unseen. Curiously or not, Argyll, having given such a saccharine view of government and government policy, then disparages both:

> In the disposal and application of wealth, as well as in the acquisition of it, are men more pure and honest when they act in public capacities as members of a Government or of a Legislature, than when they act in private capacities toward their fellow-men? Is it not notoriously the reverse? Is it not obvious that men will do, and are constantly seen doing, as politicians, what they would be ashamed to do in private life (p. 19)?

Argyll wants to accomplish two things: to render honorific the institution of property as achieved through government, and to denigrate the process of government and the people in government; the former to reify property and the latter to disable government's power to change it in a major way. This has been a strategy of Establishment parties and politicians in Britain and the United States for centuries—disparaging the government they otherwise refer to as duly constituted authority and for whose offices they are campaigning, in order to limit its use as an instrument of change in bringing about a different consolidation of social interests. Argyll is, however, more interested in promoting property than disparaging government; after all, he is a part of the governance structure. He thus reiterates the first argument, saying that George:

> is not content with urging that no more bits of unoccupied land should be ever sold, but he insists upon it that the ownership of every bit already sold shall be resumed without compensation to the settler who has bought it, who has spent upon it years of labor, and who from first to last has relied on the security of the State and on the honor of its Government (p. 22).

Nor does he stop with land ownership; he moves on, first, to tenancy and then to all property:

> Nay, more, is there any reason why the doctrine of repudiation should be confined to pledges respecting either the tenancy or the ownership of land (p. 23)?

According to George:

All National Debts are as unjust as property in land (p. 24).

Saying that 'The world has never seen such a Preacher of Unrighteousness as Mr. Henry George' (p. 25), Argyll quotes George's repudiation of the dead hand of the past:

> The institution of public debts, like the institution of private property in land, rests upon the preposterous assumption that one generation may bind another generation (p. 25).

Yet upon this assumption that ascendants may bind descendants, that one generation may legislate for another generation, rests the assumed validity of our land titles and public debts (p. 26).

(One wonders what Argyll and George would say when confronted by the proposal, by economists across the political spectrum, of an interest-free national debt coupled with the requirement that some part of bank reserves be comprised of such debt—a proposal in part predicated upon the idea that the banking system need not receive a rent for generating the money supply.) And still more, cautions Argyll:

All the other accumulations of industry must be as rightfully liable to confiscation (p. 26).

One position taken by Argyll here is in support of the Northern States in opposing slavery. He calls it 'as noble a cause as any which has ever called men to arms' (p. 27) and lauds the 'patient and willing submission of the masses, as of one man, not only to the desolating sacrifice of life which it entailed, but to the heavy and lasting burden of taxation which was inseparable from it' (p. 27). He berates George for lamenting the failure to impose a capital levy ('an act of stealing') on those who held government bonds: 'he speaks with absolute bitterness of the folly which led the Government to "shrink" from at once seizing the whole, or all but a mere fraction, of the property of the few individual citizens who had the reputation of being exceptionally rich' (p. 28).

Argyll's position is particularly interesting because he is silent on the issue that has bedevilled so many others, namely, whether the former slaveholders should have been compensated for the emancipation of their property, the slaves, or whether the slaves should have been compensated for their former loss of liberty. (We shall see below that George is similarly restrained.)[6]

When Argyll returns to his defence of landownership, he is at his rhetorical best. Notwithstanding his later call, in the early chapters of *The Unseen Foundations of Society*, for the careful construction of definitions, Argyll wants to wrap landownership in the historically growing affirmative status of capitalist, using the phrase:

the particular class of capitalists who are owners of land ... (p. 31).

Other relevant examples of his argument include:

The whole tone [of George's argument] is based on the assumption that owners of land are not producers, and that rent does not represent, or represents only in a very minor degree, the interest of capital (p. 32; again: 'a book assuming that landowners are not producers,' p. 33).
In every county the great landowners, and very often the smaller, were the great pio-

neers in a process which has transformed the whole face of the country (p. 33).

To such outlays [on improvements] landowners are incited very often, and to a great extent, by the mere love of seeing a happier landscape and a more prosperous people. From much of the capital so invested they often seek no return at all, and from very little of it indeed do they ever get a high rate of interest. ... When a man tells me ... that in all this I and others have been serving no interests but our own ... he is talking the most arrant nonsense (p. 34).

There was to be [in Bengal] no confiscation by the State of the increased value of any land, any more than of the increased value of other kinds of property, on the pretext that this increase was unearned (p. 37).

It seems that Argyll perceived no need to take up further or more directly the governance aspects of landownership. His reference to them is somewhat oblique:

the functions and duties which in more civilized countries are discharged by the institution of private ownership in land (p. 36).

The Reduction of Iniquity, by Henry George

George takes his title from an accusatory flight of language in Argyll's final paragraph. He accuses Argyll of misrepresentation on a number of issues, achieved by exaggerating or distorting George's argument (e.g.,1885, p. 43). He might have criticized Argyll for claiming distrust of the institution to which he is appealing, namely, the State (see *supra*); instead, he derides him for expressing distrust of the moral faculties, 'the very tribunal to which he appeals' (p. 43). But he, too, appeals to the work of the Creator, albeit invoking different moral lights and a different moral compass (p. 45). George agrees 'that robbery is a violation of the moral law, and is therefore, without further inquiry, to be condemned', and that robbery is 'the taking or withholding from another of what which rightfully belongs to him'. Then comes the disagreement with Argyll: 'That which *rightfully* belongs to him, be it observed, not that which legally belongs to him.' In an argument distinguishing between making one's case by appeal to human or to moral law, he writes:

Landholders must elect to try their case either by human law or by moral law. If ... by human law, they cannot charge those who would change that law with advocating robbery. But if they charge that such change in human law would be robbery, then they must show that land is rightfully property irrespective of human law (p. 46).

George states his conclusion:

For land is not of that species of things to which the presumption of rightful property attaches ... [which are] things ... that are the produce of labor ... the moral basis of property, which makes certain things rightfully property totally irrespective of human law (p. 46).

—some things, but not land. '[P]roperty in land rests only on human enact-
ment, which may, at any time, be changed without violation of moral law.' As
for property being derived from appropriation, 'Appropriation can give no
right.' Right 'is derived from labor, not from appropriation'. More than that,
the division of land, private landownership, has been effectuated by '"right of
strength,"…evidently…what they really mean who talk of the right given by
appropriation' (p. 47). George then cites Argyll on conquest:

> This 'right of conquest,' this power of the strong, is the only basis of property in land
> to which the Duke ventures to refer (p. 47).
>   … [T]he titles to the ownership of land … rest historically upon the forcible
> spoliation of the masses (pp. 48–49).

George concurs with Argyll that 'how ownership was acquired in the past
can have no bearing upon the question of how we should treat land now;
yet', he adds, 'the inquiry is interesting, as showing the nature of the institution' — which is:

> that the exclusive ownership of land has everywhere had its beginnings in force and
> fraud, in selfish greed and unscrupulous cunning (p. 49).

It is at this point where George makes the first of several references to
slavery, deriding the Duke for not following the logic of his argument to
support chattel slavery (p. 49). Another reference is to those who declared
'the slave-trade piracy [but] still legalized the enslavement of those already
enslaved' (p. 54). Still another reference makes the initial comparison much
more poignantly:

> In fact, the plea of the landlords that they, as landlords, assist in production, is very
> much like the plea of the slaveholders that they gave a living to the slaves…the gross
> inconsistency between the views he [the Duke] expresses as to negro slavery and the
> position he assumes as to property in land (pp. 66–7).

These allusions to slavery, but not to the compensation question, come amidst
a continuation of the argument; first, from natural moral law, one expression
of which is:

> Is there not, therefore, a violation of the intent of Nature in human laws which give
> to one more land than he can possibly use, and deny any land to the other? (p. 52,
> referring, in order, to duke and peasant);

and, second, from more secular reasoning:

> …property in land means…a continuous confiscation of labor and the results of
> labor. …to make so many other Scotsmen, in whole or in part, his serfs—to compel

them to labor for him without pay, or to enable him to take from them their earnings without return (p. 54).

Further, George would differentiate what Argyll would combine:

In assuming that denial of the justice of property in land is the prelude to an attack upon all rights of property, the Duke ignores the essential distinction between land and things rightfully property. ...things...produced by human exertion (p. 55).

Indeed,

to treat it [land] as individual property is to weaken and endanger the true rights of property (p. 58).

George challenges Argyll's principal assumption underlying both his defence of landownership and his critique of George. 'The Duke,' he writes, 'will justify his complaint if he will show how the owning of land can produce anything' (p. 64). The policy logic of the Georgist movement turned in part from nationalization of land to nationalization of land rent (the Single Tax) because it seemed to be more palatable to have government spend the proceeds of the tax than manage land and natural resources. The logic of Argyll's assumption was that ownership per se is productive in such a way that warrants others to have to labour for the owner, through the payment of economic rent. This policy logic succeeded because it was attractive in two ways. First, it seemed to be defended by productivity theory, notwithstanding the circularity of the argument. Second, it seemed to be negated in practice by the hope and anticipation that in the future one's children, if not also oneself, would own property. George treats the problem of governance in much the same way as he treats the land question, combining naturalistic and secular reasoning, for example:

...political corruption...springs...not from excess but from deficiency of democracy, and mainly from our failure to recognize the equality of natural rights as well as of political rights (pp. 58–9).

All the foregoing leads to the question of land ownership and governance, George writes personally of the Duke and not abstractly. Comparing slavery and property in land, he finds them 'essentially the same' as 'two systems of appropriating the labor of other men' and explicates the situation in terms of landownership comprising economic and political authority in the hands of a few over the lives of many:

...a human being is as completely enslaved when the land on which he must live is made the property of another as when his own flesh and blood are made the property of that other. ...And...the effects of the two systems are substantially the same. He is, for instance, an hereditary legislator, with power in making laws which other

Scotsmen, who have little or no voice in making laws, must obey under penalty of being fined, imprisoned, or hanged. He has this power, which is essentially that of the master to compel the slave, not because any one thinks that Nature gives wisdom and patriotism to eldest sons more than to younger sons, or to some families more than to other families, but because as the legal owner of a considerable part of Scotland, he is deemed to have greater rights in making laws than other Scotsmen, who can live in their native land only by paying some of the legal owners of Scotland for the privilege.

The situation would have as its contemporary analogy an official, i.e., con-stitutionally explicit, plutocracy in which only billionaires (perhaps adjusted for changes in the price level) may sit in Congress and for whom only billionaires may vote. Prior to the Reform Act of 1832 (which did not by any interpretation greatly reverse matters) the right to vote and the ability to control membership in Parliament were in the hands of the less than ten per cent of the English population who satisfied what amounted to property requirements.

Irish Nationalism (1893)

In Argyll's *Irish Nationalism* (1893a), he acknowledges two major themes. One theme is that nation-states were formed as a result of victories by eventual kings over other nobles and would-be kings. The consolidation of central monarchy is the means of or road to union (p. 51). He contrasts the ravaging, destructive wars of the Irish chief-led tribes with the equally ferocious but constructive wars of the English:

> They [the Irish] were tribes…hereditary castes animated with all the passions which raged throughout the land; and actually taking part in the cruel and ferocious wars to which these passions led (p. 27).

These wars had 'not one single aim or object which could be dignified by the name 'political,'…they were wars of mere plunder, slaughter, and devas-tation' (p. 27). The Irish wars were savage but also utterly useless and purely destructive, failing to generate a nation and a national government (pp. 30–31). The English people fought ferocious and barbaric wars, 'but they fought for things worth fighting for. They were re-constructive, not purely destructive' (p. 31). The English 'contended for true conquest – dominion–settlement – not for mere plunder, devastation, and ravage' (p. 31). Whereas the Anglo-Saxons had within 150 years founded kingdoms – 'political communities with well-established principles of government, of industry, and of law' – and within another 350 years 'had consolidated these kingdoms into one central monarchy, highly civilized, Christian, and to some degree even Imperial' (p. 32), the Celtic tribes had not made a single step forward, their interminable wars being mere savage raids, 'destructive alike of peaceful industry and of the very beginnings of political organization' (p. 43). In feudal and post-feudal Europe, the conquering of land as an economic and political base meant that ownership and sovereignty went together; land ownership and governance grew up simultaneously. The other theme is that the history of Europe is a history of conquest or attempted conquest. Conquest and imperialism have both economic and political dimensions, i.e., economic and political governance are inextricably intertwined. Argyll writes of the 'process which had effected the civilization of all the rest of Europe—namely, conquest by a fresh race, and a higher and an older civilisation' (p. 147). 'The thrones of kings have never been first established on abstract theories of duty; nor has the dominion of great nations ever been founded on mere philanthropy' (p. 150). Religion, in the age of the Reformation, is part of the story:

> Religion and politics were inseparably interwoven. That Christ's kingdom is 'not of this world' was a doctrine neither accepted nor even understood by anybody. ...Catholicism did not represent religion—pure and unmixed. It represented, in a preeminent degree, politics in its most fundamental principles. It represented ambitions of domination...[t]he English Government and people...the spirit of a proud nationality (pp. 186–87).

Argyll adds, '...it is quite idle to blame either party,' but the English were the cause 'best representing the lasting interests of mankind' (p. 187). The 'seventeenth century ... was everywhere an epoch of civil and of foreign wars and of political troubles—all...animated with, and some...entirely dominated by, the fiercest religious passions' (p. 189). 'It was a century mainly occupied by the completion of the necessary work of conquest [of Ireland]' (p. 195).

The Unseen Foundations of Society (1893)

As John W. Mason noted, *The Unseen Foundations of Society* 'was written partly as a riposte to Henry George's *Progress and Poverty*' of 1879 and 'revealed the embattled mind of a large property owner in the 1890s' (Mason, 1980, pp. 578–579).[7] Argyll is overwhelmingly concerned with the defence of the institution of property as it then existed and of which he was a signal beneficiary. The chief form of wealth was landed property and the first of six heads making up the definition of wealth was Possession. Possession is not appropriation, he insists. 'Appropriation is an act. Possession is a state or a condition' (Argyll 1893b, p. 40). 'Possession means, in all ordinary use, lawful and legitimate possession. ...[N]o things, however valuable, can become wealth until they are gotten or possessed. ...[N]one of them will be wealth to us until we hold them as our own' (p. 41). He goes on to say, 'It makes an immense difference in economic science if, in seeking the origin of wealth, we are compelled to begin with, and to think of, the origin of possession' (p. 42). Argyll concedes the danger arising from considering the origins of wealth, from 'the throwing down of all containing walls'. But he finds even more important the role of the social belief system in protecting the institution of property:

> If wealth does certainly include Possession, and if the mental attitude which constitutes the desire of acquisition be also included in it, then we must recognize as an indisputable fact, that religious beliefs and superstitions, moral sentiments and doctrines, legal maxims and traditions, have been the most powerful of all factors alike in its origin and growth, in its advancement or decay (p. 42).

The social belief system, including religious and legal doctrines, is the protective belt surrounding and insulating that which has come to be designated property. Against the erosion of landed property by the forces and mindset of non-landed property, Argyll seeks to restore as much as he can of the protection once given landed property and now enjoyed by the owners of capital. This means the elevation of the principles of continuity over those of change. He inquires:

> Can there be anything more durable than well-reasoned principles of law, or than well-reasoned applications of those principles to the transactions of men (p. 86)?

Thus he quotes from Adam Smith's *Wealth of Nations*:

> That security which the laws in Great Britain give to every man that he shall enjoy the fruits of his own labour, is alone sufficient to make any country flourish (1893b, p. 86).

Argyll thereby combines continuity and security in such a way (as we have seen above) as to equate income with productivity, the fruits of one's own income, with the hope that the income of land will come under the same rubric. Thus does the doctrine of productivity find its usefulness in the belt protecting property.

Argyll's *The Unseen Foundations of Society* is essentially an extended brief that assumes a landowner-dominated society, polity and economy and proceeds to argue that landownership is a, if not the, foundation of society, including governance. In such an economy, economists and ordinary people will formulate understandings of what is going on. These stories will derive from the experiences of people under the economic systems. The situation is comparable to the ruling elite contemplated by the Physiocrats. The ruling elite, essentially landlords, will dominate both the economy, including the saving-investment function, and the polity (ruling), all by virtue of their ownership of land in a legal-economic system in which rulership is vested in landownership. A story will be told of the essential services the landowning class provides to the rest of society: *their* prosperity will facilitate saving and investment and their ability to serve as rulers. What is seen is taken to be true: governance and saving-investment are provided by them. What is not seen is not taken to be true: that governance and saving-investment can be undertaken in other ways. Inasmuch as one function of social control is to promote belief in the existing order, economic ideology and religion will promote a story that reinforces the position of the landowning and ruling class, thereby further validating the story thus told. Ignorance is in this manner dissipated, created, and distributed. What is seen is a function of experience under particularly organized economic systems and of ideological training of perception. Neither experience nor trained perception picks up what remains unseen. In a variation on the foregoing, beneficiaries of the various systems can complain that critics of their system do not see what is fundamental to the existing system. Such is the gravamen of Argyll's *Unseen Foundations of Society*. What is obfuscated is the selective socially constructed nature of the existing system, i.e., that the hierarchic positions being legitimized by the story are system-specific. A system of belief substitutes for an ontological absolute. That system of belief interprets and legitimizes the system and the system validates the system of belief. Argyll thus presents defences against criticism of inequality per se, the origins of inequality in coercion and conquest, class and hierarchy, and of land ownership-based governance. We now turn to the arguments for his position that are deployed in *Unseen Foundations*.

One argument is that 'Possession means, in all ordinary use, lawful and legitimate possession' and in this sense 'enters as an essential constituent into the concept of wealth' (Argyll, 1893b, p. 41; see also pp. 42 and 281 ['the vivifying influence of possession']). Argyll wants to legitimize land ownership, in part obfuscating or diminishing the origin of ownership in conquest (which he acknowledges; see pp. 128–9, 199, 205–6, 236, 249, 369 and *passim*), and in part, as the victors in conquest, emphasizing the value of stable laws governing property and permitting the landowners to perform their function (the tension between expulsion of earlier possessors and secure possession for their successors is strikingly evident on pp. 128–9; see also 236). It is after conquest that the victors seek the 'first foundations of wealth, which consist in a general desire for the legal definition of all rights and obligations' (p. 241), thereby affirming that policy should start from the status quo. Government is used, in 'protecting property', to validate and legitimize as well as to put into economic effect the results of conquest. A corollary is that land should be seen as part of capital (*vide* 'the particular class of capitalists who are owners of land', (p. 411) and therefore in terms of the functions of ownership:

...nothing can be more certain that capital is the embodiment and representative of the very highest kind of labour—namely that in which the mental energy if forethought, expresses itself in the savings and storages of wealth already acquired (p. 72).

Can there be anything more durable than well-reasoned principles of law, or than well-reasoned applications of these principles to the transactions of men (p. 86)?

The defence of inequality and hierarchical relations under existing institutions is a further argument (the qualification 'under existing institutions' is important, because the same laudatory statements could be made about the new landlord class if class positions were reversed):

> For it is an inevitable law that equal freedom enjoyed by unequal powers is incompatible with a dead level of individual conditions. ...the inequalities of personal ability or of character...[must have] room to work (pp. 200, 201; reiterated on pp. 578–9).
> ... the gradations into which society was divided were nothing but the gradations of history and of nature—the ranks into which men have been sifted and sorted in the streams and currents of actual life, according to corresponding disparities of mind and character (p. 214; see also pp. 576–7 and *passim*).

Still another argument involves the denigration of the Ricardian theory of rent, which he calls 'one of the most extraordinary delusions which has ever been accepted by reasoning men' (p. 305; see pp. 358ff. and *passim*; see above). When he declares against 'such anarchical and immoral doctrines as those which have been founded on a belief in his [Ricardo's] theory' (p. 376; he also calls them 'subversive deductions' [p. 381]) it is clear that Argyll has Henry George in mind (see pp. 387–420).

Notwithstanding his effort to render landed property safe through the perpetuation of stable law favouring landownership, Argyll also seeks to divorce property from government, treating property as a natural phenomenon and government as something separate if not exogenous. This position is evident in his statement that 'it is [not] quite certain that any Governments, even the best, spend wealth on the whole better for the public interests than those to whom it belongs by the natural processes of acquisition' (p. 417). When Argyll takes up governance he defends those governments which were the instruments of the landed aristocracy and similarly situated folk against the charge that they sought only their own interests:

> There can be no broader mistake made in respect to historical fact than that which is now often repeated, that Parliaments and Government were careless of the interests of the wage-earning classes during the ages when these classes were not in the possession of political power (p. 550).

ADAM SMITH, EDWIN L. GODKIN AND ROSA LUXEMBURG

That quite a different story could be told is evident from Adam Smith's *Wealth of Nations*, from Arygll's contemporary, Edwin L. Godkin, the American journalist (also a lawyer) who founded *The Nation*, and the Polish revolutionary Marxist, Rosa Luxemburg. These writers address very complex topics, with quite divergent themes, so it is not surprising that they can be interpreted in different ways. But on the topic of concern here, they are clear and in agreement. Property is the interests protected as property (it is property because it is protected, not protected because it is property) and those in control of government use it to protect their interests either as property per se or rights that are the functional equivalent of property. Smith's and Godkin's stories, in Argyll's view, are both mistaken and subversively uttered. But all three men agree on the class nature of property, the ostensible role of government with regard to property, and the powers of governance inhering in property.

Adam Smith

Smith wrote the following:

> Men may live together in society with some tolerable degree of security, though there is no civil magistrate to protect them from the injustice of those passions. But avarice and ambition in the rich, in the poor the hatred of labour and the love of present ease and enjoyment, are the passions which prompt to invade property, passions much more steady in their operation, and much more universal in their influence. Wherever there is great property there is great inequality. For one very rich man there must be at least five hundred poor, and the affluence of the few supposes the indigence of the many. The affluence of the rich excites the indignation of the poor, who are often both driven by want, and prompted by envy, to invade his possessions. It is only under the shelter of the civil magistrate that the owner of that valuable property, which is acquired by the labour of many years, or perhaps of many successive generations, can sleep a single night in security. He is at all times surrounded by unknown enemies, whom, though he never provoked, he can never appease, and from whose injustice he can be protected only by the powerful arm of the civil magistrate continually held up to chastise it. The acquisition of valuable and extensive property, therefore, necessarily requires the establishment of civil government. Where there is no property, or at least none that exceeds the value of two or three days' labour, civil government is not so necessary.
>
> Civil government supposes a certain subordination. But as the necessity of civil government gradually grows up with the acquisition of valuable property, so the principal causes which naturally introduce subordination gradually grow up with the growth of that valuable property. The causes or circumstances which naturally introduce subordination, or which naturally, and antecedent to any civil institution, give some men some superiority over the greater part of their brethren, seem to be four in number (Smith, 1976a, Vol. I, pp.709–10).

It is in the age of shepherds, in the second period of society, that the inequality of fortune first begins to take place, and introduces among men a degree of authority and subordination which could not possibly exist before. It thereby introduces some degree of that civil government which is indispensably necessary for its own preservation: and it seems to do this naturally, and even independent of the consideration of that necessity. The consideration of that necessity comes no doubt afterwards to contribute very much to maintain and secure that authority and subordination. The rich, in particular, are necessarily interested to support that order of things which can alone secure them in the possession of their own advantages. Men of inferior wealth combine to defend those of superior wealth in the possession of their property, in order that men of superior wealth may combine to defend them in the possession of theirs. All the inferior shepherds and herdsmen feel that the security of their own herds and flocks depends upon the security of those of the great shepherd or herdsman; that the maintenance of their lesser authority depends upon that of his greater authority, and that upon their subordination to him depends his power of keeping their inferiors in subordination to them. They constitute a sort of little nobility, who feel themselves interested to defend the property and to support the authority of their own little sovereign in order that he may be able to defend their property and to support their authority. Civil government, so far as it is instituted for the security of property, is in reality instituted for the defence of the rich against the poor, or of those who have some property against those who have none at all (Smith, 1976a, Vol. I, p. 715).

For Smith, government itself is not exogenous to the system; government is due to and to a large extent the instrument of the propertied, of those, that is, who use government to cement and institutionalize their systemic social power. As Smith says, 'Till there be property there can be no government, the very end of which is to secure wealth and to defend the rich from the poor' (Smith, 1977, p. 404). Social control through law must be understood to be a function of social structure.

Edwin L. Godkin

Smith published his great work in 1776, well before the two 19th Century reactions to the middle-class transformation of economy and society discussed above. Smith may have favoured free markets (within the law) but he deals neither with the transformations of economy and society that transpired in the 19th Century. Godkin, on the other hand, not only lived during that period but was intellectually a part of it, and there is much more than in Smith's time to be candid about.

In his *Unforeseen Tendencies of Democracy* (1898) Godkin says of the ancient democracies of Greece and Rome that they faced the problem of 'more or less frequently...resisting the attempts of rich men to set up either a monarchy or an aristocracy. ...[T]he rich class were rarely content with the existing state of things, always felt they could do better if they had their way, and were as purely selfish as aristocracies are apt to be. They were convinced that the most important interest of the state was that they, not the many, should be happy and content' (p. 13). The point is very important to Godkin:

In all ancient democracies...the internal history is generally an account of contests between the poor and the rich; meaning by 'poor' persons who are not rich,—not the extremely poor. An oligarchy always consists of rich men; a democracy, of what may be called people of moderate means. For the most part, the rich seem never to be thoroughly content with the rule of the many, and long to rid themselves of it. ... They think themselves entitled to rule, and think their contentment the chief object of the state (p. 21).

As with Smith, for the rich (whose rights were derived from their past use of government) to advance their interests, they needed, they felt, the control of government. Godkin also says of the Middle Ages that:

The citizens or burgesses owned the state or city as property, and transmitted it to their children. They gave nothing to non-citizens but permission to reside and protection. The idea that mere birth and residence ought to give citizenship gained ground only after the French Revolutiion, and was not really received in England until the reform of the municipalities in 1832. The old confinement of the citizenship to a small body of property-holders, or descendants of property-holders, undoubtedly gave the property qualification to such of the modern European states as set up an elected legislature or council. Down to the passage of the Reform Bill in England, the exclusion of all but freeholders from the franchise seemed a perfectly natural arrangement. It was very difficult for most Englishmen, and the same thing is true of the earlier Americans, to suppose that any one could take a genuine interest in the welfare of the country, or be willing to make sacrifices for its sake, who did not own land in it. The central idea of the ancient city was in this way made to cover the larger area of a modern kingdom (p. 17).

As for the treatment of the non-propertied masses, Godkin, in contrast to the last quotation above from Argyll, argues that:

in nearly every country on the Continent, outside Switzerland, privilege reigned supreme, with harsh, even contemptuous treatment of the poor....All its political arrangements seem to have been made simply for the purpose of enabling a small class to enjoy themselves, and to indulge in their favorite amusement of command-ing armies (p. 26).

Godkin then discusses various meanings of the principle of equality, but the historical focus and foundation of much of his writing are the consequences which he felt flowed from the adoption of political democracy. He thus writes of 'the exclusion of the old landed class from the work of government, a process which began soon after the French Revolution....' (p. 39). But even in America, 'In all the colonies, and for some years in all the states, offices were reserved naturally for men of local mark, generally created by property and social position' (p. 53)—many of whom, George would argue, achieved and maintained that position through the receipt of rent. Godkin accepts as given the close historical connection between property and government, in which control of government derives from property and property derives from control of government; in short, the world whose passing is lamented by Argyll. Says Godkin:

> *In fact, from the fall of the Roman Empire almost to our time, the world was governed by property, and property was mainly land, and was associated in the popular mind, to a degree which we now find it difficult to understand, with political power and prominence.* A landless man was held to have no 'stake in the country', and therefore to have no right to manage public affairs. ...Probably nothing did as much to democratize America as the abundance of land and the ease of its acquisition. People began to perceive that a large landowner was not necessarily a great man, and the idea of government by landholders, which had held possession of the world for a thousand years, was killed by the perception (pp. 53–4, emphasis added; see also Godkin, 1966 [1896], p. 181).

Earlier, public opinion in the colonies existed largely as follows:

> The opinions of leading men, of clergymen and large landholders, were very powerful, and settled most of the affairs of state; but the opinion of the majority did not count for much, and the majority, in truth, did not think that it should (p. 184).

Instead of public opinion emanating 'from the majority of adult males':

> According to the aristocratic school, it should emanate only from persons possessing [at least] a moderate amount of property, on the assumption that the possession of property argues some degree of intelligence and interest in public affairs (p. 185).

At one point Godkin seemingly acknowledges the power of governance residing in the hands of bankers and other capitalists whose approval for loans is required (p. 242). In a market economy, that is, fundamental decisions that impact others are made by those in command of property.

Godkin writes of a Georgist tax policy adopted in New South Wales, in Australia. For our purposes it is instructive that he interprets that policy as rendering 'the state...a landlord on an extensive scale' because it receives a share of economic rent, a situation, he laments, which led to the question of rents growing 'into a great political question' (p. 247). Finally, in *Unforeseen Tendencies*, Godkin says that 'Down to a very recent period,' Americans looked 'to the government for nothing but protection of life and property' (p. 255). That property was property because it received the protection of government, and not vice versa, is an important point. But in his second relevant book there is a extremely important sequel.

In his *Problems of Modern Democracy* (1966 [1896]) Godkin in part expands, in part reiterates, and in part updates the foregoing themes. One major theme is that the wealthy should not abstain from politics/governance; they should, as natural leaders, assume the role of leadership 'to which their riches entitle them' (p. xxvi, Morton Keller's Introduction; see also pp. xxx–xxxi, regarding the 'prime constituency' of the Republican Party being that 'portion of the population "which possesses the larger share of the intelligence, public spirit, thrift, industry, foresight, and accumulated property of the country,'" quoting Godkin). Some policy issues, he believed, like the monetary standard, should be in the hands of apolitical experts (pp. xxxiv–xxxv), as if experts are not political and agree. This devotee of *laissez-faire* could not be comfortable with his prediction, in 1898 (the year of the war with Spain), that 'the government will shortly undergo great changes which will be presided over, not by men of light and learning, but by capitalists and adroit politicians ... the military spirit has taken possession of the masses, to whom power has passed' (p. xxxvi, letter to Charles Eliot Norton, 29 November 1898). The United States did not have a landed aristocracy, but he felt that no change in its transformation 'has been so marked as the transfer to wealth of the political and social influence which was formerly shared, if not absorbed, by literary, oratorical, or professional distinction' (p. xxxviii).

His principal argument, for our purposes, is expressed in various ways. The principle of equality is said to result in conceding to all persons equality before the law, from which it is a very short step 'to the possession of an equal share in the making of the laws' (p. 56; see also pp. 285–6). This represents a shift from ideal to ideal; he himself, however, emphasizes among the problems of modern democracy considerable inequality in law-making power. In the late 19th Century, he found 'as in France, Germany, and England, the poorer classes were just becoming aware of the extent of the power over the government which universal suffrage had put into their hands' (p. 175). He states his principal argument to include more than the landowning elite:

> I simply say that it was the most natural thing in the world for the working classes of England, for example, which had been so long familiar with legislation for the direct benefit of the middle and upper classes, to receive with anger or suspicion the announcement that the care of any class by the state was a mistake, and that individual independence was the true rule of industrial life. When these classes, therefore, found themselves invested through the suffrage with political power, it was inevitable that they should seek at once to improve their condition through legislation (p. 176; to not do so was to render permanent legislation benefiting others).
>
> What one learns...is the difficulty, in a democratic government, of moderation of any description, if it once abandons the policy of *laissez faire*, and undertakes to be a providence for the masses. There is no limit to the human appetite for unearned or easily earned money. No class is exempt from it. Under the old régime, the aristocrats got all the sinecures, the pensions, and the light jobs of every description. One of the results of the triumph of democracy has been to throw open this source of gratification to the multitude, and every attempt made to satisfy the multitude, in this field, has failed (Godkin, 1898, pp. 251–2).

These are remarkably important statements. Abandonment of the policy of *laissez-faire* is equated with democratization in the sense of a wide competition for benefits from the government. This wide competition replaces not a system in which the distribution of government largesse is absent; rather, under the old régime government-distributed largesse went solely to the aristocrats. *Laissez faire* = largesse solely to aristocracy; democracy = largesse thrown open to all. Affirmation of *laissez-faire* does not signify absence of government largesse, only that it is distributed to the aristocrats.

But the principal argument connecting landownership with governance is reiterated time and again:

> Now, the governing class...was...the wealthy class; and the wealthy class until the present century were the owners of the soil ...on the theory that the landowners were the country (pp. 180–1).

The theory, of course, did not lead to the institution. That was a matter of conquest. The theory came later, to provide justification.

> The 'man of property' was the landed man. He and his followers owned the country, and it seemed for ages perfectly natural and right that they should govern the country (pp. 182–3).

Godkin also presents his argument about landownership and governing power in a manner that seems to validate George's position. 'The economical or political revolutions' of the 19th Century transferred power 'from the owners of the land to people of every kind of occupation', the great landowners having been converted into annuitants forming an 'idle class...no longer render[ing] the state the service which the old feudal tenures exacted of them, and their enjoyment of large incomes...becomes increasingly difficult to defend in the forum of abstract justice' (p. 185; on status emulation and conspicuous consumption, see p. 318). They increasingly 'protect themselves by showing the danger to all property that would probably result from an attack on their particular kind of property' (pp. 185–6). He points out that while 'The labour problem' is really the problem of making the manual labourers of the world content with their lot' – clearly the view of social control from the top down – 'the existing discontent is, and not unreasonably, aggravated by the spectacle of the...idle class' (pp. 193-4. George, if he had read Godkin, might have been pleased in learning that 'The taxes paid by the annuitant or *rentier* class are but a trifling return, in reality, for the security they possess for person and property' (p. 194; see also p. 203). On land and governance reform, Godkin wrote, 'The recent Irish land laws are the dethronement of a great class, the apparent sacrifice of the few to the many, on a large scale; this is what democracy calls for, but it is never accomplished without seemingly serious violations of natural justice' (p. 279). There are several points to note here: 'Natural justice' is ambiguous but likely composed in terms favourable to the status quo prior to the reforms. No implication is intended here regarding the reforms. The main point is that a beneficiary of an old, received power structure and set of customs will inevitably have such views when confronted with a new structure and set — and our saying so privileges neither the old nor the new. Godkin also notes that the English aristocracy was alert enough to introduce 'the merit system, in time to save it from the incoming democracy' (p. 289).

Land ownership is but one form of property and wealth; governance derived from land ownership is also derived, often enough, from other forms of property and wealth. In this connection, Godkin criticizes the new phenomenon, the great corporation. 'These aggregations of capital in a few hands have created a new power in the State, whose influence on government has been very grave.' The managers defend their position and their policies with an argument consisting of a particular definition of reality, that 'they are the custodians of large amounts of other people's property, which they are bound to defend, by whomsoever attacked' (p. 293). Godkin understood the role of corporate management as social control through their influence on, if not control of, government.

> How to bring these corporations under the law, and at the same time protect them from unjust attacks, is one of the most serious problems of democratic government. …Corporations are as powerful as individual noblemen or aristocrats were in England in the last century, or in France before the Revolution, but are far harder to get at or bring to justice, from their habit of making terms with their enemies instead of fighting them (p. 294).

Godkin could have added that corporations are often instrumental in writing the legislation that covers their business. Godkin seems to object the most strenuously to the 'transfer of the government to the poor.' He again reminds his reader that, 'except during very short periods in ancient democracies, the world has been governed by rich men; that is, by the great landholders or the great merchants. …Every government has been a rich man's government.' With government transferred to poor men, 'through the taxing power rich corporations and rich individuals are at their mercy. They are…often stimulated by envy or anti-social passions' (p. 300). This type of admission brings out into the open what hitherto had been the object of ideology to obfuscate and render unseen. Godkin is candid, to the point, surely, of leading some readers to judge him subversive: such things should not be said in public. Nor is the topic of plutocracy the only one so treated. Patriotism 'has been made by the multitude to consist in holding everything [sic] that is, to be exactly right, or easily remedied.' Any man who would succeed in politics or business 'is strongly tempted to proclaim incessantly his great content with the existing order of things, and to treat everything "American" as sacred' (p. 305). It is views such as these that George confronted, even though he felt that his views were more consonant with American ideals than those of these other people.

Rosa Luxemburg

Rosa Luxemburg articulated a point of view similar to the others presented here. Not only does she, too, find that governance derived from land ownership, she identifies the governance founded on land ownership to include all three branches of what is now seen as the division of power, and, further, interprets land ownership and governance with regard to the control of the human labour force. Only two brief quotations need be given:

> ...each great noble lord of the middle ages, especially at the time of Charlemagne, was a similar emperor on a smaller scale—because his free noble ownership of the land made him lawmaker, tax-collector, and judge over all the inhabitants of his manors (Waters, 1970, p. 229).
> ...it happened that in all of Europe the formerly free peasant lands had been transformed into noble domains from which tributes and rents were exacted, how the formerly free peasantry had been transformed into an oppressed class constrained to perform labor services, to be bound to the land, even, during the later stages (*ibid.*, pp. 230–1).

Such unanimity should occasion no surprise. Otto von Gierke established that governance was an attribute of land ownership: 'Rulership and Ownership were blent' (Gierke, 1958, p. 88).

CONCLUSION

In his *Theory of Moral Sentiments*, Adam Smith uses the term 'invisible hand' to explain how spending by the rich gives employment to the poor and thereby makes the distribution of consumption more equal than the distributions of income or wealth:

> It is to no purpose, that the proud and unfeeling landlord views his extensive fields, and without a thought for the wants of his brethren, in imagination consumes himself the whole harvest that grows upon them. The homely and vulgar proverb, that the eye is larger than the belly, never was more fully verified than with regard to him. The capacity of his stomach bears no proportion to the immensity of his desires, and will receive no more than that of the meanest peasant. The rest he is obliged to distribute among those, who prepare, in the nicest manner, that little which he himself makes use of, among those who fit up the palace in which this little is to be consumed, among those who provide and keep in order all the different baubles and trinkets, which are employed in the oeconomy of greatness; all of whom thus derive from his luxury and caprice, that share of the necessaries of life, which they would in vain have expected from his humanity or his justice. The produce of the soil maintains at all times nearly that number of inhabitants which it is capable of maintaining. The rich only select from the heap what is most precious and agreeable. They consume little more than the poor, and in spite of their natural selfishness and rapacity, though they mean only

their own conveniency, though the sole end which they propose from the labours of all the thousands whom they employ, be the gratification of their own vain and insatiable desires, they divide with the poor the produce of all their improvements. They are led by an invisible hand to make nearly the same distribution of the neces- saries of life, which would have been made, had the earth been divided into equal portions among all its inhabitants, and thus without intending it, without knowing it, advance the interest of the society, and afford means to the multiplication of the species. When Providence divided the earth among a few lordly masters, it neither forgot nor abandoned those who seemed to have been left out in the partition. These last too enjoy their share of all that it produces. In what constitutes the real happiness of human life, they are in no respect inferior to those who would seem so much above them. In ease of body and peace of mind, all the different ranks of life are nearly upon a level, and the beggar, who suns himself by the side of the highway, possesses that security which kings are fighting for (Smith, 1976b, pp. 184–5).

We suspect that the 8th Duke of Argyll would have strongly objected to the first sentence of this quotation. He surely did not consider himself a 'proud and unfeeling landlord [who] views his extensive fields, and without a thought for the wants of his brethren, in imagination consumes himself the whole harvest that grows upon them'. But equally surely he understood that consumption is not the issue; the issue is the distribution of wealth, in part the accumulation of capital and in part the division of landed property. John Locke had shown, or at least argued, that the introduction of money permitted unequal acquisition of assets, whereas in the state of nature each individual could appropriate from the common pool only that which he and his family could consume and then only if as much and as good remained for others. Now Smith presents a 'trickle down' picture in which spend- ing by the rich gives employment to the poor and thereby makes the distribution of consumption more equal than the distributions of income or wealth.

The use of money permits unlimited acquisition — of consumer goods, of capital goods, of financial instruments, and of land. But land became unequally owned, historically, through conquest and favouritism by rulers; and this unequal ownership had as one of its potential features an accompanying 'monopoly' of sovereignty, that is, of governance, by landowners. Even in Smith's story, above, we read of 'Providence divid[ing] the earth among a few lordly masters.' Smith understood that land ownership brought economic and political power; owning land made one the master. George Douglas Campbell, the 8th Duke of Argyll, understood that, too. He may have been uncomfortable with the public attribution of power but he certainly understood that he had economic and political power (in a non-pejorative sense). And his claim of providing living accommodations for others, for poorer other people, is akin in intended meaning to what Smith wrote. Moreover, Argyll wrote with the purpose of maintaining the system in which he enjoyed such power. And so did Henry George understand, except that he condemned that system.

What, then, is the difference between Argyll and George? Extreme and ab- solutist claims and other statements can be put aside as so much rhetoric and/or bargaining positions; so too with flowery language. These were two motivated, indeed, ardent supporters of their positions. The Duke and the writer from the working class came from two very different worlds. One is reminded of Lord and Lady Chatterley looking upon what is supposedly Manchester and the husband wondering aloud how he would have turned out had he been raised in Manchester (Lawrence, 1928). The difference between Argyll and George seems in part to be in the language that they respectively use in describing the social world of ownership. At bottom, however, the picture is the same. The difference is almost wholly in their normative positions. Argyll is at least prepared to accept his lot in life and the system from which it emanates. Likely he more than accepts it; he relishes it. It is a system with problems, like any system. But it works, it is basically sound, it is moral, it is beneficent, it is the work of centuries of unseen forces, and, above all, it *is*, and has to be reckoned with, not lightly dismissed.

George is not prepared to passively accept his lot in life and the system that permits and gives rise to it. He detests the system. It is not merely a system with problems, it is a system which, from its origins, has condemned the majority of people to inferiority, to suffering, and, even worse, to premature death. It is a system run by and for the ruling class(es). However, the system, when not perverted, could abide by true morality, that of honest labour, hard work, and reward based thereon. The existing system is different. Its inequality derives from (1) the acquisition of the lion's share of land and its unearned income by a relative handful of households and families, (2) the majority's unequal ability to accumulate capital because others, benefiting in part from unequal ownership of land, had gotten a head start, and (3) perhaps the largest part, the landowners' historical control of government, increasingly in partnership with the owners of non-landed property.

What Argyll sees as an advantage and as the object of his program of retention, George sees as a predicament, a major obstacle, and the object of his program of reform. Both men identify and accept the reality of the power of governance derived from — and reinforced by — the ownership of land. Governance included private governance authority running with land ownership and public government position running likewise, with positions as local magistrates or sheriffs spanning both. Within their respective normative positions they also differ on their positive analyses of how arrangements work especially on the genesis of rent and the relation of landownership to human wellbeing.

Argyll considers George's program to be socialist, because it would nationalize and transfer economic rent from its hitherto private recipients into the government's treasury. George believes, however, that rent has been an unearned income for the landowners and that so far from taking from the landowners what is theirs, his Single Tax will not only prevent private receipt of unearned income but promote the values that lead to earned income. How, therefore, George believes, could such a program be socialist? It protects true earned income-based property and ends spoliation by those who took over the land and turned it over to their heirs and assigns. In response to these claims, Argyll claims that land ownership is productive and that the proof and measure of its productivity is the income that it receives. To which, in turn, George responds: landownership per se is not productive.

George believes that the capture by government of economic rent will avoid the adverse effects of progress, the poverty that has accompanied the production of greater wealth. The Single Tax will also avoid the conditions that many associate from population increase but in reality are due to the capture of land rent by private owners. George believes in the reform of governance. Government should not be in the hands of landowners; it should not be in the hands of the propertied, period. Property owners should have no greater share in making the laws than a comparable number of non-owners. In the mid-19th Century some appointed government office holders, intending both to take advantage of their positions and to foreclose the idea of a professional civil service, argued that their appointments constituted legal property rights to their positions. If they had succeeded, government itself would have been made into private property, like land.

George's position largely turns on the unearned nature of rent. The notion of unearned income can be seen in several ways. The idea of something being unearned seems to be normative to some people. To others the distinction between earned and unearned income rests on an objective, positivist basis, i.e., the growth of society. To still others, following David Hume's injunction that one cannot go from an 'is' to an 'ought' without an additional normative premise, the matter is more complicated. But more is involved in George's position than the unearned increment. Also relevant are the normative matters of whether land should be within the institution of private property and whether land ownership should convey powers of governance. Another arguable matter is whether property *is* sovereignty.

Frank H. Knight was no disciple of Henry George (see Tideman and Plassmann, 2004) but neither did he agree with Argyll that ownership per se was sufficient warrant. In his *Ethics of Competition* (1936, p. 56), Knight wrote, '...income does not go to factors but to their owners, and can in no case have more ethical justification than has the fact of ownership. The ownership of personal or material productive capacity is based on a complex mixture of inheritance, luck and effort.... What is the ideal distribution from the standpoint of...ethics may be disputed but of the three considerations named above certainly none but the effort can have ethical validity.' He also wrote, 'It [the market] distributes the produce of industry on the basis of power which is ethical only insofar as right and might are one. It [the market] is a confessed failure in the field of promoting social progress, and its functions in this regard are being progressively taken over by other social agencies' (1936, p. 58). In *Freedom and Reform* (1947, p. 67) Knight noted that the savings and dissavings determined through time in a market characterized by unequal initial endowments of income-earning rights and privileges can be expected to lead to 'cumulative increase in inequality of ...power'. And for Knight, power connoted governance.

The power that is governance is obviously political. It is also, perhaps not so obviously, economic. In the case of both landowners and capital owners, economic power resides in their constituting a saving-investment elite, the providers of income to the working class (including hired hands and tenants), and the combination of their organization for production and of production. Social functions – productivity – are latent therein. Ownership per se is a matter of who performs those functions, and is derived from historic processes and patterns of inequality.

The immediately foregoing paragraph is further revealing once unpacked or deconstructed. One element concerns Argyll's identification of the mental role of entrepreneurship in the creation of wealth. The history of economic thought on the entrepreneur turns in large part on the positions taken on two questions. One question concerns the precise nature of the role of the entrepreneur. Suffice it to say that a multiplicity of specifications of that role have been made, some possibly in conflict with others. In the preceding paragraph I have generalized (and begged) them by stipulating activities leading to the organization for production and the organization of production. Argyll makes no original contribution here. His principal lasting point, also recognized by Alfred Marshall, who made it another factor of production, is that management, entrepreneurship or whatever it is called, must be recognized as performing an important organizing function.*

The second question concerns the entrepreneurial function and whether it is performed by a specific group of people or is an aspect of the activity of all economic agents. For example, if by role is meant, alternatively, the discovery or the creation of niches—opportunities for gain—this may be undertaken by all agents or only by a select group of agents. Argyll advances an elite theory: the entrepreneur is the capitalist and landowner and their entrepreneurial role is combined with that of a savings-investment elite. The elite theory of the entrepreneur is part, a large part, of his defence of possession of private property, the second element. He wants to argue, though perhaps not so baldly, that property ownership is what enables a person to be in a position to perform that role. Again a circular argument: the role is performed by the propertied, and owning property enables them to perform the role. The inconclusiveness of the argument turns in part on whether the existing distribution of property can be shown to empower those with the most ability to organize production. (The parallel question in politics was raised with regard to lines of hereditary monarchs and their progeny's ability to govern.) Some of this was recognized by John W.

*See Alfred Marshall, *Principles of Economics*, 8ᵗʰ edit. (London: Macmillan, 1920), Book VI, Chapters vi–viii. —Ed.

Mason a quarter-century ago. Mason noted that Argyll 'became self-appointed spokesman for the landed classes in a period when they were under a great threat' (Mason, 1980, p. 579), concluded that he combined free exchange and elite theories (p. 587), and judged 'much less convincing...[Argyll's] attempt to prove that the existing distribution of wealth, both landed and non-landed, accurately reflected the distribution of potential wealth-creating talent' (p. 580). (Some, perhaps much, of this is similar to Vilfredo Pareto's theory of the circulation of the elite.)

That conclusion is reinforced by two further considerations. One is that there is no unique wealth-creating distribution of entitlements/property ownership. Each different set of entitlements, or each different distribution of property, yields a different and non-comparable result (i.e., different and non-comparable Pareto-optimal results), the non-comparability due to the absence of a metric common to all results (i.e., a non-comparable price structure specific to each result). The other is that some African colonies of European nations prevented the native population from owning land but required them to pay taxes in the ruling white man's money, thus forcing them into the white man's labour market in which free exchange could be claimed to exist.

Argyll did his argument little good by recognizing, as he must, that land ownership has been a matter of both conquest and purchase and sale. That the 'very possession of land was evidence of the successful outcome of a fierce struggle — military and economic' (Mason, 1980, p. 579) did not conduce to a belief – unless one started with it – that the talents useful in such struggle were also useful in the organization for and of production, say, in a hierarchical landowning aristocracy.

The ideas and political developments of at least the last two centuries can be seen as turning on the conflict between elitist and democratic republicanism. The former means the control of government by a more or less loosely ruling ruling class; the latter, control of the government by all people, including, and especially, the ordinary, common people — whom Abraham Lincoln meant when he spoke of 'government of the people, by the people, and for the people'. The former lauds either the special qualities of the elite or the relative ease of upward mobility; the latter condemns enormous inequalities of income and wealth, and the political power of the wealthy that conduces to further inequality through their control and use of government.

All of what is described in this article is thus played out against, or within, the working out of the pair of twin tendencies in society, hierarchy and equality, and continuity and change. Such was the stage, and Argyll and George were players in this continuing drama. Each believed he had Truth on his side, but truth or Truth has very little to do with it. Propositions, such as the inviolability of private property (Mason, 1980, p. 578), have meaning not in terms of their substantive claims but in the role to which they are put. As Ritchie (1893, p. 522) put it, 'legal security and political stability are essential to social welfare; but the greatest enemies of security and stability are those who resist every change in institutions, while such changes can still be made by legal and constitutional means.' The Duke of Argyll, for all his use of absolutist formulation in making the case for continuity of property arrangements against proposals for change he disliked, was a leader in the movement to consolidate holdings — the elimination of the runrig system of dispersed strips.* It was more than a superficial rear-rangement of holdings. It 'deeply affected' the 'circumstances of the broad mass of the cultivating population'. It 'betokened more drastic social experiment,' because it was 'entangled with conscious attempts on the part of the landlords to alter the underlying relation of land and people: to re-align tenants in new social groups: and to force industrial experiments on traditionally agricultural groups' (Gray, 1952, p. 46).[8] Argyll was thus a major player in processes which confirm de Jouvenel's dictum that history 'is in essence a battle of dominant wills, fight-ing in every way they can for the material which is common to everything they construct: the human labor force' (de Jouvenel, 1962, p. 177). Henry George understood that that was what ownership of land was all about, namely, property as governance: the organization of production, the control of the human labour force, and the control of the state and its use for those purposes.

One final dimension of seen and unseen remains. A recent study of the rhetoric in Winston Churchill's military histories includes the statement, 'The signal feature of Churchill's histories is the way they maintain an aristocratic perspective in democratic times without losing their democratic sympathies' (Valiunas, 2002, p. 2; quoted in Teagarden, 2004). How can our subjects be characterized along these lines? Argyll maintains an aristocratic perspective in a period of transformation from aristocratic to democratic structures and does so with evident relish but without the harshness or antagonism found in other defenders of hierarchy. Godkin is rather like Churchill, or Valiunas's view of him, in maintaining an aristocratic perspective in democratic times without losing his democratic sympathies. Hayek seems to have done likewise. Henry George has very different ideas. George maintains a democratic perspective in a society that continues to have strong aristocratic perspectives and structural elements. He would change society in ways that would limit certain *rentier* and other hierarchic forces of the past but is in other respects as conservative as David Ricardo. All four want to change the structure of society, system of

---

* The crofting system of land use and township organization grew up in the 18th and 19th Centuries. Previously the land was held by clans and distributed to clansmen in the 'runrig' system of widely dispersed holdings. This system was also to a large extent communal, but the focus was upon the clan. With the decline of the clan system, the community became more geo-graphically oriented. The primary difference between crofting and the runrig system was that in crofting, individual holdings were consolidated. With the Crofters Holdings Act of 1886, crofting areas were defined, and assurance was given of security of tenure, hereditary succession, and fair rent. See Ducey (1956). — Ed.

governance, path of societal development, and set of dominant policies. The doctrines of each of them render certain beliefs not only seen but salient and other beliefs not only unseen but obfuscated.

At bottom, debates over ownership and governance are part of the process of working out the legal-economic nexus (Samuels, 1989). Simultaneously worked out in this nexus are the features of the political system (or what is conventionally perceived as such) that impact the economic system (or what is conventionally perceived as such) and of the features of the economic system (or what is conventionally perceived as such) that impact the political system (or what is conventionally perceived as such). The parenthetic language is reiterated in order to emphasize selective perception and the manipulation of perception. Argyll and George were not alone in operating upon such an understanding of the recursive relations within the legal-economic nexus. For example, it has recently been written of Robert Lowe (1811–92), the English economist and politician, that he conducted a 'campaign against the extension of the franchise. Political economy was prominent in his argument, Lowe alleging that working-class voters would be protectionist, stateist and use their power to plunder the property of the rich via punitive taxation' (Rutherford, 2004, Vol. II, p. 698). At the core of the matter is power, and political and economic power are but twin aspects of the working out of the power structure governing whose interests count. And in the larger sphere of things, it is not only the rights of landed property that are involved but the rights of non-landed property and rights not designated property rights at all, as well as the legal-economic nexus itself.

NOTES

1. Property derived from financial manipulation was also anathema of George.
2. The reader should search using Google for 'land ownership in Britain' and 'land ownership in Hawaii.'
3. Data is taken from Cahill, 2001; Cramb, 2000; Wightman, 1999. See www.canongate .net/list/glp.taf?_p=5431 and www.red-star-research.org.uk/rap/rap6.html.
4. Gide and Rist's use of the term 'idle' is specialized. The landowners are idle in comparison with the productive class, the cultivators, in the Physiocrats' system; they still have the two roles to perform.
5. Argyll's 'The Prophet of San Francisco' was published in the *Nineteenth Century* for April 1884 and George's reply, 'Reduction of Iniquity', was published in the July 1884 number. The two essays were published as *Property in Land* by Funk & Wagnalls (New York, 1884). The latter is reproduced in the collection, Henry George, *The Land Question* (1982 [1884]).
6. An early reviewer of *The Unseen Foundations of Society* questioned the coherence of Argyll's notions of the laws of nature and of the role of legitimacy in the definition of wealth ('legitimate possession'), asking, 'If, then, slavery be an institution contrary to the 'law of nature,' are we bound to deny that slaves could ever be or have been a form of wealth? And if slaves were not wealth, why did the British government give compensation to the West Indian planters? If any one sincerely believes that the possession of large estates, or of vast sums of capital, is not a morally legitimate object of desire, would he, in the Duke of Argyll's opinion, be justified in treating the great land-owner or capitalist as not really owning what he seems to

own?' (Ritchie, 1893, p. 517).

7. E.A. Ross's review likewise wrote that the book is 'a defense of reactionary economic individualism' and has 'the intellectual ear-marks of the Liberty and Property Defense League …the outcome of the practical instinct of self-preservation. Throughout the book is the note of alarm at the menacing attitude that later reform movements assume toward property and vested interests… the anxious special pleading of the great landowner and capitalist' (Ross, 1893, p. 723).

8. Paralleling the enclosure movement in England, which in effect expropriated peasant rights, was the granting and enforcing of plenary mining rights to noblemen in France, effectively confiscating peasant rights. From one point of view, such enabled larger, more efficient production; but such does not negate the confiscation. More broadly, in England and elsewhere, the period *c.* 1600–1900 witnessed the transformation of the legal foundations of the economy from that of an agrarian, landed-property society to that of an urban, non-landed property society. Even the adoption and assignment of new rights of economic significance had a confiscatory effect. In none of this was compensation paid. What confiscation yieldeth, confiscation taketh away.

REFERENCES

Argyll, 8th Duke of (George Douglas Campbell) (1877), *Essay on the Commercial Principles applicable to Contracts for the Hire of Land*, London: Cassell, Petter and Galpin.

Argyll, 8th Duke of (1884), *The Prophet of San Francisco: A Criticism of the Attack on Private Ownership of Land in Henry George's* Progress and Poverty *and* Social Problems, reprinted from *The Nineteenth Century*, London: Kegan Paul & Co.

Argyll, 8th Duke of (1893a), *The Unseen Foundations of Society*, London: John Murray.

Argyll, 8th Duke of (1893b), *Irish Nationalism: An Appeal to History*, London: John Murray.

Cahill, Kevin (2001), *Who Owns Britain?*, Edinburgh: Canongate Books.

Cramb, Auslan (2000), *Who Owns Scotland Now?*, Edinburgh: Mainstream.

Ducey, P.R. (1956), *Cultural Continuity and Population Change on the Isle of Skye*, Ann Arbor, Michigan: University Microfilms (no. 00–17, 051).

Ezekiel, Mordechai (1957), 'Distribution of Gains from Rising Technical Efficiency in Progressing Countries', *American Economic Review/Supplement*, **47**, 361–75.

Gaffney, Mason (1994), *The Corruption of Economics*, London: Shepheard-Walwyn.

George, Henry (1982)[1884], *The Land Question*, New York: Robert Schalkenbach Foundation.

George, H. (1885), 'The Reduction of Iniquity' in G.D. Campbell, *The Peer and the Prophet: Being the Duke of Argyll's article on* The Prophet of San Francisco *and the Reply of Henry George*, reprinted from *The Nineteenth Century*, London: William Reeves.

Gide, Charles and Charles Rist (1948) [1915], *A History of Economic Doctrines*, Boston, MA: D.C. Heath.

Gierke, Otto von (1958), *Political Theories of the Middle Age*, F.W. Maitland, trans., Boston, MA: Beacon Press.

Godkin, Edwin L. (1898), *Unforeseen Tendencies of Democracy*, Boston, MA: Houghton, Mifflin.

Godkin, Edwin L. (1966) [1896], *Problems of Modern Democracy: Political and Economic Essays*, Cambridge, MA: Harvard University Press.

Gray, Malcolm (1952), 'The Abolition of Runrig in the Highlands of Scotland', *Economic*

History Review, **5**, 46–57.

Hawaii, Department of Business, Economic Development & Tourism (1987), *Land Ownership in Hawaii*, www.hawaii.gov/dbedt/srs/sr208.pdf.

de Jouvenel, Bertrand (1962), *On Power*, Boston, MA: Beacon Press.

Knight, Frank H. (1936), *The Ethics of Competition*, New York: Harper.

Knight, Frank H. (1947), *Freedom and Reform*, New York: Harper.

Lawrence, D.H. (1928), *Lady Chatterley's Lover*, Florence: privately printed.

Lissner, Will and Dorothy Burnham Lissner (eds.) (1991), *George and the Scholars*, New York: Robert Schalkenbach Foundation.

Mason, John W. (1980), 'Political Economy and the Response to Socialism in Britain, 1870–1914', *Historical Journal*, **23**, 565–587.

McDonald, Forrest (2004), *Recovering the Past: A Historian's Memoir*, Lawrence, KA: University Press of Kansas.

Mirrlees, J.A. (1974), 'Notes on Welfare Economics, Information, and Uncertainty,' in M.S. Balch, D. McFadden and W.Y. Wu, eds., *Essays on Equilibrium Behavior under Uncertainty*, Amsterdam: North-Holland, pp. 243–58.

Pullen, John (2005), 'The Philosophy and Feasibility of Henry George's Land-Value Tax: Criticisms and Defences, with Particular Reference to the Problem of the Land-Rich-and-Income-Poor.' Ch. 8 this volume.

Ritchie, David G. (1893), Book Review, *International Journal of Ethics*, **3**, 514–22.

Ross, Edward A. (1893), 'The Unseen Foundations of Society', *Political Science Quarterly*, **8**, 722–32.

Rutherford, Donald (ed.) (2004), *The Biographical Dictionary of British Economists*, 2 vols, Bristol: Thoemmes Continuum.

Samuels, Warren J. (1962), 'The Physiocratic Theory of Economic Policy,' *Quarterly Journal of Economics*, **76**, 145–62. Reprinted in *Essays in the History of Mainstream Political Economy*, London: Macmillan, 1992, pp. 28–46.

Samuels, Warren J. (1989), 'The Legal-Economic Nexus,' *George Washington Law Review*, **57**, 1556–78.

Samuels, Warren J. (1992a), 'Institutions and Distribution: Ownership and the Identification of Rent', *Journal of Income Distribution*, **2**, 125–40.

Samuels, Warren J. (1992b), *Essays on the Economic Role of Government*, Vol. 1, *Principles*. London: Macmillan.

Samuels, Warren J. (2003), 'Why The Georgist Movement Has Not Succeeded: A Speculative Memorandum', *American Journal of Economics and Sociology*, **62**, 583–592.

Sandilands, Roger (2004), 'What is something worth?' Received 20 February 2004 from hes@eh.net.

Schweikhardt, David (2004), 'An Examination of the Shifting Balance of Individual and Collective Legal Rights: The Case of U.S. Agricultural Commodity Programs', Michigan State University, Department of Agricultural Economics, manuscript.

Smith, Adam (1976a), *An Inquiry into the Nature and Causes of the Wealth of Nations*, 2 vols, New York: Oxford University Press.

Smith, Adam (1976b), *The Theory of Moral Sentiments*, Oxford, U.K.: Oxford University Press.

Smith, Adam (1977), *The Correspondence of Adam Smith*, E.C. Mossner and I.S. Ross (eds), Oxford: Clarendon Press.

Teagarden, Ernest (2004), Review of Algis Valiunas, *Churchill's Military Histories: A Rhetorical Study*, Lanham, MD: Roman and Littlefield. Reviewed for H-Albion and H-Net, received 19 August 2004 from conservativenet@listserv.uic.ed.

Tideman, Nicolaus and Florenz Plassman (2004), 'Knight: Nemesis from the Chicago School', in Robert V. Andelson, (ed.), *Critics of Henry George*, 2nd ed., revised and enlarged, Oxford: Blackwell, pp. 541–69.

Valiunas, Algis (2002), *Churchill's Military Histories: A Rhetorical Study*, Lanham, MD: Roman and Littlefield.

Waters, Mary-Alice (ed.) (1970), *Rosa Luxemburg Speaks*, New York: Pathfinder Press.

Wightman, Andy (1999), *Scotland: Land and Power*, Edinburgh: Luath Press.

Williamson, Chilton (1960), *American Suffrage: From Property to Democracy, 1760– 1860*, Princeton, NJ: Princeton University Press.

Young, Jeffrey T. (1997), *Economics as a Moral Science: The Political Economy of Adam Smith*, Cheltenham, U.K. and Lyme, U.S.A.: Edward Elgar.

6. The Henry George Theorem and the Entrepreneurial Process: Turning Henry George on his Head

Laurence S. Moss

ABSTRACT

This chapter offers an interpretation of the Henry George Theorem (HGT) that brings it squarely into the study and analysis of entrepreneurship somewhat loosening its ties to the subfield of urban economics. I draw on the pioneering work of Spencer Heath whose insights about the viability of proprietary communities were developed further by his grandson, Spencer Heath MacCallum who, in 1970, recognized that private real estate developers sometimes make their capital gains (mostly) by creating useful public spaces that others enjoy. I also draw inspiration from Fred Foldvary's effort in 1994 to synthesize the pubic goods problem in economics with the Henry George Theorem in urban economics. While the real estate owner–developer does emerge on my pages in a somewhat more favourable light than as originally portrayed by Henry George in his *Progress and Poverty* in 1879, I offer a realistic appraisal of the duplicitous behaviours required of such entrepreneurs in the context of the modern regulatory state. Real estate development remains a 'hot button' item in local politics, and real estate developers must become genuine 'political entrepreneurs' if they are to complete their projects in a timely way and capture business profits. It is a complicated story that the HGT helps make intelligible in terms of human action.

1. INTRODUCTION

There is hardly a major real estate developer who does not understand the basic mechanisms of the Henry George Theorem (HGT). Even the real estate *brokers* who earn commissions know that when it comes to valuing some parcel of land, it is the location of that parcel that drives a major part of its market value. By location they mean proximity to schools, fire departments and, most importantly, to central business districts (CBDs). It is a brute fact about the real world that 'economic activity tends to concentrate geographically' (Hanson, 2000, p. 477; Scott, 2005). An agglomeration of activity attracts large numbers of people to that area.

In Massachusetts, U.S.A., there are no fewer than 350 towns and cites. Each has its own CBD and sometimes several. Also, each town or city has its own local government, fire service department, police, schools and the myriad licensing departments that provide public access to the otherwise private plans and goals of the local real estate developers.

Homeowners know in their bones that a successful 'improvement', such as an elegant pedestrian mall lit by modern street lamps and designed by a noted architect, will bring higher resale values for their homes. They also know that such improvements are costly and must be paid for somehow. They worry that future real estate assessments (and later taxes) will rise.[1] Local business owners know that a tasteful lit market place with ample parking access translates mightily into large sales and profits. There is nothing that piques a local community's interest more than a real estate deal just a block or two from its homes and businesses.

These financial implications, coupled with a genuine interest in their community and what they leave behind for the next generation, make local town politics important to many people.

I am tempted to write that, just as 'all politics is local,' all local politics involves real estate deals, but that would be overstating matters a great deal. The famed economist Joseph Schumpeter noted in 1911 that economic development involved novelty. New combinations of commodities pioneered by energetic entrepreneurs and subsequently adopted by hoards of imitators are what characterized the entrepreneurial process (Schumpeter, 1961 [1911], pp. 65–68). Schumpeter would have included under his label 'new combinations' different combinations of product characteristics under brand names, and a great many other activities as well. Reflecting the colonial venturing of his day, Schumpeter included the discovery of new resources and materials and the structural organization or reorganization of industry as examples of 'new combinations'. He did not mention real estate but I think that when the real estate developers pioneer new combinations of property rights they are quintessential entrepreneurs in Schumpeter's sense of the term.

The purpose of this chapter is to make a case for the importance of the HGT, not only as an abstract theorem in urban economics (which it most certainly is), but also as a catalyst in the 'story-telling' that is an essential part of understanding the entrepreneurial process. The implications of the HGT are used to help illuminate patterns of behaviour that are observable in the market place, in the local community, and in real estate markets where claims to real property are traded under competitive conditions. In my view, the whole purpose of economic reasoning is to make the world understandable in terms of human action. As with many, if not all, economic models, the point of the exercise is to provide the social scientist with basic insights about processes at work in the real world. The theorem itself, as I shall explain in section 4 below, can help focus the mind on characteristics and features of the entrepreneurial process around us. In the next section, I shall say something about the historical Henry George, who did not hold real estate owners in high regard. While he did praise those who invested and improved land, he thought that many developers were 'mere land speculators' offering nothing of value to the whole of society.

2. THE HISTORICAL HENRY GEORGE

The life and times of Henry George are important topics for historians of what is termed the 'progressive period' in American political life (Barker, 1991). Recently, a four-volume collection of George's journalistic writings has been published and is testimony to the continuing interest among historians and admirers of this giant of American politics and social reform (Wenzer, 2003). George's best-known book was *Progress and Poverty* (1882) [1879], which is generally declared to be one of the 'best sellers' in the history of economics (Barker 1991 [1955], p. 330).

   Like Karl Marx only a decade or so before, George set out to change the world and not just intellectualize about it or assign names to patterns of behaviour around him. He remarked about how social advancement could take place in any given territorial area while in that same area so many others endured abject poverty. The problem was to explain the uneven nature of economic development. His own experience in the American West with the land speculation bubbles convinced him that an important segment of American society was growing rich without having to do any work at all. This wealthy segment of the United States gained wealth by virtue of the fact that they owned land in strategic locations, often near 'central business districts'. As the population grew and individuals competed to live within close proximity of those CBDs, the 'idle' landowners became richer and richer. They raked in large rents and real estate gains at the expense of the needy and downtrodden.

   Most important to George was that these real estate gains (allegedly) bore no relationship whatsoever to any hard-laboured-for improvements on that land. Some portion of the gain from real estate ownership was entirely independent of the landowners' efforts; that portion of the land value, following David Ricardo and the terminology of the older classical school of economics, George named 'rent'. Rent was that portion of a market-generated return on the sale or leasing of an item that was above the minimum amount that was needed for the owner of that item to provide it in the first place. In a wealth-maximizing world, economists write of the 'opportunity cost' of that item, by which they mean the amount of rental income it can earn in its next-best application. So in the case of real estate, urban rents are sometimes defined as that portion of the rental value above what that same land might earn if it were applied to agriculture.

George was one of the small group of prominent economic writers at the end of the 19th Century who insisted on distinguishing land from other forms of capital goods. The tendency of his time, and still today, is to abstract from the locational and other attributes of a parcel of land and lump the land along with machines and even intellectual property as 'capital goods' that are valued at their present actuarial value (Fisher 2003 [1906], p. 56). According to George and his followers, the returns to land are governed by vastly different economic causes than, say, the return on a machine or what is today called human capital.

Machines can be reverse-engineered and replicated, no matter how intricate or complicated they may be. Even a patented machine can be licensed and reproduced. Not so with land. Land is entirely different. It has a fixed spatial location, and one parcel of land is distinguished from all other parcels by its location. In the context of urban development, there are few other land sites with *exactly* the same location with respect to the CBD. There are substitute locations, and possibly close substitute locations, but there can never be an exact match. In a nutshell, this means that to own land is to own a particular geographical location for which there are few substitute locations. Landowners are the ultimate monopolists since they possess the exclusive rights to a unique and distinct location; in addition, the law permits them to lease some or all those rights to others not so privileged for rents.

Now with the progress of society (and this includes the growth of population flocking to urban areas), some of the landowners will rake in huge rents. These 'differential rents' are those in excess of the rents needed to cover lost opportunities and the amortized charges needed to recover the funds used for landed improvements and investments. Some sort of pure *unearned* surplus accrues. Furthermore, land speculators whose only activity is to keep land from being productively employed reap gains as if being rewarded for their antisocial behaviours. Another alleged result of this behaviour is that the wages of labour remain much lower than they would be in an economy that rewards labour according to its productivity. George's characterization of the parasitic landowners was and remains grist for the mill of radical reformers around the world.

For George, the moral or normative question was as important as the economic mechanisms. Why should a monopolist be allowed to keep his or her 'unearned' gains when the poverty of so many others could be mitigated if only the landowners were forced to share their windfalls with the rest of society? Who gained more from government than the landowners? Did fairness and justice require that the landowner give up his unjust enrichments so that others could live better? George concluded that such redistributions were required. He advocated taxing away the portion of land rent paid for the unimproved value of land—that portion of the rent that was not due to betterments or improvements made to the land. George reasoned that since the tax he advocated was on something entirely 'unearned', it would have little or no effect on incentives to supply land in the first place. There would be no reduction in the amount of land in the economy since land was fixed (or inelastic) in supply. I should also remark, perhaps with the qualification of 'last but not least', that the land-value tax is considered by most Georgists to be 'just' and fair.

And there was more good news. If the land-value tax were substituted for the myriad other taxes currently imposed on the community, the net effect would be a surge in productivity and investments. To tax is to discourage. So, if the land-value tax were substituted for the income tax, the labourer would have an incentive to work longer and harder, to the benefit of himself and the entire community.

George was not the first to call for a land tax in the history of economics, but he was one of the first to call for a tax that might replace all other taxes. This ingenious and easy-to-explain program of what others called the 'single tax movement' spawned a political movement of spirited 'single taxers'. Single taxers are still active today and they always attract a few ardent followers. In fact, the single tax movement sparked global interest; many tax jurisdictions today still rely in part on a land-value tax based on Georgist influence and analysis (Andelson, 2000). In the United States there were a half a dozen or so 'Henry George schools' that offered public lectures and provoked interest in radical land reform ideas. Currently several schools are still operating.

The HGT was not mentioned by Henry George, and it was not directly stated in any of George's major writings. The theorem was independently discovered by J. Serck-Hanson and D. A. Starrett in the early 1970s (Arnott et al., 1977, p. 336). The logic of the approach directly flows out of the seminal work of Harold Hotelling and William Vickrey both of whom (most interestingly) were aware of, and influenced by, George's writings (Hotelling, 1938; Vickrey, 1977). Still, the theorem is not really about politics and political reform. Instead, it is about patterns of economic development and how a benevolent city planner might manage a tax-spending policy that would raise living standards for all those residing in a given urban area or else planning to move into that neighbourhood.[2]

The HGT describes an equilibrium where the total utility in a region is at a maximum when an optimal population has moved to the neighbourhood of a CBD. A scientifically engineered land-value tax can be levied to finance the infrastructure improvements that provide those same taxed individuals with the financial means to pay the tax. The HGT is an *abstract proposition* that supposes an ideal benevolent government apparatus, in that there are no invisibles or unknowns and all government administrators look out for the public interest and not their own private selfish interests.

As a theorem that comes out of the armchair theorizing of modern economic analysis, it is as much fiction as are most *abstract* models in the social sciences. And as an abstract model, its value is not in the *description* of everyday life in urban settings, but as a foil or 'equilibrium apparatus' against which we can detect actual tendencies or patterns at work in the real world of everyday political life. It is to this modern apparatus – the apparatus of the HGT – that we now turn our attention.

3. PRIVATE AND PUBLIC GOODS

It is customary in introductory economics courses to explain why government intervention is needed in order to make ordinary everyday life both possible and wholesome. It is generally agreed among economists that an anarchist society (a society without a modern state, claiming a monopoly of coercive power in a territorial area) cannot possibly provide the stability and security that many of us enjoy under modern political arrangements. Part of the argument for centralization has to do with so-called 'public goods'.

Public goods provide 'positive externalities' to others in the community. For this reason they are typically undersupplied by private entrepreneurs because entrepreneurs cannot figure out a way of excluding those who have not paid from enjoying some of the benefits of these goods. Others in the community seeing the 'free riders' will also refuse to pay for the public goods. That is why a modern tax state is needed: to supply or at least subsidize the production of so-called 'public goods and services'; an example might be education. It is alleged that a literate community provides greater stability and social harmony throughout the community than if matters were left entirely to the families concerning how and whether children are to be educated and trained. Free market *laissez-faire* – so the argument for government goes – would undersupply education.

And then there are the 'negative externalities', which similarly require coercive intervention by a taxing state to mitigate certain harms. An example might be contagious diseases, which need to be bottled up by isolating the carriers in hospitals or even detention centres (Fuchs, 2005). I believe that I have offered a fair and accurate summary of the conventional wisdom in textbook education.

A public good or service (hereinafter, simply 'public good') is often sharply contrasted with a private good. Consider the simple example of an apple. An apple is a private good because, when appropriated by any member of the community, it can be entirely consumed by that member and only that member. When Joe eats the apple, Janet and Alice and Bill cannot at the same time also eat that same apple if Joe does not allow them to do so. Such a good – the apple – is a private good because the enjoyment of most of the apple's characteristics is a private affair. The image is the stereotypical one of neoclassical economics, in which each individual maximizes his own private utility by appropriating through market transactions an optimal combination of goods and services.

Joe's consumption activities to obtain dominion over goods and services rival others' attempts to do the same. Apple consumption in the community is an example of 'rivalrous consumption'. Joe, Janet, Alice and Bill do not end up struggling over the apple because they all respect the law, which provides them with a simple way of deciding who 'owns' that apple and therefore can consume it. In a political community where property rights are well defined, and when Joe acquires his apple in a lawful manner, he can lawfully exclude Janet, Alice and Bill from the enjoyment of that apple. In other words, the consumption of the apple is (often) an excludable activity. Rivalry and excludability are the defining characteristics of private goods (compare Foldvary, 1994, p. 14).

According to the story that is so often told, it is the existence of public goods in any specific location that makes the consumption of private goods at all possible. The organizations and institutions that constitute the system of 'law and order' together constitute an example of what is often termed 'public good'. Despite the long and well-established history of private de-centralized efforts to provide these valuable services, the textbooks insist that only a coercive tax state can effectively provide the vital service of defining and securing private property. The historical evidence suggests that private sector developments may also be responsible for many so-called public goods, but the conventional texts do not mention this at all (Bairoch, 1988 [1985]).

There is a sense in which 'civility' and some aspects of a well-functioning rule of law are not only non-rivalrous, but non-excludable as well. Surely it is much more economical to do business in a region characterized by trust, basic promise-keeping and civility? This combination of background conditions, or what some writers term 'social capital,' is often a major factor in explaining the strong economic performance of certain geographical regions of the world (Putnam, 1993; Asheim, 2000). Certainly these activities employ labour in the form of judges, attorneys, notaries and sheriffs and capital goods in the forms of court houses, recording offices and jails. But most importantly, when functioning well they contribute to a radical reduction in transaction costs and facilitate trade and exchange. The importance of well-defined property rights and their protection has long been a basic precondition for the successful operation of the market system. The presence of such institutions is the key to rising living standards in any region. Law and order allow an extended division of labour and knowledge and encourage the long-term planning horizons of capitalist–entrepreneurs.

The CBD shall serve as our shorthand device for that geographical space in which humans gather to trade and exchange whether it be apples, labour services or information about new technologies. Now some CBDs have evolved from early trading centres and fairs—there is a valuable and insightful literature on the city and its development that is rich in insights and illuminates important milestones in this evolution (Henderson, 1988; Bairoch, 1988 [1985]). Other CBDs are the result of conscious human planning and sometimes resemble the work of all-knowing benevolent central planners. I have in mind here the world of real estate entrepreneurs, who sometimes create CBDs as a means of accumulating wealth and profits.

Real estate developers have crafted viable shopping malls, industrial parks, medical centres, movie theatre complexes, retirement communities and hotel/resort areas. To these significant achievements, I add the creation of trade shows and 'exhibits', which create a public space in which information can be exchanged along with handshakes and promises. Trade show entrepreneurs often provide hotel space and food services. In all these cases, the revenue from the sale or leasing of private goods helps pay for the so-called public goods.

The public goods include large and luxurious common areas set up with the conveniences conducive to business discussion and contract formation. Professional associations are managed to provide 'job markets' and informational exchanges. Even in traditional towns and cities, city planners are busy at work beautifying malls with lights, parking areas, music, security guards and other protection services, and, in some cases, even mosquito-catching machines to provide a wonderful atmosphere for shopping or just 'hanging out'. Rest rooms and places for parents to tend to infants and young children are provided as well. During the holiday seasons, popular displays of religious themes are often crowd pleasers. Public goods all, provided for business reasons.

Any pedestrian can enjoy the public display so long as he or she can get in close proximity; one person's enjoyment of the overall ambience and splendid beauty of the area does not *significantly* reduce another person's similar enjoyments—at least, not up to a point. The benefits are there for the taking, but always only to a certain limit. Beyond some point, congestion sets in and one person's enjoyment reduces the enjoyment of others.

But until that point has been reached, Joe, Janet, Alice and Bill can mutually enjoy certain comforts and we have a non-rivalrous business activity. Furthermore, one person's enjoyment may not seriously interfere with another's, within broad limits, and certainly if one person is lawfully in the area, another by definition cannot choose to exclude him or her. Non-rivalrousness, and to some extent non-excludability, seem to be dramatically different in this case from the one I presented earlier concerning consuming the apple. Indeed, in this case we have the *private* provision of *public* goods and services. This wasn't supposed to happen!

4. THE HENRY GEORGE THEOREM

And there is more to the story. The average cost of providing amenities to the CBD and other public spaces often falls as more people are allowed to congregate at the CBD. This phenomenon has a long history in economics and may be referred to as the 'scale economies' phenomenon. Falling costs are not so much the result of any subtle economic analysis as they are simple arithmetic. As you divide any given expenditure on a public good by a larger divisor, the per capita or average amount that it costs falls. It is also a mathematical fact that if the average cost of providing any public good or service falls (as when the population increases in a given territorial area), the marginal or incremental cost must be *below* that level of average cost (Hotelling, 1990 [1938]).

Consider this example. Suppose a town planner or enterprising entrepreneur has provided a large, well-lit open public space with convenient rest rooms and insect-repelling technologies. The marginal cost of providing this bundle of services to one more individual may be tiny, even close to zero. Now, economic efficiency *requires* that when something is priced, the price should reflect the marginal cost of production. But this means that the provider of these public goods and services must give them away either for free or for some ridiculously low price. At this low price, there will not be enough operating revenue to cover the total costs of providing the public goods and services in the first place (Hotelling, 1990 [1938]).

What a sad state of affairs the provider of public goods finds himself in. Competition among suppliers will drive the price down to zero, and this will produce losses for all. The textbook remedy is government intervention, through its powerful tax authority to bolster or remedy this alleged 'market failure' and make certain that the public goods are provided in the right amounts. A tall order indeed.

The great insight of the HGT is that government intervention may not be needed at all. One person's 'market failure' can often be another person's key towards entrepreneurial discovery. In this way there need not be as much government involvement other than providing the minimal rule of law within which all trading occurs.

My analysis adopts Fred Foldvary's important observation that most public goods and services are intimately connected with territory in some essential way (Foldvary, 1994, pp. 25–43). You cannot enjoy the ambience and convenience of the shopping mall's food court unless you find a way to come onto the grounds where the food court is located. Public goods are nearly always provided in a given territorial area. In addition, the size of the benefit you receive from the public good often varies in a noticeable way depending on how far away you are from the CBD. Often, the closer you are the greater the benefits and/or the more frequently you can enjoy those benefits. This creates a premium for proximity to the attractive features of the CBD.

The closer one lives to the CBD the lower the transportation costs of going to work each day and participating in valuable information networks from which so much career advancement is possible. In the case of any complex urban environment, those individuals who make their livelihood in the CBD, and have the highest opportunity costs of time, will pay the highest prices for housing. One thinks of a surgeon trying to get to the operating room in the early rush hour period or an attorney hastening to court in order not to disappoint a desperate client.

Those living farther away from the CBD will have to incur larger travelling expenses, but, on the other hand, they will enjoy either more spacious housing or a given amount of housing at significantly lower rents. If the housing market were competitive, rents and real estate values would rise in the vicinity of the CBD. Although housing desirability is a complex bundle of characteristics that includes, but surely is not limited to, proximity to the CBD, there is a tendency for a gradient of real estate prices to form. Locations most proximate to the CBD rent for the highest rents and those farthest away at lowest prices (Mills and Hamilton, 1994, pp. 132–43). This is the 'differential rent' phenomenon that fascinated Henry George and the classical school economists that preceded him.

The ghost of Henry George's economics haunts these discussions. Those who invest the resources to create the CBD may not be the same group that enjoys the benefits. Then again, what is to stop real estate entrepreneurs from both creating a CBD and profiting from the expected run-up in real estate values?

Wouldn't the expectation of enhanced land values be an obvious inducement for real estate venturers? Get options on the land nearest to the CBD, and then make those options more valuable by constructing a CBD. Can one calculate the cost of the public goods provision and compare that with the expected net land-value appreciation? Under what circumstances will one just balance out or equal the other?

The HGT is all about modelling this balance. It holds that under certain conditions the difference between the total costs of providing some public goods and services *at their efficient levels*, and the revenues that can be received from pricing those goods and services at their marginal costs (which may in fact be zero), will just match and equal the total differential rents generated by those activities on the surrounding properties. This implies that it may be feasible for private entrepreneurs to supply public goods in the form of CBDs if they can tap into the capital gains by purchasing enough of the nearby real estate at economic prices.[3]

The HGT is typically presented in the context of urban economics: a public official trying to decide how large he or she should let the city grow. If the offical wishes to maximize total utility in the region, how large a population should be invited to emigrate into the area? The challenge is engineering the optimal number of people in a given geographical area and managing that area so as not to exceed that optimal number. Richard Arnott's presentation of the theorem, rooted in the pioneering writings of Harold Hotelling, William Vickrey and Joseph Stiglitz, has this focus. Arnott's discussion is about managing a region in order to achieve an 'optimal' city size in terms of individuals living in that geographical area. According to Arnott:

> The basic Henry George Theorem states that, in an arbitrarily large, spatially homogeneous economy [that is, the residential land parcels are equal in size and identical in other ways except for location to the CBD] composed of identical individuals, in which the single source of decreasing returns to scale is the production of lots via commuting costs, labour is the only factor of production, and the distribution of economic activity over space is nontrivial, optimal city size is well defined and is characterized by *aggregate land rents equaling expenditure on the pure local public good* (Arnott, 2004, p. 1085).

Here in a nutshell we have the idea that the sum of the land rents generated by the attractive CBD is just enough to finance the construction and sustained maintenance of that CBD.

Arnott suggests that one of the novel but practical applications of the HGT has been to decide whether existing urban areas, like the city of Tokyo, are really overpopulated, as some commentators contend. Alternatively, does it still have ample room to grow larger? The research team of Y. Kanemoto, T. Ohkawara and T. Suzuki has concluded that 'Tokyo is not too large [at all]' (cited in Arnott, 2004, p. 1082). Tokyo is not too large because the benefits received by people living there still exceed on the margin the additional transportation and rental expenses associated with moving to the CBD.

But the HGT is destined for other uses besides informing the work of benevolent city planners, as I show in the next section below.

5. THE BENEVOLENT CENTRAL PLANNER DEBUNKED

As we have seen in Arnott's paper cited above, there is no *logical* reason why a *benevolent* central planner cannot draw his or her insights from the HGT and design a well-meaning and bountiful downtown program of infrastructure improvements financed by an orderly growth in population and the enhanced value thus created. It would not surprise me at all if the recent torrent of urban growth in modern China produces great interest in the HGT on the part of the Ministry of Economics. The Ministry could use the theorem to argue how the Chinese Communist Party might better manage migration into the large cities in the eastern parts of China. It is possible in principle for a benevolent central planner armed with the HGT and committed to honesty and fair play to orchestrate a genuine situation of mutual advantage and gain.

Unfortunately, everyday street smarts informed by historical understanding suggest that what might happen in a fictional abstract world of angelic city officials will not happen in a world of guileful politicians and self-dealing managers. It will certainly not happen in China, where the corruption and insider trading of the Communist Party is notorious.[4] Even on the local levels of towns and cities in places such as Massachusetts, honest management by town officials is not something that anyone takes for granted, certainly not by real estate developers who often have to pay up or risk losing their projects midstream. Homeowners in the way of the bulldozer find that their property rights can sometimes be condemned under the eminent domain laws. These laws may be favoured by the real estate entrepreneurs, who get the locations they need at a reasonable price by buying the property title from the State after they have taken the title away from private persons (Peterson, 2005, p. 25).

Those in charge of the basic infrastructure design, whether they are managers in the building department or the zoning commission officials, can promote their own private interests, often betraying the public trust. The HGT shows how, by making real estate purchases secretly and through trusted cohorts ('straws'), an insider can get wealthier through private 'capital gains' at the expense of the developers. Unlike Henry George's land speculators who get rich 'doing nothing', these speculators get rich doing quite a bit of political manoeuvring. Such manoeuvring is a hard day's work. Laymen join the process as well by attending town meetings and befriending licensing commissioners.They personify the 'rent seekers' that economists are fond of mentioning in related contexts (Tullock, 1989).

Also, the costs of these projects – the projects whose expenditure will be divided among hordes of taxpayers – have an annoying tendency to rise. Each person has an interest in this not happening, but no single individual finds it financially worthwhile to expose the shenanigans associated with the award of contracts for the construction about to begin. Kickbacks, over-billing and a variety of 'tricks of the trade' now greet the weary real estate owner when dealing with the permitting processes involved. It seems unrealistic to expect any place in the urban economics literature for this topic; the abstract model of urban land use fails to account for the machinations and the dealings of everyday local politics. The potential gains of letting one property owner make the infrastructure improvements, many of which have that public goods character, while other property owners look on and capture the benefits, is a brute reality of modern administrative regulation. All successful real estate developers have to assume this risk and some way align their interests with those of the regulators if they expect to complete their projects.

6. THE ENTREPRENEURIAL PROCESS

The HGT steers us towards a fuller appreciation of the work of the real estate developer in a modern regulatory environment. Still, there are some unsung heroes of the market process who somehow manage to provide public spaces where industry can agglomerate and shoppers can gather. The idea is to capture the enhanced value of the most proximate real estate by playing by the rules of the game. Surely, it must be a tricky business to make commitments and then avoid being held-up afterwards by the canny zoning commissioners or the building inspector who questions whether the regulations are being adhered to correctly. Also, those citizens at the town meetings often grasp the potential of well-situated property rights and act accordingly to make gains.

I should not be read as stating that the real estate developer is an innocent and the government official is the corrupt extortionist of capital gains. Where there is bribery, there are both those who give bribes and those who take them. It is the classic struggle over the gains from trade. Still, it is amazing how many great projects do get completed by the private entrepreneurs despite the many rent seekers who gang up against them.

From retirement communities to shopping malls, condominium developments, hotel complexes, trailer and industrial parks, public spaces come into existence. We appreciate the pioneering work of Spencer Heath MacCallum, who recognized this important feature of modern real estate development (MacCallum, 1970). More recently, Foldvary extended MacCallum's work by recognizing the achievements of Walt Disney World, The Reston Association, Arden Village and others in the creative (but legal) financing of important communities and public spaces (Foldvary, 1994, pp. 114–93; see especially, Foldvary's explanation of how Spencer Heath MacCallum draws on the pioneering work of his grandfather, Spencer Heath). These examples suggest that this marvellous process of value creation at work is quite common and can be found in nearly every town and city where a private market in real estate exists and is allowed to function.

Consider a retirement community where the developer provides a golf course, swimming pool area, a myriad of sewage and water lines, communication cables, and so on, and a central club house with restaurant and stores. The profits come from the difference between the costs of the project and the sale of the residential and commercial properties associated with the project. The costs include the original purchase price(s) of the land, the improvements to the land, including the zoning changes and related variances that had to be petitioned down at the local town government, and the 'rents' extracted from the contractor by those connected directly or indirectly to the political process.

In this case, we have the provision of a 'public good' that is strictly tied in some way to 'location'. The good is largely non-rivalrous, but those most proximate to the public good hope to obtain the most sizeable benefits. The entrepreneur comes up with a novel combination of property rights that allows him or her to capture part of the value created by the project.

7. BUSINESS EDUCATORS LARGELY IGNORE THE HGT

I doubt that an experienced real estate developer after reading this chapter would learn anything really new about the real world of local politics and strategic insider dealing. Indeed, even real estate brokers can figure out how combining property rights in new ways can create extra value in most residential communities, and many do in brokering deals. In Brookline, Massachusetts, where overnight parking on the public streets is illegal, a broker can enhance the value of any residential property by scouting out and obtaining an overnight parking space on another privately owned property. Reshuffling property rights in novel combinations and capturing value by so doing is, as we learned from Schumpter a century ago, the very heart of the entrepreneurial process.

What I find amazing is how little of the HGT and the insights it provides ever gets into the standard and ordinary curriculum of economics major programs or even entrepreneurial programs at colleges and universities. There is an unfortunate tendency to dismiss theoretical studies as too abstract for the training and enlightenment of business leaders (Mintzberg, 2004).

Indeed, my own recent field trip to a major bookstore that contains about a score of books for sale on the general subject of 'making millions in real estate' found that, almost without exception, these texts fail to even mention how restructuring and recombining of property rights can be a major source of value creation in a market economy. One author insisted that 'most real estate books will tell you, the top three criteria for a property are: Location, Location, Location!', but nothing much seems to follow from this except that 'a good location…may be a subjective thing' (Roos, 2005, p. 106). True, a good location may indeed be a subjective thing, and that is why investing resources to create an attractive centre at which valuable public goods and services are generated, while maintaining cash and control rights on proximate locations can be a lucrative business strategy.

Another immensely popular read by Tyler G. Hicks comes much closer to the issues and insights raised by the HGT when Hicks reminds his readers that 'towns and cities usually grow in population as time passes. This growing population needs space—that is, land. To satisfy the demand for more space, almost all communities expand horizontally' (Hicks, 2000, p. 94). But the relevance of this important fact is left unexplained. The front cover of the book proclaims that over '300,000 copies [were] sold'. Perhaps Hicks and his colleagues are saving the insights of the HGT for an advanced course about how to make billions in real estate.

Both in the case of academic curriculum, and especially in the area of entrepreneurial studies in the business school environment, we find precious little about the HGT. Its related insights and dramatic examples remain largely undiscussed. Economics professors teach market structure analysis to business students, and the basic ideas of segmenting markets and price discrimination are taught as well. But the myopic focus on price theory neglects the economics of the Schumpeterian entrepreneur in modern settings. It is tragic how so much of interest and importance gets left behind.

I can only speculate on what may have caused this black-out of the real politics of public goods provision by private sector entrepreneurs. Part of the problem stems from the unfortunate direction economic theory took after 1950. The geographical location of economic activity was largely ignored. Paul Krugman attributes this peculiar turn of events to a divergence in economics between the study of economic geography and the study of international trade theory (Krugman, 2000, p. 49). He goes on to explain that the study of international trade theory does not in any way preclude the study of increasing returns, the agglomeration of industry and the enjoyment of public goods and services. Still, it is a matter of history that this literature did in fact ignore these remarkable phenomena. As a result, international trade theory in economics largely ignored the exciting problems of economic geography, such as explaining why certain industries cluster and real estate prices span out in particular ways. During the 1980s, developments in international trade theory took a turn for the better, and the 'New Trade Theory brought increasing returns, imperfect competition, and multiple equilibria firmly into the mainstream' (Krugman, 2000, p. 49). While these developments were under way, the urban economic theorists explored the logic of the HGT but not with any eye towards practical applications in entrepreneurial studies.

8. CONCLUSION

I insist that the study of location – how a competitive real estate market allocates rights to location sometimes more efficiently than at other times and how market opportunities are created for brilliant entrepreneurial venturing when inefficiencies appear – remains an important and rich part of the story of modern capitalism. The capitalist process pushes through and works around the corruptions and 'politics' of local government. The HGT shows how public goods are deeply embedded for their enjoyment in territorial advantages and how with competitive real estate markets entrepreneurs can reshuffle and redefine those rights so as to produce mutual gains.

Consumers choose private goods in different contexts and in different ways. Sometimes they are customers in stores balancing the characteristics of products and services against each other; other times they are tenants and homeowners choosing where to live and work. The HGT is an essential part of the full story of entrepreneurial venturing in the 20th and 21st Centuries.

While it has earned a noteworthy place in the texts dealing with urban planning and city government management and taxation, the HGT is much more robust and applicable to broader issues about real estate development, as I have suggested in this chapter. I have also praised the entrepreneur–landowner for his or her foresight and ability to create value by recombining property rights and navigating the regulatory maze of modern urban life. Although I have recognized the practical reality of real estate developers having to obtain permits and variances, and to struggle with the selective enforcement of regulations until certain bribes have been made, I have not elevated the real estate developer into that iconic hero of modern capitalist enterprise that we sometimes find among political writers.

All I have done is follow the lead of MacCallum and others by turning Henry George on his head. Certainly, not all gains in real estate come from the brainless speculator holding onto land and scheming to keep it off the market. There is more to making capital gains than that. Speculation is an important and valuable part of the entrepreneurial process (Rothbard, 2004, pp. 1212–14). In fact, the private provision of public goods, often in the form of CBDs, is one of the most stunning accomplishments of private entrepreneurs in the post-war U.S. economy.

I suspect a significant part of the gains on large real estate projects comes from the creative and forward-looking methods of the real estate developer who must navigate around the grabbing hand of local regulatory officials as well as other developers competing for the favour of consumers and industry leaders in order to both create and capture value. The HGT reminds us of all that is involved and some of what does not get mentioned in the private production and financing of public goods and services.

NOTES

1. Even those who are elderly, retired and managing on fixed incomes, curl up in agony at the thought of another reassessment of their home. The seniors also take some comfort in the knowledge that if the town really does make improvements, they will be able to sell their property at an even more favourable price and move to a location farther away from the CBD.
2. It also can be used by any tax-state to rationalize restrictions on human liberty and mobility. As we explain below, the HGT has been applied to the optimal size of a city analysis. If an additional migrant were found to add more to congestion and other costs than he or she adds to productivity, it might prove necessary to prohibit this migrant's move to the city or charge a 'migration fee' to discourage migration. I remark below how the Communist Party in China might draw ideas from the HGT (Section 5).
3. Of course, with the licensing and permitting processes required by local towns and city governments, the chances of 'insiders' obtaining information about future economic development and obtaining options on the best locations may make the real estate entrepreneur's

gains much smaller. That is, he or she may only be able to obtain the needed property rights at 'non-economic prices' as a result of the transparencies of the political licensing processes. The savvy real estate developer must take all this into consideration when planning the project in the first place.

4.   On the Corruption Perceptions Index for 2003, China was ranked in 66th place which is about half-way down the list from least corrupt to most corrupt (see Lambsdorff, 2004, p. 285). I suspect that one very obvious form of corruption is associated with the taking away of the land from the farmers with minimal compensation so real estate venturers can benefit. The arbitrariness of many of these incidents is the other side of a lack of a competitive real estate market in China.

REFERENCES

Andelson, Robert (ed.) (2000), *Land Value Taxation Around the World*, Malden, MA: Blackwell Publishers.

Arnott, Richard (2004), 'Does the Henry George Theorem Provide a Practical Guide to Optimal City Size? *American Journal of Economics and Sociology*, **63**, 1057–90.

Arnott, R., K. Arrow, A. Atkinson and J. Dreze (eds.) (1977), *Public Economics: Selected Papers*, Cambridge, U.K.: Cambridge University Press.

Asheim, Bjorn T. (2000), 'Industrial Districts: The Contribution of Marshall and Beyond', in Gordon L. Clark, Maryann P. Feldman and Meric S. Gertler, (eds.), *The Oxford Handbook of Economic Geography*, Oxford: Oxford University, pp. 413–31.

Bairoch, Paul (1988) [1985], *Cities and Economic Development: From the Dawn of History to the Present*, Chicago: University of Chicago Press.

Barker, Charles Albro (1991) [1955], *Henry George*, New York: Robert Schalkenbach Foundation.

Fisher, Irving (2003) [1906], *The Nature of Capital and Income*, San Diego, California: Simon Publications.

Foldvary, Fred (1994), *Public Goods and Private Communities: The Market Provision of Social Services*, Aldershot, U.K. and Brookfield, U.S.A.: Edward Elgar.

Fuchs, Victor R. (2005), 'Health, Government, and Irving Fisher,' in R. W. Dimand and J. Geanakoplos (eds), *Celebrating Irving Fisher: The Legacy of a Great Economist*, Malden, MA: Blackwell Publishers, pp. 443–62.

Fujita, Masahisa and Jacques-Francois Thisse (2002), *Economics of Agglomeration: Cities, Industrial Location, and Regional Growth*, Cambridge, U.K.: Cambridge University Press.

George, Henry (1882) [1879], *Progress and Poverty*, New York: Appleton and Company.

Hanson, Gordon H. (2000), in G. L. Clark, M. P. Feldman and M. S. Gertler, (eds.) *The Oxford Handbook of Economic Geography*, Oxford: Oxford University Press, pp. 477–93.

Henderson, J. Vernon (1988), *Urban Development: Theory, Fact, and Illusion*, New York: Oxford University Press.

Hicks, Tyler G. (2000), *How to Make Millions in Real Estate in 3 Years Starting with No Cash*, 3rd edition, New Jersey: Prentice Hall.

Hotelling, Harold (1990) [1938], 'The General Welfare in Relation to Problems of Taxation and of Railway and Utility Rates' in A. C. Darnell (ed.), *The Collected Economics Articles of Harold Hotelling* , New York: Springer-Verlag, pp. 141–65.

Krugman, Paul (2000), 'Where in the World is the "New Economic Geography"?' in Gordon L. Clark, Maryann P. Feldman and Meric S. Gertler (eds.), *The Oxford Handbook of Economic Geography*, Oxford: Oxford University Press, pp. 49–60.

Lambsdorff, Johann Graf (2004), 'Corruption Perceptions Index 2003.' In R. Hodess et al. (eds), *Global Corruption Report 2004 [of] Transparency International*, Serling, Virginia: Pluto Press, pp. 282–7.

MacCallum, Spencer Heath (1970), *The Art of Community*, Menlo Park, CA: Institute for Human Studies.

Mills, Edwin S. and Bruce W. Hamilton (1994), *Urban Economics*, 5th edition, New York: Harper Collins.

Mintzberg, Henry (2004), *Managers Not MBAs*, San Francisco, CA: Berrett-Koehler.

Peterson, Ivar (2005), 'There Goes the Old Neighorhood, to Revitalization,' *New York Times*, 30 January, A25.

Putnam, R. (1993), *Making Democracy Work: Civic Traditions in Modern Italy*, Princeton: Princeton University Press.

Roos, Dolf De (2005), *Real Estate Riches: How to Become Rich Using Your Banker's Money*, New York: John Wiley.

Rothbard, Murray (2004) [1962], *Man, Economy, and State: A Treatise on Economic Principles*, Auburn, Alabama: Ludwig von Mises Institute.

Schumpeter, Joseph A. (1961) [1911], *The Theory of Economic Development*, New York: Oxford University Press.

Scott, Allen J. (2005), *On Hollywood: The Place, the Industry*, Princeton, NJ: Princeton University Press.

Tideman, Nicolaus (ed.) (1994), 'The Economics of Efficient Taxes on Land,' in *Land and Taxation*, London: Shepheard-Walwyn, pp. 103–140.

Tullock, Gordon (1989), *The Economics of Special Privilege and Rent Seeking*, Dordrecht: Kluwer Publishers.

Vickrey, William (1977), 'The City as a Firm.' In R. Arnott, K. Arrow, A. Atkinson and J. Dreze, (eds.), *Public Economics*, Cambridge, U.K.: Cambridge University Press, pp. 339–49.

Wenzer, Kenneth C. (ed.) (2003), *Henry George: Collected Journalistic Writings*, 4 vols., Armonk, New York: M. E. Sharpe.

7. Henry George's Land Reform: The Distinction between Private Ownership and Private Possession

John Pullen

ABSTRACT

Henry George stated that the taxation of land rent would amount to the abolition of the institution of private ownership of land, thereby alienating all those who, whether for economic or ideological reasons, regard the private ownership of land as essential for social order and progress. George believed that under his proposed reform the private ownership of land would be replaced by private possession. But his distinction between ownership and possession appears to have been based on a misconception of the nature of private ownership. His proposed reform could have been more logically described as a conditional, modified, or restricted private ownership of land, rather than as the abolition of private ownership of land.

GEORGE'S REFORM POLICY: INITIAL AND MODIFIED VERSIONS

It is well known that Henry George believed that radical land reform was the essential solution to the problem of persistent poverty in the midst of progress. The reform that he proposed – viz., the taxation of land rent – is quite clear and unambiguous; but whether this reform amounts to, or was intended to amount to, the abolition of the private ownership of land as a legal institution, was left far from clear. The aim of this chapter is to explore the distinctions made by George between ownership[1] of land and possession of land, and between common ownership of land and private ownership of land. One of the conclusions of the chapter is that the lack of clarity in these concepts in George's writings has impeded the acceptance of his reform.

His initial statements of the reform appear to be an unequivocal plea for land nationalization and for the abolition of private ownership of land. He stated emphatically:

> we must...substitute for the individual ownership of land a common ownership....*We must make land common property* (George, 1956 [1879], p. 328, emphasis added)

and argued that since private ownership of land is the cause of the problem: nothing short of the abolition of private ownership of land can rectify matters. To remove an evil one must remove its cause. He regarded all other proposed remedies as mere palliatives, more or less inefficacious.

But despite having presented the case for land nationalization in such ringing terms, George then proceeded to offer a modified and less radical measure, viz., the public ownership not of the land itself but of the land value, to be achieved by imposing a tax on every portion of land equal to its annual value. He believed that this measure would amount to the abolition of private ownership of land, and he said that those who occupy and use the land after the implementation of this reform would be merely its 'possessors', not its 'proprietors'.

This distinction between possession and ownership was not formally defined, but can be inferred from statements such as:

> I do not propose to either purchase or to confiscate private property in land. The first would be unjust; the second, needless. Let the individuals who now hold it retain, if they want to, possession of what they are pleased to call *their* land. Let them continue to call it *their* land. Let them buy and sell, and bequeath and devise it. We may safely leave them the shell, if we take the kernel. *It is not necessary to confiscate land; it is only necessary to confiscate rent.*

and

> In form, the ownership of land would remain just as now. No owner of land need be dispossessed (George, 1956 [1879], pp. 405, 406, emphasis added).

Such statements indicate that for George the distinction between ownership of land and possession of land rests on the ownership of the land rent. The rights to 'buy and sell, and bequeath and devise' are merely the 'shell' or the 'form' of ownership, but the right to the ownership of the land rent is the 'kernel'. When the state takes over ownership of the land rent through taxation, George believed it effectively removes the essence of private ownership of land, and transforms private ownership into private possession, even though the possessors may still regard themselves (and may be permitted to regard themselves) as landowners.

He seems to have argued that private possession involves security of tenure for the land and its improvements, but excludes ownership of the land rent; whereas land ownership includes ownership of the land rent. By vesting the land rent in the state through taxation he therefore believed that he had transformed private ownership into private possession. He argued that the private possession of land is desirable because without security of tenure and the right of bequest, land would not be properly used or developed, and the very structure of society could be endangered. But, for George, this does not mean that the possessor of the land needs to be also its owner: 'there is no more necessity for making a man the absolute and exclusive owner of land, in order to induce him to improve it, than there is of burning down a house in order to cook a pig' (George, 1956 [1879], p. 397).

George's reform in its modified version therefore did not mean the abolition of all rights of private individuals to land. Rather, he would maintain the right of private possession of land while taking away the right of private ownership of land. If in his system it is the ownership of the land value that determines whether we have a system of private ownership or private possession, it would logically follow that the state ownership of land values could not logically coexist with private ownership in land; they would be mutually exclusive concepts.

LAND RENT AND LAND OWNERSHIP

However, George's distinction between private ownership of land and private possession of land could be challenged. There seems to be no valid reason why a person who has a secure perpetual tenure with the right of sale or bequest, and a right to the value of the improvements, should not truly be called an owner, and the holding regarded as private ownership, even though it does not include ownership of the land rent. It seems unwarranted to refuse to call a person the owner of land simply because the ownership does not include ownership of the land rent. It would have sufficed, for George's purpose, to have advocated the public ownership of the land rent and the private ownership of the land itself. Rather than describe his ideal social set-up as one of private possession of land but not private ownership, he could have simply referred to a conditional, modified, or restricted private ownership, i.e., private ownership of land in the full sense in which that word is currently used, with one exception—the land rent would be publicly owned.

When one prescribes a system of private ownership that is subject to certain exceptions or limitations, there is obviously a point beyond which the exceptions and limitations become the rule, and the system ceases to be one of private ownership.[2] The difficulty is to determine which features constitute the essence of private ownership and which are merely accidental. George himself referred to delusions that can result from confounding the accidental with the essential. If he had made a systematic attempt to expound the essence of ownership, private or public, he might have considered the possibility that the private ownership of land rent does not constitute the essence of private ownership of land.

The right of private ownership of land should be defined not in terms of one, and only one, right, but as a basket of rights. It would be beyond the scope of this chapter to attempt to provide a comprehensive list of all the rights that might conceivably be held in this basket. But the list would, presumably, include the right to use the land in question; the right to exclude others from use of the land; the right to dispose of the land by way of sale, gift, or bequest, etc. Now, in practice, these rights are often subject to restrictions. For example, one's right to use one's land might be modified by public health and town planning regulations. Your right to bequeath it to whomsoever you wish might be challenged by persons who feel they have been unfairly disinherited. And your assumed right to retain any increments in its value might be limited by government taxation.

ABOLITION OR RESTRICTION OF PRIVATE OWNERSHIP

The question therefore becomes: At what point do these restrictions amount to a negation of the right of private ownership, to its transformation into public ownership, and to its replacement by private possession? If we take out of the basket the right to use your suburban block of land as a piggery, have we in fact abolished your right of private ownership, or merely modified it? If the law states that parents must bequeath their land equally amongst their children, has their right of private ownership been destroyed or just infringed? What are the *essential* elements of private ownership, and what elements are merely *accidents,* in the sense that they can be limited or even removed entirely, without changing the essence? In the case of George's policy of land rent taxation, we are confronted with the problem of establishing a distinction between a thing and its value, and in asking whether exchange value is intrinsic to the essence of the thing or merely an external accidental quality. When the state takes away some or all of land rent, does it effect a change of ownership of the land itself, or does it merely remove one of the contingent accidental qualities of the land without altering its status as private ownership?

It could be argued that George misunderstood the nature of private ownership in land, and wrongly believed that the taxing away of the rent of land would destroy private ownership. On grounds of both logic and expediency, he could have presented his reform proposal without resorting to the distinction between private possession of land and private ownership in land. On logical grounds, he would have been quite justified in describing his policy as a restriction on private ownership rather than as the abolition of private ownership.[3]

POLITICAL IMPLICATIONS

Without being privy to George's subconscious, we may never know his reasons
for choosing to describe his proposal as the abolition of private ownership of
land and its replacement by private possession, even though he could have
described it simply as a modified or restricted version of private ownership. It
is possible that he was motivated in introducing this nomenclature by political
expediency.[4] He observed that in America in general and in California in particular the tenancy rate (i.e., the proportion of non-landowners to landowners) was
high, with many people living as tenants or lessees of houses and farms, rather
than as owner-occupiers or mortgagor-occupiers. George's aim was not merely
to have his ideas accepted at an intellectual or academic level, but to see them
implemented as practical policies; and he possibly thought that by describing
his reform as the abolition of private ownership of land it would have greater
popular appeal — and with a widening of the franchise, greater electoral force.

But here he appears to have badly misjudged the temper of the times. His
attack on private ownership of land might have appealed to some more radically minded propertyless members of society who would find comfort in a
program destined to destroy all private ownership of land; but would not have
appealed to those propertyless who hanker after private ownership, especially
of land, which has almost universally been regarded (rightly or wrongly) as a
sign and guarantee of security, individuality, and fortune. If George had been
content to express his ideas in less extreme language and to put forward his
scheme in terms of a restriction of the rights of private ownership, instead of
the abolition of private ownership, his policy might have been much more
acceptable at the time. His unfortunate choice of terminology possibly served
to alienate a considerable body of opinion that might have otherwise rallied
to his cause.

If he were alive today, and putting forward the same reform proposal in the
same terminology, he would find that his distinction between private possession
of land and private ownership of land, and his call for the abolition of the latter,
would prove to be even more politically inexpedient than when he first put it
forward. The desire to own land has shown no signs of abating over the last
100 years. There will always be some who rent because they prefer to rent than
to buy, and others who rent because, although they prefer to buy, they cannot
afford to. But by comparison with the late 19th Century the tenancy rate today
in America (and in England, Australia, and elsewhere) appears to have fallen.
Increased affluence has provided the opportunity for many of the 'propertyless
proletariat' to become owner-occupiers (or at least mortgagor-occupiers) with
a vested interest in the institution of private ownership of land. Would any land
reform proposal win their support if it were described by its proponents as the
abolition of private ownership of land?

George realized the advisability of introducing reforms with a minimum of upset to the existing order:

> It is an axiom of statesmanship...that great changes can best be brought about under old forms. ...It is the natural method. When nature would make a higher type, she takes a lower one and develops it (George, 1956 [1879], pp. 404-5).

For this reason he considered Herbert Spencer's proposal for declaring all land public property and leasing it to the highest bidders to be far too radical; it 'would involve a needless shock to present customs and habits of thought—which is to be avoided' (George, 1956 [1879], p. 404).

He could have further avoided shocking public standards if he had described his policy as one of modifying private ownership of land—which I believe it is, rather than one of abolishing private ownership of land—which I believe it is not.

LAND TAXATION OR LAND NATIONALIZATION

So far, I have assumed George's land reform proposal to be the one described above as the modified proposal—the taxation of land rent—rather than the original one (to 'make land common property'). But there remains a fundamental and difficult problem of textual exegesis. Of the two proposals (the original land nationalization, or the modified land rent taxation), which did he really prefer? His followers differ in their interpretations. Some say that as his practical policy recommendation was land taxation, he should be seen as a land taxer, not a land nationalizer. But others argue that his main concern was to nationalize land, and that the taxing of land rent was only an alternative put forward to circumvent an established prejudice against state ownership, people being more willing to accept taxation by the state than ownership by the state. According to this contention, land taxation is merely land nationalization in disguise, a clever device used by George to implement nationalization under the cloak of fiscal policy.

Henry George's own words lend some credence to this interpretation. Asking how we could secure our equal rights to the land, he stated:

> The ideal way...in a new country would be to treat the land as the property of the whole, to allow individuals to possess it and use it, paying to the whole a proper rent for any superiority in the price of land they were using....In an old country, there is a very great advantage in calling the rent a tax. People are used to the payment of taxes. They are not used to the formal ownership of land by the community and to the letting of it out in that way. Therefore, as society is now constituted, and in our communities as they now exist, we propose to move towards an ideal along the line of taxation (George and Hyndman, 1889, pp. 4–5).

It is not surprising, then, that some should interpret him as an advocate of land nationalization. For example, a 1910 British Labour Party pamphlet by G. N. Brown began: 'Henry George...was a land nationalizer, who yet objected to the term' (Brown, 1910, p. 1), and John Rae regarded George as a partial or agrarian socialist, despite the fact that George denied the label and had socialists expelled from the United Labour Party in America in 1887.

The question will probably never be solved to everyone's satisfaction. Those supporters of George who have anti-socialist leanings will continue to interpret George as an anti-socialist land taxer; and those who have socialist tendencies will continue to adopt George into their fold as a land nationalizer.

SUMMARY

This chapter has attempted to argue that George's description of his reform program as the abolition of private ownership of land, and its replacement by private possession, was based on a misunderstanding of the concept of private ownership. It contends that George's reform program is not logically inconsistent with the institution of private ownership of land. It also argues that his adoption of that terminology has impeded the acceptance of his reform proposal — and will continue to do so to the extent that present-day Georgists maintain that strict terminological tradition. The result has been, and will be, to distract attention from the major contributions he made to the evolution of economic thought on the land question. In my view his three major contributions were:

1. By insisting that 'equality' means not only political equality and equality before the law, but also equality in the use of natural resources, he has given a great impetus to the egalitarian movement and must be regarded as one of its leading figures.
2. He was one of the earliest writers to see *how* equality of land ownership could be effected without actually dividing up land into small and equal pieces [though this was how he was interpreted by some late 19th and early 20th Century governments — see Introduction to this volume], and without destroying the security of tenure necessary for long-term improvements, viz., by equality in the ownership of land value.
3. His system was a genuine attempt to find a middle way between the two extremes of private and public ownership of land. Unfortunately, he described his middle way as the abolition of private ownership of land and its replacement by private possession, whereas in my view his middle way could be more correctly described as modified, restricted, or conditional private ownership. He aimed to abolish the evils of withholding and monopoly of land, and at the same time avoid the dangers of bureaucracy,

corruption, and dictatorship potentially inherent in state ownership. This was perhaps the most important aspect of his work, and one that is still relevant today.

NOTES

1. For the purpose of this chapter, the terms 'ownership' and 'property' are taken as synonymous. George made use of both terms, but (except in quotations) the former will be preferred in this chapter, being the term more commonly used in such discussions today.
2. The question of whether, and at what point, town planning restrictions on private ownership amount to expropriation was considered in great detail in the *Report of the Select Committee on Compensation and Betterment* (The Uthwatt Report), London: H.M.S.O., 1942.
3. This was the position taken, for example, by the Commission of Inquiry into Land Tenures (Chairman, Justice R. Else-Mitchell), Canberra, Australia, 1976, where it was recommended that, while commercial and industrial land should ideally be held under leasehold tenure from the Crown, residential land should remain as freehold tenure, but with its future development value reserved to the Crown. In other words, the Commission accepted that a residential lot could remain in 'private ownership' in the usual sense of that expression even though it no longer included a right to increments in land rent.
4. George's decision to describe his reform as the abolition of private ownership of land might also have been based on rhetorical considerations. Did he deliberately adopt this revolutionary form of words, not because he really meant that private ownership of land should be abolished, but because he wished to issue a strong challenge to orthodox thinking and to attract publicity for his cause? As a skilled orator, he would have been well aware of the importance of rhetorical devices. I am indebted to a referee for this suggestion.

REFERENCES

Brown, G. N. (1910), *Henry George*, London: Labour Press.
George, Henry (1956) [1879], Progress *and Poverty*, New York: Robert Schalkenbach Foundation.
George, H. and H. M. Hyndman (1889), *The Single Tax Versus Social Democracy: Report of the Debate*, London: Justice.

PART III

Current Debates

8. The Philosophy and Feasibility of Henry George's Land-Value Tax: Criticisms and Defences, with particular reference to the Problem of the Land-rich-and-income-poor

John Pullen

Henry George's arguments for a land-value tax (LVT) have been subjected to many criticisms over the years. This paper will be concerned with criticisms on the following themes:[1]
1. Community-created values and unearned increments
2. Equal rights to land and land value
3. The Single Tax
4. Private property rights in land
5. Ability to pay
6. The land-rich-and-income-poor problem
7. Is the LVT practicable?

1. COMMUNITY-CREATED VALUES AND UNEARNED INCREMENTS

George argued that increases in land values are created by the community, not by individual owners or developers, and therefore ought to belong to the community. From this he argued that any increase in land value that accrued to an individual person or business is an 'unearned increment' (adopting the term used by John Stuart Mill), and that the private appropriation of the unearned increment is morally wrong (adopting a Lockean or labour theory of property rights).[2]

This argument is rejected by land developers who insist that it is they who create a significant part of the increased value of their estates, by their skilful design and marketing. It is also rejected by those who argue that, even if increases in land values are created by the community, the same could be said of increases in the values of other factors of production and other goods and services. Land is by no means the only recipient of unearned increments.[3] Countless instances can be cited where increments in wages, share prices, commodity prices, etc. are unearned, in the sense of occurring because of events and persons external to those who benefit from them. Life itself is an unearned increment. The community-created and unearned-increment arguments do not therefore provide a convincing basis for a special tax on land. If they are used to justify a special land tax, they can also be used to justify special taxes on labour, capital, and products.

George held that a tax on the income from land is the only legitimate way for a government to raise revenue, because all other incomes arise from human effort, and therefore, again applying a Lockean principle, they ought to belong exclusively to the individuals who have produced them, and the government has no moral right to tax them away.

Critics have replied that the productive efforts of individuals have been enhanced by the government or the community – for example, by government expenditures on health, education, and urban infrastructure, and by the more amorphous but no less influential factor of cultural heritage. Because the government has been to some extent influential in the production of individual wealth and income, it is morally justified in sharing in them through taxation. The critics thus use the same Lockean principle to rebut George. George argued that the government or the community has a right (and indeed an exclusive right) to the increases in land value that occur because of community influence. Critics argue that, because of the role played by community influences in the rewards accruing to labour and capital, land-value tax is not the only ethically justifiable tax.

A further counter-argument against George's position is that if the members of a community democratically choose to raise their government revenue by some measure instead of, or in addition to, an LVT, should they not have a moral right to do so?

2. EQUAL RIGHTS TO LAND AND LAND VALUE

Another objection to George's policy centres on his principle of equal rights to land and land value. Although George presented this as a self-evident truth that needs only to be stated to be believed, it does not command universal assent. It suffers from the fact that it is an *a priori* statement to which a contradictory *a priori* statement can readily be juxtaposed. At an *a priori* level of discourse, a statement such as 'each human being has an equal right to the ownership of the world's natural resources', no matter how vehemently and frequently repeated, is no more compelling than its contradictory statement. To carry conviction, the argument needs to descend from the *a priori* level to a utilitarian or consequentialist level of discourse, and to show that a world in which land value is regarded as a community resource and as a gift of nature belonging equally to all human beings will be, according to clearly defined criteria, a better place. An empirical proof of the benefits of an equal sharing of land value would require a series of social experiments comparing the progress of two societies, equal in all respects, except that one shared its land values equally and the other did not. As such social experiments are a practical impossibility, the question will never be completely resolved at an empirical level, but will depend on a theoretical analysis of expected outcomes, as well as on the extent to which the principle of equal rights to natural resources appeals to popular perceptions of natural rights. Although appeals to natural rights are often disparaged in philosophical circles, their influence on practical policy remains strong, and, as John King has noted, there has been a revival of interest in the use of the concept of natural rights as a defence of property rights.[4] If the equal-rights-to-land argument is to be dismissed solely because it is an *a priori* argument and has not been empirically verified, then so also should many other *a priori* principles that have come to be generally regarded as basic human rights – such as, the right to be treated equally by law, the right not to be a slave of another person, the right to vote and for all votes to be equal, and the right to life, liberty and the pursuit of happiness – none of which, as far I am aware, has ever been empirically verified.

It should be noted that although George, in arguing the case for the LVT, made use of the three arguments – equal rights to land, community created value, and unearned increment – often combining them in the one paragraph, the first can stand independently of the last two, and is not impugned if the last two are deemed to be of questionable merit. The emotive nature of the last two won widespread popular acceptance for George's ideas in his lifetime especially when supported by his rhetorical skills, but later generations have not found them intellectually compelling. In the long term, they have hindered rather than helped the case for LVT.

Critics also have pointed to an ambiguity and weakness in George's principle of equal rights to natural resources. He spoke as if there is a clear distinction between 'man' and land, or between human beings and non-human (or natural) resources; and he argued that things made by 'man' belong to the individual producer, but that non-'man'-made resources should belong to society as a whole and should not be the private property of individuals.

This dichotomy between 'man' and nature is difficult to sustain. A person's output requires the help of natural resources – even if it is only air and food and somewhere to be – and is therefore produced in a causal sense only partially by that person. Moreover, the human person not only uses external resources, but also embodies natural resources, so that when a person acts in a productive process, the output is partially attributable to the natural and internal resources that are part of that person.

The unity (as opposed to the dichotomy) of 'man' and nature was recognized by George in a number of places. For example, in a speech delivered in New York in 1895, he said: 'Our very bodies, our flesh and blood are drawn from the land and to the land they must return again',[5] and in an address given in 1894 he said: 'Take from man all that belongs to land and what do you have but a disembodied spirit. Our very flesh and blood comes from the land. To the land it must return again' (CJW, III, p. 264). However, the fiscal implications of this general concept of unity were not introduced into his economic discussions; by stressing the dichotomy between 'man' and nature, he sought to reinforce the principle that the products of land should be taxed but the products of 'man' should be untaxed.

If George's principle of equal rights to natural resources is taken literally, without qualification, then it follows logically, not that an individual's output should belong exclusively to the individual (and should not be taken away from the individual by the state through income tax) but that some part[6] of each person's income should be shared equally by everyone else. The fact that the financial success of talented people is partly the result of the natural resources within their make-up would therefore justify, on this principle, an income tax that distributes a portion of their wealth and income amongst the rest of the community. George's principle of equal rights to natural resources logically justifies taxes other than a Single Tax on the value of (external) natural resources and logically negates his principle that the individual has a full and exclusive right to whatever the individual produces.

George's principle of common or equal rights to natural resources is logically sustainable only if it is qualified in a way that distinguishes between natural resources that are external to the person and natural resources that are internal to the person. An anti-Georgist could argue that the impossibility of disentangling 'man' and nature means that George's principle of equal rights to land can never be implemented in practice. A neo-Georgist,[7] however, could argue that if the principle were re-formulated as 'equal rights to the natural resources that are external to the individual person', it remains both logically acceptable and capable of implementation.

The principle of equal rights to land has important political, ethical, and economic implications. It implies that those who are enjoying a more than equal share of the value of external natural resources are involved in institutional exploitation of those who have a less than equal share, or no share at all. The principle of equal rights to land also implies that the younger generation is suffering a monstrous intergenerational injustice.

3. THE SINGLE TAX

A very common criticism of George's position is that, if the LVT is to be the only tax, the revenue it will generate will not be sufficient for the needs of modern governments. This insufficiency allegation is often presented as an unanswerable criticism of the Single Tax, and as strong enough in itself to discredit George's entire system, irrespective of any merit in other aspects of his system.

Far from thinking that the LVT revenue might not be adequate, George usually argued that the revenue would be more than adequate, and would permit even greater government expenditure. In an article in the *North American Review* in July 1881, he referred approvingly to an expansion of the functions and revenue of government by increased taxation, provided that there was no extravagance and no increase of government debt.

> As to amount of taxation, there is no principle for any arbitrary limit. Heavy taxation is better for any community than light taxation, if the increased revenue be used in doing by public agencies things which could not be done, or could not be as well and economically done, by private agencies. ... It is a mistake to condemn taxation merely because it is high (CJW, II, p. 41).

As examples of desirable fiscal expansionism, George mentioned 'Our public schools and libraries and parks, our signal service and fish commissions and agricultural bureaus and grasshopper investigations' (CJW, II, p. 41). Speaking in Chicago in 1893, he spoke of the 'enormous income' that would accrue to the state from the LVT, and that 'could be used for public purposes' (CJW, III, p. 229). And, in his speech on 5 October 1886 accepting nomination as a candidate for the New York mayoralty election, he envisaged that the revenue from the LVT in the city of New York (for example) would be sufficient to enable every citizen of New York to have 'his separate house and land' and would generate sufficient funds 'for the beautifying and adornment of the city, for providing public accommodations, playgrounds, schools, and facilities for education and recreation'. He also believed that the LVT revenue could enable the railroads to be 'taken properly and legally by the people and run for the benefit of the people of New York' (CJW, II, p. 156). The following statement from *Progress and Poverty* is perhaps his most confident assertion of the adequacy of the LVT revenue:

> [W]e could establish public baths, museums, libraries, gardens, lecture rooms, music and dancing halls, theatres, universities, technical schools, shooting galleries, playgrounds, gymnasiums, etc. Heat, light, and motive power, as well as water, might be conducted through our streets at public expense; and roads lined with fruit trees; discoverers and inventors rewarded, scientific investigations supported; and in a thousand ways the public revenues made to foster efforts for the public benefit (CJW, II, pp. xvi–xvii).

George believed, further, that the LVT revenue would be sufficient not only to meet the aforementioned expenditures, but also to provide a substantial surplus,[8] so that the main question would be not whether the revenue would be adequate for the needs of government, but what to do with the surplus. Some of the supporters of the Single Tax advocated that the LVT should therefore be levied at a rate that would absorb less than the full annual value of the land, to avoid generating a surplus; but George argued that the rate of the single tax should be gradually increased until it absorbed the full value of the land.

In a debate with Edward Atkinson in the pages of *Century Magazine* in 1890, George attempted to show that the annual ground rent of the United States was $790,000,000, but that the necessary expenses of government were only $580,000,000, so that a Single Tax on land would yield $210,000,000[9] more than was needed. In other words, the current government's needs could be met by taking only 73 per cent of the economic rent. He also noted that Thomas Shearman had estimated that the current government's needs could be met by taking only 65 per cent of the land rent (CJW, III, p. 141). But although George insisted that 'no limit can be properly fixed for the amount of taxation' (CJW, II, p. 41), he also insisted that the *method* of taxation should be land-value taxation, which would begin at a low percentage and gradually increase until it absorbed the full value of the land. The statement that 'no limit can be properly fixed for the amount of taxation' is not therefore a literal and strictly accurate statement of his position. It was presumably his intention that ultimately the expansion of government revenue and functions would be limited in practice by the amount of revenue that could be generated by land-value taxation. This practical limitation follows also from the normative argument that, since the LVT is the only tax that is ethically justified, the LVT revenue sets a natural and divinely ordained limit to public expenditures, and is a natural and inbuilt check to any excessive expansion of government activities and expenditures.

In defence of the adequacy of the Single Tax revenue, George argued that, if the revenue is insufficient to meet current government requirements, this does not mean that the revenue is inadequate; it simply means that the government's requirements are excessive. In this respect, George's thought appeals to those who hold a minimalist vision of government, even though the policy of land-value taxation appears to some as socialistic interventionism.

Despite the belief of George and his supporters in the ability of the LVT to be a more than adequate source of government revenue, it is doubtful whether they would have been so confident if they had been aware of the extent to which government functions and government tax revenue would increase, even in 'free enterprise' economies. The conventional Georgist response is that the financial needs of modern governments have increased because the unequal distribution of natural resources has generated maldistribution of wealth and widespread poverty, and that if land values were used for the common good, there would be far less need for welfare services – for example, on education, health, pensions, and unemployment benefits. According to Blaug (1999, p. 22; citing Cord, 1965, pp. 122, 234), the expenses incurred by governments during the First World War showed clearly that the LVT could not be the only tax. The publication of *The Wealth and Income of the People of the United States* (1915) by Wilford King put an end to the idea of the Single Tax. Blaug has described the idea as 'almost laughable':

> [T]he revenue that LVT, fully and properly applied, was capable of raising may at one time have been sufficient for the expression of government but ever since 1930 the very notion of LVT as a single tax is almost laughable (Blaug, 1999, pp. 28–9).

In support of the sufficiency argument, some would argue that expenditure incurred by governments in preparation for war (including scientific research on armaments and maintenance of troops and equipment), and during war, and in post-war reconstruction (including interest and repayments of war debt), should be regarded as exceptional circumstances, and should not be used as an argument against the sufficiency of the LVT revenue as a general economic principle. Economists do not usually say that the Laws of Supply and Demand have been proved wrong because in wartime prices are often fixed by government price controls.

The outcome of the argument remains inconclusive for various other reasons. Some estimates of potential revenue take account only of *increases* in land value after the date of implementation of the tax (as John Stuart Mill proposed); others are based on the *current* value as well as potential increases. Some estimates look only at land in its everyday meaning; others look at land in the wider sense of all natural resources, including forests, minerals, oil, fisheries, and spectrum resources (radio, television, and telecommunication licences), etc.[10] Blaug (1999, p. 29) regards spectrum rent as 'the perfect Georgist rent … which, surely, ought to be taxed away to subsidise public broadcasting'.

George thought that the limit to the revenue that could be collected by a land tax from any parcel of land would be the current annual value of that land. He argued that a land tax equal to the current value of the land would remove the speculative element from the selling value of land, leaving only what he described (vaguely) as its 'use value', which he thought would be very small or 'nominal'. In an article on 'Taxation of Land Values' in Appleton's Journal in 1881 he said:

> The measure I propose … would utterly destroy the speculative value of land, and would reduce the selling value of land to but a nominal figure (CJW, II, p. 55).

This left George open to the objection that if the current value of land after taxation is very low, the LVT would be self-defeating, because it would be incapable of raising any revenue.

A related criticism is that if all land value is destroyed by the LVT, there would be no tax base, and no empirical evidence for determining the relative tax contributions for each site. This argument was used by Edward Atkinson in the Single-Tax debate at Saratoga in 1890:

> ... if Mr. George's plan, which is that of assessing land for taxation so as to destroy its market value, could be put in force, then its valuation as an article of exchange must be ended; and its valuation or rental value for purposes of taxation would depend wholly upon the arbitrary judgment of a board of assessors, who might or might not be competent to make the assessment (CJW, III, p. 108).

In other words, there would be no basis on which to levy a land tax, no way of establishing a comparable level of tax for different sites, and no incentive for anyone to buy land. I am not aware of any convincing response that George ever made to that objection. A response that could be made is that land will never be valueless. Land is essential for life; private ownership and security of tenure will always be powerful motives; and some sites will always have a greater value than others, whether for their business advantages or for their residential amenity, and this differential or allocational value will provide a basis for differential site taxation. Contrary to George's view, the revenue that a land tax could raise is not limited by the value of the land. It is limited only by the landowner's capacity to pay, and by what is politically possible in a democracy or by what can be forcibly extracted in a dictatorship.

The question of whether George's Single Tax would provide sufficient revenue for the needs of government is further complicated by the fact that, at least in his later years, George seems to have drawn back from his previous position that the Single Tax should be the only tax. In a speech in Chicago on 29 August 1893, he said that the 'central idea' of the Single Tax is 'the taking in the form of a tax that increment of land values, which grows up with the general growth and progress of the community', and that the Single Tax 'by no means excludes nor denies the idea that a community may, for police, sanitary, or other public purposes impose a tax' (CJW, III, p. 228). As examples of such other taxes, he mentioned a tax on dogs, and a tax on banknote circulation.

This idea that the Single Tax, despite its name, was not intended to exclude all other taxes is rarely mentioned in Georgist literature. It appears to contradict George's statements elsewhere on the Single Tax, and would probably be a surprise to most advocates of the Single Tax. George distinguished in this context between the letter and the spirit [of the Single Tax], saying that it is 'an adherence to the letter which killeth, not to the spirit which giveth life'.[11]

This movement away from a strict adherence to the letter of the Single Tax obviates the criticism of George's LVT based on the inadequacy of its revenue, and removes one of the major objections to George's system.

George's attitude to the 'Single Tax' label appears to have fluctuated over time. At one point he claimed to have invented the title, but elsewhere he said the title was suggested by Thomas Shearman (CJW, III, p. 227). He admitted that the title did not fully encompass the principles he stood for, but he recognized that it highlighted the policy by which the principles would be implemented, and it distanced his programme from the socialistic policy of land nationalization. He also recognized that the 'Single Tax' slogan contributed significantly to the popularity and acceptability of his programme. But in later years he appears to have had some misgivings at having adopted the 'Single Tax' slogan. In an article in the *Standard* of 6 January 1892, replying to a letter from W.W. Head, Secretary of the Shearers' Union, Wagga Wagga, Australia, George said, 'for want of a better term' we style ourselves 'Single Tax men', but our 'fundamental idea would be better expressed by some such term as equal-rights men, or individual-rights men, or natural-order men' (CJW, III, pp. 200–1). And in a speech in Chicago on 29 August 1893, he admitted that the title is a misnomer, because what he was proposing was 'not a tax, in the narrow meaning of the word, it is simply a taking by the public, by the community of a value belonging of right to the community'.[12] He came close to abandoning the title 'Single Tax' when he added: 'It does not suit us, but it is the best thing we have been able to find so far, or rather we did not find it, it came to us, and has been given to us by its seeming fitness, and its general acceptation' (CJW, III, p. 228).

In a speech he gave to the New York State Assembly on 9 March 1893, George said that 'what we aim at by the single tax' is 'equal rights to all and special privileges to none' (CJW, III, p. 207). And in a speech at Chicago on 29 August 1893, he said that the 'Single Tax' title 'sets forth clearly not our aim, but our means' (CJW, III, p. 227). This indicates that the Single Tax was for George the means to an end, not the end itself, and that the principle of equal rights was his ultimate end and therefore is the defining characteristic of George's thought. The promotion of the principle of equal rights was not of course peculiar to George; but whereas equal rights had been promoted in other domains – such as slavery and political representation – George's contribution consisted of extending the principle of equal rights to land value.

4. PRIVATE PROPERTY RIGHTS IN LAND

The belief that George's system involved the abolition of private property in land has been a source of major criticism. George interpreted the encyclical, *Rerum Novarum*, of Pope Leo XIII as a Papal rebuke on this score (see George, 1953, [1891]). Certainly there are statements in George's writings and in reports of his speeches which clearly state that his aim was to abolish private property in land, and his later writings provide no convincing evidence that he deviated from that view.

However, it has been argued (for example, Pullen, 2004) that his adherence to that policy was more verbal than real, and that the adoption of his LVT policy did not in fact constitute the abandonment of private property in land. His policy could have been more correctly and logically described as the abandonment of inequality in the private land ownerships, rather than the abandonment of private land ownership itself.

5. ABILITY TO PAY

George rarely referred to the possibility that the LVT might cause hardship because of a lack of ability to pay. He believed that landowners would not be able to pass the tax on to the tenants, basing this belief on Ricardo's theory of rent which he regarded as an unassailable truth, held by all economists. He also believed that the taxes paid by landowners[13] would be offset by 'great and actual gains', because other taxes would be abolished and because the LVT would abolish the speculative or 'selling' value of land and would thus make it easier to obtain possession of land.

A rare and brief reference to the hardship possibility occurred in an article published in *Appleton's Journal* in June 1881, where he argued that the 'only ones who would really lose [from the introduction of the LVT] would be those whose incomes are mainly drawn from the rent, not of buildings, but of land; those who are holding land in the expectation of future profit from the high prices that in time those who want to use it will be compelled to pay them'. But even they would benefit from the general improvement in society resulting from the LVT. He admitted that in some cases the relative loss might exceed the relative gain, but that would only be for those who 'could really stand the loss without being really hurt'. He hinted at compensation for hardship when he added that 'if necessary' there might be 'some provision as to widows, etc.' (CJW, II, pp. 58–9).

It seems clear that George did not envisage a society where a large portion, or even a majority, of householders would be owners (of both the house and of the land on which it stood), rather than tenants paying rent to a landlord. He himself did not own land until late in life. As he was convinced that Ricardo's theory of rent was valid and that the owner of land could not pass on a land tax, he would have been logically obliged to admit that owner-occupiers of homes have to meet the LVT out of their incomes with the possibility that some might suffer hardship because of lack of ability to pay.

George's attitude to the ability-to-pay problem can be seen in his debate with Edward Atkinson in the pages of *The Century Magazine* in 1890 (CJW,

III, pp. 117–54). Atkinson argued that the poor man with a small house should not have to pay the same tax as the rich man with a large house on a lot of the same value, thus invoking the 'ability-to-pay' canon of taxation. George replied by asking: 'Should a rich man pay any more than a poor man for a thing of a like kind? or is it just to tax men of brains for using their brains in production?' (CJW, III, p. 138), thus invoking the 'benefit received' canon of taxation, and ignoring the ability-to-pay canon.

6. THE LAND-RICH-AND-INCOME-POOR PROBLEM

The possibility that some home owners could experience financial hardship in meeting the taxes levied on them in the LVT system can be described as the land-rich-and-income-poor problem. It is a particular instance of the more general ability-to-pay problem that confronts all taxation systems. As a general rule it is probably true that home owners with high incomes tend to have a home site with a high value. But the reverse is not necessarily true. Those whose home sites are very valuable do not always have high incomes. They might have had high incomes when they bought their high-value home sites, but their incomes might have later fallen without a proportionate fall in their site values; or their site values might have increased without a proportionate increase in their incomes. It is quite likely, therefore, that in the LVT regime, home owners could find themselves in a situation where they are required to pay a high level of LVT, but have insufficient income out of which to pay it. The result could be a degree of financial hardship that would be unacceptable both personally and politically, and would make implementation of the LVT regime impossible at a practical level in a democracy.

It might be argued, on the contrary, that land-value taxation does exist in many societies already,[14] without either causing widespread hardship or proving to be politically unacceptable (or at least not to a greater extent than can be expected from any tax system). However, these existing systems of LVT differ from the Henry George proposal in one significant aspect – their scale. The current systems are usually only one part – and usually a minor part – of a system involving many taxes, whereas the Georgist LVT is intended to be, if not the single source of government revenue, then at least a major source, with far greater likelihood of causing hardship because of a disproportionality between tax and income.

The phrase 'land-rich-and-income-poor' usually conjures up images of an elderly pensioner who has lived in and cherished the family home for many years but now finds that a relatively fixed old-age pension cannot pay the annual taxes based on its escalating land value. But this conventional image disguises the fact that 'rich' and 'poor' are relative terms and that a disproportion between land charges and income can occur at any point (even the most modest) on the land value scale, owing to events such as unemployment, sickness, bereavement, family break-up; not just the coming of old age. The current volatility of the labour market and the increase in the casualization of the workforce mean that these disproportions are likely to be increasingly frequent and widespread throughout the community.

In George's proposal, when land-value taxes are introduced or increased, income taxes (and other taxes) would be either reduced or abolished. But there can be no guarantee that, for each individual taxpayer or even for the majority, the (opposite) movements in LVT and income tax will be equal. There could be windfall tax advantages for some (the land-poor-and-income-rich) and hardship for others (the land-rich-and-income-poor). It could be argued that this ability-to-pay difficulty in the case of the land-rich-and-income-poor could be overcome by selling the home with its valuable land and moving to a house with less valuable land; but this would simply mean that one form of politically unacceptable hardship would be replaced by another, as affected home owners are forced to vacate their homes and may even be obliged to move into rental accommodation, with its attendant insecurity.

Land used successfully for commercial purposes generates an income, but land used for owner-occupied residential housing is not income-producing (except in the indirect sense of providing a locus for the rest, recreation, nourishment, shelter and family life that are the prerequisites for engaging in direct income-producing activities); it does not directly generate an annual income out of which an annual LVT can be paid. To expect people to pay a substantial annual charge on land which is not producing an annual income would be generally perceived as unacceptably unfair, and is likely to be politically impracticable.

A tax that is assessed on the value of land would be interpreted as, and would in effect be, a tax on capital, or a tax on capital gains – as distinct from a tax on income, even though it is paid out of current income. Its introduction might be facilitated if presented not as a new tax but as an extension of an existing capital-gains tax that had become politically acceptable. But there is one feature of George's LVT which distinguishes it from other capital-gains taxes. George's LVT would be a tax on unrealized capital gains. It would impose a current periodical charge on capital values before they are realized.

The possibility of widespread disproportionality between a tax on owner-occupied residential land and the income of the owner-occupier is rarely discussed in Georgist literature, and, as already noted, was rarely mentioned by George; but it would seem to be a major difficulty facing the LVT, and one that would have to be resolved before the LVT could be successfully implemented in a society in which the majority of people are owners of the sites[15] on which their homes are built.

The following five proposals are tentatively suggested as ways that might resolve or at least alleviate the land-rich-and-income-poor problem.

(a) Tax deferral

One way to solve or alleviate the ability-to-pay or liquidity problem might be to allow part or all of a current LVT liability to be deferred until title to the land is transferred – for example, by sale, gift, or inheritance. George's LVT was intended as an annual or periodical tax. The undeferred portion of the LVT liability would remain as a periodical tax; the deferred portion would in effect be a tax on realized capital gains, or on realized increments in wealth.[16]

However, this deferral policy, while providing a solution to a current ability-to-pay or cash-flow problem, is not without problems of its own.

First, knowledge that one's home carries an ever-increasing debt of deferred LVT – a debt that will have to be met by one's heirs – could be very distressing for some people, especially those who identify debt with personal failure and guilt. The fact that the home owner might be bequeathing a very valuable asset to the heirs would not necessarily mitigate the distress associated with the consciousness of an accumulated debt.

Secondly, in many cases the accumulated annual deferments, especially if compound interest is added, could exceed the land value when the title comes to be transferred. The excess would thus become a remission rather than a deferment, and revenue from the LVT would be reduced.

Thirdly, if the deferred LVT becomes payable on the death of the owner, it would, rightly or wrongly, be perceived by the public and the media as a form of Estate Duty or Inheritance Tax. It would be particularly unpopular in countries that do not have Estate Duties.

Fourthly, if the deferred LVT becomes payable on the sale of the land, then a home owner wishing to sell might have difficulty in purchasing an alternative home, as the net return from the sale of the land of the existing home after deducting the deferred LVT might not be sufficient to cover the land cost of an equivalent replacement home. Owners who are obliged to move for employment or other reasons could be severely affected, and might have to change from being home owners to renters. Alternatively, the obligation to pay the deferred LVT might make it financially impossible for them to move, resulting in a decline in labour mobility and the creation of long-term pockets of high unemployment.

Unless these serious difficulties can be satisfactorily addressed, deferral of the LVT will not provide an acceptable solution to the liquidity and hardship problems arising from a disproportion between the LVT and ability to pay.

(b) Purchaser-pays

Difficulties associated with the deferral policy could perhaps be mitigated by stipulating that liability for payment of the deferred amount rests with the purchaser, rather than the seller, of the land in question. The deferred LVT would thus become a debt voluntarily incurred by the purchaser of the land, not a legal debt owed by the seller, and would not then furnish reasonable grounds for feelings of guilt arising from a perception of unpaid debts. Payment of the deferred LVT by the purchaser would also mean that deferments would not become remissions; the full amount owing in deferred LVT would be payable by the purchaser, even if it exceeded the current market value of the land.

A purchaser-pays policy could also help to alleviate (but not to resolve entirely) the deferral problems associated with deceased estates. In the case of inherited land that beneficiaries intend to sell, it would at least partially remove the perception that the deceased estate was being subjected to Estate Duty. But it would not remove that perception in the case of the land of inherited homes that the beneficiaries intend to use as homes. Children or other relatives to whom a home has been bequeathed, and who had been living in the home and expecting to go on living there, would hope to take possession and title of the home without payment of the deferred LVT. They could be faced with considerable financial and personal hardship if forced to sell in order to pay the deferred LVT. But if payment of the deferred LVT is further deferred in such cases, the deferment period could become indefinite as the property is passed on from generation to generation.

It might be objected that, even if the purchaser is billed for the deferred LVT, it will nevertheless be an indirect charge on the seller, given that the obligation to pay the deferred LVT could cause the purchaser to reduce the purchase offer; the incidence could rest, at least in part, with the seller even though payment is made by the purchaser. However, the extent of this passing-back of the deferred LVT will depend on the elasticities of demand and supply (i.e., on the relative bargaining strengths of buyer and seller) at the time. It is by no means certain that the deferred LVT will be wholly, or even partially, passed back in every case. It is quite possible that in some cases it could be met to some extent, or even fully, by the purchaser as an addition to the current market value of the land.

(c) Income-tax adjustments

If the deferral policy is not made available, or if partial deferral of the LVT liability leaves an unacceptable level of hardship in meeting periodically the undeferred portion, some alleviation of the hardship might be possible by adjustments to other taxes. For example, an annual liability for LVT could be an allowable deduction or rebate in calculating annual liability for income tax.[17]

This integration of the LVT into an income-tax system would enable unacceptable hardship for the land-rich-and-income-poor to be avoided or mitigated, but it would of course not be possible in a system where the LVT is the Single Tax. The paradoxical situation is that Henry George, as long as he advocated the LVT as a Single Tax, believed that its singleness, and the abolition of other taxes, would greatly enhance its feasibility and its popularity, but he did not recognize the possible severity of the impact of the LVT on the land-rich-and-income-poor and did not recognize that this severity could adversely affect its feasibility. He did not see that the feasibility of the LVT could in fact be enhanced by incorporating it into a package of taxes, thus providing compensation in cases of undue hardship.

(d) Equal distribution of the land-tax revenue

A way of gaining public support for the LVT and a way of alleviating the land-rich-and-income-poor problem might be to regard the LVT as a means of effecting an equal distribution or sharing of the increments in land value, rather than as a means of collecting the increments as a source of government revenue. The increments would be distributed equally as dividends to individuals (including land owners) to be used as they choose, instead of being absorbed into government revenue to be used for public works or in other ways as the government chooses. The liability of landowners for the LVT would be at least partially offset by receipt of the dividend. This would be a neo-Georgist departure from the strict letter of George's ideas, but would be a logical application of the spirit of George's principle of equal rights to land, and would be consistent with his general (but not universal) emphasis on an individualist rather than collectivist organization of society.[18] It would give practical expression to the idea that the right to land is an equal right rather than a common right.

(e) A tax on land value, or a tax on land-value increments

This ability-to-pay problem for those who are land-rich-and-income poor would be mitigated in the early years after the implementation of the LVT if the tax is applied only to increments in land value that occur after the date of implementation of the tax, rather than to the full value of the land, although the degree of mitigation would diminish as the implementation date receded into the past. John Stuart Mill recommended a land tax based on increments after the implementation date, but George insisted that the LVT should be based on the value of the land in the implementation year and in all future years. He appears to have been quite unmoved by pleas that recent purchasers of land prior to the implementation date would suffer unfair hardship – having paid the current market value of the land in the expectation of future capital gains, but then finding that the expected gains might only be partly realized, or not at all, because of the new tax, and that the current value might also fall. Responding to claims that such recent purchasers should receive some compensation or tax relief, George adopted the somewhat harsh and radical position – which must have alienated many prospective supporters – that it had never been the custom for people to be compensated for changes in taxation.

The compensation issue was particularly relevant for a relatively new country like Australia, where land owners had only recently bought land (freehold or leasehold) from the government. Buyers obviously felt that the capital sum they had paid was in effect a land-value tax that was equal to the full capital value of the land at the time of purchase, and that to require them to pay an annual tax equal to the annual value of that capital sum would be double taxation. They argued either that an annual LVT should be levied only on the increments that had occurred after the date of purchase, or that their annual LVT liability should be reduced to compensate for the capital sum they had recently paid.

Choosing a tax on only the increments in land value after the implementation date rather than the full current value at that date would of course mean that the revenue raised by the tax in the early years would be relatively small, and that it would be some years before the benefits of the LVT began to be perceived. George would obviously have been aware that popular political support would be necessary to introduce the LVT and to ensure its continuance in the face of the political opposition that would be aroused amongst land owners and investors. To ensure popular political support, it would be necessary to establish a strong vested interest in its retention by showing that the LVT was capable of generating considerable revenue, even in its early years, and that this revenue was being spent on clearly identified and well-publicized public improvements.

7. IS THE LVT PRACTICABLE?

George was convinced that the LVT policy was just, and must therefore be practicable – 'That which is just, that which is right always is practicable' (article in the *Standard*, 26 February 1887; CJW, II, p. 201) – and he asserted that 'We are, ... in all that we propose, the most practical of men' (speech in New York, 1895; CJW, III, p. 276).

Implementation difficulties – in particular, the ability-to-pay issue in the case of the land-rich-and-income-poor – do not appear to have been adequately addressed by George or subsequent Georgist literature, but would need to be addressed and resolved if the LVT proposal is ever to become politically viable and administratively practicable.

George was fully aware that what he was proposing would require a major shift in attitudes towards the ownership of increments in land value. In his day as much as in ours, and in other countries as much as his, the belief that landowners are morally entitled to appropriate any increases in the unimproved value of their land is deeply and fervently held. In a democratic society where the majority of voters are landowners, it will always be difficult to implement a policy that deprives them of their land-value increments. The land-value increments might be 'unearned', but they are certainly not unappreciated. Indeed, being 'unearned' probably enhances the appreciation. Political success for the LVT might have to wait for the time when 'the landed are few and the landless many'.[19]

NOTES

1. This list of criticisms is not intended to be comprehensive. See, for example, Andelson (1979, 2003). Blaug (1999, pp. 19–20) classifies all the objections to George's arguments under five headings, which he labels: '(1) The Anti-landlord Thesis; (2) The Inseparability Thesis; (3) The Adverse Incidence Thesis; (4) The Inelasticity Thesis; and (5) The Moral Hazard Thesis'.
2. 'man, by being master of himself and proprietor of his own person and the actions or labor of it, had still in himself the great foundation of property' (Locke 1952 [1690], p. 27).
3. See, for example, the comments of E.R.A. Seligman in the Single-Tax debate at Saratoga in 1890, in CJW, III, pp. 81–4.
4. See King (1988), p. 102: 'Many modern political philosophers would be inclined to take seriously George's moral claim that landowners have no legitimate right to the land and therefore no entitlement to compensation if it should be taken from them .... [T]he ethical basis of George's system is considerably stronger than contemporary critics were prepared to admit'.
5. George (2003 [1890], p. 281). (This title is referred to hereafter as CJW. The author of this paper and all students of Henry George are deeply indebted to Ken Wenzer for his efforts in recent years in republishing so many of the writings and speeches of George that had previously remained scattered in relatively inaccessible locations.)
6. The insurmountable problem of disentangling the part of a person's output that results from the external natural resources used in the production process and from the natural resources that are internal to the person, from that part of the output that is attributable to the rest of the person, is similar to the disentanglement problem that featured prominently in the early years of the Marginal Productivity Theory of Distribution. J.B. Clark (1956 [1899]) believed that the output caused by the marginal unit of a variable factor could be disentangled from the part of the marginal product caused by the fixed factors. It is interesting to note that J.B. Clark became interested in economics in order to refute the land-tax policies of Henry George.
7. 'Neo-Georgists' could be defined as those who align themselves with what they perceive to be the essential elements of George's ideas, while modifying them in the light of modern events and valid criticisms, but rejecting those elements of George's ideas that they perceive to be inessential and questionable.
8. 'There would be a great and increasing surplus revenue from the taxation of land values' (pp. 455–7; CJW, II, pp. xvi–xvii).
9. The text has $220,000,000.
10. For a recent study of the value of Australia's natural resources, see Dwyer (2003), which concludes that 'land-based tax revenues are indeed sufficient to allow total abolition of company and personal income tax' (p. 40).
11. CJW, III, pp. 228. cf. Second Epistle of Paul to the Corinthians, Chapter 3, Verse 6: '[God] also hath made us able ministers of the New Testament; not of the letter, but of the spirit: for the letter killeth, but the spirit giveth life'.
12. CJW, III, p. 228. Some modern Georgists prefer to use the expression 'land-value charge' rather than 'land-value tax', and regard that charge as a payment for a privilege granted by society to the landholder, viz., the privilege of holding exclusive possession of a community asset. Blaug (1997, p. 18) gives a further reason for 'land-value taxation' being a misnomer: 'It should never have been called "land value taxation" but rather "land *rent* taxation" for it was the rent from land and not its selling value that George wanted the government to tax'. George proposed a tax on the annual value, rather than the capital value of the land, but obviously the two are related.
13. He thought that, after the introduction of the LVT, landowners would in fact be possessors rather than owners, even though they might persist in thinking of themselves as owners, and

might be permitted to continue to call themselves 'owners' if that would help to facilitate the introduction of the LVT.

14. This hardship problem could of course also occur in the case of a property tax levied on the combined value of a house and its land, not just in the case of a tax levied on the value of the land.

15. Or, in the case of multiple dwellings on one site, credited for taxation purposes with a proportion of the value of the site.

16. The policy of imposing the LVT in two ways – partly as an annual (or periodical) tax and partly as a deferred tax on capital-gains – has advantages. The former, undeferred, portion of the LVT would exert the anti-withholding influence that is traditionally attributed to unimproved-value taxes. The latter, deferred, portion of the LVT, would be a tax on *realized* gains, and would avoid the objection that George's LVT is unworkable because it attempts to tax a capital gain that, until it is realized, exists only as a book entry.

17. Land taxes are traditionally associated in some countries with local, regional or state governments, and income taxes with central or national governments but, for ease of administration, an integration of land-value taxes and income taxes would presumably require that both taxes be administered by the same authority.

18. This distinction in George's writings between equal rights and common rights, or between individualist and collectivist approaches to social organizations, is treated more fully in Pullen (2004).

19. George (2003) [1890]; CJW, III, p. 183.

REFERENCES

Andelson, R.V. (ed.) (1979), *Critics of Henry George: A Centenary Appraisal of Their Strictures on 'Progress and Poverty'*, Cranbury, New Jersey: Associated University Presses.

Andelson, R.V. (ed.) (2003), *Critics of Henry George: An Appraisal of Their Strictures on 'Progress and Poverty'*, 2nd ed., revised and enlarged, 2 vols, Malden, MA: Blackwell.

Blaug, M. (1999), 'Henry George – rebel with a cause', Walsh Bequest Lecture, Sydney: Macquarie University typescript.

Clark, J.B. (1956) [1899], *The Distribution of Wealth: A Theory of Wages, Interest and Profits*, New York: Kelley & Millman.

Cord, S.B. (1965), *Henry George: Dreamer or Realist?*, Philadelphia: University of Pennsylvania Press.

Dwyer, T. (2003), 'The taxable capacity of Australian land and resources', *Australian Tax Forum*, **18**, 21–68.

George, H. (2003) [1890], 'Land purchase for Ireland', *New Review*, reprinted CJW, III, pp. 182–9.

George, H. (1953) [1891], *The Condition of Labour. An Open Letter to Pope Leo XIII*, New York: Robert Schalkenbach Foundation.

George, H. (2003), *Henry George. Collected Journalistic Writings*, Kenneth C. Wenzer, (ed.) 3 vols, Armonk, New York: M.E. Sharpe. (Title abbreviated in the text above as CJW.)

King, J. (1988), 'Henry George (1839-1897)', in *idem*, *Economic Exiles*, London: Macmillan, pp. 82-108.

King, W. (1915), *The Wealth and Income of the People of the United States*, New York and London: Macmillan.

Locke, J. (1952) [1690], *The Second Treatise of Government*, Thomas P. Peardon (ed.), New York: Bobbs-Merrill.

Pullen, J. (2004), 'Henry George on property rights in land and land value', in T. Aspromourgos and J. Lodewijks (eds), *History and Political Economy: Essays in Honour of P.D. Groenewegen*, London: Routledge.

Wenzer, K.C. (ed.) (1997b), *An Anthology of Henry George's Thought*, Vol. I of the *Henry George Centennial Trilogy*, Rochester, New York: University of Rochester Press.

Wenzer, K.C. (ed.) (1997), *An Anthology of Single Land Tax Thought*. Vol. III of the *Henry George Centennial Trilogy*, Rochester, New York: University of Rochester Press.

Wenzer, K.C. (ed.) (2002), *Henry George's Writings on the United Kingdom*, Research on the History of Economic Thought and Methodology, Vol. 20-B, Oxford: JAI (Elsevier Science Ltd).

9. Equal Rights, Competition and Monopoly: Henry George's Insight into Current Debates on Regulation of Common Use Infrastructure

Terry Dwyer

GEORGE'S NATURAL LAW APPROACH TO ECONOMICS

Jeremy Bentham adopted a radical utilitarian philosophy to critique the theory of legislation, and later economists have often critiqued economic policy on the basis of utilitarian underpinnings to their normative economic theories. Most theories of economic justice, welfare economics or trade-offs from income distribution have a neo-utilitarian basis, traceable back to Bentham.

However, not all economic writing rests on utilitarian foundations. The philosopher John Rawls challenged utilitarianism with his *Theory of Justice* in 1971, arguing for a Kantian approach. He, in turn, was challenged by Robert Nozick who, in his *Anarchy, State and Utopia* (1974), argued that economic justice consisted of justice in distribution of original endowments and commutative justice. Hence, he argued that income redistribution by taxation was unjust if there was no injustice in the distribution of endowments or in exchange. Nozick's was an approach which argues that an individual's property rights cannot justly be taken away to improve the well-being of the majority.

Nozick noted that John Locke had wrestled with the same problem, and in his *Two Treatises on Government* had enunciated a labour theory of property ownership along with the 'Lockean proviso'—that so long as one left enough and as good for others, one could appropriate the gifts of Nature for oneself and claim ownership by admixture of labour to them. Writers, such as John Locke, the Physiocrats, Adam Smith and Henry George can be better regarded as deriving their economics from a natural law, rather than a utilitarian, philosophy.

While Henry George effectively accepted an approach to the problem of economic justice in the same terms as Nozick, and while both rejected utilitarianism, George was basically asserting that the 'Lockean proviso' could never be satisfied in the real world unless there was equal access to natural resources. If simultaneous equal access was physically impossible, then equal justice could only be assured by requiring those using such coveted resources to compensate their fellow human beings for their equal rights by paying full-market rent into a common fund.

A non-utilitarian, individual rights, approach is not the usual approach taken to economic justice by economists (who tend to think in terms of a benevolent government maximizing a neo-utilitarian 'social welfare function'). The Physiocrats, Adam Smith and Henry George took a 'rights-based' approach to economics rather than a Benthamite utilitarian approach. As in most philosophical debates, what matters is the internal consistency of a theory and the insights it provides; and one can well argue that 'individual rights' or 'natural law' theories of economic justice can display more philosophical consistency than neo-utilitarian theories which are in practice bounded by what James Buchanan and other public finance theorists would describe as 'constitutional' or 'quasi-constitutional' limits on the permissible trade-offs allowed to economic policy makers.

Henry George is best described as a 'natural law economic philosopher'. The key to understanding Henry George is that he was a convinced and passionate 'natural law' theorist; for George there had to be a congruence between economic law and moral law. The theme is overt in the Physiocrats, more muted in Adam Smith, and blazes forth in Henry George. He questioned the nature and meaning of economic equality, liberty and competition. These questions are of continuing importance and value to economic inquiry. Essentially, his central thesis was that economic liberty was both ethically right and economically optimal.

It is wrong to see George as just a 'single taxer' — a term which he did not invent and the use of which he later somewhat deprecated: see Barker (1955, pp. 519–20). His tax principles follow from his identification of unequal inter-generational and inter-temporal access to land as a fundamental source of inefficient, anti-competitive, monopoly and of inequity in terms of inequality of opportunity. As Geiger (1933, p. 13) puts it: 'George must be approached not just as the "single taxer", as is so often the case, not as an economist concerned primarily with the technical details of a practical scheme of taxation, but as a moral and social philosopher who has attempted to secure an inseparable union of economics and ethics.' In this quest George was very close to Adam Smith and the Physiocrats, and, before them, John Locke. His economic and tax principles follow from a dual track of argumentation — an ethical theory of natural liberty and labour as the basis of property rights, coupled with an economic theory of the efficiency of free competition. The use of land rent for public revenue comes from a policy of preserving equality of rights to natural resources between not only for those alive today but also for generations yet unborn.

As Adam Smith recognized, the true founders of economics as a mode of systematic theorizing were the French Physiocrats such as Quesnay, Turgot, Mirabeau and du Pont de Nemours. The Physiocrats taught that only land produced a taxable surplus and that there were natural laws that should be respected in designing fiscal systems or economic regulation. As Henry George himself later acknowledged (*Progress and Poverty*, (1971) [1879], bk VIII, ch. 4, pp. 423-4), his conclusions on taxation policy were much the same, though he had arrived at his conclusions independently. George's natural law philosophy of equal freedom and equal rights comes out clearly in passages such as the following (*ibid.*, bk VI, ch. 2, p. 328):

> This, then, is the remedy for the unjust and unequal distribution of wealth apparent in modern civilization, and for all the evils which flow from it:
> *We must make land common property.*
> We have reached this conclusion by an examination in which every step has been proved and secured. In the chain of reasoning no link is wanting and no link is weak. Deduction and induction have brought us to the same truth—that the unequal ownership of land necessitates the unequal distribution of wealth. And as in the nature of things unequal ownership of land is inseparable from the recognition of individual property in land, it necessarily follows that the only remedy for the unjust distribution of wealth is in making land common property.
> ...The laws of the universe are harmonious. And if the remedy to which we have been led is the true one, it must be consistent with justice; it must be practicable of application; it must accord with the tendencies of social development and must harmonize with other reforms.
> All this I propose to show. I propose to meet all practical objections that can be raised, and to show that this simple measure is not only easy of application; but that it is a sufficient remedy for all the evils which, as modern progress goes on, arise from the greater and greater inequality in the distribution of wealth—that it will substitute equality for inequality, plenty for want, justice for injustice, social strength for social weakness, and will open the way to grander and nobler advances of civilization.
> I thus propose to show that the laws of the universe do not deny the natural aspirations of the human heart; that the progress of society might be, and, if it is to continue, must be, toward equality, not toward inequality; and that the economic harmonies prove the truth perceived by the Stoic Emperor [Marcus Aurelius]— 'We are made for co-operation—like feet, like hands, like eyelids, like the rows of the upper and lower teeth.'

Essentially, in *Progress and Poverty*, George was arguing that persistent widespread poverty, widely unequal distributions of wealth, industrial depressions and involuntary unemployment were not natural states of society nor the inevitable Malthusian result of over-breeding by the masses. He wrote (*ibid.*, 'Conclusion', p. 558): 'It is impossible to reconcile the idea of an intelligent and beneficent Creator with the belief that the wretchedness and degradation which are the lot of such a large proportion of human kind result from his enactments'.

His argument was that those evils flowed from a violation of natural social and economic laws, from a lack of equal access to God-given natural resources (land), and that an economic system which provided equal inter-generational access to land by requiring payment of economic rent by land users to the community would be more productive, more equitable, more efficient and less prone to speculative manias. Taxation would be unnecessary, competition would be fair rather than predatory, and civilization would advance to new heights, based on a broad elevation of the masses, instead of being undermined by the growth of under-classes.

Similarly, in *Social Problems*, George wrote ((1963) [1883], ch. XXII, 'Conclusion', pp. 241–2):

> The domain of law is not confined to physical nature. It just as certainly embraces the mental and moral universe, and social growth and social life have their laws as fixed as those of matter and of motion. Would we make social life healthy and happy, we must discover those laws, and seek our ends in accordance with them.

The common theme in *Social Problems* is social and economic liberty and equality of opportunity. George wrote (*ibid.*, ch. XV, p. 160): 'We can never abolish slavery, until we honestly accept the fundamental truth asserted by the Declaration of Independence and secure to all the equal and unalienable rights with which they are endowed by their Creator.' Accordingly, George criticizes big government and monopoly business (*ibid.*, ch. XVII) and the loss of individual opportunity (*ibid.*, ch. V) in terms which recall the ideals of Jeffersonian democracy.

In *A Perplexed Philosopher* (1965) [1892] George challenges Herbert Spencer's apparent repudiation of his original views on the philosophical origins of the right to private property and equal access to use of the earth. The book is essentially about ethics and philosophical first principles in assigning property rights; but its discussion in chapter XI on the principle of whether there should be compensation for legislative change which destroys the value of a capitalized monopoly right has strong contemporary relevance. It bears directly on normative economic issues such as compensating for abolition of tariff quotas or whether economic regulators should have regard to prices paid for monopoly utility franchises instead of the actual cost of capital works.

In *The Condition of Labour* George places his view on taxation *as a moral question* to the fore. He argues ((1947) [1891], ch. I, pp. 8–17) that taxes and tariffs are inherently immoral and corrupting methods of raising public revenue and that the use of land rent for public revenue conforms to natural moral law. He argues (*ibid.*, ch. IV, pp. 64–72) that the Pope [Leo XIII] should not expect government regulation of wages or working conditions or trade union cartels to help labourers in a world of surplus labour. Only equality of opportunity to use the earth's resources can provide a natural economic guarantee of a living wage (*ibid.*, ch. V, pp. 82–85). It is notable that Henry George expressly disavows any leanings to socialism in the sense of equality of outcome, but stresses equality of opportunity as the moral basis of his economic philosophy (*ibid.*, p. 80).

In *The Science of Political Economy* (1932) [1898] George presses the contrast between 'value from production' versus 'value from obligation' in bk II ch. XIV. George draws a sharp distinction between produced capital goods and capitalized values of monopoly rights or franchises. At pp. 207–8 he notes that for an individual investor it matters not whether one invests in buying a monopoly or creating a new capital asset, but stresses that it matters to society as a whole. In modern terminology, George was saying that rent-seeking behaviour by investors is not economically productive for society as a whole.

The overall messages from Henry George's writings are that economic liberty is natural and desirable for human progress, that it requires equality of opportunity which can only be based on equal rights of access to scarce natural resources (land), and that public revenue should not, and need not, be derived from taxes on labour or capital as opposed to collecting resource rents. Monopolies should not be legislated for in any form and should be removed wherever they have been created. Further, there should be freedom of trade so that society can progress through free, full and fair competition rather than predatory competition based on inequality of starting position. George advanced these views on both moral and economic grounds.

Like Adam Smith (1976 [1776], bk IV, ch. ix, p. 687), who invoked 'the obvious and simple system of natural liberty' and accepted the idea of a benevolent Deity, Henry George saw the workings of economic systems as being affected favourably or unfavourably by whether human beings in their economic legislation and conduct respected the natural laws laid down by the Creator. There is nothing surprising about this. Just as the physical laws discovered by Isaac Newton were seen as the work of the Creator, so the Physiocrats, Adam Smith and Henry George, had little difficulty in seeing the invisible hand of the Creator behind apparent natural economic laws.

Socialists have sometimes tended to criticize George as inferior to Marx in not going the 'the whole way' in advocating wholesale nationalization of all the means of production. Others of a different persuasion have criticized him as an 'agrarian socialist'. But John Locke's approach to the origins of property rights is remarkably parallel to George's,[1] while Adam Smith shared George's distaste for those who engrossed or monopolized what might be seen as the 'bounty of the Creator' and loved to reap where they never sowed.

While Henry George is most prominently identified in the minds of most economists with the 'single tax', his writings have contemporary relevance in several important areas of economic inquiry. These areas include fiscal policy, globalization, tax competition, patent monopolies, competition policy, externality, the financing of public urban goods through land rents, marginal cost pricing and lump sum financing of infrastructure, development economics, rent seeking, and theories of economic justice. Against this background of George's views on equal rights, I want to explore his approach to competition policy and contrast it with an archetype of current neo-classical arguments in favour of deregulation of monopolies.

GEORGE ON COMPETITION AND MONOPOLY

Patent Monopolies

Economists and others are debating the proper role of patents and copyrights following the adoption, under the World Trade Organization treaties, of the TRIPS [trade-related aspects of intellectual property rights] agreement for greater international protection and longer terms for enforcement of intellectual property — for example, the 2002 meeting of the American Economic Association featured a debate on the pros and cons of intellectual property. Brazil and South Africa objected to paying high prices for patented AIDS drugs. Indian peasants have objected to paying for patented seeds. Henry George opposed monopolies. He made a contribution to this debate that finds echoes today in movements such as the 'free software' movement and debates on Third World income transfers to the West. He wrote that patents checked discovery and invention rather than encouraging them and could not be justified on the same grounds as copyright (*Progress and Poverty* (1971) [1879], bk VIII, ch. 3, p. 411, later footnote):

> Following the habit of confounding the exclusive right granted by a patent and that granted by a copyright as recognitions of the right of labor to its intangible productions, I in this fell into error which I subsequently acknowledged and corrected in the *Standard* of June 23, 1888. The two things are not alike, but essentially different. The copyright is not a right to the exclusive use of a fact, an idea, or a combination, which by the natural law of property all are free to use; but only to the labor expended in the thing itself. It does not prevent any one from using for himself the facts, the knowledge, the laws or combinations for a similar production, but only from using the identical form of the particular book or other production — the actual labor which has in short been expended in producing it. It rests therefore upon the natural, moral right of each one to enjoy the products of his own exertion, and involves no interference with the similar right of any one else to do likewise.
>
> The patent, on the other hand, prohibits any one from doing a similar thing, and involves, usually for a specified time, an interference with the equal liberty on which the right of ownership rests. The copyright is therefore in accordance with the moral law — it gives to the man who has expended the intangible labor required to write a particular book or paint a picture security against the copying of that identical thing. The patent is in defiance of this natural right. It prohibits others from doing what has been already attempted. Every one has a moral right to think what I think, or to perceive what I perceive, or to do what I do — no matter whether he gets the hint from me or independently of me. Discovery can give no right of ownership, for whatever

is discovered must have been already here to be discovered. If a man make a wheel-barrow, or a book, or a picture, he has a moral right to that particular wheelbarrow, or book, or picture, but no right to ask that others be prevented from making similar things. Such a prohibition, though given for the purpose of stimulating discovery and invention, really in the long run operates as a check upon them.

Monopoly and Competition Policy

Debate continues between economists today over monopoly and competition policy. Some, such as Israel Kirzner (1973), in his *Competition and Entrepre-neurship*, argue that monopoly may represent the outcome of competition for scarce essential inputs and therefore pro-competition legislation may deter investment. The Australian Federal Government's Productivity Commission, in its inquiries into Australia's regulation of airports, its national access regime for infrastructure and the gas access regime for pipelines, seems to express considerable sympathy for such arguments.

Henry George's writings would lead one to argue that such competition is competition *for* a monopoly and not genuine competition at all. (J. S. Mill, (1965) [1848–71], also wrote about competition for a monopolized commodity[2]). George gave the example of men gaining an island to claim it and then asserting the right to exclude others. [3] This is not real competition since each generation of would-be producers can never compete on an equal basis unless the resource is leased at a market rent from time to time. George's point is that one can *never* have free and fair competition in a 'first come, first served – or first grab' world because space and time in such a model of appropriation of natural resources inevitably create ineradicable advantages for the first incumbent to seize a site or resource. The Henry George prescription of leasing natural monopoly resources or sites can thus be seen as a prescription for competition policy—in line with his defence of *laissez-faire*, once competition is equitable in the first place. This aspect of Henry George's thought flows from his passionate concern for inter-generational equity. (For example, a reader of Henry George can see the Sydney property boom [see Chapter 10, this volume] as an example of inter-generational inequity as young homebuyers are driven to the affordable fringes.)

Rent Seeking and George's 'Value from Obligation'

A modern economic literature has arisen in respect of 'rent seeking'—the be-haviour of industries or individuals seeking incomes insulated from competition by cornering a particular advantage or monopoly position or privilege. This is particularly important in the study of regulatory economics and how market participants seek to 'buy' the regulators or legislators.

In his *The Science of Political Economy* (1932) [1898] Henry George wrote of 'value from production' and contrasted it with 'value from obligation'. 'Rent seeking' is seeking to manufacture 'value for obligation' for one's own benefit, to use Henry George's terminology. For example, if an airport is to be sold a government may instruct a regulatory body to bring down a report favouring deregulation of airport charges for such a natural monopoly, so that a high price is bid for the purchase of the airport. That would be described as a successful exercise in rent seeking—the purchaser pays a lump sum for the right to 'tax the public' and is in reality partly a tax farmer. Another, historical, example of 'value from obligation' was the value of slaves. Sometimes economic historians say the American South suffered a loss of capital as a result of the Civil War and the emancipation of the slaves. A reader of Henry George would dispute that and say (in my view, perfectly correctly) that nothing of real economic value was lost. The labour power still existed after emancipation. What was lost was a capitalized 'value from obligation'—the right to live off the labour of others and to sell that right.[4] (The example of slavery was fresh in the American mind when George wrote and he used it to make moral or economic analogies.)

An essential theme of Henry George is freedom and equal access to resources. A Georgist approach would have been to oppose extended protection of intellectual property for multinationals in the W.T.O. rounds and would have urged governments and parliaments world-wide *not* to legislate to extend patent terms. Similarly, George's fundamental idea of equal freedom would tell against legislating for plant breeders' rights, and a reader of George might question the social value of computer software protection and simply view the Microsoft litigation as an example of the inevitable abuse which is made possible by all legislation upholding monopoly rights.

Henry George wrote against monopoly: where monopoly did not exist, he did not want to see it legislated for; where it did exist (as he saw it in land titles excluding newcomers) he argued that society should 'open up', rather than permit the 'lock up' of scarce common resources. In his passionately pro-competition and anti-monopoly stance, Henry George echoes the ancient hostility of the common law to monopoly.

George on Externality as a Blessing, not a Problem

Economists often think of externalities as 'market failures' which always need to be corrected. They are usually seen as causing misallocation of resources because the creator of a benefit cannot charge for what he has created. Henry George took a different view—he saw externality as the outcome of a beneficent Creator's providence which ensured that all together could create a superabundance over what any individual could create by himself. George recognized (1) that external benefits exist, (2) that it is not necessary for them to be captured by their immediate producers to induce production if the producers are earning a competitive return on their capital or labour, and (3) that such external benefits will be capitalized in land rents where it reflected a community-generated surplus. That surplus is in turn available to fund public common use infrastructure which no private investor might otherwise undertake. Thus he writes (*Progress and Poverty*, (1971) [1879], bk IX, ch. 1, pp. 435–6):

> For there is to the community also a natural reward. The law of society is, each for all, as well as all for each. No one can keep to himself the good he may do, any more than he can keep the bad. Every productive enterprise, besides its return to those who undertake it, yields collateral advantages to others. If a man plant a fruit tree, his gain is that he gathers the fruit in its time and season. But in addition to his gain, there is a gain to the whole community. Others than the owner are benefited by the increased supply of fruit; the birds which it shelters fly far and wide; the rain which it helps to attract falls not alone on his field; and, even to the eye which rests upon it from a distance, it brings a sense of beauty. And so with everything else. The building of a house, a factory, a ship, or a railroad, benefits others besides those who get the direct profits. Nature laughs at a miser. He is like the squirrel who buries his nuts and refrains from digging them up again. Lo! they sprout and grow into trees. In fine linen, steeped in costly spices, the mummy is laid away. Thousands and thousands of years thereafter, the Bedouin cooks his food by a fire of its encasings, it generates the steam by which the traveler is whirled on his way, or it passes into far-off lands to gratify the curiosity of another race. The bee fills the hollow tree with honey, and along comes the bear or the man.
>
> Well may the community leave to the individual producer all that prompts him to exertion; well may it let the laborer have the full reward of his labor, and the capitalist the full return of his capital. For the more that labor and capital produce, the greater grows the common wealth in which all may share. And in the value or rent of land is this general gain expressed in a definite and concrete form. Here is a fund which the state may take while leaving to labor and capital their full reward. With increased activity of production this would commensurately increase.

The insight of Henry George that public works can be funded from land rents has earned him the distinction of having a general theorem in spatial economics named after him by two Nobel prize-winning economists—the 'Henry George Theorem', or the 'George–Hotelling–Vickrey Theorem' [see Laurence Moss's chapter in this volume—Ed.]. This was enunciated by Joseph Stiglitz[5] and by William Vickrey.[6] Both these Nobel Prize winners demonstrated that, under certain conditions, a tax on site rents could cover the cost of public goods as the benefits of the expenditure were capitalized in land values.

This insight solves one of the most celebrated problems in economics—the problem of financing economically efficient marginal cost pricing for common use infrastructure. Harold Hotelling, in his famous 1938 *Econometrica* article (see References), explicitly pointed out that land taxes could cover fixed infrastructure costs allowing pursuit of marginal cost pricing where there was unused capacity over a spatial network such as railway system or an electricity transmission system. He was not unaware of his intellectual debt to Henry George, as he explicitly acknowledges in that article the work of Professor H. G. Brown, an academic supporter of land value taxation, well known as sympathetic to the ideas of Henry George.

CURRENT DEBATE ON REGULATION OF MONOPOLY INFRASTRUCTURE

Legal and economic history both record the well-founded distrust—even hatred—of the common people and their Parliamentary representatives towards monopoly. In England this was manifested by Queen Elizabeth's contrition in her 'Golden Speech' of 1601*; in France it was manifested in the Revolution which swept away the tax farming monopolies of the *Ancien Regime* and sent king and nobility to the guillotine. In the United States, it was manifested in the antitrust legislation against the Standard Oil trust and its kin.

Against this history of hostility to monopoly, often enjoying the sympathy of economists such as Adam Smith and John Stuart Mill (who both criticized monopolization of land, for example), it is bracing to realize that Henry George's philosophy is deeply grounded in a theory of equal rights which abhors monopoly. Increasingly, however, neo-classical economics appears to be assuming away the regulatory problem of monopoly. This benign approach to monopoly is reflected in the work of the Australian Productivity Commission, which relies heavily on academic literature in favour of 'light handed' regulation. The revisionist thesis[7] is that, when it comes to network infrastructure such as toll-roads, railways, pipelines, telephone lines and water supply systems, natural monopoly is not so bad, after all, and if it does really exist, it often has no market power and we are best advised to let monopoly infrastructure owners make the decisions that are efficient and those decisions will be best for us. Any attempt to limit or regulate away monopoly rents would do more harm than good by deterring useful investment in network infrastructure.

In short, it seems we live in Dr Pangloss's best of all possible worlds and we are best advised to gloss over the minor inconvenience of large monopoly profits being extracted from the general community by those munificent benefactors who build and operate network infrastructure. Thus, monopoly has its modern neo-classical defenders who sometimes employ arguments such as the following to oppose or limit regulation of natural monopolies:

1. Anyone can apply for licence to build a railway, toll-road or pipeline.
2. *Ex ante*, in deciding to build, the investor looks at expected costs and returns. If the anticipated internal rate of return is higher than market

---

*The speech revoked a number of 'letters patent' previously granting monopolies to various companies after high prices had caused widespread hardship.—Ed.

threshold, the infrastructure is socially worth while and should be built.

3. If, *ex post*, the investor's returns are liable to be truncated by regulation of the monopoly infrastructure, he will revise down his expected returns but not his expected costs.

4. If, after revision, the internal rate of return on the investor's cash flows falls below his threshold, he will choose not to build the infrastructure.

5. Regulatory attempts to stop monopoly pricing, that is, extraction of monopoly rents, therefore do more harm than good. Anticipated monopoly rents are factored into the investment decision itself. The attempt to protect infrastructure users and consumers ends up by denying them the very infrastructure they wish to use.

6. In conclusion, competition between would-be infrastructure monopolists, not regulation, is what will benefit users and consumers and prevent the public from being exploited.

So stated, the argument has all the appeal and elegance of a theorem by Euclid. Unfortunately, it happens to be wrong.

To see why it is wrong, it is worth examining how this argument was put – better and more carefully – some years ago in *Competition and Entrepreneurship* by Israel Kirzner (1973), an economist in the Austrian school. It is even more interesting to realize that this argument had in turn been anticipated by Henry George's idea of equal inter-generational access to natural resources.

A Neo-Austrian Defence of Acquired Monopoly

Kirzner argued, well enough, that competition was a process, not a static situation as in textbook diagrams.[8] He then observed that 'to speak freely of a lack of competitiveness in a market process, we must be able to point to something which *prevents* market participants from competing. What is it that might succeed in rendering particular market participants secure from being competed with—that might make it possible to them to continue to offer inferior opportunities to the market, immune from the pressure of having at least to match the more attractive offers which other participants might be making available? What is it, in other words, which might halt the competitive process? Clearly this formulation of the question points to its answer. Competition, in the process sense, is at least potentially present so long as there exist no arbitrary *impediments to entry*'(original emphasis).[9]

Kirzner then observes, fairly enough, that 'in the absence of government restrictions on given activities the only possible source of blockage to entry into a particular activity must arise from restricted access to the resources needed for that activity. Without oranges, one cannot produce orange juice. All imaginable obstacles to entry can be reduced, in basic terms, to restricted access to resources.'[10]

The result is that 'there is no room for possible confusion between monopoly profits and entrepreneurial profits. In fact it should be apparent that in our view of monopoly the term profits is hardly in place in this context in general. What the monopolist is able to secure for himself (beyond any possible purely entrepreneurial profits which his alertness may discover) is a *monopoly rent* on the uniquely owned resource from which he derives his monopoly position.... Monopoly rents can, after all, be captured not only by monopolist producers but also by monopolist owners of resources selling their resources to entrepreneur-producers' (original emphasis).[11]

Kirzner thus realized that the problem with the Euclidean argument above lies in step 1. The reality is that no one can just get a licence or a title to a unique natural resource. A licence to build network infrastructure results from an exercise of sovereign power, of eminent domain, whereby the sovereign grants an interest in and over public and private lands. An easement for a road, railway or pipeline is a strategic natural resource.

Faced with this problem, viz., that there *are* strategic, non-reproducible natural resources, Kirzner goes on to argue '*a monopoly position may be won by alert entrepreneurial (and hence competitive) action*. With monopoly understood as a position which confers immunity from the entry of competing entrepreneurs (this immunity arising out of unique ownership of resources), it becomes of interest to inquire into the *source* of such a monopoly position. Clearly the source may be simply the prevailing pattern of natural resource endowment as recognized by the relevant property rights system.'[12]

While Henry George would immediately question the justice (in terms of equal rights) of the relevant property rights system, Kirzner then tries to define away monopoly by appealing to the idea that in the long run, everyone has an equal chance to bid for strategic natural resources. '*From the point of view which takes his monopoly ownership of the resources as given, one must describe them* [production and pricing decisions] *simply as the decisions of a monopolist* ... he may find it possible to secure a monopoly profit by restricting the utilization of his monopolized resource. ... If we attempt to categorize the case in hand from the long-run point of view, that is, as of a date before the *acquisition by our "monopolist" of the entire supply of the essential resource*, things appear in a quite different light. Before our producer acquired unique control of resource supply, he was in no sense a monopolist.... Other producers could, if they wished, have purchased some (or all) of the resource supply and proceeded to make the product ... from the long-run point of view these profits arise not from resource ownership but from the decision to acquire the resource' (emphasis added).[13]

The result is that 'The long-run interests of the consumers have, in this case, been well served by the would-be monopolist. At the time when he acquired sole control over the resource, every part of the entrepreneurial plan (even his planned restricted use of the resource) meant an improvement in resource allocation, as viewed by consumers, over the alternative entrepreneurial plans then being attempted. ... A long-run view may, we have seen, reveal that the consumer's interests have been furthered by the creation of monopoly.'[14] The conclusion then follows that 'Abrogating the rights of the monopolist cannot, it is true, nullify the advantages which have already accrued to consumers from the earlier transactions completed by the would-be monopolist [e.g., creation of gas pipelines]. But a social policy which arbitrarily confiscates from entrepreneurs the profitably secure positions their entrepreneurial alertness has achieved cannot fail to discourage such alertness in the future. And since such alertness, even when it leads to monopoly positions, may very well improve the extent to which consumer tastes are satisfied, any discouragement of it must be deplored [e.g., consumers will lose because no one will invest in natural monopolies again].'

The Flaws in Defending Monopoly as the Outcome of Free Competition

One notes that Kirzner does recognize the problem with step 1, the opening assumption that anyone can compete *ab initio* for a monopoly position. He admits this is a monopoly right but tries to sidestep the adverse normative welfare economics implications of that admission by assuming that everyone is free to compete for the monopoly advantage in the first place.

Unfortunately, as Henry George realized, the argument fails. It is not true that all persons are free to bid for strategic natural resources or rights. Real economic activity takes place in space and time. Not only does spatial monopoly exist for network routes, but also, not all economic actors exist at one point of time with equal knowledge. Monopoly licences may be allocated on a 'first come, first served' basis, with or without a competitive tendering process. By definition, unborn future generations are locked out of the auction. Future generations of producers and consumers are excluded from the bidding (or asking, or granting) process. Further, how can one describe competition to acquire a monopoly strategic resource as free, fair and open when the future is inherently uncertain, a resource may have future unknown uses and there is unequal knowledge?

The Neo-classical Argument that Entrepreneurial Monopolies are not Welfare-reducing Ultimately rests on the Concealed Assumptions of a Spaceless, Timeless, Economy

In this unreal, J. B. Clark, economy,[15] only capital and labour exist and all investment returns are returns to entrepreneurial investment decisions. The trouble is that, in forgetting space, one excludes location rents for land or land assets such as easements. One is then driven to argue that all monopoly rents are really returns to capital, not to land (natural resource rights). Unfortunately, to argue that monopoly resource rents are a necessary inducement to capital investment is to admit that capital is not getting its normal return and is being mal-invested due to cross-subsidization from captured monopoly rents.[16]

Monopoly cannot be Perceived in the Common Two Factor Model

At the back of neo-classical arguments against price regulation of monopolies is a mental room where the only factors of production are labour (largely ignored) and investors with capital weighing up *ex ante* risk-adjusted rates of return on investment possibilities. 'Capital' is the precious factor of production which needs to be invested to increase economic welfare.

But in this J. B. Clark model of the economy, where the only factors of production are capital and labour, monopoly rents cannot exist by definition. Labour is reproducible, as is capital. Capital is only a fund of value. If a monopoly exists, it will be bid for and the return to the investor will equate with the return on investing his capital anywhere else.[17] As Bohm-Bawerk pointed out, in criticizing Clark some ninety years ago, it is a huge analytic mistake to confound 'capital' as a factor of production with 'capital value' representing a process of capitalization. Once a monopoly profit is capitalized, the investor in that monopoly will naturally be heard to argue that he has no super-normal profit—that he is only getting the going rate of return. That is perfectly true, but it does not mean the monopoly has ceased to exist through a process of competition—it has simply been valued, traded and capitalized, and is therefore now treated as 'capital'.

Virtually anything can be capitalized, including a monopoly rent or a licence to tax or the right to enjoy an import quota. But it is very wrong to think some of these 'capital values' have anything to do with being a factor of production: on the contrary, they represent the value of tribute which may be extracted from production. This is what Henry George was driving at in his distinction between value from production and value from obligation. George recognized that transfers due to monopoly rents are mere transfers, and that there is deadweight loss to society from rent-seeking behaviour and the accompanying process of capitalization and dissipation of monopoly rents.

In this regard, many neo-classical models of monopoly are literally 'clueless': they lack both a language and a model to start analysing the costs and benefits to society as a whole from monopoly. At their base lies the idea that 'Regulation reduces returns on investment in infrastructure. Investment is good. Therefore regulation is bad'—a thesis which should earn a quick 'Fail' from a competent examiner.

Instead of focusing on achieving the driving of prices for essential infrastructure towards the economically efficient short-run marginal cost, under the guise of looking at dynamic investment effects, the apologists for 'light handed' regulation cavil at the idea that monopoly regulation should be about eliminating monopoly rents. Instead, the idea is emerging that monopoly rents might have to be paid as the price necessary to bring forth investment in new physical infrastructure. Readers of Henry George will recognize the exploded argument that the 'unearned increment' in land values was necessary to induce exploration and settlement and the idea of taxing land values was therefore a discouragement to investment. Once again, in modern dress, we have the old failure to distinguish between land and capital as factors of production.

Another parallel to the old land value tax debates may be seen in renewed attacks on the idea that natural monopoly even exists. Opponents of Henry George used to argue that he was wrong to say that land was monopolized. Were there not many different blocks of land held by many different owners, each to some extent competing with each other? Similarly, in modern times, advocates of complete deregulation of monopolies argue that there should, for example, be no economic concern if two highways are privatized and sold to two 'competing' merchant banks. In each case, there would be competition for drivers and trucks going between two cities. The market power of each highway would be constrained by the other. Of course it would be—but in a very weak sense. The real issue for motorists and the economy is whether anyone seriously believes that two privately owned highways would charge prices equal to short-run marginal cost. On the contrary, it is more than a fair bet that both highway owners would be racing to extract as much as they could on the way of monopoly rents. And why can they extract monopoly rents?—because, as with blocks of land, no asset is reproducible at the same original real cost.

The point is that so long as you can extract monopoly rents you have market power. You can extract monopoly rents so long as no one else can enter into ownership of a like asset on the same terms and conditions as you did. It does not matter that it is not absolute power (only a monopolist of all the earth's air or water might achieve that happy position!). Buyers will always have *some* alternative—even if it is only to walk on foot. At the end of the day, so long as you can persistently charge a price in excess of short-run marginal cost and extract monopoly rents, you have market power that matters. Practical businessmen do not worry about theoretical alternatives like customers choosing to walk between cities. They realize that 'Monopoly is a terrible thing—until you have it.'[18] The very point of having a monopoly is the ability to extract monopoly rents.

The Strange Death of Marginal Cost Pricing

A curious feature of recent regulatory economics is that writers often admit that prices set equal to short-run marginal cost are optimal, yet proceed to spend zero mental effort on how to get to that desirable position. The obvious difficulty lies in financing large fixed capital costs where short-run marginal costs are low. But this should be a challenge on how to recoup or write off such costs as fast as possible so they are no longer a financial obstacle to short-run marginal cost pricing. Instead, many regulatory economists seem to consider it acceptable for infrastructure prices to be set at long-run marginal cost in perpetuity.

The traditional Australian land-value rating system captures external benefits of infrastructure and thereby amortizes the fixed costs of infrastructure. The economically and financially shrewd way for a municipality or rural town to operate if it wants network infrastructure would be to levy a rate on land values to pay for network construction and capital maintenance costs by tender, and then to offer the market (operation of the system once built) by tender at the lowest cost for servicing it. Land rates would service the capital costs while user charges on throughput would be priced merely at operational cost plus the wholesale price of gas, for example, bought at the transmission connection. Harold Hotelling realized that land-value rating could provide the key to pricing at short-run marginal cost in the 1930s, and William Vickrey (1977) endorsed the optimality of the concept.

If land-value rating cannot be used and capital costs must be recovered solely from users, then regulatory authorities should be looking to see that these initial capital costs are amortized out of prices as soon as possible and that any 'double dipping' on actual capital costs is prevented. This issue is also often passed over in silence. What is worse is that there sometimes seems to be a confused idea among some regulators that competition for the market means offering a franchise (e.g., for gas pipelines) to the highest bidder who is left with unrestrained monopoly pricing power. In that scenario, one can never get prices down later to short-run marginal cost: the successful bidder will plead that he has to service forever his capitalized cost of purchasing the monopoly.

Competition for the market should be different. The purpose should be to get the infrastructure built and made available to the community at the lowest cost. The tender should be on the basis that you will only be allowed to charge short-run marginal cost plus a mark-up which will be eliminated over time as the capital cost is recouped. The community offering up the monopoly market is really asking who is willing to charge us least as a community for the monopoly infrastructure.[19]

In the case of a monopoly infrastructure franchise, there is a publicly sanctioned grant of a monopoly easement which overrides the rights of private and public landholders. As with patents, the Crown grants this monopoly for the public benefit. Why should the public be deprived forever of the possibility that prices should be set equal to short-run marginal cost? Increasing returns are a blessing, not a curse. The object of economic policy should be to take advantage of them as quickly as possible, rather than let them be used as an excuse to keep up monopoly rents.

CONCLUSION

Privatization of natural monopolies, such as railways, roads, telecommunications networks and gas pipelines, has been in fashion since the 1980s. At first, it was argued that there was no threat to the public interest because these monopolies would be subject to regulation, which would prevent price exploitation. More recently, critics of regulation have argued that no or, at most, 'light handed' regulation is necessary, lest infrastructure owners fail to invest in maintaining or expanding necessary public infrastructure. Monopoly rents have come to be seen as the price of infrastructure investment by the private sector.[20]

Against this, Henry George would object that the public does not have to (and should not) suffer the overweening pretensions of infrastructure owners demanding monopoly rents. It is the public, through their governments, which grants titles to land and easements for infrastructure networks. The public can therefore insist that such networks be operated on the basis of a fair return only on capital actually invested (as opposed to what was paid to buy into the monopoly or its revalued assets). As to the argument that a monopolist who has bought his monopoly is entitled to a legitimate expectation of enduring monopoly rents, Henry George would have responded, as he did to former slave owners, that it is enough for bygones to be bygones upon the abolition of unjust property rights and those who have gained profits unfairly in the past should count themselves lucky not to be required to pay them back, rather than complaining of lost opportunities for future exploitation.

George's focus on justice led him to think of property rights in terms of 'mine', 'yours' and 'ours', not solely 'mine' and 'yours'. He would therefore have thought it foolish and wrong to grant a monopoly easement to a private owner of common-use network infrastructure who might charge as he pleased. He would have seen it as foolish a situation as if the residents of an apartment block gave over the stairs, lifts and landings to some investor who was then left free to charge them as he pleased for the privilege of leaving or going to their apartments. As George wrote in *Progress and Poverty* ((1971) [1879], bk VIII, ch. 3, p. 412): 'And it may be said generally that businesses which are in their nature monopolies are properly part of the functions of the State, and should be assumed by the State. There is the same reason why Government should carry telegraphic messages as that it should carry letters; that railroads should belong to the public as that common roads should.' George would have said some land must be used separately and therefore should be rented to the highest bidder from time to time for exclusive use; but other land rights, such as network easements, which can be enjoyed in common, should continue to be held in common and any investment necessary in roads, bridges, pipelines, etc. to make these common land rights useful should be financed by a rate on the holders of the lands serviced. In that manner, the public would be free to use roads, pipelines, airports, etc. without being charged monopoly rents but only the marginal cost of use (if any).

NOTES

1. One might say they shared the idea that creation, not appropriation, is the original justification for property. You own what you create and your title is good as against the world, but you cannot assert ownership of the Creator's natural bounty as against the other descendants of Adam. This is not a labour theory of *value* but a labour theory of *title*.
2. See his *Principles of Political Economy*, (1965) [1848–71], bk II, ch. xvi, 2. Although Mill drew criticism from Schumpeter (*History of Economic Analysis*, (1954), p. 672), Mill's point is not at all silly. Of course, there can be competition to secure a non-reproducible advantage. Mill's point is the same as Kirzner's.
3. See *Progress and Poverty*, (1971) [1879], bk VII, ch.1, pp. 344–6 and *Social Problems*, (1963) [1883], ch. XV, pp. 148–9.
4. Income taxation may be described similarly, as in the popular usage of the term 'tax slaves'.
5. Formerly Chairman of the US Council of Economic Advisers, World Bank chief economist and now (2004) at Columbia University.
6. Formerly Professor of Economics at Columbia University and President of the American Economic Association.
7. 'pc' or 'political correctness' seems to take many (and inconsistent) forms, the only unifying feature seeming to be a surrender of one's critical faculties to some current fashion.
8. Kirzner (1973, pp. 89–94).
9. Kirzner (1973, p. 97).
10. Kirzner (1973, p. 99).
11. Kirzner (1973, p. 109).
12. Kirzner (1973, p. 131).
13. Kirzner (1973, pp. 199–201).
14. Kirzner (1973, p. 240).
15. See Clark, John Bates (1907–27) *Essentials of Economic Theory*, Macmillan: New York. At p. 37 is exemplified one of J. B. Clark's semantic attempts to translate land into a manifestation of capital, an approach which has heavily influenced subsequent economic theory. As I noted in my 1982 article (see References), this evolution was clearly a reaction to Henry George's writings, but one which I—like Bohm-Bawerk—consider to have been essentially misconceived.
16. In a related context, the argument was often made in the nineteenth century that land-value taxation was unwise because the 'unearned increment' on land was necessary to promote railroad and other investment. This argument proved sufficiently embarrassing once its sub-optimality implications became apparent that it was quietly abandoned. See Dwyer (1980, pp. 205–9).
17. The 'profits' from rent-seeking behaviour are usually dissipated either *ex ante* or *ex post* through 'competitive' processes, as noted in Hylton (2003, pp. 13–14, 18–19). That is why talk about 'competition' for a monopoly is hopelessly naive. Until and unless one can distinguish and define the differing meanings of the terms 'capital', 'investment' and 'competition' one will be in a perpetual muddle.
18. Attributed to Rupert Murdoch by Lawrence Grossman (1995, pp. 173–4).
19. Which doubtless explains why U.S. drug company lobbyists seem to hate the Australian pharmaceutical benefits scheme and hope the new U.S.–Australia 'free trade' agreement can be used to eliminate it.

20. It would be an interesting thesis topic for a bright Ph.D. student to explore 100-year cyclical
     'cobweb' fashions in economic thought.

REFERENCES

Andelson, Robert V. (ed.) (1979), *Critics of Henry George: A Centenary Appraisal of
     their Strictures on Progress and Poverty*, London: Associated University Presses.
Barker, Charles Albro (1991) [1955], *Henry George*, New York: Oxford University Press,
     reprinted by the Robert Schalkenbach Foundation.
Blaug, Mark (ed.) (1992), *Henry George (1839–1897): Pioneers in Economics 34*,
     Aldershot: Edward Elgar
Bohm-Bawerk, Eugen von (1959) [1921], *Capital and Interest*, 3 volumes, translated
     by George D. Huncke and Hans F. Sennholz, South Holland, Illinois: Libertarian
     Press.
 Brown, Harry Gunnison (1974) [1924], *The Economics of Taxation*, Chicago: University
     of Chicago Press.
Clark, John Bates (1907–27), *Essentials of Economic Theory*, New York: Macmillan.
Dwyer, Terence M. (1980), *A History of the Theory of Land-Value Taxation*, Ph.D. thesis,
     Harvard University (Ann Arbor, Michigan: University Microfilms).
Dwyer, Terence M. (1982), 'Henry George's Thought in Relation to Modern Economics',
     American Journal of Economics and Sociology, **41**(4), 363–73.
Geiger, George R. (1933), *The Philosophy of Henry George*, New York: Macmillan.
George, Henry (1971) [1879], *Progress and Poverty*, New York: Robert Schalkenbach
     Foundation.
George, Henry (1963) [1883], *Social Problems*, New York: Robert Schalkenbach
     Foundation.
George, Henry (1966) [1885], *Protection or Free Trade*, New York: Robert Schalken-
     bach Foundation.
George, Henry (1947) [1891], *The Condition of Labour*, London: Land & Liberty Press.
George, Henry (1965) [1892], *A Perplexed Philosopher*, New York: Robert Schalken-
     bach Foundation.
George, Henry (1932) [1898], *The Science of Political Economy* (edited by Henry George
     Jr), London: Henry George Foundation of Great Britain.
Grossman, Lawrence (1995), *The Electronic Republic*, New York: Viking.
Groves, Harold M. (1974), *Tax Philosophers* (edited by Donald Curran), Madison, U.SA.:
     University of Wisconsin Press.
Hotelling, Harold (1938), 'The general welfare in relation to problems of taxation and
     of railway and utility rates', *Econometrica* **6**, 242–69; reprinted in K. J. Arrow and
     T. Scitovsky, *Readings in Welfare Economics*, London: AEA and Allen & Unwin,
     1969, pp. 284–308.
Hylton, Keith (2003), *Antitrust Law: Economic Theory and Common Law Evolution*,
     New York: Cambridge University Press.
Kanemoto, Yoshitsugu (1984), 'Pricing and investment policies in a system of competi-
     tive commuter railways', *Review of Economic Studies,* **LI**, 665–81.
Kirzner, I. (1973), *Competition and Entrepreneurship*, Chicago: University of Chicago
     Press.
Lincoln Institute of Land Policy (2001), *The Legacy and Works of Henry George*, 2
     volumes CD-ROM set, Cambridge, Massachusetts.
Mill, James (1965) [1844], *Elements of Political Economy*, 3rd edition revised and cor-

rected, New York: Augustus M. Kelley.

Mill, John Stuart (1965) [1848–71], *Principles of Political Economy with some of their applications to Social Philosophy*, edited by J. M. Robson, Toronto: University of Toronto Press.

Nozick, Robert (1974), *Anarchy, State and Utopia*, New York: Basic Books.

Productivity Commission (2001), *Price Regulation of Airport Services*, issues paper, Canberra: AusInfo, January.

Productivity Commission (2001), *Review of the National Access Regime*, position paper, Canberra: AusInfo, March.

Productivity Commission (2001), *Price Regulation of Airport Services*, draft report, Melbourne, August.

Productivity Commission (2001), *Review of the National Access Regime*, Report no. 17, Canberra:, AusInfo, September.

Productivity Commission (2004), *Review of the Gas Access Regime*, report no. 31, Canberra: AusInfo, June.

Ricardo, David (1951) [1817–21], *On the Principles of Political Economy and Taxation*, edited Piero Sraffa, Cambridge, U.K.:Cambridge University Press.

Schumpeter, Joseph A. (1954), *History of Economic Analysis*, New York: Oxford University Press.

Smith, Adam (1976) [1759], *The Theory of Moral Sentiments*, Indianapolis: Liberty Classics.

Smith, Adam (1976) [1776], *An Inquiry into the Nature and Causes of the Wealth of Nations*, edited by R. H. Campbell and A. S. Skinner, Glasgow edition, Oxford: Clarendon Press.

Vickrey, William (1977), 'The city as a firm', in Martin Feldstein et al. (eds), *The Economics of Public Services: Proceedings of a Conference held by the International Economic Association at Turin*, London: Macmillan, pp. 334–43, reprinted in Richard Arnott et al. (eds) (1994), *Public Economics: Selected Papers by William Vickrey*, Cambridge, U.K.: University Press, pp. 339–49.

10. Land Tax in Australia: Principles, Problems and Policies

Frank Stilwell and Kirrily Jordan

INTRODUCTION

There has been a recent revival of interest in Georgism. In part it is driven by the crisis of housing affordability and recognition that this reflects the failure to develop appropriate policies for land. It also derives from 'green' concerns about the need to restructure tax policies so that they discourage wasteful uses of natural resources and promote ecologically sustainable development.

Such concerns are currently evident in Australia, further fuelled by widespread disquiet about the existing taxation arrangements. Australia's tax system has been described as the most complex anywhere in the world.[1] Existing under nine Federal and State jurisdictions, it has evolved in a fragmentary and often incongruous way, with taxes being added or changed in response to current objectives and with no view to a cohesive underlying logic. The result is duplication and contradiction between the taxes levied in different jurisdictions, Federal-State financial imbalance, and a blowout of tens of thousands of pages of tax law which is 'so complicated that it is difficult for many tax accountants and lawyers, let alone taxpayers, to understand'.[2] For example, Mason (1991) reports an addition of 15,000 pages of tax legislation and regulations in the seven years prior to 1991, and Banks (2003) cites the phenomenal growth of the Income Tax Assessment Act, expanding from around 1,000 pages in 1985 to nearly 7,000 in 2003.[3]

The need for an overhaul of the existing tax arrangements is clear. By developing a more cohesive tax system on sound economic, social and environmental principles, opportunities also exist to restore the financial viability of the public sector, to promote more ecologically sustainable development and to produce a more equitable society. What taxation principles can promote these goals? The following standards are essential criteria upon which any tax system should be judged:

- simplicity—the legitimacy of the tax system depends upon its being readily understood;
- equity—tax rates should reflect people's ability to pay;
- efficiency—the tax system should not discourage productive economic activity nor encourage unproductive pursuits;
- potency—the tax system should generate the revenue required to finance a good quality public sector;
- sustainability—the tax system should provide disincentives to ecologically unsustainable economic activity.

Can Georgist analysis contribute to the development of a tax system that serves these various goals? This chapter explores this question in some detail, as a contribution to a broader debate on progressive tax reform. The focus is both on Georgist principles and on Australian empirical data, particularly from the State of New South Wales (N.S.W.) and its capital, Sydney, where land prices have become the highest in the nation. This does not purport to provide a comprehensive analysis of all the possibilities for tax reform, and the figures used in the discussion are indicative only. The general aim is to consider the potential for addressing tax reform, both in principle and practice, from a radically different perspective.

TAXING THE USE OF NATURE

Progressive and ecologically responsible tax reform can usefully begin with a philosophical emphasis on taxing the use of nature. It is now a common tenet of the environment movement that the earth is not ours to 'own'. Rather, we are its temporary stewards, with responsibilities to care for the earth and not to compromise the needs of future generations whilst meeting our own. This is the cornerstone of the widely accepted concept of sustainable development, and reflects a 'necessary humility regarding the human place in nature'.[4]

Flowing from this logic is the idea that natural resources are the common gift to all who share the earth, such that those who alienate them from the community for exclusive use should be taxed for the privilege, with the revenue thus raised funding the community's economic, social and environmental needs. In this way our economic system would better reflect an ecological view of the earth.

TAXING THE EXCLUSIVE RIGHTS OF ACCESS TO LAND

Perhaps the most obvious place where the economic system deviates from these principles is in the private ownership of land, through which much of the earth is divided up into parcels held by individuals having rights of exclusive access and use. This practice was alien to most indigenous cultures and is a relatively recent phenomenon, taking hold with the Western European 'enclosures' from the 14th to the 19th Centuries that privatised and fenced off what had previously been common land. The tradition of 'the commons' has been supplanted by a society in which private land ownership and exclusive rights of access to land have seemingly come to be accepted as natural and almost pre-ordained phenomena.

The exclusive right of access to land raises particular equity concerns. Land is fundamentally different from other forms of capital in that it is limited in supply and geographically immobile. That is, some land is more desirable than other land, and neither the total supply nor its location can be modified to match this pattern of demand. Because land cannot increase as demand increases, there is never enough land for everyone to own a plot in practical, preferred locations. Those with the financial capacity to be top bidders in the property market alienate this most strongly sought-after land from the rest of the population, while those who might want to buy but cannot afford the rising property prices are forced to pay rent to landowners. As populations continue to grow and land prices continue to rise, more and more land is parcelled up into housing developments, further straining the capacity of future generations to own their own plot of land.

While current Australian evidence does not yet point to a substantial decline in overall levels of home ownership as a consequence of rising land prices, it does suggest an increasing stress on households entering such an inflationary property market. The nationwide index of housing affordability, compiled by the Housing Industry Association in conjunction with the Commonwealth Bank, fell by 23.7% between 2002 and 2003 alone. In Sydney, the median price of new homes was $571,300 in December 2003, rising to $700,000 for established houses.[*] Mortgage repayments for first home buyers reached an average of 48% of household income. No wonder that the proportion of first home buyers among total house purchasers had fallen to only 13%, historically the lowest level ever. A median-priced house in Sydney in 2003 cost over 12 years' worth of average personal earnings, compared to just under 4 years of average earnings in 1986.[5]

Home ownership is not necessarily a desirable social norm, renting being the preferred option of many people. However, there is a critical equity issue: under present arrangements land is alienated from the community by private ownership, with the landowners enjoying exclusive access to that land and its rising values while others are denied this opportunity. The intergenerational aspect of this process is especially pertinent, for landowners typically pass on the title to their land to their heirs, such that future generations are denied equal access to land and its benefits.

---

[*] All amounts are in Australian dollars.

Can, and should, the benefits of exclusive access to land be shifted back into the public realm through a system of land taxation? Such a system would be based on taxing the unimproved value of the land, whereby those enjoying exclusive access to more valuable land would 'rightly pay society proportionally more for the privilege'.[6] Essentially this would operate as a system of land rentals, with the rent being collected by the state for reinvestment into public expenditure.

TAXING COLLECTIVE BENEFITS PRIVATELY APPROPRIATED THROUGH RISING LAND VALUES

Rising land values, which currently result in wealth accruing to the land's private owners, are typically the product of societal processes rather than individual efforts. For example, land values increase in an area when new public works or amenities are built nearby, such as a new rail link or shopping centre. Landowners can also receive tremendous 'windfall' gains in land values when their land is rezoned to allow development. Yet more fundamentally, the driving force for increasing land values, particularly in urban areas, is the nature of the urban growth process itself. Whilst demand for sites in these areas is continually growing, the supply remains fixed, with the resultant increase in value generating enormous increments of unearned wealth for existing landowners.

Individual landowners may have some impact on the value of their land; for example, when they renovate or landscape their property. This is more marked when a number of landowners in a neighbourhood do so and thereby push up market prices.[7] However, it is seldom the sole efforts of the individual landowner that cause the increase in the value of their land, but rather the productive efforts of the community in general.

Without adequate taxation on land to recoup this social dividend, land value increases resulting from the community's productive efforts are captured by the individual landowner, while those unable to afford land are further excluded from the market. These processes are a major contributor to ongoing social and economic inequality, as those fortunate enough to have owned land in desirable areas capture the economic surplus at the expense of those making a productive contribution to its creation, and at the expense of future generations saddled with higher prices for access to urban land and housing.

LAND INFLATION AND INCOME REDISTRIBUTION

It is possible to indicate the extent to which landowners have privately appropriated social wealth in the Australian case by examining the increase in land values and incidence of land taxes over the last decade. The State of N.S.W. can be taken as a case in point: its increase in land values, particularly in Sydney but also, more generally, along the eastern seaboard, has vastly outstripped land-based taxation revenue in that State. This reflects a more general trend of inflationary real estate pressures and low levels of land taxation in other States too: so the data presented here have a broader national significance. They have further international significance as an illustration of what happens generally to land values in a city or region experiencing substantial economic growth.

As Table 10.1 shows, total land values in N.S.W. more than doubled in the decade 1993–2003, with a total increase in value of 153% or $361.5 billion. Land value increases were particularly marked in the years 2001–02 and 2002–03, with increases of over 17% in total land values in each of those years. Residential land was the major contributor to total land value, and accounted for 80% of the total land value increase over the whole period 1993–2003.

Table 10.1 Land Values in N.S.W., 1993–2003

Year	Value of Residential Land ($b)	Value of Commercial Land ($b)	Value of Rural Land ($b)	Total Land Value ($b)
1993	185.3	32.1	18.2	235.6
1994	194.1	33.5	18.5	246.1
1995	207.9	34.1	18.9	260.9
1996	200.8	33.5	37.1	271.4
1997	227.7	36.7	38.3	302.7
1998	252.2	38.8	40.8	331.8
1999	279.2	40.9	43.2	363.3
2000	304.4	42.9	45.4	392.7
2001	334.6	45.2	52.7	432.5
2002	399.6	49.3	60.0	508.9
2003	475.5	53.8	67.8	597.1

Notes:
The value of land in hobby farms and residential rural land was classified as 'rural' land for the first time in 1996.
Mining and industrial land are classified as 'commercial' land.
Source: Australian Bureau of Statistics.[8]

Table 10.2 shows that various Federal and State government taxes and local government rates have captured a small proportion of this increase in land values. State land taxes and local government rates, the most direct policy instruments, generated revenues of $8,525 million and $13,139 million respectively in the period 1992–93 to 2002–03. Additional taxes on property transfer capture some of the increase in land values, but only when properties are sold or exchanged.[9] Total land-related stamp duty revenue collected by the N.S.W. Government in the period 1992–93 to 2002–03 was $20,383 million. This is more than double the total State land tax collected in the period. Capital Gains Tax (C.G.T.), a Federal Government tax, also captures some of the increase in land values, with an estimated C.G.T. revenue from real estate assets in N.S.W. of $1,920 million in the period 1992–93 to 2002–03.

Table 10.2 Land-based Tax Revenue in N.S.W., 1993–2003

Year	Land Tax Revenue ($m)[a]	Land-related Stamp Duty Revenue ($m)[b]	Land-related C.G.T. Revenue ($m)[c]	Local Govt. Rates Revenue ($m)[d]	Total Land-based Tax Revenue ($m)
1992–93	549.3	882.0	—	566.3	1,997.6
1993–94	519.2	1,206.5	118.2	—	1,844.0
1994–95	509.7	1,122.5	74.6	1,049.6	2,756.4
1995–96	580.0	1,131.0	113.7	1,045.9	2,870.6
1996–97	625.0	1,472.0	171.5	1,061.0	3,329.5
1997–98	839.3	1,820.5	283.4	1,744.7	4,687.9
1998–99	961.0	1,824.0	391.8	1,806.3	4,983.1
1999–00	889.0	2,249.0	436.3	1,868.3	5,442.6
2000–01	919.0	2,075.0	330.9	1,955.0	5,279.9
2001–02	999.0	3,050.0	—	2,042.3	6,091.3
2002–03	1,134.0	3,550.0	—	—	4,684.0
Total	8,524.6	20,382.5	1,920.4	13,139.5	43,967.0

Notes:
Capital Gains Tax Revenue data are unavailable for the years 1992–93, 2001–02 and 2002–03. Available C.G.T. revenue data include tax on capital gains in a range of asset types and, being a Federal tax, in all States. While total annual revenue has not been consistently disaggregated into asset type, capital gains tax on real estate assets has typically accounted for less than 15% of the annual total in the period 1993–2003. Hence, 15% of the annual C.G.T. revenue is a sensible estimate of the proportion attributable to real estate assets. While no figures are available to illustrate the proportion of this total revenue that is generated in N.S.W., 33% is a rough guide, based on the 2001 Census data that found that 33% of the total number of dwellings in Australia are situated within N.S.W..
Local Government rates data were collected in calendar years for 1992 and 1993, and subsequently in financial years. For the years 1992 and 1993–94 to 1996–97 the available Local Government Rates Revenue data include only residential rates. For subsequent years, farmland and business rates are also included. Figures for the years 1993 and 2002-03 are not available.

Sources:
a. N.S.W. Treasury Budget Papers.
b. N.S.W. Treasury Budget Papers.
c. Calculated from N.S.W. Treasury Budget Papers.
d. N.S.W. Department of Local Government, N.S.W. Local Government Councils Comparative Information.

These figures allow us to estimate what proportion of the increase in land values has been captured for public purposes. From 1993 to 2003 the total land-based tax revenue collected by all levels of government was approximately $44 billion. This was only 12% of the $361.5 billion increase in land values over the same period. The other 88%, comprising $317.5 billion in increased land values, was left in the hands of private landowners.

This prodigious increase in the wealth of landowners raises all sorts of questions about efficiency, equity and sustainability. It creates a politico-economic context in which thoughtful reconsideration of Georgist principles and their applicability is warranted.

GEORGIST PRINCIPLES

Concerns about the private appropriation of rising land values are not novel. The case for using land tax as the antidote found its most powerful expression in the work of Henry George (see George, 1966 [1879]), and has been promoted by his followers for over a century (see, for example, Day, 1995; Hemingway, 1998). George's powerful exposition of the social and economic ills arising from the private appropriation of social wealth by landowners has been discussed in preceding chapters in this book. So too has his 'remedy', consisting of the replacement of taxes on productive economic activity by a uniform tax levied on the unimproved value of land (sometimes called site revenue).

Underpinning the strong following George's ideas gained in both the United States and Australia in the late 19th Century were both ethical and economic propositions. Ethically, land tax was seen as the best form of taxation, as no individual had the right to privately appropriate the benefits from land and to exclude others from their rights to a share of these benefits. It was also regarded as the most economically rational tax because it would not discourage productive endeavour. George argued that most taxes, including income taxes, company taxes, goods and services taxes, and payroll taxes, did just that. In contrast, land tax encourages active endeavour by encouraging landowners to put their land to the most productive use.

As Cord (1965) notes, George argued that land prices would fall as land rent was collected through taxation, discouraging land speculation and eliminating depressions brought about by booms and busts in the housing market. With land prices reduced, workers would have more access to land and home ownership. Moreover, as land speculation diminished, a bigger share of total production would be available for wages and interest. Meanwhile, as taxes on income and production were abolished, economic growth would receive a great stimulus and unemployment would disappear. Economic disparities would diminish too; since land ownership was a 'source of great wealth and privilege, the public collection of land rent would end the gross inequality in the distribution of wealth'.[10] The revenues raised could then fund vast improvements in welfare programs and public benefits.

While George's arguments won the support of many followers, including many in government, they also encountered fierce opposition, particularly from academics and business people in the United States and from the wealthy landed classes in countries like Britain and Australia, all of whom had vested interests in the *status quo*.[11] Some conservatives of the time misinterpreted George's ideas as promoting the socialisation of land and so forcefully railed against him, claiming that the adoption of the single tax would mean the confiscation of land by the State. George had suggested no such thing, being opposed to government ownership of land because he feared it would lead to corruption and the abuse of a community resource.

George's assertion of the capacity of a single uniform land tax to finance all government expenditure also alienated many economists and academics. Influential economists at the time argued that the single tax was a naive idea unfounded in scientific or rigorous economic analysis. They pointed out that George was not formally trained in economics and that no professional economists supported the single tax. For example, George Seligman, Professor at the University of Columbia, dismissed George as an ill-informed enthusiast who supposed that he had 'discovered a world-saving panacea'.[12]

Rejecting George's ideas along these lines, much of the early debate against the single tax was lacking in analytical critique. One exception was Francis A. Walker, a leading American economist of his time.[13] Walker criticized George's claims about the inequalities created by the capture of rents. Like the earlier classical economist David Ricardo, George had argued that as industrial society developed, rents would be correspondingly increased, such that the advantages gained by material progress would be absorbed by rents and captured by landowners, thereby limiting the possibility of a general rise in wages. Walker used empirical evidence to show that the condition of waged workers had actually improved over time. This was possible, he suggested, because some increases in production, such as improvements in quality rather than quantity, involved an increase in the demand for labour but no corresponding increase in the demand for land. Walker argued that such a scenario could lead to a growth in wages that outstripped any growth in rents. This was in opposition to George's claim that 'the increase of land values is always at the expense of labour'.[14]

Walker also criticised George's analysis of rents and land speculation. George had argued that land speculation was the primary cause of economic depressions, whereas Walker emphasised that economic depressions can be caused by other factors, and that speculative activity is not always associated with land. Moreover, while Walker did not dispute George's theoretical arguments about the ethics of the community's right to claim land rent, he added a proviso that if land rents were to be collected by the State, landowners should be paid compensation, at least in the transition period, as they had bought the land under the belief that they would own any increases in its value. Here was a foretaste of the ethical and practical problems of implementing any tax reforms that run counter to the expectations of citizens who had made economic decisions based on previous tax arrangements.

Others to discuss the 'single tax' proposal included the businessman Edward Atkinson,[15] noted for his contributions to contemporary economic debate, who objected to George's proposal on the grounds that landowners would seek to shift the tax onto consumers in the form of increased rents for housing and commercial property. This argument continues to underlie concern about who would bear the incidence of the tax. But land tax is different from other taxes in this respect. It is a tax on an economic surplus and must be borne by the landowner if competitive conditions prevail in the market for land. As Cord puts it, such a tax 'cannot increase the price of land... because it cannot decrease its supply': it would simply divert land rent from landowners to the government.[16]

Debates on these issues raised by Henry George and the Georgist movement have continued to this day.[17] However, for the most part, George's ideas have been largely ignored in contemporary economic analysis. This cannot wholly be explained by the vested interests opposed to the Georgist 'remedy', although that is undoubtedly a major influence on the broader reaction to Georgism. The utopian or even evangelical approach taken by many of George's followers may also have played a part, serving to alienate the non-committed. But from an economist's viewpoint, the key issue is the incongruence of George's ideas with the dominant mode of economic analysis. Neo-classical economics treats land, like labour and capital, as a factor of production whose rewards are determined by marginal productivity, and leaves out land and natural resources from any deeper consideration. This is part of the general push by neo-classical economists to purge economic theory of the notion of an economic surplus on which classical political economists, from Ricardo to Karl Marx and Henry George, had focused their analyses. The combination of these factors means that there is now little in the way of explicitly critical responses to George's ideas.

This neglect of George's ideas in economic debate is unfortunate, as his fundamental points about the ethics of land ownership and the redistributive effects of land taxation continue to be relevant. It is pertinent to ask, then, what aspects of George's analysis remain sound, and how might his ideas be selectively adapted in today's economic and political climate? The following section of this chapter explores these issues, with particular reference to the potential of land taxation to combat speculation, to moderate inflation and to generate necessary government revenues. It is on these practical concerns, rather than on historical debates, that the contemporary significance of the Georgist position now seems to rest.

PRACTICAL EFFECTS OF A UNIFORM LAND TAX

It is one thing to assert that a policy of increasing land taxes is philosophically sound, but what might the effects be on the economy, on society and on the environment? As the data in Table 10.2 clearly show, the N.S.W. Government's capacity to tax wealth deriving from land ownership is extremely limited under current taxation arrangements. We need to consider the likely practical consequences of a policy that seeks to increase the impact of land taxation.

COMBATING SPECULATION AND MODERATING LAND PRICE INFLATION

As discussed above, proponents of land tax often assert that one of its major benefits would be as a disincentive to property speculation. The rationale for this argument is that a tax on land value would 'cream off' part of any potential capital gain, thereby reducing the attractiveness of land as a speculative investment. This has important implications for housing affordability, which has become a significant concern and the subject of much public debate and media attention in Australia, as it has in major cities the world over.[18] The key point to establish here is that no policy to promote greater housing affordability can sensibly ignore the impact of land price inflation. Land prices are a significant component of housing prices, and usually the major contributor to general housing price increases. While buildings deteriorate and hence decline in value over time, it is usually the land values that continue to escalate and hence push housing prices up. Increased land taxes could affect this process via various means.

Other things being equal, the reduced speculative demand engendered by increased land taxes could be expected to reduce property price inflation. That is, by reducing the attractiveness of property relative to other assets, and hence reducing demand for investment housing (i.e., houses and flats that are not occupied by their owners), increased land taxation could be expected to facilitate a reduction in land prices and therefore allow a significant increase in housing affordability. It should be noted, though, that for this effect to be experienced nationwide, the land tax would need to be applied uniformly across Australia. If this were not the case, higher land taxes in one State would simply push property speculators into other States with lower incidences of land tax.

However, this general argument needs to be qualified by attention to particular complexities. For example, will property speculation continue to look attractive whenever the share market enters a downturn? Would the taxation advantages to buyers of 'investment' properties (known in Australia as negative gearing) and the Capital Gains Tax provisions that encourage property investment cancel out any effect of increased land taxes in reducing demand? These questions are difficult to answer in general terms. An appropriately cautious inference would be that, while an increased and nationally uniform land tax could go part of the way in combating property speculation, it must be accompanied by broader changes to Australia's taxation arrangements to create a coherent tax system underpinned by desirable social, economic and environmental goals.

In addition, it is necessary to ask what rate of land tax is necessary for it to be a sufficient disincentive to property speculation. As a general benchmark, one may surmise that reducing capital gains on property by around half could be expected to significantly reduce its attractiveness as an investment. This is particularly the case where such a move would reduce the annual capital gains to less than the current bank interest rate, in which case the more sensible investment would be depositing the money in a term deposit in a bank.

We can take N.S.W. as an example again to see, in general terms, how capital gains in landed property interact with land taxation. In the decade 1993–2003, median house prices in N.S.W. increased by an annual average of 10.1%.[19] As Table 10.1 shows, this is very similar to the rate of land price inflation, averaging about 10% per annum, and compounding to a 153% increase over eleven years.

Owner-occupied property in Australia is currently exempt from land tax.[20] Some simple fiscal arithmetic can be used to establish a 'ballpark' figure of what the rate of land tax would need to be to reduce the typical capital gain on real estate assets to 5% annually if the current owner-occupier exemption were removed. To halve the rate of capital gain on real estate assets to 5% annually, land tax over the 1993–2003 period would have had to capture about $180 billion (i.e., 50% of the $361.5 billion gain in the value of land). To produce a land tax revenue averaging $18 billion annually would have required a tax rate of about 5%. A 5% uniform land tax rate on all current land values in N.S.W. would currently generate about $30 billion annually. This is slightly more than the current total of land tax and land-related stamp duty revenues (as shown in Table 10.2). In other words, the introduction of such a tax would allow the State Government to dispense with stamp duty on landed property transfers altogether.

While such a rate of land tax might not entirely eliminate speculation, it would be instrumental in reducing and smoothing out long-term cycles in the housing market. In addition to its effect on land speculation, land tax may also increase housing affordability by fostering an increased supply of properties in the housing and rental markets. Levying an increased tax on land would encourage landowners to put their land to its most productive use. For example, vacant land would have to be developed and empty housing would have to be rented out in order to bring in returns to cover the increased costs to landowners resulting from the land taxation. Landowners who did not use their land productively would be forced to sell to others who would. In this way, more land and housing would be released for occupation, with the additional supply potentially acting as a downward pressure on housing prices, assuming that the increased supply was in areas in which people chose to live.

This issue, however, also has significant equity considerations. For example, might increased land taxes mean that middle and lower-income families cannot afford to keep an unoccupied holiday home, while wealthier landowners can keep their holiday property as they can afford to carry the increased cost? Will small-scale farmers and primary producers on the outskirts of metropolitan areas be forced to sell up their properties or subdivide to make way for more profitable developments? These are specific concerns to be set against the general characteristics of land tax as a highly equitable tax; one that redresses the inequality caused by the capacity of landowners to capture unearned income at the expense of the community.

GENERATING REVENUES WHICH CAN BE USED AS A 'SOCIAL DIVIDEND' OR TO REDUCE OTHER TAXES

How potent would a uniform land tax be as a source of government revenue? In general, it seems that even quite low rates of land tax can generate substantial annual revenues. The discussion above illustrated that a land tax rate of 5% would generate an annual revenue of $30 billion in N.S.W., based on the most recent land values. Even a tax at the 2003 land tax rate of 1.7% would generate revenues of $10.2 billion annually (i.e., 1.7% of the total value of land shown in Table 10.1) if the owner-occupier exemption and tax-free threshold were removed. Such revenues could be used for a variety of public purposes.

One possibility would be to return the revenue to the community as a 'social dividend' in order to satisfy social goals and address inequality through redistribution. That would give a highly visible return to the community, helping to promote the perceived legitimacy of the uniform land tax. A more targeted variation on this theme would be to return the revenues raised from land tax (or some part thereof) to the original custodians of the land, recognising their prior relationship with the land and its resources. This could be in the form of provision of additional services to indigenous Australians or increased funding of Aboriginal Land Councils, for example. Any action along these lines would need to be done in proper consultation with and active involvement of indigenous communities to ensure appropriate outcomes.

The potency of land tax as a revenue raiser means that the revenues generated may also be targeted to a range of other social, cultural and environmental programs. Restoring and raising the quality of public infrastructure would be to the broad benefit of the economy and society. Of course, the alternative, more in tune with Georgist thinking, is to use the extra land tax revenues to fund a reduction in other taxes, including taxes on labour, capital and financial transactions. One specific possibility would be to utilise the increased land tax revenue to fund the reduction or abolition of stamp duty on property exchanges. Originally, stamp duty in Australia was intended to cover the cost of stamping and filing documents that transferred an interest in property, but with the stamp duty[21] payable on a median priced house in Sydney now above $23,000[22], its original purpose has been superseded. The stamp duty payable is calculated on the current market value of the property when it is exchanged, and this is a progressive tax because as property values increase so too does the rate of stamp duty applicable.

However, stamp duty has a number of intrinsic problems. As an impost on buying and selling property, it has a 'lumpy' characteristic, with large amounts paid at once rather than small amounts over a period of time, and it often impacts at times of particular financial stress (as when moving house). As a tax on transactions, it also discriminates between movers and non-movers and thereby has a negative effect on spatial mobility. The large amount of stamp duty incurred by moving house acts as a disincentive to relocation, discouraging people from relocating to a more practical location. In turn, this has effects on society's use of resources, such as increased need for transportation, causing problems of traffic congestion and atmospheric pollution. By substantially reducing stamp duties on property transactions and replacing their revenues with a system of annual land tax, these problems could be alleviated.

Again, some fiscal arithmetic can illustrate the orders of magnitude involved in these possible tax changes. If the owner-occupied exemption on land tax were to be removed, a land tax rate of 0.63% (i.e., just over a third of the former standard rate of 1.7%) would generate more than enough annual revenue to replace the current land-related stamp duty. Such a rate of land tax would generate around $3.8 billion annually compared with the current land-related stamp duty of $3.5 billion in N.S.W.

Alternatively, using revenue raised through land taxation to fund reductions in taxes on income and capital would shift the balance of taxes away from productive activities and could thereby improve the nation's productive capacity. Terry Dwyer (2003, Chapter 9), one of the contributors to this book, has examined the implications of such a move, suggesting that land income in Australia is a sufficiently large tax base to enable very substantial reductions in company and income taxes. While national income tax and company tax revenues in the year 1998–99 totalled $76.7 billion and $20.7 billion respectively, Dwyer estimates that national land income in the same period was $132.7 billion.[23] By utilising this revenue (or some substantial part thereof) to fund reductions in taxes on mobile factors of production, Australia could compete for global investment without losing its ability to fund a viable public sector.

The possibility of utilising land tax revenues to fund a reduction in taxes on capital and labour also has another important implication. Were increased levels of land tax to reduce land prices, the revenue-raising potential of the tax would be diminished over time. This might necessitate an eventual increase in other taxes (or the tapering off of previous reductions) in order to recoup the balance of revenue. This reflects the general tension in all tax arrangements: if a tax is effective in discouraging a socially undesirable activity it simultaneously becomes less effective as a revenue-raiser. This is a tension that is particularly relevant to taxes imposed on activities that have damaging environmental and/or health effects.

Dwyer suggests, however, that this may not be a significant problem in the case of land tax. While increasing the rate or coverage of land taxes would exert a downward pressure on land values, when combined with reductions in taxes on capital and labour, land values may actually continue to rise. This is because reducing taxes on capital and labour may stimulate an increased demand for land. Dwyer cites Hong Kong as an example of this phenomenon,[24] where high rates of land taxation and low tax rates on labour and capital have resulted in vigorous demand from international business for operational space in Hong Kong, such that land values have continued to grow strongly.[25]

TOWARDS LAND TAX REFORM IN AUSTRALIA

The extention of Georgist principles in the Australian context would not involve starting 'on a clean slate'. Indeed, since the idea of land value taxation became popular in Australia in the late 1800s, it has found various supporters across the political spectrum, including individuals within the Australian Labor Party, the Liberal Party, and, in recent times, the Australian Democrats and the Greens. It has also had considerable impact through public policy 'on the ground', albeit in half-hearted and inconsistent forms.

The States were the first to introduce land taxes in Australia, beginning with Victoria in 1877. Other States soon followed, and legislation was brought in to also allow the developing cities, towns and shires to levy rates on land. In 1910 the Federal Labour Government introduced an additional land tax at the national level. The rationale behind these taxes was to break up large landholdings by forcing landowners to subdivide, to encourage the productive use of idle land, and to raise the revenues needed for expansion of settlements and defence of the nation. For the most part, this rationale was based on the pragmatic response of settlers trying to adjust to a new environment rather than any political, social or economic theory, although some legislators later pointed to Henry George's philosophy to justify or amend land taxes.

Perhaps the closest approximations to Georgist principles in Australia have been the leasehold systems in the Australian Capital Territory (A.C.T.) and Northern Territory. These were originally designed in principle to recover the unearned increment in land values through the collection of rents subject to periodical adjustment based on land value increases. In practice, however, these attempts were largely unsuccessful, perhaps partly due to their deviation from the essential principles of leasehold in allowing payment for land use rights in the form of a capital sum rather than rent. Their eventual abandonment has left the freehold system of land tenure as the national norm. Along with the concentration of population and economic activities in the coastal cities, this has been the basis on which land ownership has facilitated prodigious amounts of private capital accumulation. Speculation in land has been called the 'national hobby'.[26]

Now, after decades of adjusting land tax and rating regimes in response to different pressures in different State and local jurisdictions, only vestiges of the original land taxes remain. Significant differences exist across State or local government borders, adding up to an incoherent mix of policies with scarce reference to any underlying rationale. It is important to take stock of these current arrangements before considering possible initiatives for reform.

CURRENT ARRANGEMENTS FOR STATE LAND TAXES

Land tax in all Australian States and the A.C.T. is calculated on the unimproved value of the land, determined by professional valuers. Each of these jurisdictions has introduced numerous exemptions such that land tax does not apply to all landowners. These include exemptions on land owned by non-profit religious societies, and charitable or educational institutions as well as land that falls below a certain value threshold. In many jurisdictions, exemptions or rate reductions are also given to different classes of land, particularly to rural land used for primary production.

Notably, all States and the A.C.T. also exempt landowners from paying land tax on their principal place of residence, thereby limiting the tax to investment properties. However, as noted earlier, the land tax arrangements in N.S.W. have differed from those in the rest of the country because of the existence of a 'premium property tax', which taxes land used as the principal place of residence where the value of the land is above a threshold level. This threshold was indexed to the rate of inflation, such that as property prices rose, so too did the premium property tax threshold. It was originally set at $1 million when introduced in 1998: by 2004, just before it was abolished, it had risen to $1.97 million.

Land tax in N.S.W. prior to 2004 was also unique in the Australian context in being calculated at a flat rate. For the current year (2003–04) this rate is 1.7%. All other States and the A.C.T. have calculated land tax on a sliding scale, imposing a higher marginal rate of taxation on more valuable land. N.S.W. in 2004 adopted a similar principle. Queensland has the largest number of land tax brackets at fourteen. The Northern Territory is unique in that it does not levy a land tax. Full details about these land tax arrangements in each of the States and Territories are set out in the Appendix to this chapter.

CURRENT ARRANGEMENTS FOR MUNICIPAL RATES

Municipal rating arrangements also vary widely across the country, with different rating requirements applying under different State or Territory legislation. Most municipal councils calculate rates on the unimproved value of the land. There are, however, some notable exceptions. Councils in Western Australia calculate rates on one of two values. Unimproved Value is used for calculating rates on rural land, while Gross Rental Value (including improvements) is used for rating urban land. In Victoria, councils have three valuing options — to calculate rates on the unimproved value, on capital improved value, or on net annual rental value of the land. In some areas in the Northern Territory, council 'rates' are not actually rates as they are not calculated on land values at all, being determined instead as a flat sum per property.

Complicating the picture still further, most councils provide differential rates for different land uses, such as commercial, residential, industrial and rural, although some charge a flat rate across all rateable properties. Some councils have a two-tiered rating system, with a higher rate applied above a certain land value.

A number of Australian States and Territories provide rate rebates or pensioner concessions on rates, and in some areas rates can be deferred until the sale of a property. In Queensland, land owned and occupied by the State or Commonwealth Government does not pay rates unless used for commercial activities. In the A.C.T. landowners do not pay rates on the first $19,000 of the value of their land.

In most instances the rationale for rating is to raise revenue. In fact, in many States and Territories the rate is determined by the amount of revenue a council calculates that it needs in order to meet its financial responsibilities. In local governments in N.S.W., annual increases in general revenue are capped by the State Government, essentially limiting council rates and meaning that rate revenues do not necessarily increase in line with land values.

This jumble of municipal rating structures across the country illustrates how far removed the notion of rating has become from any consistent ethical or philosophical considerations of the sort considered by Henry George. It would not be credible to claim that the current arrangements systematically reflect the Georgist rationale of capturing the economic rent of the land. On the contrary, many municipal rating arrangements undermine this philosophical position by taxing improvements on land, i.e., improved rather than unimproved capital values. This is anathema from a Georgist perspective because it is a disincentive to making capital improvements that increase the economic productivity of land use.

Summing up a confused situation, it is appropriate to look at the total revenues raised by State land taxes and by municipal rates. Table 10.2 shows the overall situation for N.S.W. (with some years missing because of data unavailability). Comparing the first and fourth columns, we can see that land tax revenues have grown at a much slower rate than municipal rate revenues, being the equivalent of 97% of municipal rate revenues in 1992–93 and only 48.9% in 2001–02. Full information on land tax rates is shown in the Appendix to this chapter.

POSSIBLE INITIATIVES

Considering these existing land tax and municipal rate arrangements, what would be the most appropriate way of implementing a broad-based system of land value taxation?

To have the desired effect on land speculation, land tax arrangements would have to be nationally uniform to prevent speculators from simply shifting their investments interstate. One option, then, would be to replace local government rates with a nationally uniform land tax scheme managed through the Federal or State Governments. Such a scheme could be linked to a reform of local government finance. For example, a policy change that replaced local government rates with an apportionment to local governments from a uniform land tax could be an economically efficient, and electorally palatable, reform. A land tax rate of 1.7% would raise annual revenues in N.S.W. by an estimated $6.8 billion, based on current land values if the owner-occupier exemption were removed, and assuming that one-third of properties fall below the existing tax-free threshold. This is more than enough to replace the revenues currently generated by municipal rates in N.S.W. Of course, the implications of such a shift in the means by which local government would raise revenue would need careful consideration. Councils currently guard their relative autonomy to determine the arrangements for rate revenues, and regard this as part of the process of local democracy. But even if they had a guaranteed apportionment from a more nationally uniform land tax scheme they would still have autonomy regarding the way in which the revenues are locally spent.

Alternatively, a nationally uniform land tax scheme could be linked to a replacement of local and State governments by regional governments to be funded from a uniform nationwide system of land taxation (as advocated in Stilwell, 2000, chapter 20). That could provide an institutional basis and a fiscal means of seeking more balanced regional development. In general terms, the extension of the existing land tax provisions would tend to 'cream off' more revenue from those regions where land price inflation is most pronounced. In practice, this would mean that the metropolitan areas would be more highly taxed, tending to favour regional decentralisation of population and industry. A formula for redistribution between regional governments would be needed in order to ensure reasonably equitable standards of local service provision, akin to the formula currently used by the Commonwealth Grants Commission for inter-State redistribution of revenues. Whether metropolitan landowners as a whole would contribute a higher share of total taxation than they do currently through stamp duties on property transfer would depend on the detailed structure of these arrangements. Any such additional revenues could be used for regional redistribution (e.g., financing infrastructure in non-metropolitan areas necessary for them to act as effective 'counter magnets' to the major cities). How best to use the revenues for such purposes, and indeed whether to do so rather than simply use them to improve the quality of public services across the board, would necessarily be a matter of political judgement and choice.

CONCLUSION

The arguments and evidence marshalled in this chapter provide the basis for a serious consideration of the potential for land tax to be a substantial element in progressive tax reform in Australia. We can sum up by seeing how a more broadly based uniform land tax would perform according to the five criteria for judging a tax system outlined in the Introduction to this chapter.

Simplicity

A nationally uniform land tax in itself is a relatively simple tax, although provision for exemptions applying to certain types of land would increase its complexity. To keep it simple and transparent in practice, the land valuing process would need careful attention: existing arrangements have often been the subject of concern over their legitimacy and fairness. In introducing a nationally uniform land tax it would, therefore, be prudent to establish a land valuing process with which the community could feel confident. But all tax systems — whether income taxes, capital gains taxes, or wealth and inheritance taxes — need to face up to this challenge of transparency and consistency of application. In the case of land tax, the land and housing market constitutes an ever-present check on reasonably consistent valuations.

Whether a greater emphasis on land tax would reduce or add to the complexity of the tax system overall would depend on whether the land tax would supplement or replace other taxes. In the former case, it would add yet another layer of complexity to Australia's taxation arrangements: only in the latter case could it properly be regarded as contributing to a simplified tax system. Yet that is obviously a very tall order.

Equity

The essential nature of a nationally uniform land tax is highly equitable in that it redresses the inequality caused by the capacity of landowners to capture unearned income at the expense of the rest of the community. It is also progressive, in that it offers significant scope for utilizing the revenues raised as a social dividend to address further social and economic inequalities.

However, a nationally uniform land tax would potentially have a greater impact on some types of landowners, such as pensioners and others who are 'asset rich but income poor' (cf. Pullen, Chapter 8, this volume). There is scope to alleviate these impacts through concessions such as rate reductions or deferred payments, such that the social impacts of the tax would depend on the specific details of its application. As was currently the case with the N.S.W. 'premium property' land tax, for example, deferral of tax liabilities until the death of the property owner, at which time they are taken from the estate, can be an effective means of marrying the principle of land tax with inheritance tax. The current absence of any such tax on inherited property in Australia is a significant element in perpetuating socio-economic inequalities.

Efficiency

Land taxation is an efficient tax in that it does not provide disincentives to productive economic activity nor encourage unproductive pursuits. On the contrary, it encourages landowners to bring their land into its most productive use and acts as a disincentive to the unproductive activity of land speculation. The Australian experience indicates that controlling the speculative processes that have fuelled rapid land price rises in Sydney, for example, can be a crucial factor in producing a less inflationary overall economic environment.

Potency

A significant advantage of land tax is its potency as a revenue raiser. There is little scope for tax avoidance or evasion. While corporations can shift other assets overseas in order to reduce their other tax liabilities, the geographically fixed nature of land means that land tax obligations cannot be avoided. The tentative estimates presented in this chapter indicate that the revenues that could be generated by a uniform land tax, even at a quite modest rate, are very substantial. These revenues could be used to fund other social infrastructure expenditures. Funding the expansion of public housing, which has been getting a shrinking share of public investment in Australia over the last two decades, is one direct means of contributing directly to easing the problem of housing affordability. Alternatively, the revenues raised could be used to fund reductions in other taxes such as payroll tax, income tax or the Goods and Services Tax (G.S.T.), Australia's equivalent to the value-added tax (V.A.T.) that exists in many other nations.

Sustainability

From a 'green' perspective, it is crucial that any tax system should promote ecological sustainability and discourage ecologically unsustainable economic activity. In general, a uniform land tax system could be expected to serve this goal by limiting the profligate use of land resources associated with 'urban sprawl'. However, there are specific environmental concerns needing to be addressed. Binning and Young (1999), for example, have raised concerns about the impact of land taxes on the conservation of native vegetation. Indeed, as discussed earlier, any increase in land taxes will encourage landowners to increase the productive capacity of their land in order to cover the additional costs. This may have an adverse impact on conservation where land in its natural state is cleared to make way for developments that will generate financial returns. It would therefore be essential to ensure that adequate controls are in place to prevent such developments and protect conservation values through planning, zoning and development-approvals processes. In addition, it may be prudent to subject areas of high conservation value to reduced rates of land tax or exempt them from land tax obligations altogether.

Essentially, however, land tax can be seen as an 'environmental tax' in that it taxes people for their use of a natural community resource. It is therefore consistent in principle with other 'environmental taxes' such as carbon taxes and resource rental taxes. Introducing changes to land tax as part of a coherent tax system aimed at encouraging socially, economically and environmentally useful activity, and discouraging destructive activities, may sensibly involve a planned mix of such taxes. Not surprisingly, among the political parties in Australia, the Greens are the most enthusiastic proponents of this approach to radical reform.

Political Challenges

Changes to taxation structures invariably produce both winners and losers, whatever their aggregate benefits. Not surprisingly, any efforts to increase land taxes can be expected to face fierce opposition from those who perceive that they would be worse off under the new arrangements. This opposition may be heightened in the case of land tax because the tax bill would have to be periodically paid by the landowner. In this respect, a land tax differs from taxes such as the G.S.T. (where the tax increment is effectively 'hidden' in the normal retail price of goods and services, other than for major payments such as home building) and income tax (where the tax liabilities are regularly and automatically deducted at source). Like council rates, any 'lumpy' periodic payments are predictably problematic in terms of the visibility of their impact. This makes it all the more important for effective land tax reform to be seen in the context of the demonstrable benefits and objectives of a broad tax reform package. The acceptability of any package of tax changes depends ultimately on what relief is given from existing taxes and how effectively it is presented to the public as a means of making the tax system as a whole more equitable and efficient.

An array of broad political and social as well as economic judgments must necessarily be made in considering such reform. For example, in the Australian case, the extension of land taxation would impact on the overall structures of Federal–State financial relations, because land taxes (and stamp duties) are currently collected by State Governments, while the major taxes, including income tax and company tax, are Federal taxes. Under current arrangements the States rely on the Federal Government passing on some of its tax revenues to help them meet their major expenditure commitments on health, education, roads and so on. That is the principal feature of the long-standing 'vertical imbalance' in Federal–State financial relationships in Australia: the Federal Government raises most of the taxes but the State Governments do much of the spending. It is also why the allocative formula applied by the Commonwealth Grants Commission is such a politically contentious issue.[27] Not surprisingly, the States have been eager to exploit whatever revenue-raising sources are directly available to them, such as stamp duty, payroll tax and gambling tax. Any shift in the balance of these and other taxes, including land tax, would have significant implications for Federal–State financial relationships and therefore for the Australian political system as a whole.

A Challenge Worth Embracing?

Georgist ideas evidently have significant contemporary relevance, notwithstanding their marginalisation in 'respectable' economic opinion. As this chapter has demonstrated, they can make a useful contribution to a consideration of options for reforming Australia's taxation arrangements. Such consideration is timely, because the current tax arrangements seem ill-suited to produce the social, economic and environmental outcomes that a good tax system should provide. The problems of housing affordability in the major cities and the challenge of restructuring for ecological sustainability currently bring the issue of tax reform into particularly sharp relief. Land tax warrants attention as a key element in any such reform. It offers significant possibilities for aligning the fundamental goals of social justice, economic efficiency and ecological sustainability. It should properly be the subject of carefully considered community debate.

NOTES

1. Grbich (1991), p.247.
2. Mason (1991), p. 244.
3. Banks (2003).
4. The Earth Charter Commission (2000).
5. Stilwell, F. (2003), p.7.
6. Williams, K. (n.d.), p.12.
7. While the crucial factor here is land values, *house* prices prevailing in the market are relevant as they are one element in the Valuer-General's determination of land values.
8. Australian Bureau of Statistics (2003) *5204.0 Australian System of National Accounts. Table 83. Value of Land, Land Use by State—as at 30 June.*
9. While property prices cannot be directly equated with land values, a large proportion of the capital gains in real estate assets is derived from the land component of the asset, with the value of the existing buildings typically depreciating over time.
10. Cord (1965), p. 26.
11. For a discussion of attempts by those with vested interests to silence George and his followers, see Gaffney and Harrison (1994).
12. Seligman, quoted Cord (1965), p.33.
13. For further discussion of Walker's critique of George's ideas, see Cord (1965), pp. 37–47.
14. George (1966), p.244.
15. For further discussion of Atkinson's critique of George's ideas, see Cord (1965), pp. 49–50.
16. Cord (1965), pp. 49–50. See also Gabbitas and Eldridge (1988), pp. 151–154, for a further discussion of these issues.
17. See, for example, Lindholm and Lynn (1982); and Gaffney and Harrison (1994).
18. See, for example, the draft report of the recent Australian Productivity Commission Inquiry into First Home Ownership (2003).
19. Real Estate Institute of N.S.W. (2003).
20. The exception applying in the State of N.S.W. between 1998 and 2004 was owner-occupied property with a very high land value, set at $1 million in 1998 and subsequently indexed to inflation.
21. All subsequent references to 'stamp duty' refer to stamp duty on land transfer unless otherwise indicated.
22. Stilwell, F. (2003), p.9.
23. Dwyer, T. (2003), p.39.
24. Dwyer notes that Hong Kong may be unique in that it is a city state with scarce and valuable land. However, he suggests that the experience of Hong Kong may be translatable to the Australian context where the demand for land is so densely concentrated in urban areas.
25. Dwyer (2003), pp.26-27.
26. Sandercock (1979), p.xi.
27. See, for example, Totaro, P. (2004).

REFERENCES

Banks, G. (2003), 'The good, the bad and the ugly: economic perspectives on regulation in Australia', address to the *Conference of Economists, Business Symposium,* Canberra, 2 October 2003.

Binning, C. and M. Young (1999), *Conservation Hindered: The impact of local government rates and State land taxes on the conservation of native vegetation.* National R&D Program on Rehabilitation, Management and Conservation of Remnant Vegetation, Research Report 3/99, Canberra: Environment Australia.

Commission of Inquiry into Land Tenures (1973), *Report of the Commission of Inquiry into Land Tenures*, First Report, Canberra.

Commission of Inquiry into Land Tenures (1976), *Report of the Commission of Inquiry into Land Tenures*, Final Report, Canberra.

Cord, S. (1965), *Henry George: Dreamer or Realist?* Philadelphia: University of Pennsylvania Press.

Day, P. (1995), *Land: The elusive quest for social justice, taxation reform & a sustainable planetary environment,* Brisbane: Australian Academic Press.

Dwyer, T. (2003), 'The Taxable Capacity of Australian Land and Resources', *Australian Tax Forum*, No. 18, 21–67.

Gabbitas, O. and D. Eldridge (1998), *Directions for State Tax Reform,* a Productivity Commission Staff Research Paper, Canberra: AusInfo.

Gaffney, M. and F. Harrison, (1994), *The Corruption of Economics*, London: Shepheard-Walwyn Publishers.

George, H. (1966) [1879], *Progress and Poverty,* New York: Robert Schalkenbach.

Grbich, Y. (1991), 'Australian legislation: a recalcitrant child', *Taxation in Australia,* **26** (5), 247.

Hemingway, L. (1998), *Sharing the Earth,* Warrnambool: Les Hemingway.

Lindholm, R. and A. Lynn, Jr (eds) (1982), *Land Value Taxation: The Progress and Poverty Centenary,* Madison: The University of Wisconsin Press.

Mason, A. (1991), 'Simplification: enough to give you a complex', *Taxation in Australia,* **26 (5)**, 244–5.

Productivity Commission (2003), *First Home Ownership*, Melbourne: Productivity Commission a discussion draft.

Real Estate Institute of N.S.W. (2003), *Property Focus* (December Quarter).

Sandercock, L. (1979), *The Land Racket: The Real Costs of Property Speculation,* Canberra: Silverfish.

Stilwell, F. (2000), *Changing Track: A New Political Economic Direction for Australia,* Annandale, N.S.W.: Pluto Press.

Stilwell, F (2003), *Submission to the Productivity Commission Inquiry Into First Home Ownership*, URL: www.pc.gov.au/inquiry/housing/subs/sub212.pdf.

The Earth Charter Commission (2000), *The Earth Charter*, URL: www.earthcharter.org/files/charter/charter.pdf.

Totaro, P. (2004), 'Carr fury over $376m cut in share of tax take', *Sydney Morning Herald*, 4 March.

Wade, M. (2004), 'Interest rate rise ahoy as economy steams ahead', *Sydney Morning Herald*, 10 February.

Williams, K. (n.d.), *Economic Justice in Australia: A Guide to Real Prosperity for Everybody,* Melbourne: Prosper Australia.

APPENDIX: COMPARISON OF STATE LAND TAXES, 2003–04

1. New South Wales

Total Unimproved Value	Land Tax Rate
0–$260.999	Nil
$261,000 and over	$100 plus 1.70 cents for every $1 of the value that exceeds $261,000

Note: A premium property tax applied to owner-occupied property with a value of $1.68 million or above at the end of 2003. The N.S.W. Government's 'mini-budget' of 2004 abolished this tax. It also changed the land tax scales in general, removing the tax-free threshold and lowering the top rate of tax.

Source: Office of State Revenue, N.S.W. Treasury.

2. Victoria

Total Unimproved Value	Land Tax Rate
0–$149,999	Nil
$150,000–$199,999	$150 plus 0.1 cents for every $1 of the value that exceeds $150,000
$200,000–$539,999	$200 plus 0.2 cents for every $1 of the value that exceeds $200,000
$540,000–$674,999	$880 plus 0.5 cents for every $1 of the value that exceeds $540,000
$675,000–$809,999	$1,555 plus 1.0 cents for every $1 of the value that exceeds $675,000
$810,000–$1,079,999	$2,905 plus 1.75 cents for every $1 of the value that exceeds $810,000

Source: State Revenue Office, Victorian Department of Treasury and Finance.

3. Queensland

Total Unimproved Value	Land Tax Rate
0–$275,997	Nil
$275,998–$349,999	$1,895 plus 1.20 cents for every $1 of the value that exceeds $200,000
$350,000–$499,999	$3,695 plus 1.37 cents for every $1 of the value that exceeds $350,000
$500,000–$649,999	$5,750 plus 1.54 cents for every $1 of the value that exceeds $500,000
$650,000–$799,999	$8,060 plus 1.71 cents for every $1 of the value that exceeds $650,000
$800,000–$949,999	$10,625 plus 1.89 cents for every $1 of the value that exceeds $800,000
$950,000–$1,099,999	$13,460 plus 2.01 cents for every $1 of the value that exceeds $950,000
$1,100,000–$1,249,999	$16,475 plus 2.23 cents for every $1 of the value that exceeds $1,100,000
$1,250,000–$1,299,999	$19,820 plus 2.44 cents for every $1 of the value that exceeds $1,250,000
$1,300,000–$1,349,999	$21,040.00 plus 2.66 cents for every $1 of the value that exceeds $1,300,000
$1,350,000–$1,399,999	$22,370 plus 2.87 cents for every $1 of the value that exceeds $1,350,000
$1,400,000–$1,449,999	$23,805.00 plus 3.09 cents for every $1 of the value that exceeds $1,400,000
$1,450,000–$1,499,999	$25,350.00 plus 3.30 cents for every $1 of the value that exceeds $1,450,000
$1,500,000 and over	1.80 cents for every $1 of the value

Source: Office of State Revenue, Queensland Treasury.

4. South Australia

Total Unimproved Value	Land Tax Rate
0–$50,000	Nil
$50,000–$300,000	$0.35 for each $100 or part $100 of the value that exceeds $50,000
$300,001–$1,000,000	$875 plus $1.65 for each $100 or part $100 of the value that exceeds $300,000
$1,000,001 and over	$12,425 plus $3.70 for each $100 or part $100 of the value that exceeds $1,000,000

Source: Revenue S.A., South Australian Department of Treasury and Finance

5. Western Australia

Total Unimproved Value	Land Tax Rate
0–$50,000	Nil
$50,001–$190,000	$75.00 plus 0.15 cent for each $1 in excess of $50,000
$190,001–$550,000	$285.00 plus 0.45 cent for each $1 in excess of $190,000
$550,001–$2,000,000	$1,905.00 plus 1.76 cents for each $1 in excess of $550,000
$2,000,001–$5,000,000	$27,425.00 plus 2.30 cents for each $1 in excess of $2,000,000
$5,000,001 and over	$96,425.00 plus 2.50 cents for each $1 in excess of $5,000,000

Source: Office of State Revenue, Western Australian Department of Treasury and Finance.

6. Tasmania

Total Unimproved Value	Land Tax Rate
0–$15,000	Nil
$15,000–$99,999.99	$25 plus 0.55 cents per $1 above $15,000
$100,000–$199,999.99	$492.50 plus 1.25 cents per $1 above $100,000
$200,000–$499,999.99	$1,742.50 plus 2.25 cents per $1 above $200,000
$500,000 and over	$8,492.50 plus 2.5 cents per $1 above $500,000

Source: State Revenue Office, Tasmanian Department of Treasury and Finance.

7. Australian Capital Territory

Average Unimproved Value	Land Tax Rate
0–$100,000	1.00 %
$100,001–$200,000	1.25 %
$200,001 and over	1.50 %

Note: Average Unimproved Value includes the 2001, 2002 and 2003 unimproved land values of the property.

Source: A.C.T. Revenue Office, A.C.T. Department of Treasury.

8. Northern Territory

There is no land tax in the Northern Territory.

11. Enduring but Unacknowledged: the Georgist Inheritance in Australia

Philip D. Day

ORIGINS

Georgist philosophy is undoubtedly evident and enduring in Australia. Not in the consistent and purposeful development of economic thought, but evident nevertheless, both in fiscal practices and in land planning and administration. A difficulty, however, is that manifestations of Georgist influence have been essentially disjunctive, both in substance and temporal sequence.

European settlement in Australia in 1788 introduced conceptual issues of sovereignty and ownership, and practical questions of land administration. Tracing their subsequent evolution requires some spelling out of the early historical background to the extent that space permits. In 1770, Lieutenant (later Captain) James Cook claimed sovereignty over eastern Australia on behalf of King George III. The British Admiralty's 1768 instructions to Cook[1] convey something of the generally high-principled attitude of the Imperial government towards the indigenous population, and subsequently towards the administration of a raw frontier settlement and its sometimes fractious non-indigenous population:

> You are likewise to observe the genius, temper, disposition and number of the natives, if there be any, and endeavour by all proper means to cultivate a friendship and alliance with them, making them presents of such trifles as they may value, inviting them to traffick, and shewing them every kind of civility and regard; taking care however not to suffer yourself to be surprised by them, but to be always on your guard against any accident. You are also with the consent of the natives to take possession of convenient situations in the country in the name of the King of Great Britain, or, if you find the country uninhabited take possession for His Majesty by setting up proper marks and inscriptions as first discoverers and possessors.

Sir Stephen Roberts's (1968) definitive *History of Australian Land Settlement* records the incremental expansion of Australian settlement following Captain Arthur Phillip's arrival in Sydney Cove in 1788 with 700 convicts and 200 soldiers to establish a colony of felons at a cost assumed to be less than that of keeping them in hulks on the Thames. They were modest beginnings, preceding the flowering of empire in the Victorian era. 'There was no notion of a colony as a colony. Pitt and Sydney, the responsible statesmen, merely wished to solve a troublesome problem in the cheapest manner. ... Accordingly, little provision was made for anything beyond the actual transportation. ... More regard was paid to markets than to seed-wheat, to military precedence than to food supplies. There was no land policy...' [2] In 1788 Britain was disentangling its North American involvement and was about to become involved in the momentous struggle against Napoleon. India was still governed by the (British) East India Company, and while Phillip's three immediate successors as governors of New South Wales were also naval captains, there seems little evidence to support the surmise that Sydney was envisaged as a significant naval base and trading port.

EVOLUTION OF LAND LAW

Land tenure and land speculation were issues from the outset. The early decades of the 19th Century were characterised by *ad hoc* gubernatorial land grants: by the institution for a time of attaching modest quit-rents to land grants, and the prohibition of selling within five years; by conflicts with the Colonial Office in Whitehall (six months away by sea); and later by the intense and protracted controversy over the phenomenon of 'squatting' by pastoralists over huge areas of Crown lands at very low rentals, which the Colonial Office viewed as impeding the general development of population and industry. The vociferous public exchanges between William Charles Wentworth, pastoralist, leader of the free settlers, and campaigner for self-government, and Governor George Gipps are a matter of record. Gipps, arguably one of the ablest and most principled of the early governors (1833–46), frustrated Wentworth's bizarre attempt to buy from Maori chiefs some 20 million acres of New Zealand (then a dependency of N.S.W.) at the rate of one hundred acres per farthing.

Following Earl Grey's memorable 1848 instruction, reservation clauses were written into colonial leases; but his sentiment that 'the settlers in Australia have incurred a moral obligation of the most sacred kind', and his hope that the Imperial government had made every effort 'to avert the destruction of the native race as a consequence of the occupation of the territory by British subjects' were imperfectly reflected in subsequent colonial (and post-Federation) practice.[3] A century and a half later, landmark decisions of the Australian High Court in 1992 and 1996 refocused attention upon indigenous land tenure. The *Mabo* decision in 1992[4] disposed of the doctrine of *terra nullius* and established that, while *sovereignty* passed to the British Crown when Cook raised the union flag, indigenous *ownership* was not necessarily extinguished— a difficulty of course being that ownership as understood by Aboriginal Australians has always been conceived as communal rather than individual. The *Wik* decision in 1996[5] held that Aboriginal ownership could coexist with pastoral leases. Uncertainty about native title still prevails. The High Court decisions are not a reflection of any significant Georgist influence, but they underscore the difficulties inherent in any concept of absolute private ownership of land. Federal and state legislation has since provided mechanisms for establishing Aboriginal land claims – but not over land already alienated in freehold.

Clear evidence of the influence of Georgist philosophy emerged in the latter part of the 19th Century. After the cessation of (convict) transportation and the influx of population following the gold discoveries in the 1850s, the 19th Century saw profound changes in colonial society and in the character and emphases of political and economic debate, along with considerable innovation in land administration.

In the absence of a comprehensive overview of the evolution of Australian land law and administration, Justice Rae Else-Mitchell's lucid monograph *Legacies of the Nineteenth Century Land Reformers from Melville to George* (1974) goes a long way towards filling the gap and spelling out the chronology. Land speculation, leasehold tenure and land taxation were dominant themes. Else-Mitchell pays tribute to the remarkably high quality of intellectual activity in the late 19th Century in what was still a relatively small society. He discusses the pervasive influence of Henry George and the rapturous reception accorded him during his visit to Australia in 1890—his 1879 masterpiece *Progress and Poverty* 'took on some of the qualities of a book of gospel'. In Queensland, the Lands Minister Charles Dutton, who introduced far-reaching and enduring reforms, was strongly influenced by Henry George. In Tasmania, however, Henry Melville's (1835) *History of the Island of Van Diemen's Land from the Year 1824 to 1835 inclusive* (see Else-Mitchell, 1974) in which he urged that the whole of the colony's revenue should be chargeable upon the land, preceded Henry George by forty years.[6] Another who preceded George was William Gresham, a friend of J.S. Mill, who established the Land Tenure Reform League in Victoria which urged 'the gradual abolition of all indirect taxes whatsoever, the revenue of the state to be derived solely from the rental of land.'[7] Notorious land speculation in Victoria in the 1880s associated with railway and tramway extensions[8] increased the pressures for reform.

Land reform (in the six separate self-governing colonies prior to federation) was not uniform or contemporaneous. Nevertheless, citing the extension of leasehold tenure and progressive experiments with it in the case of perpetual, homestead and conditional purchase leases, Rae Else-Mitchell, respected lawyer and valuer, concludes his tribute to the 19th Century reformers with a significant observation: their practical achievements 'far exceeded anything which had been accomplished in the United States of America or the United Kingdom' — a judgement borne out by the fact that land reformers in the U.S. and U.K. have yet to achieve Georgist reforms in land valuation and municipal rating practice commonly accepted in Australia a century ago.[9] (Rating on land only, i.e. excluding improvements, dates from about 1887.)

THE COMMITMENT TO LEASEHOLD IN CANBERRA

Henry George certainly influenced the leading protagonists of Federation in 1901 and the decision to adopt leasehold tenure for the 900 square-mile seat of the Commonwealth Government, now the self-governing Australian Capital Territory. It was envisaged that leasehold tenure would fund the subsequent development of the national capital. But the early administrators made the fatal mistake of providing for reappraisement of land rentals in Canberra at twenty-year intervals. After a period of accelerated growth in the 1960s, a reassessment of Canberra land values in 1970 led to such a dramatic increase in rentals that – prior to an election — the (Commonwealth) Government abandoned leasehold as a fiscal instrument and bestowed upon existing leaseholders an absurdly munificent windfall gift of public revenue forgone. Instead of lease rentals it resorted to a dubiously founded system of rating, coupled with a betterment levy on land value increases attributable to any changes in the permitted use of leases. Thereafter leases for terms of years were sold virtually as freehold.[10]

Thus the incongruous outcome in Canberra reflects a diluted Georgist inheritance in that the residual leasehold system in the A.C.T. acknowledges that land ownership is still vested in the Crown; and betterment, when it is levied, accords with Georgist philosophy. However, the practical significance of vesting ultimate land ownership in the Crown is debatable. Outside urban areas, most of Australia is held from the States under various forms of Crown leasehold. The Crown is the acknowledged owner and lessor. Unoccupied land is referred to as Crown land. But whether the Crown really has any residual ownership rights in respect of land after it has been alienated in fee simple, i.e. in freehold title, is open to question. As early as 1834 the first Chief Justice of the N.S.W. Supreme Court sought to dispel any doubts about whether the vesting of all land in the Crown had been translated to colonial Australia.[11] In the course of a judgment he referred to all lands in the colony being vested in the Crown 'as the representative of the British Nation'. The legal fiction remains in the case of freehold, but as a pale shadow of feudal possession subject to communal obligations (although the term 'resumption', used to describe compulsory acquisition for public purposes, implies that the State is 'resuming' its underlying ownership).

LAND TAXES

Whether current land taxes in Australia are indicative of Georgist influence is likewise debatable. In the latter part of the 19th Century, land taxation in the colonies was aimed both at revenue-raising and at breaking up excessively large estates, particularly those held by absentees. After the turn of the century it seems Labor (State) Governments were attracted by the prospect of taxing land into use, but the land tax introduced by the Commonwealth (Federal) Government in 1910 had, strictly speaking, no purposeful Georgist rationale (but see Introduction to this book). Georgist purists would, correctly, prefer to refer to land *value* taxation (and better still to *resources rental*). But the rationale of land taxes has never been explicitly Georgist. The Commonwealth discontinued land tax in 1952. Land taxes in Australia, now imposed by the State Governments, are essentially an arbitrary wealth tax. For fifty years taxing the unimproved value of land was a frequently debated plank in the policy platform of the Australian Labor Party. However, it was omitted in unexplained circumstances in a revision of 1963 conference proceedings according to the Hon. Clyde Cameron in a paper 'How Labor lost its way' published by the South Australian Henry George League in 1984.

Frank Stilwell and Kirrily Jordan's Chapter 10 in this volume reviews land tax and its presently confused and depressingly diverse implementation in Federal Australia, while at the same time demonstrating the potential of land taxation as a revenue source which could permit the abandonment of irrational tax imposts like payroll and stamp-duty taxes currently levied by State Governments in pursuance of the arbitrary apportionment of fiscal responsibilities prevailing in Australia. Even (conservative) Prime Minister Howard, whose party has traditionally opposed the centralization of government in Canberra, has conceded that dispensing with state-level government might better serve the national interest than retaining the compromise apportionment of powers and responsibilities negotiated by the framers of Australian Federation in 1901. But an end to the present wasteful and fractious overlapping of jurisdiction is not imminent.

SAMUEL GRIFFITH'S NATURAL LAW BILL

Before pursuing the Georgist inheritance in the 20th Century, a surprisingly little known event occurred in 1890. It reflects the fertility of intellectual debate which then prevailed and at the same time ranks among the accidents of history which have frustrated the pursuit of land reform (like the curtailment of potential tax reform by the French Revolution, Henry George's narrow failure to become mayor of New York, and the defeat of the reforms proposed by the Asquith and MacDonald governments in 1910–11 and 1931 respectively).

Some of the unfortunate consequences of the commodification of land might have been effectively negated in Australia at the end of the 19th Century if a Bill introduced in 1890 by Sir Samuel Griffith, Premier of Queensland, had become law. The Bill was for an Act to be cited as *The Elementary Property Law of Queensland* 'to declare the Natural Law relating to the Acquisition and Ownership of Private Property'. Seeking to ensure a 'proper distribution of the products of labour', it enunciated 'First Principles', among them that 'The right to take advantage of natural forces belongs equally to all members of the community'; that 'Land, by natural law, is the common property of the community'; and that 'All property, other than land, is the product or result of labour'.[12] The text of this remarkable document is reproduced as an appendix to this chapter. One can only surmise about the evolution of land law and public and political perception of land as a resource if the Bill had proceeded. Alas, because of parliamentary instability and the looming financial crisis of the early 1890s, the Bill lapsed. (Griffith became Chief Justice of Queensland and went on to become the first Chief Justice of the High Court of Australia, but continued to espouse the principles of Natural Law after his retirement in 1919.)

TAX REFORM

Agitation for tax reform is an enduring legacy of Henry George (and his predecessors[*]). In Australia, it simmered throughout the 20th Century and became a lively focus of debate in the 1980s and 1990s, the outcome of which, however, did not reflect any significant Georgist influence.

While a number of respected economics texts explicitly endorse the taxation of land, the Henry George Foundation-sponsored Association for Land Value Taxation was denied attendance at (Labor) Prime Minister Hawke's much publicized and purportedly widely representative 'National Tax Summit' in 1985. In 1996 a comprehensive analysis prepared by four well-qualified professionals on behalf of the Land Values Research Group suffered a similar fate. It was submitted to the 'National Tax Reform Summit' jointly convened by the Australian Chamber of Commerce and Industry and the Australian Council of Social Service, but was ignored on the conference agenda and by the popular media. Arguments for and against a goods and services tax were the main focus of debate. Subsequently, the H.G.F.A. sponsored a 'Challenge', offering a $25,000 prize for the most convincing *refutation* of the L.V.R.G. submission. The competition was widely advertised and attracted professional and academic attention, but little editorial attention in the media. In the event, it attracted only 17 entries of indifferent quality, none of which impressed the respected inde-

[*] See J. Morrison Davidson (2003) [1899], *Concerning Four Precursors of Henry George and the Single Tax*, Honolulu, Hawaii: University Press of the Pacific — Ed.

pendent economists who evaluated them (Emeritus Professor Russell Mathews and Professor Rod Jensen).

Not echoed in Australia were the sentiments of the U.K. Conservative Government's committee which, in 1995, reported in favour of 'a gradual move away from taxes on labour, income, profits and capital towards taxes on pollution and the use of resources'. Billed as a once in a lifetime opportunity, the opportunity for real reform was squandered. By the time of the 1998 Federal election, Prime Minister Howard's 'great adventure' had degenerated into a pro- and anti-goods and services tax debate, and a tawdry auction for votes in the course of speculation fostered by the popular media about the likely winners and losers of a few short-term dollars. The lure of lower taxes was more potent than the prospect of serious tax reform.

By common admission the Australian tax system is seen to be defective because of its absurd complexity, its high compliance costs and its vulnerability to avoidance and evasion. Yet the protracted tax-reform debate of the 1990s was very narrowly based and the end result was an anti-climax. After a very close vote in the Senate, in 2000 the Howard Government's extravagantly publicized 'new tax system' introduced a regressive thirty-year-old value-added approach to taxation which vastly increased its complexity, particularly for individual professionals and small businesses. There were no overt indications that the Government or the Commonwealth Treasury ever considered the merits of land-value taxation, or the wider concept of natural resources rental and ecological taxes comprehensively argued by Clive Hamilton of the Canberra-based Australia Institute. In effect, tax reform in Australia was stillborn in 2000 — a testament to an entrenched mindset which instinctively rejects any reformist proposition which involves rethinking the nature of land. In the new millennium it remains to be seen whether smouldering resentment generated by the Goods and Services Tax rekindles agitation for reform.

Nevertheless, while the actual outcome in 2000 was totally anticlimactic, there were concurrent indicators of the endurance of Henry George's legacy. In mid-1997, for example, Georgist philosophy was revisited by one of the nation's most respected economic commentators. In feature articles headed 'An idea for tax reform, by George' in both the Melbourne *Age* and the *Sydney Morning Herald*, Maximilian Walsh recalled the vociferous welcome accorded Henry George at his first hour-long meeting in Sydney in 1890, reportedly interrupted 46 times by cheers. Reviewing George's influence on pre-Federation Australia and on Sun Yat Sen's land reforms in Asia, Walsh pointed out the surprising relevance of Georgist philosophy now to nation-states confronted with the erosion of their traditional tax revenue bases by globalization and communications technology. The need was to shift taxes 'to assets or activities anchored in the domestic economy such as land and land usage taxes'.[13] Also in 1997, P.P. McGuinness, another *S.M.H.* columnist, said that George preceded modern environmentalists in seeing land 'as a common resource belonging to future generations as well as the present' and land taxation 'as a means of opening it up, pushing unused or monopolised land into productive use'.[14] And in his column in the *Australian Financial Review*, former (Labor) federal finance minister, Peter Walsh, seldom missed an opportunity to assert that taxing the unearned increment was the most rational and least economically distorting form of revenue raising. Contemporary major reports, notably by H. Pender of the Australian National University and M.T. Young of CSIRO (the Commonwealth Scientific & Industrial Research Organisation), urged the capture of the unearned increment by broad-based land and resources taxes in the interests of both equity and sustainable development.

Earlier, in 1979, Edward Nash, the economics editor of the *Adelaide Advertiser* used the centenary of *Progress and Poverty* to review the legacy of Henry George, who had addressed three public meetings in Adelaide in 1890: 'The survival of the American's ideas to this day says something about their appeal. ... The philosophical base for George's economic views was simply that a landholder had no more right to charge rent for land he did not create than he would have to monopolise the air and charge others for the right to breathe it'. Nash used the occasion to deplore the situation in South Australia where (unlike Queensland, N.S.W. and the A.C.T.) home owners' local government rates rose with the improvements they made to their properties.[15] (Stilwell and Jordan refer to these differences in interstate practice.)

THE GEORGIST MOVEMENT

One indicator of the endurance of the Georgist legacy in Australia (and its likely future endurance) is of course the influence and status of the Australian Georgist movement. Now distant in time from the heady days of the 1890s, the formal organization of the Georgist movement in Australia has had a somewhat chequered and less than inspirational history.

Early benefactors assured the establishment and continuance of the Henry George Foundation of Australia Incorporated, based in Melbourne with a board of trustees, and the Henry George Foundation of N.S.W., an incorporated company located in Sydney. The latter has had a protracted litigious relationship with a factional offshoot, the Association for Good Government. The most active propagation of Georgist philosophy in recent years has been undertaken in Victoria by Prosper Australia (formerly Tax Reform Australia), with funding from the H.G.F.A. The journal *Progress*, in an attractive format, celebrated its centenary in May 2004, amidst some evidence of a recent resurgence of interest and a less elderly membership. Small associated bodies with a mere handful of mostly ageing members exist in the other States. Some substantial research was undertaken in Victoria in earlier years[16] and again more recently by the Land Values Research Group, which has an interstate membership coordinated by respected valuer Bryan Kavanagh. The Group's ecumenical patrons are a former Federal Liberal (conservative) minister and a former Federal Labor minister (the Hon. Sir Allen Fairhall, K.B.E. and the Hon. Clyde Cameron, A.O.).

There is, however, no one all-embracing nationally acknowledged Georgist body in Australia. The Georgist movement has been diminished by disputation about terminology; by the conviction of many disciples that the overnight conversion of the unenlightened requires only a reading of *Progress and Poverty* and reiteration of the 'single tax' mantra; and by a corresponding reluctance to acknowledge that, in any society, there is a legitimate place for user charges, and for ecological penalties and sumptuary taxes on things like alcohol, tobacco and petrol (and even a place for tariffs if the economic rationalist pursuit of freer trade in a globalized economy has intolerable *social* consequences). There has been too little research into the real-world implications and administrative pre-conditions associated with implementing Georgist philosophy in practice (and, realistically, in stages), plus too little analysis of the fundamental enigma: society's seemingly purblind resistance to what, to Georgists, is so logical and obvious. (One H.G.F.A. trustee, disenchanted with the movement's otherworldliness, is known to have found the bi-annual meetings of the trustees evocative of Alice in Wonderland.)

In the 21st Century the Georgist movement could identify – and consolidate – Georgism's contribution to economic policy in Australia. But not by simple regurgitation of late 19th Century doctrine. Nor by extravagant assertions that the Georgist panacea would eliminate unemployment in a society whose adopted lifestyle is dependent upon labour-*displacing* technology. Or by unqualified assertions about increasing housing affordability. Land rental could reduce to zero the capital price (but not the *value*) of land and thereby eliminate the initial capital cost of the land component from the house and land package. Housing would be *relatively* less expensive. But in expanding metropolitan areas and in other premium locations of high demand, land values will continue to rise and low-income affordability will remain a social problem warranting public policy intervention.

Paradoxically, there are factors present now which are insufficiently appreciated by the Georgist movement but which make the basic Georgist argument demonstrably more persuasive. Firstly, comprehensive land-use planning schemes make it easier to demonstrate that, regardless of its natural attributes and access to services, the market value of any parcel of land is ultimately determined by the use to which the community, via its public planning agencies, allows it to be put, either as a permitted or conditionally permissible use. The inequity of allowing private landholders to appropriate increases in land value attributable to public land-use decisions can thus be demonstrated more precisely than in George's day. The status of land as a community resource is demonstrably more apparent than in 1879.

Secondly, the technical feasibility of annual (or more frequent) revaluations means that valuations to calculate annual rental can now be kept up to date and more accurately reflect changes (upwards or downwards) in market value attributable to economic circumstances or public decisions about land use and the provision of public infrastructure.

Thirdly, the proliferation of transnational industry and commerce and technological advances in communication have vastly increased the mobility of capital and widened the scope for both legitimate tax avoidance and money laundering. Thus, far more so than in 1879, contemporary economic circumstances highlight the merits of an *immobile* revenue source for nations confronted with a shrinking traditional revenue base.

A fourth circumstance is the increasing recognition and endorsement of the notion of environmentally sustainable development, any meaningful pursuit of which must come to terms with the valuation and pricing of the planetary community's natural resources, and eliminate development pressures primarily motivated by the prospect of unearned private profit from natural resource exploitation.

In other words, at least four factors render Georgist philosophy more relevant and more persuasive than in George's time and administratively more capable of practical implementation. Thus the Georgist inheritance in Australia, however defined and by whatever name, seems more likely to wax than to wane. Nevertheless, its actual impact on future economic policy remains to be seen.

Within the Australian Georgist movement there has been some unproductive speculation about the interpretation of *Progress and Poverty* and George's voluminous other writing, but in academic circles there has been nothing like the volume of discussion which Georgism continues to generate in America. In part of course this is a reflection of a smaller society. But it also reflects the fact that, in much of Australia (and New Zealand), municipal rating on unimproved land values has been taken for granted for more than a hundred years. Far from being a focus for Georgist activism, it is not explicitly recognized as reflecting Georgist doctrine, and this, paradoxically, doesn't assist in logically urging the extension of Georgist philosophy into other areas of revenue-raising. It is one of the factors which make identifying and quantifying the Georgist inheritance in Australia difficult.

In the terms in which it was conducted, Henry George's memorable disputation with Malthus (see Chapters 1 and 4 of this volume) is not particularly relevant in 21st Century Australia. George's contention that more people could be fed if productive land were not held out of production by speculators and monopolists remains intrinsically valid, regardless of scientific (and fossil-fuel dependent) advances in food production. A 21st Century Malthus might be more disposed to argue that the planet's capacity to employ people meaningfully and equitably may well be a valid reason for curbing population growth.

The forcing of vacant or underdeveloped land into productive use was of course a cornerstone of George's 1879 thesis. Whether it threatens or conflicts with the principles of ecological sustainability and the preservation of environmentally significant undeveloped land or other natural resources has been canvassed in some academic writing (for example, by Backhaus and Krabbe [1991], writing in the *American Journal of Economics and Sociology*). But in any well-conceived land-use planning system this is a needlessly contrived non-issue. The natural environment *can* be protected by well-conceived land-use controls. Whether they are adequate in any given circumstances will depend upon the public will and governmental competence in devising and enforcing them.

In Australia a more puzzling issue is the seeming tardiness of the environmental movement to appreciate the status of land and to recognize that Georgist philosophy goes to the very core of environmental concerns. The unearned increment, if not captured for the community, renders all land vulnerable to private developmental pressures motivated by the prospect of windfall land-value profits.

THE IMPACT OF TOWN PLANNING

Reflecting the difficulty of observing a chronological sequence which was foreshadowed at the outset, it is necessary to revert to the first half of the 20th Century in order to trace the emergence of town planning as a significant responsibility of government (which in Australia means the six State and two Territory Governments and not the Federal Government, to which the 1901 Constitution did not allocate any specific jurisdiction in respect of regional and town planning). Over time, land-use planning has both widened the scope for public revenue-raising and more overtly exposed the ravages of the unearned increment.

Town planning *theory* has a respectable Georgist congruence. Thus the 1932 English *Town and Country Planning Act* acknowledged the logic of capturing a percentage of the betterment conferred on landowners by public planning decisions which increased the value of their land, and conversely it envisaged compensating landowners who were disadvantaged and suffered detriment. The 1932 Act was the model for town planning legislation adopted in the Australian States following World War II. However, governments shied away from imposing betterment levies and sought to confine very narrowly landowners' entitlements to compensation. Nevertheless, a decision of the N.S.W. Land and Valuation Court in a compensation case in 1954[17] acknowledged the concept of betterment. In assessing the compensation claimed, Judge Sugerman held that it should be offset by the betterment conferred on other land held by the claimant. While acknowledging that planning restrictions such as those in respect of setbacks, building heights and minimum lot sizes restricted the rights of landowners, the Court held that these so-called 'good neighbour' restrictions did not confer any entitlement to compensation. Thus in respect of compensation, this case (*Bingham* v. *Cumberland County Council*) established a restrictive precedent which has since prevailed in town planning law. As for betterment, the only examples of specific betterment levies are the levy that has operated in the A.C.T. since 1971, and the levy which the N.S.W. Government imposed between 1971 and 1973 in respect of land controversially released from Sydney's Green Belt.

In the absence of any means of capturing the windfall increase in land value conferred on private landowners by the decisions of public planning agencies, the town planning system is fundamentally flawed. As C.S. Keyworth, a State Planning Authority valuer and town planner, stated in evidence before the N.S.W. Royal Commission of Inquiry into Rating, Valuation and Local Government Finance in 1967: 'Before the introduction of prescribed town and country planning schemes the present system of council rating siphoned off some of the unearned increment ... (but) once a town planning scheme is prescribed, rural land becomes residential, commercial or industrial in the time it takes a Minister to sign a document. Values increase threefold overnight. Lucky owners, participants in the land lottery, by selling immediately at the enhanced figures are able to pocket the unearned increment' (transcript of evidence, p. 555). This evidence was a key factor in the Commission's recommendation that some of the unearned increment, or betterment, be captured for community purposes, a recommendation which the N.S.W. Government subsequently implemented in the case of the green belt release. But not thereafter. A solution compatible with Georgist philosophy (though not referred to as such) was not pursued.

In *Land: The elusive quest for social justice, taxation reform and a sustainable planetary environment* (Day, 1995), the economic and environmental ramifications of the 'fatal flaw' in the planning system are reviewed at length, including their implications for national development. In 1993 a (Commonwealth) Economic Planning Advisory Council research paper alluded to the disposition of individual Australians 'to direct their savings towards property rather than new business investment'.[18] In 1996 the Land Values Research Group compiled statistics showing that, at the peak of the real estate boom in 1989, the *land* value component of property sales was approximately 70 per cent.

PRAGMATIC RESPONSES

Meanwhile, in the absence of betterment levies, a pragmatic alternative had begun to evolve in the 1960s which exhibited an identifiable but similarly un-stated Georgist influence. Confronted with a severe infrastructure backlog in the post-war period, hard-pressed local government councils resorted to imposing conditions upon planning approval requiring a contribution of infrastructure from land developers. Modest and tentative at first, such contributions became increasingly substantial, resisted by the development industry and viewed am-bivalently by State governments. In Queensland, for example, the government appointed a commission of inquiry into the allegedly arbitrary practices of the Brisbane City Council.

As the practice of extracting contributions evolved, the kinds of infrastruc-ture which could legitimately be required (or a financial contribution in lieu) were – and remain – a matter of legislative controversy. Practice has varied among the States. In Western Australia a condition of approval of some major subdivisional developments was the provision of a percentage of lots for lower-income homeseekers. The N.S.W. *Environmental Planning and Assessment Act* of 1979 became the most sophisticated and comprehensive legislative statement, which, as amended, enables councils to require contributions to a wide range of community infrastructure (though not to as wide a range as that embraced by 'planning gain' in the U.K.).

The evolution of development conditions was reviewed in *Land Value Capture* (Day, 1992). While the concept remains controversial and ill-defined, planning authorities and government ministers have long been fully cognizant of the fact that planning approvals can confer very large windfall profits on landholders. Nevertheless, a problem in ascribing the practice of extracting development contributions to the endurance of Georgist philosophy in Australia is that their rationale has never been clearly spelt out, and the quantum of contribution in any given case is not explicitly related to the increase in land value attributable to development approval. While the practice is clearly compatible with Georgist philosophy, there has never been any overt attribution to Henry George or his predecessors.

There are no recent estimates of the windfall land value profits which are *not* offset by development contributions or capital gains tax. In 1993 an estimate by the National Capital Planning Authority quoted by the Commonwealth's Industry Commission was that throughout Australia some $300 to $400 million of potential infrastructure investment funds was forgone every year.[19] A com-prehensive analysis of the enormous revenue potential of land value taxation in Australia will be found in Terry Dwyer's chapter in this volume. As for the merits of land charges as a *means* of municipal revenue raising, in 1987 a broadly representative committee of inquiry into valuation and rating was appointed by the Lord Mayor of Brisbane (the nation's largest local government authority) in response to widespread public concern at the assumed impact which the Valuer-General's substantially increased city-wide valuations would have on council rates.

In the course of two-and-a-half-years' research, the committee reviewed the philosophy and principles of taxation, compiling a matrix of all the desiderata against which revenue-raising alternatives could be tested in the pursuit of equity and efficiency. It concluded that, in seeking to recover the cost of the public works and services it provided, a revenue-raising authority should charge the beneficiaries or users of such works and services to the extent that such works and services and their beneficiaries could be identified. Where works and services could not be separately identified and charged for, their cost should be recovered by some form of basic general charge, which should nevertheless as far as possible reflect the benefit principle. The committee then evaluated poll taxes, taxes on income and sales, taxes on land value and on improved property value, and licence fees (as well as the scope for local government trading enterprises and joint ventures). It came to the unanimous conclusion that rating on the unimproved value of land was the most efficient and equitable general revenue base for Brisbane, and, significantly, it expressed the view that, in principle, the unimproved value of land was a logical and appropriate basis for revenue-raising *irrespective of the level of government.*

Henry George would have applauded this finding, although the committee's orientation was not avowedly Georgist. In the event, the committee's two-volume report in 1989 did not attract a great deal of attention from media representatives indisposed and ill-equipped to explore the intricacies of a seemingly arcane subject area. In effect, the committee's findings served to confirm and validate long-standing municipal practice in eastern Australia.

Some random occurrences contribute to the difficulty of systematically quantifying contemporary Georgist influence in Australia. For example, in 1976, Australia endorsed the recommendations of the United Nations (Habitat) Conference for National Action on Human Settlements, the so-called 'Vancouver Plan for Action'. The recommendations on land emphasized its special quality: 'Land, because of its unique nature and the crucial role it plays in human settlements, cannot be treated as an ordinary asset controlled by individuals and subject to the pressures and inefficiencies of the market. ... The unearned increment resulting from the rise in land values resulting from change in the use of land, from public investment or decision, or due to the general growth of the community must be subject to appropriate recapture by public bodies [the community]. ...'[20] However, no practical consequences attributable to Australia's endorsement of the Vancouver Plan are readily identifiable.

In 1990, a private consortium proposed to build a new rail line between Sydney and Melbourne via Canberra and run a 'Very Fast Train' to cover the

800 km journey in as little as three hours. It was to be funded in part by rezoning land along the route. Contemplating this form of public/private partnership, using land value profits to provide *public* infrastructure to be operated for *private* profit (reminiscent of the 19th Century North American railways) requires a degree of philosophical agility. For environmental and other reasons the V.F.T. project did not proceed. But in the U.K. the suggested recoupment of land-value increases generated by the new Jubilee underground line in South London as a means of funding other transport infrastructure has attracted the attention of the Greater London Council and the U.K. Treasury, and endorsement in principle by the financial press and English Georgists. At the time of writing, the Australian government had not displayed any similar interest. It is interesting, however, to recall the remarks of Judge Foster in the Arbitration Court in 1947, when he observed that, far from being a morale-destroying proposition owing some 30 million Australian pounds, Australia's railways would be in credit to the order of about 100 million pounds if the land-value increases they had created were entered on the credit side of the ledger.[21]

BETTERMENT AND COMPENSATION

In 2004, interest in the related concepts of betterment and compensation resurfaced, promoted by the sensitive issue of vegetation clearing in response to the greenhouse gas emission targets proposed by the Kyoto Protocol and widespread environmental concern generally at the extent of clearing, particularly in Queensland. The Queensland Government imposed new limits on clearing which evoked plausible demands for compensation from landholders who had purchased or leased land specifically for agricultural or pastoral purposes, demands which funding constraints and the traditionally narrow public policy concept of compensation established in the *Bingham* case (*supra*) have induced governments to resist.

A 2000 report entitled 'Encouraging Conservation through Valuation' prepared by the Queensland Department of Natural Resources, Mines and Energy (Skitch, 2000) canvassed the possibility that lower valuation of uncleared land would be reflected in lower municipal rates (or State land tax and leasehold rentals where applicable) and accordingly would operate as an incentive to preserve vegetation (and reinforce planning objectives in urban areas). The proposal accords with Georgist principles; but the incentive impact would regrettably not be significant because municipal rates on land are presently only a minuscule proportion of public revenue in Federal Australia.

While often paired in common parlance, betterment and compensation have no functional relationship. However, a betterment levy on land-value increases could certainly raise funds to help offset compensation claims. But a specific levy would be a politically unpalatable new tax. Moreover, while on the face of it betterment levies (and development contributions) have a persuasive logic, they have significant limitations.

Firstly, in the case of land-use planning decisions, the land-value increase derived from immediate before-and-after valuations for the purpose of a one-off betterment levy may understate the true increase since in many situations the change to a more intensive use will have been anticipated by the market months or even years in advance. Secondly, betterment levies, or their development contributions surrogate, cannot work in reverse and compensate detriment or 'worsenment'. And thirdly, a once-off betterment levy cannot recoup the betterment conferred on landowners over time by the incremental extension of public infrastructure and community development. A small percentage of this benefit is currently recouped by municipal rates levied on annually reassessed land values, whereas virtually all the benefit could be recouped if public revenue were to be wholly dependent on land-value charges. Or, as some Georgist activists have put it, if national revenue were raised 'by municipal rating writ large'. Betterment from whatever cause would be automatically recouped, and worsenment from whatever cause would be automatically compensated – an outcome completely in accord with Georgist doctrine. As alluded to earlier, however, enlarging the contribution of land-value taxation to public revenue in Australia is frustrated by the arbitrary but currently accepted apportionment of revenue-raising responsibilities between Federal, State and local government. Meanwhile controversy over land clearing awaits final resolution.

ATTEMPTING AN ASSESSMENT

Confronted with disparate threads, a moving target and unrelated events, any attempt to draw the threads together and conclusively evaluate Henry George's continuing influence in Australia must unavoidably be subjective. Given the interest commonly expressed in many quarters in the scope for, and desirability of, raising an increased proportion of public revenue from expanded taxes on land, coupled with the widely acknowledged concern about the windfall profits accruing to land developers, a Georgist influence is certainly identifiable. In mid-2004, for example, the then Lord Mayor of Brisbane, Jim Soorley, addressing a planning conference, related infrastructure funding directly to betterment. The billion dollars spent by the State on upgrading the motorway between Brisbane and the Gold Coast had created a land boom for broadacre landholders along the route, 'but the State had failed to capture for future generations any of the value it had created'.[22]

But the Georgist influence is nowhere explicit. Partly because a century after the widespread enthusiasm which Henry George's visit and writings inspired, his name is virtually unknown in Australia today, even among graduates in economics and commerce, let alone sociology. Partly this is because, to the extent to which it is known, Georgism has come to signify something which is unrealistic and unattainable — and academically not entirely respectable. A related difficulty in assessing the influence specifically of Henry George is that his impact cannot be asserted prior to 1879, whereas awareness of the basic ingredients of Georgist doctrine owes something to his predecessors like William Ogilvie, Adam Smith and the Physiocrats and, indeed, to his predecessors in Colonial Australia (see footnote * above, and Craigie, n.d. *c.* 1950 — Ed.).

Another difficulty is that some policy decisions in Australia since 1788 have arguably been responses to circumstances and do not warrant specific doctrinal attribution. If so, it can of course be argued that, to this extent, Georgist doctrine is an expression of the logically obvious which ought to be pursued by whatever name. Indeed, given the ineffectual endeavours of the formal Georgist movement over the past century, preferably not in Henry George's name.

Summing up, the trail is a convoluted one and the evidence is disjunctive and chronologically elusive. An identifiable Georgist inheritance is tangible and enduring. The Georgist legacy undoubtedly survives in Australian fiscal practice. But it is not the result of explicit pursuit of Georgist philosophy, or an obvious product of Georgist advocacy. The latter has been relatively unsuccessful for some of the reasons which have been alluded to, not least a single-minded preoccupation with tax reform, and a lack of appreciation of the land-use planning process and the interrelated revenue and infrastructure funding issues which are of topical interest. Simple reiteration in the 21st Century of the gospel according to George will not suffice. The fundamental illogic of taxing productive labour and capital does not need Georgist attribution. Nor does the fact that massive revenue is *potentially* available to finance public infrastructure and public housing. Or the demonstrable practicability, over time, of automatically capturing betterment and awarding compensation, and eliminating the threat to environmental sustainability and public morality posed by the insidious unearned increment.

To those who have 'seen the cat' and believe that the logic of land and resources rental is irrefutable, debate about the extent of attribution specifically to Henry George is academic. His place in history is sufficiently assured. He should not become an overworked standard-bearer. Tactically, it may be counter-productive (and historically inaccurate) to describe the pursuit of resources rental as the resurgence or resurrection of Georgism.

For reformers, the essential practical target is the pervasive mindset, inadequately confronted by the Georgist movement, which so obdurately resists implementation of the logically irrefutable.

Notwithstanding the enormous revenue potential, the scope for vastly simplified revenue-raising, and the prospect of automatic resolution of betterment and compensation, the mindset is sustained by cultural and political inertia compounded in part by misconceptions and terminological confusion, and by assumed obstacles. The vital distinction between absolute *ownership* of man-made property, and exclusive conditional *possession* of natural resources, is not commonly understood. There is general public ignorance about valuation and rating and the difference between rates and taxes. And the history of State land taxes in Australia clouds the issue. At the forefront of popular resistance is apprehension that a land-rental regime would eliminate the culturally ordained right to engage in speculative property investment— whereas land rental does not inhibit outright ownership of, and trading in, property *on* land. Nor, indeed, does it inhibit profiting by transferors from inducements paid by transferees to secure the transfer of land which has increased in value.[23] Assumed obstacles include the impact of universal land-value taxation on the 'asset-rich but in-come-poor' (discussed by John Pullen in Chapter 8), and the possible differential impact on some industry sectors. For pensioners and other low-income property owners living in inner urban areas where land values have escalated – as well as property owners confronted with illness or sudden hardship – land-value tax can be *deferred* (like municipal rates, but preferably not *remitted*, since the li-ability properly runs with the land). Whatever concessions or relaxations needed initially are likely to be infinitely less complicated than those which currently litter the Income Tax Assessment Act and associated G.S.T. (Goods and Services Tax) legislation. Yet it all seems too hard (although to some, incredibly, Georgist doctrine has seemed too simple).[24] And a time lag is inevitable in democratic societies sustained by universal adult franchise, particularly, one is tempted to add, if voting, as in Australia, is compulsory.

The target of reform needs to be clearly focused. It is not really the commodi-fication of land. The fateful commodification of land in the later Middle Ages is almost certainly irreversible. And while the notion of commodifying air and water is repugnant, it is not in fact impossible, as evidenced, for example, by the strata titling of vertical development and commodification of the radio spectrum. One practical issue for Georgists is a concomitant fiscal outcome of commodifi-cation. Ironically, its commodification should have made land a potential target for taxation like any other commodity. But the Middle Ages also bequeathed to Anglo-Australian society one of the elements of the pervasive enigma, namely, the relative immunity of land from taxation and the persisting sanctity associated with land ownership. Both derive from the dominance of landowners, elected by landowners, in the parliaments of England until the extension of the franchise in the 19th Century. As Richard Cobden graphically demonstrated in the House of Commons in 1845 in the course of a powerful denunciation of the notorious Corn Laws, the whole of the revenue of feudal England had been derived from the land of the realm for the first 150 years after the Norman Conquest, but by 1845 the proportion had declined to a mere twenty-fifth.

Australia can accommodate commodification, even if the concept may be unintelligible to many. Individual title and communal title can both subsist. The real evil – as Henry George so clearly perceived and consistently emphasized – is the unearned increment derived from the private exploitation of land and other natural resources (irrespective of tenure).

Private capture of the unearned increment has conferred the seal of approval on private profit-seeking – the satirized 'greed is good' syndrome of the 1990s, which has become obsessive throughout Western society, with the blessing of neo-classical economics. A powerful case can be argued that virtually all the symptoms of the widespread malaise lamented by the social commentators — the erosion of communitarian values and institutions, the increasing disparities of wealth and influence, the structural unemployment, and the consequential alienation and despair in an increasingly violent, insecure and underemployed society — derive from cultural acceptance of the unearned private exploitation of the community's natural resources in the ruthless pursuit of economic efficiency at the expense of social efficiency.[25]

The unearned increment is the instrument of creeping *dollar Darwinism*. Its elimination would be an enduring tribute to Henry George and an ultimate reaffirmation of his legacy.

ACKNOWLEDGEMENTS

The author is very grateful to Geoffrey Edwards of the Queensland Department of Natural Resources, Mines and Energy for his advice and encouragement.

NOTES

1. Quoted by G. Nettheim (1993), p. 103.
2. S.H. Roberts (1968), p. 3.
3. See Henry Reynolds (1995).
4. *Mabo and Others* v. *Queensland (No. 2)* (1992), 175 Commonwealth Law Reports.
5. *Wik Peoples* v. *Queensland; Thayorre People* v. *Queensland (1996)*, 141 Australian Law Reports.
6. R. Else-Mitchell (1974), pp. 7–14.
7. Frank Brennan (1971), p. 11.
8. See Michael Cannon (1967).
9. Else-Mitchell (1974), p. 30.
10. Brennan, op. cit.
11. C.H. Currey (1968), pp. 464–5 and 480–2.
12. *Queensland Parliamentary Debates*, Legislative Assembly, 1890, Vol.61, pp. 306 and 688, Vol.62, p. 1329.
13. *Sydney Morning Herald*, 6 June 1997; Melbourne *Age*, 6 June 1997.
14. *Sydney Morning Herald*, 11 December 1997.
15. *Adelaide Advertiser*, 25 August 1979.

16. Notably A.R. Hutchinson (1979).
17. *Bingham* v. *Cumberland County Council*, 20 N.S.W. Local Government Reports, I.
18. Research Paper No. 34, *Income Tax and Asset Choice in Australia,* Canberra: Australian Government Publishing Service.
19. *Taxation and Financial Policy Impacts on Urban Settlement*, Vol. 1, Canberra: Australian Government Publishing Service..
20. United Nations Habitat Conference on Human Settlements, Vancouver, 31 May–11June, 1976 Preamble and Preface of summary document *Vancouver Plan of Action.*
21. In the Standard Hours case on 21 May 1947, *Proceedings*, p. 7480.
22. *The Courier Mail*, 12 June 2004.
23. The amount of the premium would be reflected in the next revaluation.
24. E.g. Leonie Sandercock (1979), *The Land Racket*, Melbourne: Australian Association of Socialist Studies, p. 79.
25. Anon. (1999), *Measuring Progress*, Collingwood: CSIRO, compares Gross National Product with wellbeing measured by 'genuine progress indicators'.

REFERENCES

Andelson, R.V. (ed.) (1979), *Critics of Henry George*, New Jersey and London: Associated University Presses.

Anon. (1967), *Report of the Royal Commission of Inquiry into Rating, Valuation and Local Government Finance*, Sydney: N.S.W. Government Printer.

Archer, R.W. (1976), 'The Sydney Betterment Levy, 1969–1973: An Experiment in Functional Funding of Metropolitan Development', in *Urban Issues*, **13**, 339–42.

Backhaus, J. and J. Krabbe (1991), 'Henry George's Contribution to Modern Environmental Policy', *American Journal of Economics and Sociology*, **50**, 485–501.

Brennan, Frank (1971), *Canberra in Crisis*, Canberra: Dalton Publishing.

Brisbane City Council (1989), *Report of the Committee of Inquiry into Valuation and Rating*, Brisbane.

Cannon, Michael (1967), *The Land Boomers*, Melbourne: Melbourne University Press.

Churchill, Winston (1970), *The People's Rights*, London: Jonathon Cape.

Commission of Inquiry into Land Tenures (1973), *First Report*, Canberra: Australian Government Publishing Service.

Craigie, E.J. (n.d. *c.* 1950), *Land and Wages: The Economic Effect of Land Values on Labor and Wages—A Study of the Colonisation Schemes Associated with the Swan River Settlement in Western Australia and the Foundation of South Australia*, Adelaide: Reliance Printing Company.

Currey, C.H. (1968), *Sir Francis Forbes*, Sydney: Angus & Robertson.

Day, P.D. (1992), *Land Value Capture*, Brisbane: Local Government Association of Queensland.

Day, P.D. (1995), *Land: The elusive Quest for Social Justice, Taxation Reform & a Sustainable Planetary Environment*, Brisbane: Australian Academic Press.

Eckersley, R. (ed)(1999), *Measuring Progress*, Collingwood: C.S.I.R.O.

Else-Mitchell, Rae (1974), *Legacies of the Nineteenth Century Land Reformers from Melville to George*, Brisbane: University of Queensland Press.

Hill, M. (1999), *Churchill: His Radical Decade*, London: Othila Press.

Hutchinson, A.R. (1979), *Natural Resources Rental Taxation in Australia*, Melbourne: Land Values Research Group.

Jupp, Kenneth (1997), *Stealing Our Land*, London: Othila Press

Morrison Davidson, J. (2003) [1899], *Concerning Four Precursors of Henry George and the Single Tax*, Honolulu, Hawaii: University Press of the Pacific.

Nettheim, G. (1993), *Essays on the Mabo Decision*, Sydney: Law Book Company of Australia.

Reynolds, Henry (1995), *The Other Side of the Frontier*, Victoria: Penguin Books.

Roberts, S.H. (1968), *History of Australian Land Settlement*, Melbourne: Macmillan.

Sandercock, L. (1975), *Cities for Sale*, Melbourne: Melbourne University Press.

Skitch, R.E. (2000), *Encouraging Conservation through Valuation* (2 vols), Brisbane: Department of Natural Resources.

Stilwell, Frank (2000), *Changing Track: A New Political Economic Direction for Australia*, Annandale: Pluto Press.

APPENDIX

SIR SAMUEL GRIFFITH'S 1890 NATURAL LAW BILL

1890
A BILL
To declare the Natural Law relating to the Acquisition and Ownership of Private Property

Preamble
WHEREAS it is essential to the good order of every State and the welfare of the People, that all persons should have and enjoy the fruits of their own labour, and to this end it is expedient to declare the natural laws governing the acquisition of private property: BE IT DECLARED AND ENACTED by the Queen's Most Excellent Majesty, by and with the advice and consent of the Legislative Council and Legislative Assembly of Queensland in Parliament assembled, and by the authority of the same, as follows:-

Definitions

'Land'
1. The term 'land' means land in its natural condition resulting from the operation of natural forces unaided and undirected by man, and does not include any improvements made upon it.

'Value' of land
2. When the term 'value' is used with reference to land, it signifies the extent of the difference between the advantage of having the use of the land in question and the advantage of having the use of the nearest other land the use of which can be obtained by mere occupation without making payment to any person for such use.

'Rent'
3. The return or payment demanded by persons having, by positive law, the right to the exclusive possession of land, for the permission to use that land, is called 'rent'.
Rent is therefore a measure of the value of land.

'Labour'
4. The term 'labour' includes all modes of exercise of the human faculties, whether of mind or body. It therefore includes the function of supervision or organisation of other labour.

'Wages'

5. The immediate remuneration of labour is called 'wages'.

'Property'

6. The term 'property' includes all forms of material things in the possession of man which have a value for the purpose of exchange or use. It also includes inventions and other immaterial results of the exercise of the faculties of the mind.

'Production'

7. The term 'production' includes any act or series of acts by which labour is applied, either directly or indirectly, to property, and the result of which is new property, or property in an altered form, or in a different place.

It also includes the exercise of the faculties of the mind or body, the result of which is property, although the exercise of those faculties was not applied to property.

'Capital'

8. The term 'capital' means and includes all forms of property not being land which are in use for the purposes of production. It therefore includes as well property which is consumed or destroyed as property which is not consumed or destroyed in the process of production.

'Interest'

9. The term 'interest' is used to denote either the immediate return derived from the use of capital for the purpose of production, or the payment received by the owner of capital from another person by way of return for the use of that capital.

Interest is therefore a measure of the value of the use of capital.

'Productive labour'

10. The term 'productive labour' means labour applied for the purpose of producing some property which is, or is intended to be, of greater value than the value of the property (if any) to which the labour is applied.

'Net products'

11. The terms 'net products of labour' and 'net products' mean the net increase in property resulting from productive labour, after allowing for the cost of production.

'Cost of production'

12. The cost of production may include all or any of the following elements:

(1) The replacement of the property which is consumed, or destroyed, or altered in form, or changed in place, in the course of the process of production;

(2) The wages of the labour engaged in the production;

(3) Interest on the capital used in the production;

(4) Rent of the land used for the purposes of the production;

(5) Incidental expenses not falling under any of the foregoing heads.

'Positive law'

13. The term 'positive law' includes all written laws enacted by a competent legislative authority.

It also includes all unwritten rules declared by any competent judicial authority to be the law of the State.

First Principles

Equal right of all persons to life and freedom of opportunity

14. All persons are, by natural law, equally entitled to the right of life, and to the right of freedom for the exercise of their faculties; and no person has, by natural law, any right superior to the right of any other person in this respect.

Natural forces common property

15. The right to take advantage of natural forces belongs equally to all members of the community.

Land common property

16. Land is, by natural law, the common property of the community.

Positive law

17. Positive law is the creation of the State, and may be altered or abrogated by the State from time to time.

Functions of positive law with respect to natural law

18. The application of the natural law of equality and freedom may be modified by positive law, so far as the common advantage of the community may require, but not further or otherwise.

Private rights to land

19. The rights of individual persons with respect to land are created by, and their incidents depend upon, positive law.

Property the result of labour

20. All property, other than land, is the product or result of labour.

Measure of wages

21. The natural and proper measure of wages is such a sum as is a fair immediate recompense for the labour for which they are paid, having regard to its character and duration; but it can never be taken at a less sum than such as is sufficient to maintain the labourer and his family in a state of health and reasonable comfort.

Ownership of net products

22. The net products of labour belong to the persons who are concerned in the production.

If one person only is concerned in the production the whole net products belong to him.

If more persons than one are concerned in the production, the net products belong to them, and are divisible amongst them, in proportion to the value of their respective contributions to the production.

Application of labour to property

23. When labour is not applied directly or indirectly to property, the whole products belong to the labourer.

When labour is applied directly or indirectly to property, the person who is lawfully entitled to the use of that property is deemed to be concerned in the production as well as the labourer.

Rights of possessors of land receiving rent

24. When for the purposes of production the use of land is required, then the rent (if any) payable for that use is a part of the cost of production.

The person who receives the rent is not, by reason only of his permission to use the land, concerned in the production, but may otherwise be concerned in it.

He is therefore not entitled, by reason only of such permission, to any share of the net products.

Rights of occupiers

25. For the purpose of ascertaining the net products of productive labour applied to land, and the persons entitled to share in those products, the land to which the labour is applied is to be considered as if it were capital, and were the property of the person who for the time being is entitled to the possession of it.

The amount of that capital is to be taken to be equal to the value of the land burdened with a perpetual rent equal to the rent (if any) payable by him for the time being.

Ownership of products

26. The share of net products coming to each person who contributes to the

production from which they arise is the property of that person, and may, subject to any positive law, be disposed of by him at his pleasure during his lifetime or by will.

Enforcement of rights to share of products
27. Any person entitled to a share of the net products of any productive labour may enforce that right by proceedings in a Court of competent jurisdiction.

Duty of State
28. It is the duty of the State to make provision by positive law for securing the proper distribution of the net products of labour in accordance with the principles hereby declared.

Short Title
29. This Act may be cited as *The Elementary Property Law of Queensland*.

Name Index